2 00

D0457171

The CLUB RULES

The
CLUB
RULES

Power, Money, Sex, and Fear– How It Works in Hollywood

PAUL ROSENFIELD

WARNER BOOKS

A Time Warner Company

A DOVE BOOK

Warner Books, Inc., 1271 Avenue of the Americas, New York, NY 10020

W A Time Warner Company

Printed in the United States of America
First printing: April 1992
10 9 8 7 6 5 4 3 2 1

Library of Congress Cataloging-in-Publication Data

Rosenfield, Paul, 1948–
    The Club rules : power, money, sex, and fear—how it works in
Hollywood / Paul Rosenfield.
        p.   cm.
    ISBN 0-446-51528-0
    1. Motion picture industry—California—Los Angeles—Anecdotes.
2. Hollywood (Los Angeles, Calif.)—Social life and customs.
I. Title.
PN1994.9.R6   1992
384'.8'0979494—dc20   91-50404
                                                                    CIP

Book design by Giorgetta Bell McRee

For Shelby Coffey and Mickey Ziffren

Not a word of this book would have been written without Irv Letofsky, who taught me.

Not a word would ring true without Shirley MacLaine, who taught me to disclose.

CONTENTS

A Selective Who's Who in the Club

The
CLUB
RULES

"Friendship in Hollywood is a romantic notion. It's only your enemies you can count on."

—Steve Shagan

"In our business you have to know who your friends are. Because your enemies don't reveal themselves."

—Sue Mengers

1

The Leg

Y̲ou have to be able to go into their houses.

This was my first goal in Hollywood, to get into the houses. Now that's not as simple as it sounds. The real houses in Hollywood have many meanings, and owners, and histories. They have great bones. When you sit at breakfast with Ray Stark you have to know that Bogart had the same view of the sculpture garden; it was the Bogart & Bacall house. Ray Stark may have added some priceless Henry Moores, but it was Bogart's sculpture garden.

There are various ways to get into these houses. The people people really get close to here—the ones they confide in—are the service people. I know. I was a service person—that's how I got into my first real house. (I was from a good house myself, mind you, but it was in Ohio. And I knew the difference.) In 1969 I was the clip-and-file boy for the last heavyweight gossip columnist in modern Hollywood. Joyce Haber was the *Los Angeles Times's* successor to Hedda Hopper, and five mornings a week the community trembled in her wake. She invented A and B parties, and A and B players. And even were you foolish enough not to read her, you knew she was the only power base in town. But this is not her story, or mine, because the journalist is never a player, or a member, in this club. The journalist is the watcher here. They called me the leg because I was her legman.

1

My first real Hollywood house, her house, was haunted by the late actor Clifton Webb, who had lived there forever with his mother, Maybelle. In the very late '60s when I first went to this house, it was also a salon, replete with an apple green screening room and powerful club members as guests. The club—which controls show business—is provocative because it's based not just on connections or power or style—but all of these together, and it prefers to remain private. It's not an underworld, but an overworld, mysterious and unexplored. These are people who walk out the door in the morning, but don't see the same world other people see. And I wanted to see what they saw.

So I went to the séances in the screening room, where Clifton Webb and Maybelle appeared as an ethereal, and very devoted couple. Which I thought was very appropriate. Because the club members, I soon discovered, were primarily little boys (or girls) looking for good mommies. Like Clifton. That's why they often play guardian angels for each other. That's what the movie business is about: The real drive is to be unconditionally loved.

I discovered that club members are more alike than they are unalike: Most of them are white males, forty or older, Jewish for the most part, heterosexual for the most part, usually fathers, of shorter-than-average height—and they tend to go to bed early. (Usually in Pacific Palisades, north of Sunset, or in the Beverly Hills blocks of Maple or Elm, south of Sunset.) These houses are usually idealized versions of Ozzie and Harriet Nelson's house, except that Harriet Nelson didn't employ Oriental help.

In Miss Haber's screening room right away—I mean within a week of being hired—I saw what happens when you are the assistant to someone powerful. Automatically you're the stand-in, an intimate at the table, and it's the best kind of understudy job. Because if you stay long enough—and I stayed six years—you know how you want to play the game. Or even if you want to play at all. Maybe, like me, you'd just want to watch.

This particular screening room was like something out of *Shampoo*. The right Rauschenberg graphics and the warm ermine pillows and the romantic needlepoint homilies ("BIG HUGS TO J!"). And the people. At night you'd see artist Ed Ruscha all over actress Samantha Eggar, who'd been "discovered" by producer Mike Frankovich, who was there with his actress wife, Binnie Barnes—even though he couldn't stop talking about choreographer Onna White. (Hadn't Frankovich, the president of the Academy, been the one to get Onna that special Oscar for *Oliver?*) And the perfection of the accessories: I most remember the Louis Vuitton ashtray from the store in Nice, a gift from the summer Bob and Ali MacGraw Evans went to the South of France and came back looking more beautiful than Greek gods. Or the night Henry Kissinger, with Secret Servicemen attending, held court at table about Pakistan while Michelle Phillips pretended to understand. ("I always forget they're actresses," Dr. Kissinger would say later, privately.)

In the understudy role—or the role of the leg—all one does is listen. Home truths are revealed very quickly. One discovered that every visit to Merle Oberon in Acapulco meant returning with the trots. ("Pilar Wayne has the trots, after Merle's," I heard one Christmas. The next year it was, "Lyn Revson got the trots at Merle's.") One discovered that at dinner Stanley Jaffe and Sherry Lansing had such chemistry—long before they became partners—that together they could solve impossible arithmetical problems—their compatibility was such that one could have predicted their success together years later. One saw the duenna of the piranhas, Edie Goetz, joined at the silk-draped hip of Rosalind Russell, trailed by Russell's husband, who everyone called the Lizard of Roz. (Actually, Freddie Brisson was a talented Broadway producer who just never made it as a movie producer.)

So those were the kinds of things I saw. Tented parties and little intimate evenings and big mistakes on the part of important people. I was there in the kitchen the morning Diana Ross came to apologize for not showing up at a dinner party the night before—and the party was in her honor. Standing there in Joyce Haber's kitchen with her youngest child strapped to her back, she seemed like a secretary who got her days off mixed up. This was the year Diana Ross was close to winning an Oscar, and it may have been her last real Hollywood moment—that morning in the kitchen.

That's what I learned. It's all moments, and they don't necessarily add up. Certainly they matter, but they don't really count. Almost nobody remembers you six years later—should you run into each other—because there have been so many "wonderful little moments" in the meantime. So many new faces. Very quickly I saw how people go through people here. Like the six-year friendship of Sally Field and her *Flying Nun* co-star, the handsome Alejandro Rey. After daily soulmate closeness for years and years, the actor one day asked the actress, "If you never saw me again, it would be okay by you? Right? As close as we've been?" Sally Field shook the best head of hair in Hollywood and said, "Yes." That was the end of the friendship. It was also the last season of the series. People are gone from each other's lives real quickly.

I myself was almost gone real quickly. My original ploy to be hired had backfired. On the first Sunday in December 1969, my would-be boss printed a readers' poll asking them to write in their favorite films of the decade. So when I first had the guts to call her, two days after it ran, it was to offer to count the ballots. I counted them wrong, and she had to stay up all night recounting. So she had every right to fire me, which she did. I didn't blame her, but I couldn't bear it. "Let me work for free," I pleaded; nothing in my life meant what this job meant. So she let me stay on, which, in retrospect, seems kind. I was, after all, less than useful. I didn't know anyone and I hadn't worked anywhere, except in her wonderful guest house, walled with file cabinets and framed photos of the members of the club. I was a film student at USC worried about being drafted. So I worked for free and finally got raised to $1.25 an hour. Had I any money at all, I would have paid her. The job itself was the best gift I ever got.

Or the second best. One night in the screening room I found myself eyeing the Watch. A Tanexis is a certain kind of inexpensive, direct-black Swiss watch that people in Hollywood considered sacred and lucky. People very carefully passed these watches around. It's a tribal thing, at a certain level. The first time I saw one was on the late Gladyce Begelman, who got it from her husband's former partner, Freddie Fields. ("David and Freddie are beyond brothers, beyond family," Gladyce told me gravely.) I wondered just when did Freddie give Gladyce the watch. To pass around one of those watches—there were maybe two dozen floating around Hollywood in those days—that was a real moment. That kind of moment got remembered—it got told around town.

One night—for some geometric reason, certainly it wasn't status—I was seated at the head of the table at dinner. And the producer Leonard Goldberg let me wear the watch. For like two hours, while everyone sat in the screening room making fun of the Beatles movie *Let It Be.* ("Let *Let It Be* be," one producer howled.)

It was tacitly understood by me (and Leonard) that I was to give the watch back at the end of the evening, and I did. But such was the effect of his generosity that I never wrote an unkind word about Leonard. Not in the nineteen years since then that I covered Hollywood for the *Los Angeles Times.*

I wanted to understand these people somehow. Not that I was fooled. I eavesdropped, I heard, I knew what they really thought of the press. One day at La Scala Boutique I overheard David Janssen telling someone, "Oh, he's a barrel of laughs if you want to bore yourself to death. But my wife likes to see her name in the paper. So we invite him for dinner once in a while." I understood. But even the journalist is part of the machinery here, and the machinery must be oiled at all costs. People who are part of the machinery have various things in common. All of them have a kind of radar. They can smell it at twenty feet when you want something. So you learn never to want anything, ever. Only the story.

I was probably drenched in sweat for most of the social evenings for almost two decades. And for the interviews, too. Each subject, each host, naively gives you so much, well, ammunition. You could really trample these people if you print what they tell you. You hear Howard Koch beg Warren Beatty to give his son Howard Jr. billboard credit as associate producer—"for the billboard on Sunset Boulevard, at least, Warren"—on *Heaven Can Wait*. Then you wonder what to do with it. Candy Spelling tells you about discussing at dinner with Barbra Streisand how outrageously expensive chinoiserie has become; you can picture the conversation.

Once you have your own byline, and you are no longer one-legged, you really worry. Barbara Walters tells you about her retarded sister, then cries. ("You could have razored me," she said after the story ran. The reason for Walters' staying power became clear when I walked in from a tennis game and heard on my machine the weekend the piece ran, "This is Barbara Walters. I'll be in all day Saturday and all day Sunday. Please call me.") Jane Fonda talks about her mother's suicide, and watches you write it down. Johnny Carson reveals himself by his dime-store ashtrays in a $10 million house, a barren symbol. You see that show business is not all gorgeous—but you also see how gorgeous parts of it can be. An afternoon with Billy Wilder is worth growing up for.

It goes on and on because they are as nervous as you are; all a powerful person has, finally, is the image. So it must be guarded at all costs. Al Pacino calls from Jamaica to make sure you got the quotes right; he's worried. Jeffrey Katzenberg calls back "to make sure you got enough." Dawn Steel tells you three times in a half hour how young you look. Liz Smith lets you sit in her office and take down every word, but seems surprised you're there day after day. Lucille Ball gets angry if you are even five minutes late ("Traffic, honey, or what?"). Mike Nichols is a complete snob. Anne Bancroft gets offended when you offer to walk her home—questions she was prepared for, but she's not prepared for you to walk her home. That's too close.

You're not allowed many violations here. The faux pas—my Donna Rice story everyone hates because I like her—will (I am told) "go away," and it does. But you do not print most of the above information because you know better. That's the radar you aim for—the sense of knowing how far to go in a company town so closed that many members don't even know each other. What Ray Stark says about Mike Ovitz isn't to be used in the hometown paper because the business managers and the children and the spouses and the lawyers and the service people, for God's sake, read it.

So you make people bright, or brittle, but you don't make fun of them or be mean. Because they remember every mention of every dribble of coleslaw sliding off the chin—every slight mention of bad manners is remembered for years, and verbatim.

For many of these people identity itself comes from being mentioned in a column—that's where their "character" lives, and stars. Always the right angle, please. The journalists—the A journalists—get the best two hours of a star's life. For a brat from Ohio with a movie magazine mentality and an understanding of neurotic personalities—this was the true path.

Even though withholding is considered the major metaphor of the movie business, I found very little information withheld—from what I could tell, anyway.

But first I had to get into the houses. And this is really a book about getting into houses.

Four weeks before she died, Bette Davis got on the phone and said, "I hear you're doing a book on power in Hollywood. Remember, there are only forty stories. Four-O. But they keep repeating themselves."

Miss Davis didn't live long enough to explain what she meant. But these are forty stories of Hollywood, more or less. I hope they don't repeat themselves.

By the way, I finally did get one of the lucky watches. It was the one Sylvester Stallone gave producer Gene Kirkwood the day after *Rocky* won the Oscar for Best Picture. Gene Kirkwood gave it to publicist Howard Brandy, who gave it to actress Brian Ann Zoccola, who gave it to me one night over an omelette at Nate 'n Al's. I don't wear it anymore. But I carry it in my bag in case I run into Howard Brandy. Howard's sentimental.

2

The Club

S*am Warner and Sam Spiegel and Sam Goldwyn were club founders. Sam Goldwyn, Jr., is a child of the club. Alan Ladd, Jr., is a child of the club who grew up to be an officer of it. Jane Fonda and Michael Douglas are the club children who turned out the most productive. Desi Arnaz, Jr., was the club child with the most troubled youth. Anjelica Huston was the club child with the most to overcome. Gloria Katz and Willard Huyck got in because their script about untroubled youth,* American Graffiti, *caught George Lucas' eye, and he liked them. They stayed in because Mike Ovitz and Steven Spielberg liked them, even after* Howard the Duck. *George Lucas got in because he was Francis Coppola's assistant and because Coppola took a chance on him. Toni Howard got in because of Anjelica Huston, and because she was Freddie Fields' secretary, not because she was Wendy Goldberg's sister. Wendy Goldberg got in by marriage, first to David Mirisch and then to Leonard Goldberg. Wendy Goldberg stays in because she's smart and because of her friendships with Barbara Walters and Barbara Davis, her two "Bs". Barbara Walters did not get in by marrying Merv Adelson, but it didn't hurt. It also didn't hurt Barbara Walters when she separated from Merv Adelson. Merv Adelson got in because of*

7

La Costa. Andrea Jaffe did not get in by booking stars on Barbara Walters' specials, but it didn't hurt. She got in because her father was Columbia chairman Leo Jaffe and that's also why her brother Stanley Jaffe got in. Stanley Jaffe stayed in because of brains and Sherry Lansing. Peter Hyams got in because he was a sibling, of Nessa Hyams. David Picker got in by marrying Nessa Hyams. David Picker goes in and out faster than any producer in the club. Irwin Winkler has stayed in as long as any modern producer in the club. Irwin Winkler got in by producing Rocky. *Gene Kirkwood got in by shepherding* Rocky. *Sylvester Stallone got in by dreaming up* Rocky. *Mickey Rourke got in by making a movie for Gene Kirkwood and becoming friendly with Sylvester Stallone. Sylvester Stallone spent his fortieth birthday with Mickey Rourke and Gene Kirkwood and Irwin Winkler.*

It was only days after the milk-toast opening of TriStar's $60-million-plus epic *Hook*, and the studio production executive was carrying on at lunch at Celestino about everything else in the world. About Richard Gere's wedding to Cindy Crawford, and how the actor was given away in true Hollywood style by not one but three people (photographer Herb Ritts, songwriter Bruce Roberts, and Gere's agent Ed Limato). The executive was talking about how great it was that *Bugsy* was winning the critics' awards, and how TriStar also had critics' darling Gus Van Sant's next project. The executive looked a little worried, though.

"I dunno . . . it may just be the ultimate nonmovie that Gus Van Sant wants to make. It scares me."

"Let him make it," whispered one of the people at the table. "Gus Van Sant should be able to do anything he wants."

"That's what people told us about Steven Spielberg," said the executive, "and look at the grosses of *Hook*."

The Spielberg star opus had just opened, and already the executive was talking about how they only needed to gross—"all in"—$120 million to walk away smiling. Maybe *Hook* would break even, and maybe not, but nobody at the table at Celestino even flinched at this kind of talk. Club members talk this way about each other's product every day. So Steven's movie was going down the tubes. So? Steven was in Hawaii, and the club marches on. Hopefully to the next blockbuster. The leg never understood why a movie that cost $60 million was supposed to open bigger than a movie that cost half that. It seemed neurotic to the leg, but not to the club.

There are a thousand people floating around the top of this world—and they all know each other. They make money together, and sometimes they make magic—and almost always they protect each other. They are the club that controls show business—the attorneys, agents, talents, studio chiefs, and bankers—and they know who they are. In any given decade the names may change—members vanish and new ones appear (or reappear)—but there really are only a thousand people in this world. And if they mostly see each other in airports, so what? Yes, they make commitments they can get out of—but not with each other.

The following story may or may not be apocryphal. One night in 1977, five of these people were sitting around an upstairs table at Ma Maison, playing poker for upward of $475,000—when Pierre Groleau, host extraordinaire, walked in. On his arm was Gladyce Begelman. The two of them stood in what had come to be known as the power arch. "This is what's left of Hollywood power," Pierre Groleau said knowingly—he was brought to Hollywood from Paris to be gigolo to the late Mrs. Joe Pasternak. Now all these years later, Groleau had learned how to sniff power like a King Charles spaniel.

"This is the club," Groleau told Gladyce Begelman in a hushed tone.

"It's the boys' club," she whispered, looking straight at the poker table. "The whole world is downstairs. Jackie Bisset is with Marty Ransohoff and Michael Cimino is down there, for God's sake—with Francis! . . ."

"Yes, darling," responded Groleau. "But the club sits upstairs."

"You mean club as in monastery," said Mrs. Begelman darkly. "Or casino!" Mrs. Begelman watched the poker game with interest—she knew these men for whom gambling is such a release. For whom the kinship with one another is paramount. She knew that this poker game was not very different from the games in the '50s at Billy Wilder's house. Only the stakes were higher, not the emotions.

In every case the members know who they are. They have a sixth sense about each other, too—even though there may be no true intimacy. Often you can get only so close to these people, and no closer. Dan Melnick eating at Mortons with Steve Martin is as close as it gets in the club; that, or Christmas at the Eisners in Aspen. When members run into each other at charity evenings, they acknowledge each other the way members in a country club do, with light casual air kisses on both cheeks. They know each other's Hollywood histories, and they know each other's status of the moment. Also, as in a country club, they might ignore each other, or be in a feud—but ultimately club blood is thicker than water.

The club is the family structure for these people who left home a very long time ago. When Guy McElwaine sits with Steven Spielberg and talks about nothing of importance, or something of importance, it's real. It counts.

Yet it's not a country club. It's a metaphorical club, the kind you've known about since sixth grade—when you got included, or didn't. It's the invitation to the dance that comes, or doesn't. It's the unspoken *knowing* that you're inside, and not out. All the tribal rituals can change—and in Hollywood they do change, often—but the rituals are secondary to the actual membership. If you belong, you know it. Brandon Tartikoff knows he belongs. You have a security that insecure people envy, and whine about. Ultimately it's a club of nonvictims. Victims bore the club, and so do hard-luck stories. That's what makes it different from a club in Detroit: On some unconscious level, it's completely unforgiving.

In a country club, if your job changes, you stay a member—if you can pay the dues. (At Hillcrest Country Club the joining dues are $1 million, but you don't get booted out if your movie flops.)

In the club everyone plays a role. There has always been a fixer and there has always been a provider. In the '60s the provider role was played by a Merle Oberon social understudy named Mrs. Lee Anderson. She was then a publicist with a fetish for ladies' lunches, at the old Bistro on Canōn. (Hosts Casper and Jimmy took good care of Mrs. Anderson, and she got Jimmy enough publicity to eventually open his own place.) The lunches were stacked with would-be A club wives, each of whom knew inside that she was really a B club wife. Rosemarie Stack (who would go to the opening of a door) would be there, usually, and Mrs. Stuart Whitman and the newest guest would be a wife who paid Lee Anderson (later Minnelli, as in Mrs. Vincente) at least four figures for the introduction. (Lee, impeccably British, tried to model herself after Miss Oberon, but she wasn't beautiful.) When a newly divorced Joanne Carson arrived in Hollywood, Lee went after her like a barracuda. "We must have lunch," Lee told the former game show hostess.

Said Mrs. Carson, who knew the rules, "I'd love to, Lee—but I don't have any money." That ended it.

(Joanne Carson's settlement from Johnny gives her $100,000 a year for life, if she doesn't remarry—and it doesn't look like she will. The divorce was final in 1970.)

A hundred thousand a year is like no money at all in the club. Seven-figure incomes are essential—that's the great good shimmer of the movie business. The potential to become not just rich but rich-rich. The sums of money are so enormous they can't be counted. Club windfalls come in the form of blockbuster hits; a franchise like *Beverly Hills Cop* can easily make you a hundred million if you're the producer. That's why money is a given, and why it's not thrown around, in spite of Marvin Davis, and in spite of what you read in Hollywood novels. In the club, for Christmas, you send cards or give donations or give gifts that would fit in an evening bag.

This is a club that protects itself, that's why what I'm writing here is so dangerous. Probably they'll never let me watch their antics again. No more club sandwiches in Carol Matthau's kitchen, I assure you. But once you realize you can't really play and can only watch, you don't really care anymore.

No bitterness—just resolve to capture the club as it really is. What it *isn't* is heartless and mean. There are some of the strongest, truest friendships in American business in the club, and some of the most idealistic adults on earth. The generosity of thugs, after all, is historic. Monsters make major million-dollar donations to charity, and nicer men, like directors Mark Rydell and Billy Wilder, say yes when a crony from the old days calls for wheelchair money. I know. I was there when Vince Edwards (*Ben Casey*) called Mark Rydell for $5,000, cash—overnight— for gambling debts. Vince Edwards got Mark Rydell his first job directing episodic TV when Mark was a nobody. I heard Mark say yes to Vince, and five minutes later I heard him handle Katharine Hepburn in Hartford, with such love in his voice, even Hepburn softened. Mark Rydell isn't in the club for nothing. He knows when to be smooth and when to be soft. He knows how much to say and how little.

That's the first club rule: Don't say too much. After years of weekly contact, you can say anything provided you only talk to four or five people—and never talk about those people to each other. I have the three best mentors in the club, and you can believe they are not mentioned in this book. They will remain my friends. *Real* friends, the kind you have in Syracuse or Santa Rosa. "What you are in the club," Joyce Selznick told me, "is whatever you came in with. People don't change."

That's why there are no fakes here, not really. They would be weeded out. You need billions to *buy* your way in, and even then it's iffy. When I began writing about the club, for the *Los Angeles Times*, I realized that more than anything else you had to play by the rules. And I began writing the rules down in the early '70s: I did this not so much for the future as for survival. Each rule gleaned from each member—slowly—got me into another house. Another lesson, another season. Each club rule has been tried and tested.

"There are no kids in the club," says half billionaire Ted Mann, the strongest movie exhibitor in club history.

"Ted knows," says Jeffrey Katzenberg. "He's seen them come and he's seen them go."

Club Rule Two (the first one, remember, is about not talking too much): Know who to kiss and who to kick. (This is knowledge gained in one's twenties, or not at all.) A great way to learn it is to be an assistant. Jeff Katzenberg was assistant to Barry Diller; Jeff Berg was assistant to Freddie Fields. Larry Mark was assistant to David Picker. Kathleen Kennedy was assistant to Steven Spielberg. They listened firsthand, and they learned.

Club Rule Three: Niceness counts. Producer Suzanne de Passe, who's black, blushes when Barbara (Mrs. Marvin) Davis says hello to her at a party. She's as soft as a kitten, and she purrs. It isn't fake. There are screamers in the club, but they scream in private. Joel Silver yells at his harem girls in private—and until recently said nothing whatever in public. A lot of the screamers are sweet in other situations—truly. "I happen to connect well with monsters," Disney VP Ed Pine told me candidly. "I see the soft parts, I recognize those parts, and these people treat me well."

Club Rule Four: Candor is acceptable, even de rigueur, as a mark of membership. It shows how quick you are. At a convention in New Orleans in 1990, Columbia chief Peter Guber told a writer, "I'm the most powerful person you'll ever meet." At a lunch in Los Angeles, Fox chairman Barry Diller told a group, "Nobody in Hollywood is happy anymore. The days of opening *The Godfather* and going to the opening, and celebrating, are over. Nobody is having fun." Accept this candor as gospel; these people mean what they say.

Club Rule Five: Love applies, and so does sex. Jon Peters turns women on, and they turn him on, and they deliver. Barbra Streisand was remade as a sexual creature when Peters took her from playing Fanny Brice to playing lovestruck in *A Star Is Born*. It was Peters' stroking that got the *Batman* performance out of Kim Basinger. Blake Edwards' adoration of Julie Andrews made *Victor/Victoria* one of the best movies of the '80s. The love is for real.

Club Rule Six: Prepare for creative differences and turbulence. In other words, be very wary. The classic line "He won't do it to me" is the line executives use about troubled, tortured, talented people (as in Michael Cimino or Bruce Willis). Creative people are allowed a higher level of turbulence—if they are truly talented, and ultimately deliver. (The jury is out on Willis, if not Cimino.) But the club is comprised of more business people than creative people. And these businessmen believe they are not going to be played with by the talent. Michael Cimino may have wasted great sums of money on a United Artists picture, but if his next project is going toward Fox, the executive there will say—and mean it—"He won't do it to me." Ultimately he does do it to them, of course, but the creative pool is so small he will be given more chances, other times at bat. Since the club operates largely in the moment, nobody much dwells on past behavior.

Club Rule Seven: Humor helps, because it's sorely missing in the club now. Standing at an elevator at the Plaza Athenee in New York, Malcolm Forbes (of all people) made a play for Elizabeth Taylor.

"What would it take to get you to let me come upstairs?" the tycoon asked the star.

"A big thing in a little blue box," said Elizabeth Taylor. "From Tiffany."

Then she went upstairs, alone. But at Metro—they trained them to be glib. The real stars never lost the knack.

Club Rule Eight: In the club nobody gets sick ever. If you think about yourself all the time—you see a different world from other people. Your entire day is about being listened to, and coddled, and reassured. Norman Lear looks better in his sixties than he did at forty. The self-obsession extends to physical care taking in the extreme. Male executives, at the development level, talk excessively about facials. Personal trainers are taken for granted. Look at John Belushi in *Continental Divide,* before he had status, and look at his later pictures. You see how well pampering works. In spite of addictive behavior.

Club Rule Nine: Look for the loneliness. People in the club really are lonely. The cliché is true because they really don't want to put energy into other people. They want the energy put into them. That's the privilege that comes with admittance; no more having to take meetings with people who drain you, or turn you off. That's why you sometimes see slightly disguised entourages instead of true friendships. Very often for "friend" you can substitute the word "publicist" or "manager."

Club Rule Ten: It works synchronistically when it works. When Billy Wilder was at his peak, he would simply call his producer Walter Mirisch and Mirisch would say, "What do you want to do next, Billy?" It was a ten-minute conversation and the wheels were set in motion. The movie would get made. One phone call. The same is now true of Walter Hill and Joel Silver, or Barry Levinson and Mark Johnson, or Bill Murray and Ivan Reitman. It's still one phone call.

Club Rule Eleven: Loyalty counts, and doesn't. Jack Lemmon was in a play in London, in early 1989, and his longtime (twenty-seven years) agent Lenny Hirshan was in town. They were on the phone, and Lenny wasn't sure he'd come to the play that night. They'd been talking about having supper afterward.

"No, don't," said Lemmon softly. "Listen Lenny, what the hell, while we're on the phone—I've been meaning to tell you . . . I'm leaving the agency. I'll, uhm, see you, Lenny."

Twenty-seven years. One phone call. It's a good rule to know.

These rules are only the beginning. There are club rules for every chapter of this book—and every home truth.

But what is this club, finally? It's the place you come to when you leave New York. On New Year's Eve in 1980 the ICM agent Joan Hyler was dancing on a rooftop on Central Park West when she made up her mind. She would come to California after all. New York was over for her—she'd found *The Elephant Man* off-Broadway, she was there in the bleachers, getting the backers—she'd done it. So she came to Hollywood, to the club.

Why did she get in? Why her, this former secretary from Dayton who took the Greyhound to New York, her Ph.D. in religious history counting for zip in the club? Why her? She didn't get in because she put Candy Bergen in *Murphy Brown*. That happened years later. She got in because she didn't swim with minnows. By New Year's Eve 1989 she was swimming around the Hollywood parties, and hosting them—a little lonely maybe. Maybe she was missing Dayton or Manhattan. Just a little. In 1990 she met her dreamboat husband.

But she wasn't swimming with minnows. So she felt at home.

Because nobody in the club is a minnow.

MONEY

The leg never understood money, even remotely, so he never reported on the business side of Hollywood. Figures were too unemotional for the leg—he chased after style and drama like most men his age chased women.

As the leg got into more houses—and saw how alike they were—he began to be fascinated with money. Peter Guber's obsession with Japanese furniture completely overrides his fascination for movies; even his secretaries would arrive in flats. (Kabuki gowns are optional.) Grant Tinker's and Mary Tyler Moore's perpetual moving in and out of houses in Malibu and Bel Air was a saga of restlessness—and high finance—worth following. The Sidney Sheldons lived in thirty-one houses in twenty-five years. The houses told a story of upward mobility.

Finally the leg understood that in the club having money really is the first given: Denise (the third Mrs. Vincente) Minnelli got in the club without money—but she had style to burn, and even more drive, having survived the Nazis in occupied Yugoslavia. ("Hollywood was then easy," said Denise, "after Yugoslavia.") Denise could give nothing little dinners at home, without help, and get everybody from the Wilders to the Starks. Because she was vital and funny. And smoother than the doctors at the Betty Ford Center.

Conversely, the leg saw how has-beens like Merle Oberon stayed in (at least socially) *only* because they had money. Merle's extraordinary Louis Quinze chairs and Porthault bedrooms brought out even the recluses, people like Jennifer Jones and Norton Simon. Just to gawk. Things haven't changed much: Money still gets listened to.

One night at a dinner party, at the Bistro, the leg saw Marvin Davis tastelessly ogle his busty dinner partners, Joan Collins and Evie Bricusse, and get away with it. Because he has more money than God. The same is now true of Lucille Ball's rich widower, Gary Morton. However, if money isn't your priority, you can invite people like David Geffen's classy English butler to share Christmas dinner—like Ali MacGraw does every year. But that takes real social security.

The first thing that the leg had to face was that the press has power without money. Always. (Unless you inherit.) Having money in the club means you have money *plus power*. Otherwise it doesn't count. I'm talking here about club members like Jeffrey Katzenberg. Or Dawn Steel in her days as president at Columbia. (When Dawn moved to Disney in 1990, she acquired real money, but lost power. It was her choice.) The really smart money people in the club—Ray Stark being the smartest— know that the best combination is money *plus* independence. Dawn Steel would rather be the future Ray Stark than the future Lew Wasserman. The thing about Wasserman *and* Stark is that both were agents—and agents are more mad about money than anyone.

Finally the leg had to face the fact that money runs the club—not style or class. "Look who's in power now," suggested former Columbia co-chairman Jon Peters one afternoon. "Look at who the players are: I was a hairdresser, Ovitz was a bartender, and [CAA President] Ronnie Meyer was a stevedore, or whatever the hell he was." Peters is a capo in Holly-wood's new mafia. It's him, Geffen, Diller, Ovitz, Eisner, Meyer, Guber, Jake Bloom, Mike Medavoy, Alan Ladd, Jr., almost all of them godfa-thered by Ray Stark. Almost all of them agents or former agents.

This isn't the first club generation to be dominated by agents: The last group—Guy McElwaine, David Begelman, Freddie Fields, Dick Shepard, Jay Kanter, the young Medavoy, John Foreman—were also ten-percenters. And if Ovitz became the kingpin of the town, instead of a studio man, it was simply, really, a matter of the eminence grise baton being passed. From former agent Lew Wasserman to agent Mike Ovitz. One thoroughbred workhorse to another. In the club, the baton always passes, even if unwittingly.

These names terrified me for fifteen years. I couldn't even imagine a phone conversation with one of these people. What would I say to Univer-sal's (and then Paramount's) Ned Tanen? I perspired at the thought. I'm not exaggerating. I wanted to interview people like Robert Redford, for

God's sake, and Kim Basinger, and Billy Wilder—not Frank Mancuso. Not, heaven forbid, Sid Sheinberg. Not Lew. Not me. I can't balance a checkbook or read a financial page. Yet somehow as I got into the bones of the club, I realized I had to follow the money. Money is one of the six major reasons people get in the club. The others are ego, love, sex, status, and—particularly—fear.

Agents are motivated by all six reasons, sometimes all at once. But the reason I always begged off writing about agents wasn't the cliché one. The one about how double-crossing they are. After stars like Bette Midler tell you for years about how even the best agents "cheat on you," you get scared off meeting agents.

I was always sure I would be outsmarted by agents. And I always was. But an agent is going to bring the most to the club table, always. He always knows where the bodies are buried. He might have the eyes of a pawnbroker, like David Begelman, but he's also the member who's the hardest working, closest to the edge, and most privy to everything. Especially the tsuris that descends on Hollywood every day like trade papers. You better believe Jeff Berg knows every detail of every major Sam Cohn deal. Sometimes before Sam Cohn knows.

3

The Reign
of Terror—
The Agents

Jeff Berg got in because he was in Freddie Fields' office when 200 calls a day were coming in, and he was an assistant who paid attention. Jeff Berg was also born into the business, as was his brother Scott, via their producer-father Dick Berg. Jeff Berg stayed in because Freddie Fields left the agency business, and because he was literate in dealing with smart directors like Bernardo Bertolucci and Jim Brooks and Paul Mazursky. Jeff Berg also worked instead of partied, and thus became the only rival to Mike Ovitz and a kind of nonsocial bookend. He lacked only Ovitz' tightly knit team. Berg had to stroke his colleagues and he didn't have foot soldiers—or full partners either, in the true sense. But Jeff Berg could get along with complex peers like Sue Mengers and Ed Limato. Sue Mengers got in because of moxie and a Germanic tough-mindedness. Sue Mengers dropped out because of ennui. She dropped back in after Stan Kamen died. Sue Mengers got a more important title at William Morris than Norman Brokaw, but Brokaw had Bill Cosby. Cosby kept William Morris at the top of the TV agency heap, and agent Joan Hyler putting Candy Bergen in Murphy Brown didn't hurt. Joan Hyler got in because Stan Kamen made her an offer *to leave Freddie Fields and New York for William Morris and Hollywood. Ames Cushing stayed in at William Morris because she appealed to people, and because she was often escorted by Douglas Cramer. Arnold Rifkin of Triad got in by co-opting Bruce Willis and putting him into Schenley commercials. John Kimble of Triad stayed in because he and Alan Nierob took Victoria Principal from* Dallas *to TV movie queendom. Triad was the agency that made it okay to cash in and do commercials. William Morris was the agency with all those millions stashed away; it was the one that played rich father. ICM was the personal attention agency, and Ed Limato the shoulder to cry on. By the early '80s, CAA was the power and the future. Bauer-Benedek was the loyalist agency; Larry Kasdan was the college roommate of Peter Benedek. Peter Benedek's wife co-wrote* The Big Chill *with Larry Kasdan, and Bauer-Benedek did the deal.*

Two heterosexual women agents were waiting for an elevator at the ICM Building on Beverly Boulevard. One woman looked at the other and said, "You turn me on so much I want to fuck you with my dick." Then they took separate elevators. Nobody in earshot was even slightly shocked.

When people call the club "the boys club," I always remind them of the girl mafia that surfaced in Hollywood in the '80s. By the end of the decade women like Martha Luttrell and Boaty Boatwright and Rosalie Swedlin were running their own shows. In 1990 when Mike Ovitz called then-William Morris agent Elaine Goldsmith to say he represented Steven Spielberg—and that Steven wanted Julia Roberts, Elaine's client, to play Tinkerbell in *Hook,* Elaine said no. When Mike called the second time, he was more persuasive—and Elaine talked to Julia about the movie. People said Elaine was angling for a job at CAA, but no. She was on her way to ICM. But she was playing in the club. Along with Toni Howard, who'd gotten Anjelica Huston her first million dollars, for *The Addams Family.*

I finally decided in the mid-'80s to write about agents when CAA looked like it would become the most powerful company in town. I didn't start small. I started with Paul Kohner, the pioneer agent whose longtime clients included John Huston and Ingmar Bergman. I called up Mr. Kohner out of the blue, and told him John Huston suggested I meet him. Kohner was Huston's oldest friend in town. The courtly Mr. Kohner kept me entertained for hours, in his '30s baroque office on Sunset Boulevard designed by Lutah Mae Riggs.

Paul Kohner was in his eighties when we met in 1987. The first time I walked in I realized all the best conversations were in German. Since I learned it at home, I knew what Kohner was saying. Right away I grasped a hard simple truth: Agents want desperately to be accepted by the town, and by the people they represent. They need validation. They study modern art and high finance and the subtleties of Mandarin cooking. Stan Kamen would rather talk about Hawaii than Hollywood. These people educate themselves about the stripes of Frank Stella, and the habits of Kirk Kerkorian, and the cuisine of southern Italy. And they have antenna like nobody else in the club. Also the best ones dress beautifully, and they tend toward a style of life that's high, wide, and handsome. When Freddie Fields gave a party, you went. Or when Fran and Ray Stark did.

Kohner was fatherly enough that I finally relaxed. I was just the latest in a long line of people who sat at his feet, lapping it all up. Who I was didn't really matter. So I gave up worrying about wearing the same khakis three days in a row. He wouldn't know the difference if I walked in in a gym suit.

Mr. Kohner gave me enough confidence to walk up the street, one block west, to the office of the late Evarts Ziegler. The handsome Ziggy was the first Princeton-educated literary agent in town—he got William Goldman the historic $425,000 for the script for *Butch Cassidy and the Sundance Kid*, and he pacified people like Arthur Krim and Bennett Cerf. In the '30s, Ziggy wrote about Manhattan for *Esquire*—he always knew the mise-en-scène, and shared what he knew. He not only dropped names of clients like "the Didions" and the Sydneys—Pollack and Lumet—he also had a superb Cary Grant act. (Years later I would discover it really was an act. Zig was a phony.)

Then I went up a few blocks to Trousdale to the immaculate modern, cozy house of the other living legend, Irving Paul Lazar. Lazar tried to convince me that George S. Kaufman and George Gershwin had been to his legendary Oscar night parties—but the parties only began in the '60s, long after these men died. But it hit me that I must listen to what a club legend has to say. No matter what. And not contradict. If you're not well behaved, you will never get back into the houses. So I took everything everyone said not only as gospel, but as truth. Then, after sifting, I printed it.

Gradually, I began to see how the machinery worked—and the egos; I watched how agents brought index cards to interviews, with figures on them to impress the leg. After meeting with William Morris agents, and dating Triad agents, and having dinners with ICM agents—and over a couple of years getting very close to Sue Mengers and Jennings Lang and Stan Kamen—I was finally ready for CAA.

In the world of being taken care of, CAA is it.

Example: One day in 1986, Mike Ovitz, by then the most powerful agent in Hollywood, took a call from Marty Klein, a friendly, longtime competitor, a co-founder of Agency for the Performing Arts (APA). The call was about the very bankable character actor John Candy, whom Ovitz wanted to sign at CAA. The other agent didn't want to lose his star.

"You have everyone else in town," said Marty Klein to Mike Ovitz. "Must you have John Candy, too?" Ovitz understood immediately. The actor stayed with the competition—and stayed a character actor. Five years later Candy left Klein, not for Ovitz but Guy McElwaine. Go figure. The point is, the club takes care of its own. The club also competes ferociously and plays for high stakes, not always as gentlemen.

The reason: Power travels in the agency business. It travels as if on a slow train. Since the '60s, this train has made only four major stops— from Freddie Fields at Creative Management Associates (CMA) to Sue Mengers at International Creative Management (ICM) to Stan Kamen at William Morris to Mike Ovitz at CAA. When a train stops only four times in twenty years, the other passengers (read "agents") are bound to be restless.

More to the point: Are modern agents happy being agents? In years past an agent was almost always on his way elsewhere—usually to a studio job or his own production company. Three of the four people named above are no longer agents—Freddie Fields became a producer, Stan Kamen died in 1986, Sue Mengers took a "breather" from the business (twice)—and that leaves Ovitz. If he's the top of the heap, it's a very small heap.

Are the other players alike in any way, other than being collected into categories like "nurturer" and "pleaser" and "shmoozer" and "killer"? Do they merely reassure insecure people all day long and send them out the door with false hopes? In *The Way We Were* Barbra Streisand is introduced at a Hollywood party to Allyn Ann MacLerie, a woman referred to as "the greatest agent in town." MacLerie looks up from her croquet mallet and shoots Streisand an ironic glance.

"If I were a great agent—would I be an agent?"

The line referred to the self-deprecation historically heaped on agents by themselves. And if agents didn't do it, there were others who were willing. The following story is not apocryphal.

In the early '50s, Paul Kohner and John Huston and writer Peter Viertel spent some time with Ernest Hemingway in the South of France. It was just after Viertel wrote *White Hunter, Black Heart* about Huston. But it was the agent Hemingway connected with. In fact Hemingway was so taken with Kohner that he invited him to visit him in Cuba. Even Huston was impressed.

"Hemingway sure went for Paul," Huston told Viertel. "Is he always that chummy with agents?"

"You'll get a kick out of this," replied Viertel. "When I told Hemingway that Paul was an agent, he flinched. 'An agent!' Hemingway bellowed. 'Jesus, I thought he was a money man.' "

In modern Hollywood, agents are money men—some of them are major players in the same club echelon as studio executives. ICM topper Jeff Berg carries more weight in town than Alan Ladd, Jr.; CAA TV Head Bill Haber is as powerful in the club as the president of ABC. Agents' bonuses can be seven figures; their partnerships are like annuities; their clout in getting a picture made is considerable. (In the early '80s more pictures were put together in Stan Kamen's office than were put together at MGM or Columbia. Kamen's client list included Streisand, Diane Keaton, Warren Beatty, Goldie Hawn, Chevy Chase, Kurt Russell, et al.) But power shifts in the agency business—it travels exactly as if on a train. People get on—and off.

Since the '30s when Myron Selznick and Frank Orsatti began playing David to William Morris's Goliath, agents began to take on different colorations. The job—selling the client—hasn't changed, but the style has. The first power twins—the buckarooing MCA and the paternalistic William Morris—were as different as Daniel Inouye and Oliver North. The private grammar—the lingo—that agents speak changes in each decade, even if the power doesn't. In the '80s the power was high stakes but the profile was low. In the '70s the opposite was true. In the '90s, style is taboo—it's too expensive to give lavish little dinners, and nobody wants to appear extravagant.

To be very specific: The flamboyant Freddie Fields was the most powerful agent of the early '70s. Paul Newman and Robert Redford were his clients at CMA, which in 1975 merged into ICM—the same year Fields became an independent producer. The most powerful agent of the mid-'80s was the completely nonflamboyant Mike Ovitz. The difference between the two is everything: Fields lived in the high-rolling tradition of agents like Charlie Feldman and Leland Hayward—a showplace house on the best block in Beverly Hills, Christmases in Acapulco with cronies Ted Ashley and Jim Aubrey—with parties to match; Ovitz spends weekends at an almost unknown cove beyond Malibu and quietly got the legendary I. M. Pei to agree to design the new CAA headquarters in Beverly Hills. Ovitz is more a throwback to the late MCA founder, Jules

Stein, who believed that the client is the star, and not the agent. (Jules would have liked Mike Ovitz' reclusiveness.)

Does a decade make that much difference? The decade of the '80s did. The last intoxicating incident that any agent can remember was the late '70s lunchtime imbroglio between has-been club agent Bobby Littman and has-been club producer Sidney Beckerman on the patio of Ma Maison: Littman (who at the time was dating the producer's daughter) was slugged by the producer, and the patio came to life. Times change. Ma Maison is as much a memory, albeit a glamorous one, as Ciro's or the Hillcrest Country Club in its prime. It's Mortons that replaced Hillcrest— and the club members sit in front. On a given night at Mortons, quiet business dinners are served to agents in Armani suits who go to bed early and don't talk about drugs, let alone do them. It's likely they've gone to Yale, and not just pretended to (as people like Begelman did).

Most importantly the new breed understands the rules of the club. They know by heart the first law of Uncle Abe Lastfogel (the late longtime chief of William Morris): Don't poach a client from a smaller agency. The second law: Agencies are the one place that males begin in the mail room then become secretaries (as Rick Nicita and Lenny Hirshan did) and wind up as executives. Women are not in the mail room, but very much in the secretarial pool.

The third and latest law: Certain clients (Dustin Hoffman and Robert Redford are examples) are not going to pay the full 10 percent commission. Those who do best at raise time are the ones who know what constellates around an agent—the hype or lack thereof, the client signed or lost. Agents' incomes rise or fall on such signings: A good year means you signed a star, or someone who will become a star; a fair year means you held on to everyone you signed, that there were no deserters. Salary is only half of the income—the Christmas bonus is the other half. (Any agent at a club agency—CAA, William Morris, ICM—is earning a minimum $200,000 a year unless they're still in training. And it goes up from there.) The topmost agents earn $2 to $3 million a year—and they also know the ultimate rule of the business: Agents are players but not personalities. They only represent personalities.

So how do they play? They play with rituals, but without flash or fireworks. The family birthday party has replaced the dinner party. At Richard Dreyfuss' first birthday party for his son Benjamin, agents from competing offices, friends of the family, sat together and huddled—but didn't shmooze. (The semantic difference is important: "Shmooze"— which CAA agent Jane Sindell has as a license plate on her Volvo—is what agents call shoptalk. "Huddling" is just huddling—it isn't business.) Also unsurprising is the notion of agents from different companies socializing. Rival agents are often closer to each other—Stan Kamen and Sue Mengers dined every four weeks—than to their clients (though the client gets the empathy). But there is an artificiality to competition within the club; grown-up agents understand "the long day," as one put it, "and we get together to celebrate another long day, another client lost or kept, another contract, another season." They also understand the unspoken spy system that exists within studios; when a script is sent from an agent to a studio, a piece of gossip may be attached. The return? An answer as to which executive liked which script.

The power shift right now is generational, toward agents who came of age in the '60s, who have ego but also pride—and a political framework. (The only big party that anyone remembers Mike Ovitz giving in the '80s was for presidential candidate Bill Bradley, which Ovitz co-hosted with Disney chairman and friend Michael Eisner.) The modern framework includes teamwork; setting up your colleagues for a fall is frowned upon. Teamwork is one major reason for the enormous rise of CAA—within twenty-five minutes of a script submitted for client Bill Murray, every CAA agent is apprised. The callbacks are faster there than at, say, rival ICM, which is widely regarded to be less organized and more like a collection of boutiques. (If not a collection of misunderstandings.) Access to top material—and the processing of it—is any agency's strength.

It's a trench mentality—"We are in this together"—that's now at work. The instant philosophies behind *The One-Minute Manager* are not unknown at modern agencies. (Ovitz had his foot soldiers read the book before a Palm Springs retreat.)

What studios were until the '60s—a home base—is what agencies have become. Bicoastal teams of agents within a single company "look after" a star, maybe even groom him, much as a studio once did. The next possible shift: a return of the studio as a home base, as seen in Disney's signing of Tom Hanks and Carol Burnett to Midler-like deals. Burnett, for instance, is used by Disney's development teams for TV projects as well as features; her longtime ICM agent Bill Robinson is involved in the material—and Disney in the process acquired a major TV asset. All because it hit Michael Eisner that Carol Burnett should be a TV star, again.

But don't expect agents to leap ships to join studios. Not in the '90s. Agents today are staying agents more often than not. Jeff Berg has already said no to every studio. In the '70s, agents wanted to be producers or studio executives for two reasons: money and more control. In 1948, a court decision led MCA to move out of the agency business and concentrate on the movie business; chairman Lew Wasserman became a role model. Former agent Ted Ashley further paved the way by having Jack Warner personally hand him the keys to Warner Brothers, when ex-agent Ashley took over the studio in 1968. (Other ex-agents who went on to become producers or studio executives include Mark Rosenberg, Paula Weinstein, Joe Wizan, Gary Lucchesi, and Guy McElwaine.) Agents like Freddie Fields saw star clients like Paul Newman becoming very rich; producers too can become very rich—richer than all but the topmost agents. Another incentive: a reduced workload—no job is more time consuming than an agent's. It's an eight-day week, whether an agent is reading scripts or answering phones, or answering to partners or clients. He must be findable.

"It's a calling," says Sue Mengers, the first female major player, a former William Morris secretary who rose to become Hollywood's most important woman (and agent) in the late '70s. Mengers understood timing; she was key in the New York–to–Los Angeles shift that radically changed the agency business—and put the focus on Hollywood. In the '70s, the emerging actors and directors (and thus agents) were Manhattan-based (Meryl Streep, Bob Fosse, Al Pacino, Robert Benton, Kevin Kline, Treat Williams, Richard Gere). The last real New York influences were *Saturday Night Live* and the lower Manhattan club scene (Madonna and Cyndi Lauper). In the '80s the Hollywood-based Brat Pack appeared (Judd Nelson, Ally Sheedy, Sean Penn, Demi Moore, Molly Ringwald, Rob Lowe). Also, actor-clients began coming to Hollywood for representation—from Chicago (John Malkovich) and London (Gary Oldman, Julian Sands). Hollywood became 90 percent of the world.

And in a world where the term "baby moguls" is no longer heard, agents are staying put. Studio jobs are fewer, and agency jobs offer mound building (read "career building"). An agent's background can be anything—Nicole David and Paula Wagner were actresses, Peter Benedek and Alan Rifkin were lawyers. And yes, there's inbreeding, and coupling: ICM's Hildy Gottlieb is married to director Walter Hill, who is the best friend of ICM's Jeff Berg. CAA's Paula Wagner and Rick Nicita are married; Jack Rapke and Laurie Perlman have a marriage born at CAA (though Perlman eventually left to become a producer at Warner's). At William Morris the couple was Carey Woods and Cynthia Shelton.

But how did they get from there to here? How did their names get on the map? What puts an agent on the map is one of two things: (1) an impenetrable relationship with a client or (2) an event. An example of an event would be the sleeper success of director Robert Zemeckis with *Romancing the Stone*. The director's agent Jack Rapke got put on the map. (The first studio check for Zemeckis was in the low seven figures;

such checks constitute getting on the map.) A client-agent relationship, a solid joined-at-the-hip one, is the other ultimate way to get on the map. It's understood, for example, that Steve Martin will probably never leave Marty Klein at APA. It's assumed that Amy Irving and agent Nicole David are in it for the long run. Ed Limato at William Morris is Richard Gere's first and only agent. William Hurt was never even approached without the understanding that Triad's Gene Parsehegian was the conduit. It's the only way you could talk to William Hurt. Of such arcs are careers built.

It's wrong, however, to think agent-client marriages are any more binding than other marriages. In one three-year period, Mark Harmon was with William Morris, the Gersh Agency, and APA. The revolving door applies even to an actress like Anne Bancroft, who perennially shops for agents like people shop for shoes. If after thirty-five years in the business an Anne Bancroft is still prowling for representation, the schism is clear: Agents are disposable and necessary all at once. Thus an agent can never be truly secure. Clients, even the cream of a crop, come and go and sometimes come back again (as Burt Reynolds did with Sue Mengers). Clients also blame the agent for any rotten career moves, and praise the agent almost never when things go right. Why? Because dealing with a person's career and his money make for an emotionally loaded relationship. "There's always a cloud over the relationship," explains the knowing William Morris agent Joan Hyler, "especially if it's a friendship, too."

And yet agents are a fact of show business life. Or are they? In 1986 Debra Winger made a much-publicized exit from CAA (after her unhappiness at being part of the package called *Legal Eagles*). Debra Winger did not sign with another agent for two years. Debra Winger got herself a lead in a movie directed by Costa-Gavras (*Betrayed*) without an agent. Debra Winger used only an attorney (Barry Hirsch). Ultimately she surprised nobody and returned to CAA: see Chapter 18. Is it a trend? A throwback to the '70s when Paul Newman announced he didn't need an agent, after all, then Robert Redford followed suit? Then Newman and Redford, in the '80s, both signed with Ovitz?

"If you are Steven Spielberg and you have relationships," once explained Stan Kamen, "you don't need an agent. But Steven is one of maybe five exceptions. In Hollywood nobody is to the manor born."

CLUB RULE TWELVE

The smartest ones in the club are agents—or former agents.

Here's why Lew Wasserman was the ultimate agent and the smartest one: For years he pulled a stunt that never failed. When an MCA executive would threaten to quit—an executive Lew *liked*—Lew would take a little black book out of his top drawer. "The name of my successor is in this book," Lew would say, then let his voice trail off . . . "Your name is the one in the book," was the implication. More than one Wasserman protégé was fooled that way—into thinking he was Lew's favorite. The point is, the smarter an agent is, the more he is apt to outsmart you. The smartest ones in the club are (or were) agents, almost without exception.

That's why Lew Wasserman was the most powerful man in the club and not Jack Warner. Or why Mike Ovitz is, and not Bob Daly.

4

Studio System—
Bette Midler and
Jeffrey Katzenberg

Bette Davis got in because of Hal Wallis and stayed in because of William Wyler. Elvis Presley got in because of Hal Wallis. Martha Hyer married in when she finally became Mrs. Hal Wallis, and not just his mistress. Minna Wallis got in because she was Garbo's best friend, and Hal Wallis' sister. Shirley MacLaine got in because of Hal Wallis, and stayed in because of determination. Warren Beatty did not get in because he was Shirley MacLaine's brother. Warren Beatty got in because he wanted it so badly, and because of what independent club agent Charlie Feldman saw in him. Warren Beatty stayed in because Jack Warner let him produce Bonnie & Clyde. Arthur Penn got in for a decade because of Bonnie & Clyde. Faye Dunaway got in because of Bonnie & Clyde and dropped out because of Mommie Dearest. Gene Hackman got in because of Bonnie & Clyde. (Bonnie & Clyde and The Graduate were the favorite club movies of the '60s.) Warren Beatty stayed in the longest because he made the most out of the fewest movies—and because of seduction. Warren Beatty and Natalie Wood became the club couple of the '60s after they met at a Sunday brunch at Minna Wallis', and went back to the Chateau Marmont together. Robert Wagner did not drop out when Natalie Wood *dropped him for Warren Beatty. Robert Wagner got in by marrying Natalie Wood in the first place, and then remarrying her. Robert Wagner also stayed in when he married Stanley Donen's ex-wife, Marian. Stanley Donen got in because of Elizabeth Taylor and Gene Kelly. Gene Kelly got in because of talent and Lew Wasserman. He got back in because of* That's Entertainment *and Joyce Haber. Dan Melnick got in because of David Susskind and* That's Entertainment. *He got back in because of* Footloose *and Craig Zadan and Ray Stark. Jack Haley, Jr., got in by birth, and stayed in because of* That's Entertainment. *He dropped out when he dropped Liza Minnelli as his wife—while her father was still alive. Vincente Minnelli was the club director of musicals. Vincente Minnelli was also club husband to ultimate club wife Denise Minnelli Hale. Liza Minnelli got in because her mother was Judy Garland, and her father was Vincente Minnelli, and she stayed in because of* Cabaret. *She dropped out because former club agent Stevie Phillips talked her into doing* Lucky Lady. *Stevie Phillips got in because she was David Begelman's secretary. Freddie Fields got in because his brother was a famous bandleader and his wife was Polly Bergen. David Begelman and Freddie Fields got in as a team because of Judy Garland, whom both of them coddled. David Begelman stayed in because of Warren Beatty and* Shampoo. *David Begelman was only dropped temporarily because he forged Cliff Robertson's name on a check. He got back in because of* The Fabulous Baker Boys, *and because of a triangular friendship with Billy Wilder and Walter Matthau (and their wives). Freddie Fields got back in because of the prestige success of* Glory. *Polly Bergen dropped out because she left Freddie Fields and Hollywood for New York and a younger husband. She could get back in anytime she wanted to because of how well she understands the club, and because she's Judy Quine's best friend. Judy Quine got in because she was Barney Balaban's daughter and Jay Kanter's wife and Grace Kelly's best friend, and bridesmaid. She stayed in because of class and style.*

At the most important Hollywood evening of 1989—the American Cinematheque dinner honoring Steven Spielberg—MCA president Sid Sheinberg uttered perhaps the ugliest line in social Hollywood history. "Good evening ladies and gentlemen and Jeffrey Katzenberg." Sheinberg was talking about his arch-rival, Disney president Jeffrey Katzenberg. (Both Katzenberg and Sheinberg are second-tier Hollywood executives— Sheinberg is second-in-command to MCA chairman Lew Wasserman and Katzenberg is second—if that's the word—to Disney chairman Michael Eisner. But it's Katzenberg and Sheinberg who run the studios.)

Since Katzenberg is widely considered to be both smarter and more capable than Sheinberg, the remark was particularly gratuitous. It also showed how low Hollywood has sunk: Would Donald Trump have introduced Felix Rohatyn like that? The feeling that night at the Spielberg dinner was that maybe Lew Wasserman made a mistake in picking Sid Sheinberg as his heir apparent—but that Wasserman is a company man above all else. And once he chose Sid, he chose Sid. Even though he can't tolerate him at table. But Wasserman stood by Sheinberg right through to the profitable Matsushita buy-out. Lew could ease his conscience by seeing to it that Sid was taken care of. (All of this is rudimentary, anyway: The ultimate successor to Lew Wasserman is Mike Ovitz. Somewhere, subconsciously, Sheinberg knows this. So does Ovitz.)

The irony: Universal, under Sheinberg and Tom Pollock, was finally having its season of seasons—what Steven Spielberg calls a "sweet circle"—the revolving democratic flow of each studio getting its share of hits. Out of the Universal stable that year were *Field of Dreams, Born on the Fourth of July,* and *Parenthood,* among others. So why was Sid Sheinberg behaving so badly at a dinner he was co-hosting for the all-time wunderkind of Hollywood—whom he discovered?

Brattiness.

"Or maybe it's envy," said an executive who used to be at Columbia. "The two of them are like cats and dogs. Sid has more money but Jeffrey is still under forty. Barely, but . . ."

At Table Number One, Katzenberg simply clutched his wife, Marilyn's, hand more tightly as Sheinberg read (not even memorized!) from index cards the prepared remarks about Steven Spielberg.

"I stand corrected," said the ex-executive from Columbia. "Sid's envy isn't about Jeffrey's age. It's about Jeffrey's star, Bette Midler. She's the kind of star Louis B. Mayer used to have—and Sid wants one of those."

Bette Midler is the modern version of the quintessential studio star— the executive's pet, the bankable favorite. Five hits in five years at one studio, and $255 million in film rentals. That she became a movie star doesn't surprise anyone; that she had to become a well-behaved studio employee to do so is a stunner. "Every executive on this lot—every day— drives to work, and the first thing on their minds is—*you have to believe me*—Bette Midler." Jeffrey Katzenberg was being specific about his star as an asset. The businessman was exposing his vulnerability to a creative resource.

"Even myself," continued Katzenberg, "I still drive past a billboard at Crescent Heights and Sunset Boulevard, and I think, 'Well, there's an obligation here—an obligation to be enthusiastic.' This whole success is 98 percent her and 2 percent us."

"Bette and I go to Jeffrey's office for a meeting, and it's wild," said Bonnie Bruckheimer, the producer (*Beaches*), who's probably Midler's closest friend. "Fourteen things are going on, and we're on our way somewhere else—one of us is, anyway—and we talk in shorthand. I don't think it's formal like people think. Jeffrey and Bette both have this sense of humor."

That doesn't mean these two are alike. "Do you think alike?" Katzenberg was asked. He replied with a prolonged pronounced laugh. "Are they alike?" Bruckheimer was asked, and she responded with, "Nobody's like Jeffrey." Only Midler thought before she responded. "Jeffrey and I are very much . . . two equals. He never pulls rank on me, and I never pull rank on him. We never threaten each other, and we never blackmail each other. And we never talk about personalities. It never gets to that level. We never say, 'I hate so and so.' We never talk like that. He's very amusing, but it's never anything personal or dirty. Also, it's not that intimate. Because I don't think it can be . . . It shouldn't be."

"She's very amusing," said Katzenberg, using Midler's word. "And so is her husband. [The commodities trader Martin von Haselberg.] But I would say we have had moments of contentiousness."

The major misconception about Bette Midler is that she gave away her power to the powers at Disney. "She handed her career to Jeffrey Katzenberg and Michael Eisner," is the way one agent puts it. "And then the power came back to her." Midler listened closely as the line was repeated to her.

"The power, hmm . . ." she said, tugging at an orange cashmere turtleneck and thinking. "I didn't give it away, I gave it up. 'Gave it away' means I actually gave it to someone, that someone received it. No—I just gave it up."

And, she agreed, it came back to her: "I would say that that was true. But I'm much more cautious about the use of it now. I'm not interested in misusing it; that would be easy. I'm not even really interested in using it." Midler made a distinction: "One has to be in charge of where one's career is going, but that's personal power. That's not getting other people to do what you want. *For the Boys* was different because I was obliged to say more, because I co-produced. But if I had my way, I wouldn't have said anything. I was obliged to do the job, I did the job. I cared, and I think it shows on the screen, but . . . right now, I just want to know I have a body of work."

So there's a kind of compromise. "The truth is that it pays not to care," confided Midler. "It's better if you don't have your soul on the line. I haven't found anything that I'm ready to sell my soul for. If I do, I will, but I haven't yet. Not so far with these people. Although I like them, I'm enjoying myself. I mean, I love the relationship we have."

There's love, and there's love. What's sometimes missing in Midler's voice is a kind of passion, and she knows it. "I just don't have the fever now," she'll say, when asked. So that's one Midler misconception cleared up—the one about her still being a careerist at all costs. But there are other misconceptions about Bette Midler, seven-figure movie star. They are taken as truth only because real information is harder to come by. But Midler has no problem prioritizing them.

1. After seven lean Hollywood years, Bette revels in playing queen of the lot. Use the phrase and she looks at you like you are crazy. "I hear that, and I don't know who they're talking about. It's like some balloon over there"—she points out a window—"it's like this ephemeral cloud of vapor. Do you think I should behave like the queen of the lot? Sometimes I'd like to. I see pictures of Barbra Streisand in a limousine with a bodyguard, and I think, 'Oh—I really should do that.' But I don't want to meet any new bodybuilders. Debra Winger says every six months she puts some dirt out there—that's what a star does. I thought, 'Why didn't I think of that?' But then I knew I'd have to make something up. And that would be like playing another role, and I don't have the time."

2. In those seven lean years Midler acquired a "get-even" philosophy. "No," she countered. "I don't have any axes to grind. I don't need my enemies, and it's very freeing. Not to have another agenda is very freeing. Think of the amount of time you spend trying to knife the people who stiffed you. Or trying to get back at them . . . I'm not saying I've forgiven anybody. I hold a grudge, definitely, absolutely. I just don't need my enemies any longer. When I was younger I needed them. I was mad, and I'm not even sure why I was so mad. It's from when I was a kid. It got me through many, many years in New York, that anger, from like '65 to '75. Ten years of it, and I grew out of it. This stardom is like a major payback. I used all that anger," she said almost convincingly. "I've really used it all up."

3. When cream rises—and you're the cream—it's fun. "Wrong," corrected Midler. "All this is work. You don't know what it's like to think about hair and makeup all the time. When Joan Collins says she's a

product of the old studio system and she never goes out without hair or makeup—it's like four hours to do that. You could be in the garden. Growing something. It's like why bother? Bette Davis asked me one night how could I come to a party looking like that? I looked perfectly respectable! I had on a nice black dress, I combed my hair. I said to myself, 'Well that's the way Bette Davis does things.' But I would never be so mean-spirited as to say that about somebody. I don't think she was always like that. Maybe it was the smoking and getting older and being lonely. In the '40s when she broke her contract, and went to England, I thought that was powerful. That was a strong thing to do." (Irony: Bette Midler was named for Bette Davis.)

4. Midler as star is in a galaxy with other stars; she is part of a peer group. This time she really looks at you like you are crazy. "Most of the time you are so wrapped up in yourself, you don't really look or see. Suddenly I opened my eyes and saw that there are people out here in the same position I'm in. But most of us are so self-involved, looking at ourselves through a microscope. I'm always self-consciously prejudging, and judging my own actions."

5. Since her self-proclaimed nervous breakdown, in 1985, Midler has put on blinders about her movie stardom, and become completely gung-ho. "No, I still have my withdrawing days. Definitely. But it's a balance. If there's a crisis on the lot, I know how to jump out of bed, quick, rush over and put my two cents in. But only if I'm needed. It's a tough, hard lesson to learn that other people have imagination and vision, too—but I learned it. Mostly from being in the music business, where you deal with more gangsterish-type people. Not gangsterish—maybe they're just tougher, more from the street. The budgets in music aren't as huge as in pictures. People in the movie business are more elegant; they have a shinier veneer. But once you scratch the veneer, the bottom line is the thing that counts. Sometimes I get a little vague," Midler said vaguely, "but I always know where the bottom line is."

6. Bette Midler, millionairess, is still basically tight with a dollar. She laughed the way a teenager laughs about her biggest secret being revealed. "You mean that I'm cheap? I am quite cheap. I don't own shopping centers, I don't have any tax shelters, I don't have stock in any bank, I don't do any wheeling and dealing. But I can get very agitated, and I can say, 'Where's the money?' I'm interested to see how they work these schemes in business. And then when I find out, I want to practically throw myself on a funeral pyre, because I think, 'Ohmigod, I'm broke.' But I'm conservative about money because I see constant waste around me. People are so damned mindless, brainwashed almost, about buying

up everything. People want to be on the top of the trend. With these leveraged buy-outs, stock market gambits, and ways of buying money, people are just going nuts."

She's been on top of a trend for almost two decades. Why her? Comparing careers is tricky, but if you look at three stars who came from musical comedy to movies—Barbra Streisand, Liza Minnelli, and Midler—you see that Midler had the hardest road. Barbra Streisand was a major recording and Broadway star at age twenty-two; she had then–star agents Freddie Fields and David Begelman paying attention, even when she was singing for nothing at the Bon Soir. Liza Minnelli won a Tony at eighteen, and she had bloodlines. Midler was the eldest daughter on Broadway in *Fiddler on the Roof,* not a star-making bit. It took Midler combining tragic torch songs with camp humor—and jokes at her own expense—to rivet early audiences at the Continental Baths. In 1972, even before her debut at Hollywood's Troubadour, there was talk that producer Ray Stark wanted to star her in a movie called *Ruby Red,* but she was already thirty years old. The week before the Troubadour, a publicist was talking to a journalist about "someone called Bette Midler, who's going to be an enormous star—a monster in the business."

Midler tears up when talking about her ambition then, her need, her fever. She becomes the loneliest, homeliest preswan ugly duckling, with all the rough edges showing. So you have to ask her about wanting the power of movie stardom. Part of the legend of Barbra Streisand has her as a young singer at the Bon Soir refusing a CMA agency contract for recording and TV—because she wanted to be a movie star, period. And Freddie Fields agreed. Midler had a rockier road—Freddie Fields never came backstage to woo her. But she can relate.

"I intended to be a movie star because I thought it was the high end," she said simply. "I thought it was where the work would survive, that if you had something beautiful and good to offer, it was worth the effort. I still feel that way, but not as strongly. Because I know how hard it is to make something good and beautiful. With your own personal vision. You almost have to be a giant of some sort."

No, she wasn't talking about *Yentl,* the movie most actresses talk about in terms of a star having a vision. Midler was asked to drop a name. "Okay, let's take Orson Welles," she responded in a flash. "A giant, who was beaten down by the system, and couldn't survive. I'm not saying he didn't contribute to his own demise, but he should have found the way to survive. He should have found the path. He didn't, he couldn't. And if he couldn't, who of us can?"

But Orson Welles didn't have the resources of the Disney empire behind him. "So are you saying I have an obligation to force my views on the studio?" Midler retorted. No, but this phase of her career should feel like a dream come true, at least a little. "It does," Midler admitted. "But my situation is one I don't want to jeopardize by beating them with a stick of my ego and my personality. My situation is one that I want to remain calm and polite. So the steps I take are cautious ones."

So she's paying strict attention, ignoring the emotional roller coaster that made *The Rose* such a signature film. There is a Hollywood proverb about seven years lucky, and seven years unlucky: *The Rose* was 1979 and her comeback *Down and Out in Beverly Hills* was exactly seven years later. In the middle of a lucky period, Midler became a political animal. Without malice, but very straightforwardly, she said: "My steps are very considered. I think a lot about what I'm doing with these people."

More to the point: "I think a lot about the things I want the studio to do for me. And I know they think a lot about the things they want me to do for them. It's give-and-take." Whether it's the *Georgette* animation film Midler did for Disney, as a kind of favor, or a tour film she did for Disney's Epcot Center. "I did *Georgette* for almost nothing. Not nothing, but almost no money. I'm doing this little tour picture for them, for Epcot. I did a little Mickey thing for Michael [Eisner]. Little things, you know, here and there." She makes it sound like day work.

Then what does Disney do for Bette? "They listen," she said, like it was a gift from God. *Somebody in Hollywood listens.* "They're obliged to listen to pitches, but they also bend over backward to see my point of view." Midler cracked up at her own phrasing, and her eyes went mock-lewd. "They'll listen again and again and again. It's like whittling away at the people who are under Jeffrey. Who, for the most part, have been pretty much in my corner. But it's about saying 'You have to take another look' or 'This might be eccentric but it's good' or 'You just don't understand.' I manage to convince them a lot, and sometimes they go to bat for us, too."

At one point Midler said, "I'm not a gentle person" and because Katzenberg is himself not considered soft, the chemistry became clear. Where they are alike is in their willingness to intrude, in terms of the final cut of a picture. Both can be brutal. As Norman Mailer put it, if two people can kill equally—they can love each other.

"In certain cases the directors and Jeffrey have both asked me, 'What do you think?' I'll say, 'Oh, I think you shaved too much off this scene.' Or, 'I don't like the music' in a scene. Sometimes they listen, and sometimes they don't. If I feel very strongly about something I don't want used on a picture, Jeffrey listens."

The executive listens and not the director? The myth is that directors at certain levels wield the editing power. Midler nodded in agreement.

"Usually that's true. When a director makes his cut, an actor just has to shut up. Unless the director asks them, and then he's leaving himself open for any number of complaints. In my case, it has happened that they ask me what I think, and I tell them."

Garry Marshall, who directed *Beaches*, says, "She can be insecure. She hadn't sung on screen in six years when we did *Beaches*. But something happens to her between 'Action' and 'Cut.' She comes to life. She understands that Disney is a studio with both hands on, and sometimes even an elbow. Bette's fearless when she works with them, and she can be obsessive. I mean, she couldn't stop talking about her hair. There must have been a hundred hair jokes. Such insecurity. And then you say 'Action' and the insecurity is just gone."

But there's a catch-22 here—the Midler-Disney marriage is not without outside temptations, especially for the star. There are Bette Midler projects at 20th Century-Fox and TriStar, which Disney has passed on, and Midler is just canny enough to know that friction could ensue. Bonnie Bruckheimer says, "Oh well, Bette is exclusive to Disney now." Jeffrey Katzenberg says, "We had a first look at those other projects." But it's Midler who sees the situation most clearly: "If he [Katzenberg] turns something down, I have it in my contract that I can go elsewhere. So I have something at Fox, something at TriStar. Nobody minds that. Because until *For the Boys* we hadn't gotten to the point where we're going to make those pictures. But they don't really have to feel that I'm deserting them."

One day arriving slightly late for an afternoon meeting at her All-Girl production office, Midler was almost unrecognizable. The wiry librarian glasses, the shapeless butterscotch sweater, the pleated '50s sophomore skirt, the quietude of her personality that day. Talia Shire in the original *Rocky*. Bette talks about gaining enormous sums of weight "between pictures, even now, and then going to exercise class, and everybody's shocked how fast I take it off." But it's not the weight or the schoolgirlish looks—it's the seriousness of Better Midler that's surprising. "The mood swings in the last few years are less frequent," says Bonnie Bruckheimer, but one senses that Midler's still volatile enough to change moods in the middle of a corridor.

And indeed she seems to sense when a curvy question is coming. The Disney comedies blur in some people's minds—*Big Ruthless Outrageous Fortune in Beverly Hills*. Didn't Midler hesitate ever before saying yes? "I had hesitation, oh yes I did," she insisted. "But I was in an I-want-to-work mode. I would have done cameos, I just wanted to get my feet wet again. I did ponder over *Ruthless People*. I thought, 'Oh God, I can't do this, it's so vulgar.' Then I thought, 'Oh the hell with it, who cares, they all think I'm totally vulgar anyway. Why not really go for it?' I didn't look good in it at all, and I was definitely confused. I wasn't all there. Lucky it was a hit. I don't think I got a lot of guidance on that one."

Guidance. Career moves. Actresses desperate for direction. One either works all the time, like Jessica Lange, or waits for what seems like forever, like Barbra Streisand. Midler didn't want to wait six years again between movies. She didn't want to wait for another *Rose*. "I'm not that kind of person," she admitted. "If I waited, I wouldn't have a body of work, and I wanted a body of work. Sometimes I wish—when I look back at the body—that the body I had was a little better. But it's what I've gotten, it's my fate." Very quickly she added: "I would never bemoan my fate. I'm happy to be working."

Happy but not surprised. Midler tensed up a little on the topic of stardom. "I'm not surprised because I know I have it. I have what it takes. I'm a hard worker, too. But I'm surprised at the strength of the popularity. Or not so much surprised as relieved. Not to be in the unemployment line. You don't ever forget that phase of your life."

This phase—the house in Coldwater Canyon, the land in Hawaii, the husband and child, the baby showers for friends, the balance—is a little cushy for die-hard Midler fans who remember her when. "I'm not as driven anymore. It comes from having been around. You begin to see what's valuable, what will and won't waste your time." This new life wasn't what Midler originally envisioned for herself. Ask her to drop a name, and she says, "Anita Loos, or Dorothy Parker. Alone at the end, I could see myself heading that way. I didn't want it to happen though. I didn't want to end up on the last bar stool. With a drink in my hand. I may yet, though," she added with a kind of knowing look—the old Divine Miss M twinkle—that encompasses many possibilities. "Or maybe I'm too bourgeois to end up on the bar stool."

So what has this movie star learned in Hollywood? . . .

Hmm . . . "This period is giving me a chance to really solidify my instincts. I'm finding out what I care deeply and passionately about."

And?

"I'm finding out that sequins are my life."

And?

"I'm finding out that I'm completely and totally superficial."

And?

"I'm finding out that movies are like propaganda. They are like instruction, like messages, and you can't be vague about what you are saying.

If you don't have a vision, you are just acting someone else's point of view. So what I have to do is solidify my point of view. Every five years or so I go through a life change."

That's one reason why Jeffrey Katzenberg still pays such close attention to Bette Midler.

CLUB RULE THIRTEEN

You get what you want by giving the club (or studio) what it wants.

Bette Midler worried that Jeffrey Katzenberg wouldn't like it when she made pictures for other studios. Not after she'd made $255 million for Disney. "There will be a little bit of friction," worried Bette. So, to outsmart everybody, she went after two non-Disney movies that were, finally, beyond Disney's scope: the musical life of legendary Lotte Lenya (with Dustin Hoffman as Kurt Weill) and the lavish musical *For the Boys* directed by Mark Rydell, who made her a movie star in *The Rose*.

That way *how could Jeffrey get mad?* His star made two expensive star-enhancing movies at somebody else's expense. That's why Bette Midler is not just a star, but a club star. Because she keeps the studio brass dancing to her tune.

5

The Fall of Dawn— Dawn Steel

Dawn Steel got in because she marketed Gucci toilet paper, got some publicity for it, and Michael Eisner saw something in her. Dawn Steel stayed in because of speed, smarts, and a friendship with Jeffrey Katzenberg. She continued to stay in first because Ned Tanen liked her, and then—when he didn't like her—she stayed in because of Victor Kaufman. By the time she got to Disney (and back with Katzenberg) she was a full-fledged member. One of the few girls who's also one of the boys. Victor Kaufman got in because of Ray Stark. Guy McElwaine stayed in because of Ray Stark, and so did Frank Price. Peter Guber got in because of Ray Stark and David Begelman. Jon Peters got in in spite of Ray Stark. Richard Dreyfuss stayed in because of Ray Stark and Sherry Lansing, and so did Neil Simon and Herb Ross. Jon Peters stayed in in spite of exiting the co-chairmanship of Columbia. He stayed in because of Peter Guber, and street smarts. Dawn Steel changed roles because of Peter Guber and Jon Peters.

The club watches each studio executive's pet movies almost with vengeance. Every true club movie—*Children of a Lesser God* or *Working*

Girl for example—has a mentor in the club. *Lesser God* was Ned Tanen's movie; *Casualties of War* was Dawn Steel's movie as much as it was Brian De Palma's. *Born on the Fourth of July* first belonged to Al Pacino (who got within three weeks of shooting, in 1977) until finally it belonged to Oliver Stone and the CAA agent who nurtured it, Paula Wagner. Then it belonged to Tom Cruise.

Chinatown was Robert Towne's movie until it became Robert Evans' movie, too, and then finally it belonged to Evans and director Roman Polanski. The movie never belonged to stars Jack Nicholson or Faye Dunaway. The sequel (*The Two Jakes*) belonged (unfortunately) to Nicholson. In the original, *Chinatown*, Dunaway was second choice to Jane Fonda. The day Dunaway got cast, someone close to the movie said (presciently—perhaps foreseeing what trouble would ensue)—"That cunt is Chinatown. We wanted Jane." Because *Chinatown* was Evans' first commitment from Paramount when he left executive status to become an independent producer, the studio was completely behind it. Evans and Polanski were given their heads.

Everyone in the club knows every history of every major studio club movie. Let's take one club movie, and one studio executive, one director, one producer, and see how a club movie is really a case study in muscle at work.

The fact is that people in the club create their own mythologies. The first half of 1989 was the season of Dawn Steel. Suddenly the first woman executive star since Sherry Lansing came into media flower. But if Sherry was the cheerleader from Northwestern, Dawn was more the anxious little girl from Long Island. The Queen of Mean was what *California* magazine called Dawn; *Time* called her Steely Dawn. Mostly because she wouldn't cooperate with articles—for *Time*, *Vanity Fair*, *California*, *Rolling Stone*—she started becoming legendary. (See Pacino in Chapter 17: The club wants what it can't have; the same is true of the media.) A woman with a mouth, how unusual some of the boys said, and a woman with real power, too. Her moment came in the summer of '89 when she spoke at a Women in Film luncheon: None of her movies had failed yet. So she had magic. The speech was videotaped and it made some kind of Hollywood history. Dawn Steel played to the toughest audience of all like a movie star. Savvy people were studying the videotape. Suddenly she was like Madonna.

Once I knew how much the New York media craved her, this first female president of a studio, I decided to talk to Dawn Steel. I was so determined, I bent my own rules. I only asked for thirty minutes. That was a mistake: She could have talked all day. Another mistake: I didn't tape her. The third mistake: I told her people were studying her like a role model. The fourth mistake: I left her office so transfixed I walked right past Ray Stark, who was waiting to have lunch with her. So affected was I by the Steel magnetism I barely noticed the producer who had a lot to do with putting her in place. I barely got home without hyperventilating; she has the intensity of a star. And the same capacity to break hearts and wills.

People at Paramount told me that *Casualties of War* was really the story of a jilted love affair between Dawn and Paramount, the studio that groomed her. When I walked into her Burbank office, I knew that—but she didn't know I knew it. A part of fusing with club members is playing dumb; after all, they are smarter than you are, no matter who you are. So go along with the fiction of the moment.

When I walked in, she pointed to a priceless framed *From Here to Eternity* poster that hung above the leather sofa in her all-beige office. "There have been four regimes here in six years," she said bluntly. "And nothing was saved. Our seventieth anniversary is coming up—or is it our seventy-fifth?—and we are buying up memorabilia. I actually had to buy that poster." She shrugged. Dawn Steel understands purchase power—and executive shuffles. Exactly two years after she made her very publicized shift from Paramount to Columbia, *Casualties of War*, the first Columbia movie she green-lighted, was released nationwide in 1,500 theaters. This dark and controversial $22.5 million Brian De Palma saga of the rape and murder of a Vietnamese woman was based on a 1969 *New Yorker* piece by Daniel Lang. The movie co-starred Michael J. Fox and Sean Penn as soldiers ultimately pitted against each other. Ultimately, it may have cost Dawn her presidency at Columbia.

From the start, there were obvious financial ramifications—why was she releasing a war movie in August? insiders asked. But for Steel there were emotional ramifications, too. *Casualties* was originally developed at her longtime home base, Paramount; her former colleagues are the people who developed this film from scratch. The movie's producer, Art Linson (*The Untouchables*), claimed, "There's no real downside for Dawn." (He meant the foreign take on the movie would put it in profit—eventually.) Still, there was a detective story here.

When Brian De Palma said, "This is the first war movie with a woman as the pivot," he didn't just mean onscreen. He meant the pivot off screen is also female. There are many theories about what Dawn Steel saw in *Casualties of War*. ("She was so obsessed with it, she actually went to the Thailand location!" said one stunned producer.) In 1988 Steel profitably rereleased David Lean's *Lawrence of Arabia*—her first "success" at Columbia—which led to speculation that she had a childhood thing for all-male combat movies. She laughed out loud at the notion.

"I haven't heard that one," Steel said, swiveling in a chair in the middle of her second-floor office. "The first war movie I ever saw was *Platoon*, and I was eight months' pregnant. So my husband [producer Charles Roven] wasn't sure I'd make it. *Lawrence of Arabia* is a whole other thing; *Lawrence* is flawless. The day I sent David Lean a check was the most thrilling day of my life. *Casualties* is a commercial endeavor. I admit it's also an epic, and I do like epics. An epic is the canvas Brian De Palma paints on. De Palma thinks David Lean walks on water—not only *Lawrence*, but he also loves [Lean's] *Bridge on the River Kwai*. There's this classic photo of De Palma at the *Lawrence* premiere looking at Lean with such awe . . . I don't want to keep comparing the two, but *Casualties* is probably a direct result of *Lawrence*."

And nobody else wanted to make it. At Paramount the movie was fully developed and cast, but when the budget abruptly jumped from $17 million to $20 million, the studio pulled out. After eighteen months of support. "Nobody else was breaking down our doors, nobody but Dawn," remembered producer Linson, who was based at Paramount until he left in early 1991 to headquarter at Warner's. Her support put Steel in the David Puttnam position with her first Columbia acquisition. (Puttnam, her predecessor, left the studio in 1987, with almost $100 million in write-offs, primarily movies nobody else wanted to make.)

After Steel's Sequel Summer (both *Ghostbusters II* and *Karate Kid III* performed below capacity for Columbia) the studio found itself defending a movie most people in the club were ready to dismiss. Even her Christmas gamble on Jane Fonda's long-postponed $31 million *The Old Gringo* seemed more logical to some people than *Casualties of War*. But some people aren't Dawn Steel. As De Palma put it over dinner one evening, "I think *Casualties* appealed to Dawn because it offers an emotional dilemma that could take place anywhere. It could take place in a high school." (Or Hollywood. Some of playwright David Rabe's lines—"Are you on my frequency?" or "Kill the bitch"—sound like studio conversations.) "The fact of it being in Vietnam gives it a whole other dimension. Vietnam is America's wound. No Vietnam movie has ever lost money. Especially abroad, war movies make money." De Palma continued almost defensively: "Women adore this movie more than any other focus group. Pauline Kael [*The New Yorker* critic] has called it a life-changing experience. And Pauline hasn't liked a movie of mine in eight years. And Pauline discovered me!"

"Okay, it seems risky," admitted Steel, agreeing that the fifteen days between opening day and Labor Day ultimately determined *Casualties* shelf life—or, rather, the lack of it. "So it was risky. So? What I do for a living is risky." She leaned in close to elaborate. "We are gamblers. We bet on people. That's what we do. So as a gambler I bet on Art Linson and Brian De Palma." (The three of them did *Untouchables* while Steel was at Paramount, with a $101 million gross domestically—the movie was De Palma's first mainstream hit, and as the director said recently, "We also made Kevin Costner a star.") Continued Steel: "After *Untouchables* I wanted to do it again. These are people I believed in. I was the first studio executive to meet with Sean Penn after *Taps* in 1981. I was anxious to develop things with him when nobody knew who he was."

But why this movie? The answer was surprising from the "Queen of Mean" in a community where the "King of Mean" would be a redundancy; only Dawn Steel's gender got her her labels. "Nobody is black and white," she said carefully, "and here's a big movie that says that. There's a moment when Michael [Fox's] character says, 'We can't keep treating people this way.' It's a modern moment. We are alive at a time when there's a hole in the ozone. Crazed fans are killing people . . ." She started to fan herself; the steam machine in the corner of her office overheats the room, and even the executive was warm. "I don't want to depress myself. But this movie is about how we all have gray areas. I was moved by it."

No, this isn't a *Yentl* saga of a movie nurtured by a nineteen-year believer: Steel was actually on maternity leave from Paramount when De Palma and Linson finally put *Casualties* into development in 1986. The movie only became a Steel project after it was cast and almost ready to shoot. Steel found herself, in October of 1987, named Columbia president four days after meeting Columbia's reclusive CEO Victor Kaufman—and found herself in need of a slate of movies. Sequels, yes, to be sure: Columbia under Steel was planning remakes or sequels to *Pal Joey*, *The Way We Were*, *The Deep*, *Jagged Edge*, *St. Elmo's Fire*, *The Big Chill*, ad nauseam. But what else? All participants agree *Casualties* wouldn't have been made without Dawn Steel. But exactly how did this movie get to Columbia?

"I'll trace it for you," she said openly. There's almost a nakedness to Steel that draws emotion from people, positively or negatively. She's like a star actress in a way—when she's in a room, you focus only on her. Said Steel, dramatically: "There was an appetite for this movie at Paramount. But there was also some fear. And then it got a smidge expensive." (Paramount sources put the smidge at $3 million, after the picture had been green-lighted. Other sources said $8 million. Linson attributed the extra expenses to "odds and ends across the board. Fringes and drivers, a whole collection of things.") Steel continued: "So the question is, 'How much is too much? Or how much is enough?' The pocketbook has to match the appetite." Paramount had exclusive hold on producer Linson at the time: He produced their dismal Robert De Niro–Sean Penn 1989 Christmas release *We're No Angels*. So Paramount could have contractually withheld *Casualties* from Columbia but relented—at a price. They listened to their in-house producer. (Also at a price.) The switch from one studio to another meant the movie went from costing $20 million to $22.5 million, or more.

"Paramount didn't make it easier for us to acquire it," complained Steel. "They added things to make it more expensive."

What things?

"Stuff.

Added Linson: "We built this movie from the ground up. Every set you see was built in Thailand. Paramount was well vested in this movie, and they got every dollar back from Columbia." Another off-the-record Paramount source explained that the studio "believed in the picture we green-lighted, at the price agreed to. Seventeen million. Good business means you don't suddenly come back with a figure of $20 million." Countered Linson: "Costs add up even before you shoot in a foreign country. You're on their turf. Suddenly it was going to cost a little more. I think that was a little frightening to Paramount. One phone call to Dawn, and the movie was set at Columbia. Who knew it was her cup of tea?"

She knew. "Do you remember Charlie Bluhdorn?" Steel was invoking the name of the legendary Austrian founder of Gulf & Western, and one of her mentors. "Charlie used to say we needed Bank of America awards, like Academy Awards, for the bankers who back our passions. We have to make some movies we have only passion for, only respect for. You do sequels because they are tent poles: They open well, and they hold the tent up. But in between you make a movie you respect. A movie like *The Accused* would be an example. Sometimes that movie surprises you."

At Columbia, Steel was suddenly competing directly with Paramount, going up against Paramount's acknowledged state-of-the-art marketing and distribution network. She nodded. "Paramount sets the standard, from a marketing standpoint. And, yes, you are trying to compete with them. You are competitive with everybody. What I was trying to accomplish at Columbia was to get the top couple of slots for Columbia." You could feel her anxiety, her need, to get Columbia out of being the ninth-place studio she found when she arrived. (When she left, in early 1990, Columbia was third of nine studios, due mostly to the sequels. Steel's own movies—*Awakenings, Postcards from the Edge*—hadn't been released yet.)

"But I'm glad Paramount didn't do this picture," she went on. "Obviously they were waiting to see what this picture would do. One man's turnaround is another man's hit. I've been there. I know. And the lesson is always the same lesson: Nobody knows nothing."

Ironically Steel chose as an example the 1989 Disney summer hit *Honey, I Shrunk the Kids.* (Two years later she would produce the sequel.) She remembers calling Jeffrey Katzenberg "at eight-thirty on the Saturday morning after it opened. He seemed startled. I said, 'C'mon, Jeffrey, don't tell me you don't know the numbers.' The picture did $5 million on a Friday night! He thought they'd do five for the whole weekend. But Disney knows how to make movies that open, not just movies with intentions."

Steel's intentions were obvious, but her battle at Columbia was so uphill it even staggered her: "It's more uphill than I ever dreamed. It's all so . . . operational. It's like a tanker floating on an ocean. Have you ever seen a tanker on a newsreel? Do you know how hard it is to turn a tanker around? I don't know that I turned it around, but . . ."

But they were watching, they were observing her like Richard Zanuck was observed in the '60s, or Peter Guber was observed in the '70s. Suddenly she verged on being a household name. Articles she didn't cooperate with were being written around her. The people who remember her in her baby Fiat, obsessive and single and *looking*, were now asking questions like "What are the colors in her office?"

Almost nobody doesn't now know the former Dawn Spielberg (her father, a semipro weight lifter, changed the name to Steel). The press was having its field day. When Steel visited writer Nora Ephron in New York's Hamptons, even hard-edged New Yorkers were gaga. Dawn Steel's arrival was Topic A at the choicest Easthampton softball games.

"I want them to write about me less," she said as if she meant it. She knows Jacqueline Onassis was uncanny and correct when she said privately that the worst thing a person can give up is anonymity. "You become this persona and you become mythic," said Steel. "Visibility is dangerous because if a guy cuts you off in traffic you can't call him an asshole—it might get to the press. But I wanted to build a stable and I wanted to build momentum. So . . ."

Brian De Palma has the table manners of someone who just got out of prison. He tackles a Musso & Frank's prime rib like a hungry inmate; he turns a head of lettuce into a victim. His friend Martin Scorsese claims De Palma simply puts on a "tough front," that he's actually loyal and devoted. To his friends, maybe, and his movies certainly. Twenty movies in twenty years, in a spiral that's gone upward and more toward middle of the road: *Hi Mom!*, his 1968 debut, was as underground as the late '60s ever got; *The Untouchables* made him a mainstream director. *The Bonfire of the Vanities* almost unmade him.

But it's power—the power of working all the time—that De Palma relishes. The misconception is that he's still living in the two-bedroom Greenwich Village apartment, apart from Hollywood. Whereas he in fact had a house in the Hollywood Hills forever, and feels no estrangement from the company town. He's married to *Terminator's* zillionaire co-producer Gale Ann Hurd. He has his own table at the club restaurant Mortons. "This is our industry," he says, without apology. "I don't distance myself from it." But *Casualties of War* was like a casebook history on how hard it is to get movies made—for De Palma or anybody. Even without any distance from Burbank.

The director, like everyone associated with *Casualties*, remembers reading *The New Yorker* piece by Daniel Lang in 1969 and wanting to film it. He talked with James Woods early on about playing one of the soldiers. The twenty-year saga is not a new story: A Robert Redford with *Ordinary People*, or a Robert Benton with *Kramer vs. Kramer*, can tell the same story. De Palma, the workhorse, simply (compulsively) did other things while waiting for a green light: He sat next to Angie Dickinson at a dinner for the mayor of Montreal and wrote *Dressed to Kill* for her, then directed it; he spent eighteen months with writer David Rabe on *Prince of the City*, before they were paid off, and replaced by Sidney Lumet and Jay Presson Allen. "Not until *The Untouchables* did I have any real muscle."

Muscle may be the single favorite asset in the club; it ranks right up there with empowerment. But how much muscle anyone has depends on whom you listen to, and how closely, and what questions you ask. By all accounts Brian De Palma's success with *The Untouchables* got Paramount to develop *Casualties* and finally to green-light it, at $17 million. When the studio balked at another $3 million, it pissed off De Palma. "I just made $100 million for them [on *The Untouchables*], and they say things to you like, 'We love being in business with you. But what else have you got?' Paramount listened very carefully and seemed very excited, so to be told no . . . A director of my stature, they wind up paying you because it's a pay-or-play deal. But I was so infuriated I couldn't stand it. Because they have Eddie Murphy, they have Indiana Jones, so it's not like Paramount can't afford to release a few important or serious movies."

How strongly did De Palma fight? "Oh yeah, we had heated debates," he says, lighting an umpteenth cigarette. "I was never in a more impassioned debate. I'd hear lines like, 'Does anybody want to see another

Vietnam movie?' And this was shocking to me because they'd developed it, and got it passed."

De Palma invoked every argument; when he recounts them, fearlessly, you can see two things. First, you see how even in the club everybody fights at every level for every important gain. (And as Ned Tanen put it, "Everybody hates everybody.") You also see how successful you must be, how independent à la De Palma, to speak up about it. The power structure is so small, the list of names so short, you have to be big bad Brian De Palma—a man who ultimately is fighting for a movie and not personal power—to talk.

"All the good war movies made money," he said as if it was conventional wisdom. "Francis' movie [Coppola's *Apocalypse Now*], *Deer Hunter*, *River Kwai*, and *Platoon*, obviously. Also Vietnam is not like something people aren't interested in. It's an unclosed book to Americans. It's something that's never been exorcised in the American psyche . . . So we were begging them at Paramount. It was a 'go' at $17 million and then it went up a couple million, and in a day we were in turnaround."

De Palma doesn't just want to answer this question, he wants to address it. "I pulled out all the stops, I wanted to give them a package. They want a contract producer? So, okay, Art Linson [who has a long-term contract there]."

De Palma quieted down a moment: "It's like you can't get too excited about these things. In the movie business it's like they move the zeros over here, and get rid of some guys. Like the executives who passed on *Dressed to Kill* went to Filmways, and their contracts were bought by Orion—which ultimately released the film. So then we have to sue Orion for monies owed us. So these same people who passed on the movie originally are now the ones we are suing for monies owed."

De Palma waited for a reaction. "Part of doing business in this community is that you normally have to litigate to collect money owed you. So the executives who passed on a project can be the executives you wind up litigating against, because they change companies so fast. Imagine in eight years what interest you could have been collecting! Tell me this isn't ironic."

Suddenly the director shifted gears so effortlessly it felt like a De Palma movie moment. Like when Angie Dickinson vanished from *Dressed to Kill*. He went from stone to soft. "Where we were fortunate, was with Dawn. She's been a great believer in me and the project. She's an entrepreneur, and yet she understands the cry of the last decade: *What are the numbers?* What's brave about Dawn is that she knows there are no mistakes in the movie business. You make a mistake and you are watching it the rest of your life. This was a tough call, this movie. This was Dawn's baby. Usually you start a movie and when you finish, the executive is no longer there. In that case, it's better to be paid off than to make the movie. You should not spend time with administrations without heart."

"Heart" isn't a usual label for the director. So you have to ask him what are the appropriate adjectives for Brian De Palma, club provocateur? Chief titillater? He answered spontaneously: "Master manipulator, wry, cackling, witty, violent, anarchic, which means I'm from Anarchia, I guess. Outrageous. I'm like Dan Quayle, it'll never change. Once the media gets a fix, they get control. That's the whole problem."

"The relationship of Alfred Hitchcock and David O. Selznick intrigues me," said Brian De Palma, "because Hitchcock worked best with a strong producer. Like Gene Kelly with Arthur Freed, or Orson Welles with John Houseman. The lesson I learned from knowing Orson so well was 'Don't try to do it all yourself.' " The problem is, success gives strong directors complete control. And there are no David Selznicks today. "It's dangerous how your ego grows," admitted De Palma. "You get successful enough, you say to yourself, 'Oh no, I don't want to do another meeting with that guy.' When that guy might be the ultimate right guy."

The guy, the producer, for De Palma on *Casualties* at least, was—unsurprisingly—Art Linson. Both of them come from '60s sensibilities, and *The Untouchables* took both of them to another level. It made them millionaires strictly from their percentages. Linson knows who the artist is, and so does De Palma, and Linson knows how to handle an artist. His "relationships" with complicated people like Robert De Niro, David Mamet, and Sean Penn are enough to give him a status of sorts. He's a "writer's producer."

Mamet wrote *Speed-the-Plow* about Linson and his long friendship (dating back to the music business in the late '60s) with Ned Tanen. Though the roles as written aren't really flattering—Mamet being Mamet—Linson doesn't mind. He's one of the luckiest people in Hollywood, knows it, and thus far has stayed lucky. He's also a pragmatist. When his directing career didn't work (*Where the Buffalo Roam*, *The Wild Life*) he stayed a producer.

In the Robert Evans–Otto Preminger office on the Paramount lot, Linson looks the part: cashmere socks, hand-cuffed khakis, tan silk shirt. He says Ron Silver, the actor who played Linson in the Mamet play on Broadway, is better-dressed, but that's debatable. Why this producer in cashmere socks wanted to make a war movie in Thailand (where one sweats profusely) was a question.

"The theme of this movie was: A guy turns on the men who befriended him," said Linson. "What a dilemma. Originally I said to Brian, 'What a tough movie. Must we pick this one?' " That could be the same question Paramount was asking, once the budget hovered over $20 million.

"I didn't want to walk across the street," Linson said, meaning his momentary segue to Columbia. So what happened? "This is vague, this is speculation. But frankly Paramount, and every other studio, felt the elements weren't as certain as they later became. Sean hadn't had a hit since *Fast Times at Ridgemont High*, which he did with me, to be boring about it. But then suddenly you have Sean in *Colors*, a moderately successful movie. But at the time nobody wanted this movie. Look, I know this story from scratch. The guys at Paramount said, 'We have enough on our plates.' And Dawn said, 'I will make this picture.' "

The producer sees a club object lesson here: "Studios should be judged on the movies they make and not the ones they passed on. I'm not an executive, and nobody ever asked me to be. The only given I see right now in Hollywood is that they all want to make sequels to hits."

De Palma talks about fighting for *Casualties*—"pulling out all the stops"—but Linson presents a cooler version. "I would have liked Paramount to make it. The movie was there to be made if Paramount felt they needed it. Did I throw a fit and stamp my feet? No. I said, 'Yes, it is tough, and no, it shouldn't have to be a blockbuster to justify itself.' "

There was a reason Linson could stay cool, an ace in the hole, so to speak. "At all times I knew I could say, 'If you guys don't want to do it, Dawn will.' " And no hard feelings? He shook his head no. "If Dawn didn't step up, would Paramount still make other movies with Art? Sure. To be frank, Paramount could have allowed this picture not to be made. So if this was a personal thing, there would have been no movie. It was very cordial. This was a business decision."

But business being business, are all things equal? Is one Hollywood studio not so much different from another? Is *Casualties* the same movie at Columbia it would have been at Paramount? "It's the same movie. Paramount has the best marketing and distribution system in the movie business. Other than that, there's not much difference between companies. I hate being put in the middle here. I'm out of the loop."

Yet sources at Paramount suggested Linson was a little in the loop. Said one studio executive, "We developed, we green-lighted, we even cast this picture. The budget was set, the movie was going forward. And one day Art came back and said, 'It's going to cost a little more. Art is great with writers and creative people, but budgets concern him less. He came back on this picture and said, 'It will be another $3 million.' This was after we had approved everything. That's his MO. But don't get me wrong. He was very well liked at Paramount."

Some observers cite how risky *Casualties* was, but every picture is risky, even *Godfather III*. *Born on the Fourth of July* was risky, too—except that Tom Cruise is a bigger star than Sean Penn and Michael J. Fox put together.

"The up side was for Dawn," Linson said confidently. "If nothing else this movie was a loss leader. It offered proof that she was in the movie business, and not in a silly frivolous way. It's proof she was president of a movie studio. It's a prestige picture that keeps you on firm ground. Sequels are not it. There are so many sequels now it's like we are watching TV. Why sequels? Because you can open them. But this movie took Dawn out of the sequel business. I'm serious. She wanted to be in the movie business with something good."

And so it came down to the David Rabe screenplay, according to both De Palma and Linson. "She read the screenplay David Rabe wrote," said Linson. "She knew what was there. And Dawn knows one of the major secrets of the movie business."

Which secret?

"The writer is the real deal in Hollywood. That's the secret. The writer is the thing. Would Bob De Niro have played Al Capone if David Mamet hadn't written it? I doubt it. And I am not underestimating the genius of Brian De Palma."

Mea culpa: Club members really do create their own mythologies. Dawn Steel, I discovered much later, originally hated *Casualties of War.* It only became her "baby" when it became expeditious for her to take it from Paramount to Columbia—and maybe show Paramount a thing or two. And show the club, too. But the movie wound up grossing under $17 million internationally, less than its estimated $28 million cost. It had no legs.

In the fall of 1989 when Guber-Peters began to take over Columbia, one of their first moves was to dump every Dawn Steel project. Announcements were made about Guber-Peters asking Dawn Steel to stay on, but nobody believed them. The omen was already there. In the reign of terror expected to be called Guber-Peters, Dawn Steel was yesterday's news.

She was also rich ($7.6 million was her settlement from Sony)—and furthermore she was on the brink of becoming a role model for working women, and she knew it. In 1990 she began writing her life story. And she told Mike Nichols she was really pissed he'd already used her title, *Working Girl.*

CLUB RULE FOURTEEN

The time to make up your mind about club members is never.

People at Columbia started to really appreciate Dawn Steel only after she left. Especially the first Christmas after she left. Guber-Peters gave the Columbia troops sweatshirts with the Columbia logo. *Sweatshirts,* for Christmas. Dawn has been called tight about money—but Dawn gave champagne, and it was Cristal or Dom Perignon. And so the first Christmas she was gone, they missed her.

In the club, perceptions about people do change. That's why you need to keep on top of things. You need to know who's who. Otherwise you might bitch the wrong target.

EGO

When I was eighteen, and a college student in Boston, I ushered at the Colonial Theater. On Valentine's Day, 1968, Neil Simon's *Plaza Suite* opened a pre-Broadway run directed by Mike Nichols. A month earlier Nichols had changed my life—I saw *The Graduate* and decided to move to California, and transfer to USC. All because of Benjamin Braddock's open-air drive along the California coast—and because of the Oedipal urges all over *The Graduate.* So when I saw Mike Nichols enter the lobby of the Colonial Theater, on a snowy matinee day, I stopped him to say thank you. Then, boldly, I asked him if I could interview him. In effect he referred me to the show's producer, just as he should have, and kept moving.

That same week I introduced myself to Neil Simon. This was not something I did then, or even do now—but I did it that week. And to show how even show people differ—Neil Simon was charming. He took me into a lounge at the Colonial and for twenty minutes gave me great advice. "Be one thing, like a writer, a director, or an actor. In show business, people get sidetracked. So if you are one thing, you stand a shot at succeeding. Don't scatter yourself." Two and a half years later I was in California, in my first job as a journalist, when I saw Neil Simon at an intermission of *California Suite* playing at the Music Center. He was gracious and remembered the encounter—or seemed to.

I'd heard forever that Neil Simon has an ego the size of an apartment—and I don't disbelieve it. Ego is a common bond in the club. Traditionally, ego propels the Sam Goldfishs of the world to leave the Lower East Side, and become Sam Goldwyns. Ego in the club is one of the givens—it's understood. When David Geffen talks to Mike Ovitz over lunch at Le Dome, the interplay is interesting to watch. (First of all, they rarely have lunch: In the club it's hard for members of equal status to carve out time for each other, even though they enjoy each other. When Richard Dreyfuss talks regretfully about seeing his good friend James Woods only once a year, he's telling the sad truth. Richard Dreyfuss' lunches, and James Woods' lunches for that matter, are more likely to be with members of their team—assistants, trainers, business managers, lawyers, agents, etc.—than with peers.)

But ego sustains you: The helpers help you keep your membership shipshape. Relationships are discussed; the tending of the more important relationships is particularly discussed. It's why Ovitz and Ron Meyer for years have always vacationed together: They are tying up loose ends at all times. Playtime with nonbusiness friends is an indulgence.

Club egomaniacs run the complete gamut from hostesses to executives. Hall of fame egomaniacs have one thing in common: no competition in their category. Edie Goetz was the duenna of the social piranhas, never simply one of the piranhas. Edith Head was Edie Emeritus when it came to being the star movie dress designer. She was a self-promoter, but she stood alone.

6

Club Genius—
Mike Nichols

Mike Nichols *got in because of Neil Simon and Elizabeth Taylor and Richard Burton. Neil Simon got in because of Robert Redford. Robert Redford got in because of Sydney Pollack. Rob-*ert Redford stayed in because of William Goldman (and Butch Cassidy and the Sundance Kid) *and Natalie Wood. Natalie Wood got in as an adult, because of Elia Kazan and Warren Beatty. She stayed in because every six months she told Abe Lastfogel she wanted to hear the pitter-patter of little feet—and Abe Lastfogel got her the best scripts in town. Elaine May got in because of Mike Nichols and Sydney Pollack and Warren Beatty. She dropped out because of* Ishtar *and personal choice. Mike Nichols dropped out because the movie he made with Warren Beatty and Jack Nicholson,* The Fortune, *cost a fortune, and lost a fortune. Mike Nichols got back in because of Meryl Streep and* Silkwood. *Meryl Streep got in because Bobby Lewis took her from Yale to Milton Goldman, the ICM agent who took her to Joe Papp. Meryl Streep stayed in in spite of Jack Nicholson rumors and the two Jack Nicholson bombs,* Heartburn *and* Ironweed, *mostly because she is a club archetype: the leading lady. Mike Nichols stayed in because of a string of hits on Broadway, and because of his marriage to Diane Sawyer—and*

59

because he's the club genius. Almost everything he touches turns to gold. In the club only David Geffen and Sidney Sheldon and Barbra Streisand and Steven Spielberg have that kind of track record, where almost everything turns to gold.

I began wanting to write about these people after I met Mike Nichols. Nichols may have the biggest ego of anyone in the club. I finally *really* met him, eighteen years after the meeting in the lobby in Boston. As I was leaving his apartment at the Carlyle, I told him of the eighteen-year-old whose life got moved to California because of *The Graduate.*

"I seem to remember . . ." he said, putting his hand to his chin, in a mock pose.

I stopped him.

"Don't pretend," I said. "That was an important memory for me. Don't pretend you remember . . . That's not nice." If I had liked him on any level, I would never have said that. Then I realized he was improvising. The truth is, Mike Nichols may be forever improvising. The former improv comedian who (with Elaine May) brought psychoanalytic humor to America in the '50s does it by rote. For example I asked him to explain the failure of two of his Jack Nicholson movies, *The Fortune* and *Heartburn*, the comedies that almost worked, but didn't. Nichols was on the spot, in his own living room. (Maybe I was getting even, or trying to.) Nichols was taking his time with the answer. He might have been improvising the role of the English dentist he used to do onstage. (Leaning over the patient, who was Elaine May, the dentist said, "I knew before I met you I loved you. There I've said it! Rinse out, please.") Nichols has this forbidding way of looking at you, not unlike a demon dentist, or a shrink. He seems to be asking, "Did you get it? If so, how much did you get?" But before saying a word he takes a very long time.

Mike Nichols has been the ultimate critics' darling since his debut play *Barefoot in the Park* and his debut picture *Who's Afraid of Virginia Woolf?* For years there were no mistakes, only hits. So he understandably operates with noblesse oblige—even in the midst of chaos. Example: When Mandy Patinkin left *Heartburn*, a week into shooting, there were no leaks to the press as to why, no public explanations. (The movie could have been called a top-to-bottom Sam Cohn project. Cohn, the Manhattan-based club member and ICM agent, represented Nichols, Streep, Patinkin, and novelist-screenwriter Nora Ephron.) Ask Nichols now about the Patinkin exit and he goes into turnaround. "Let's talk about Jack," he says. "Let's talk about how Nicholson [who replaced Patinkin] is a master of bringing life to every scene."

But about Patinkin? "The chemistry was better between Meryl and Jack. Period." (The gossip said Patinkin was too unwilling to take direction from Nichols.)

To really change the subject, Nichols went so far as to credit Nicholson with creating "my first painless experience shooting a movie, on *Carnal Knowledge.* I always loved the preproduction work on movies, and I loved the editing process. But I abhorred the actual shooting. I was terrified. I would always sigh with relief," sighed Nichols, "when something was finally shot. Most people would give anything in the world to make a living the way I do, and they are right. But not until Nicholson, on *Carnal,* and Meryl, on *Silkwood*—and then the two of them on *Heartburn*—did I love the actual shooting."

Nichols not enjoying movie making? Even after his celebrated debut (*Virginia Woolf*), after winning an Oscar for *The Graduate,* and after becoming the first star director to command a seven-figure salary (*Catch-22*)? In 1969, Nichols found himself barely thirty-five and stuck with the nickname "Midas." ("A journalistic figment," he calls the label now.) But for a solid decade he had almost owned Broadway (*Luv, Plaza Suite, Streamers*), if not Hollywood. Then in 1975, after the failure of *The Fortune,* Midas Nichols vanished. A lot of time was being spent reclusively, in Connecticut. In 1976 he tried to come back, but there was a shutdown during the first week of production on his Robert De Niro–Marsha Mason–Neil Simon comedy *Bogart Slept Here.* (All members of the *Bogart* quartet—Simon, Mason, Nichols, De Niro—insist the movie was simply half baked.) And Mike Nichols walked out of Hollywood, almost like Esther Williams, or Norman Maine, and didn't make another movie until *Silkwood* eight years later.

Regardless of what one reads in trash Hollywood novels, major studio movies almost never shut down completely, especially in the first week of production. Among the rare examples, in the last twenty years, are *A Glimpse of a Tiger,* first starring Elliott Gould, and then in a reworked version called *What's Up, Doc?* starring Gould's ex-wife Barbra Streisand. Another example: *No Small Affair,* which originally starred Sally Field and eventually starred Demi Moore. The point is obvious: By the time a major studio movie gets as far as preproduction, it is going to get made. Badly or well, it is almost certainly going to get made. *Bogart Slept Here* did not get made—though Neil Simon incorporated bits of the story into *The Goodbye Girl.*

And the question became: Did Mike Nichols abandon the club or was it the other way around? In 1983, Nichols made *Silkwood* (and made a movie star of Cher); and got Oscar-nominated. The popular thinking was that Hollywood had forgiven Mike Nichols his commercial failures—*The Day of the Dolphin, Catch-22*—or forgotten them. But the Directors Guild of America didn't nominate him as Best Director for *Silkwood*. It was a clear and cruel slight. So maybe all was not forgotten, after all. He remained in his suite at the Carlyle when he wasn't in Connecticut. He did Broadway. Traditionally, wunderkind directors—names like Elia Kazan and Joseph Mankiewicz—would return east with bodies of work behind them when they were like fifty. But Nichols was only in his middle thirties, and he was finished in Hollywood. People said.

"In California," said Nichols slowly, "I always feel I'm missing out on something. I pick up the trade papers, and I feel other people are doing things I don't know about." The look in Nichols' eyes was conspiratorial, a glint. As though he wasn't sure anyone knows about his 375-acre horse ranch near Santa Barbara—even if he is ambivalent about California. (He also is private—if not reclusive—about the details of his five marriages or his three children.) "California is a swell place to live if you imagine yourself an anthropologist," he decided. "It reminds me of . . . well, it's like when Elaine [May] and I were performing. And I would worry about things like 'Is this the best dressing room?' or 'Did you check our billing on the marquee?' That's the baby part of me, and in California I take a little slide toward the baby part. I find California easier for living, but it's also easier there to avoid real life."

Yet again Nichols had almost maneuvered his way out of a question, or had he? "Had I had it with the movie business after *The Fortune?*" Nichols asked himself out loud. "No . . . and it wasn't movie people I didn't like. One of the lessons of *The Fortune*, in my view, and God knows who else's view, is that it's not enough just to put together good people. You have to have an idea. You can't just wait for the idea. I don't believe in picking fruit before it's ripe. Eventually you have to either find an idea or forge one."

Eventually can stretch to eight years between pictures. "Yes, well, I wanted to be sure before I made a picture again that there was a movie there. That it would have enough weight for me to spend a year and a half on. With a play, there's time to discover what it is you're making. You go to another town and make it better. But by the time you are sneak-previewing a movie, there's only so much you can do. Eighty-eight percent of the work on a picture has been done by the time you sneak it. Also, making a picture is a somewhat mysterious process. I've said before that movies are dreams, and plays are public. Thus you have to be a little careful what you invest in, with a movie. For years I couldn't find one I wanted to do enough, and I found things I wanted to do onstage. But with a movie, I had to be sure it wasn't just an idea or a combination of people or a situation."

As his sometime producer John Calley (*Postcards from the Edge, Catch-22*) puts it: "Mike left the movie business like I did, to move away. I went to Europe to live, Mike went to Broadway. Years go by, and you wonder if you're missing something. Or if it's changed. So you come back. You try another movie, like we did with *Postcards*. And you realize nothing changed. Nothing. A club doesn't change fundamentally, that's what makes it a club. That's what I realized after ten years of being away."

But Mike Nichols isn't an executive, like Calley was. And when you debut, as Nichols did, with *Who's Afraid of Virginia Woolf?*, you get a privileged early look-see at the club; after all, *Virginia Woolf* was one of Jack Warner's last personal productions. The most expensive black-and-white movie made up until that time. "Do you think *Virginia Woolf* was a gamble?" Nichols asked coyly. "That's funny. A very bright woman friend of mine said it was not enough of a challenge. She said it was a sure thing. Actually, for me it was a learning film. You can see me learning as we go along."

Example: Nichols demanded the title sequence be shot in Northampton, Massachusetts, "because I had this crazy notion that a soundstage wouldn't look authentic. And they indulged me, because I felt so strongly." Here Nichols' boyish-modest front appeared: "They indulged me" is not unlike his *Graduate* acceptance speech at the New York Critics Awards when, after thanking his associates, he added, "I can't tell you who did what. I hope I did some of it."

Under the boyish-modest attitude, however, are more revealing admissions. "God, the things I didn't know about movies!" Nichols confessed. "I had to check a print of *Virginia Woolf* recently for one of those Lincoln Center tributes, and I took one of my kids along. We saw the first three reels, and I thought, 'This is not what my kid wants to watch.' Then I realized it got better as it went along, because I was learning. On that movie I was like a kid taking things for granted, making things up, diving in. Kids do things relatively unquestioningly. I was diving in, but not really in the deep end."

How not? "I really understood the play," Nichols said without a pause. (The play, as he once put it, "isn't complicated. It's about a man and a woman named George and Martha who invite a young couple over for drinks after a faculty party. They drink and talk and argue for ten to twelve hours, until you get to know them.")

But to direct Elizabeth Taylor and Richard Burton, the couple of their decade, the first time out? "Elizabeth was set before I came along, but

Richard wasn't; he needed to be suggested, which seems impossible now, but it's true. Richard and I once shared an alley on Broadway. *Camelot* was at the Majestic Theater, and *An Evening with Nichols and May* was at the Golden Theater. He was a pal, and Elizabeth I was getting to know pretty well, and . . ." (Almost unknown is the fact that Taylor insisted on Nichols. During her Roman fracas on *Cleopatra*, and the brutal publicity surrounding the Burton-Taylor affair, Nichols was one of the only friends to fly to Italy to be with the couple. The stars didn't forget. And they saw to it that Nichols was properly launched in Hollywood.)

The follow-up film, the one that got him a generation of devotees, was *The Graduate*. It made Nichols a culture hero because Nichols made Southern California look like another planet, sexy and rich and full of new chances. Especially for Benjamin Braddock (Dustin Hoffman) and Mrs. Robinson (Anne Bancroft), if not the clones they inspired. Bancroft admitted she "never worked harder in my life! Mike's theory about Mrs. Robinson was very clear: All grown-ups were bad and all kids were wonderful."

Nichols now disputes this notion. "I don't remember telling Anne Bancroft that," he said thoughtfully. "What *The Graduate* is about for me is something very different. The movie always was, and still is, about finding yourself surrounded by objects, and people who are concerned with objects. It's about saving yourself from becoming an object, through passion and, if necessary, madness."

Nichols admitted that, yes, Doris Day had been sought to play Mrs. Robinson. ("I believe we did ask her, and she turned it down because of the love scenes, but my memory is not so strong now and wasn't even then.") The very married, very available Mrs. Robinson struck nerves, and made everybody obsessed with California, and its seduction. "Mrs. Robinson," said Nichols, "is a person who did not like what she let her life become. She's angry at herself, and therefore angry at others. And then there's Benjamin, who felt he was drowning in things. He determines to become prouder of himself by going as far as he can. He hits bottom, then bounces back. That's what usually happens, in life and movies, and it's dramatic to see it."

But what happens next? A sequel to *The Graduate* seems, if not inevitable, then intriguing, and Nichols doesn't disagree. Some time went into speculating over who and how and in what way a sequel could be done. Would Ben and Elaine (Mrs. Robinson's daughter) return middle-aged to Beverly Hills? Or would they split like the couple in *Heartburn*? "Partly you don't want to tamper with it," reasoned Nichols. "Also it's hard to know where they all are. But let's think about it: Do they all forgive each other? And in what manner? They can't go on, you know, until they forgive each other, which is true in life as well. But do they have Mrs. Robinson over for dinner? I mean, here you have this seductive mother-in-law . . . I don't know. Maybe it ends like *Down and Out in Beverly Hills.*"

The irony of Nichols and Beverly Hills is how little time he'd spent there before so accurately catching it on film. (It was twenty-two years before he came back, to do *Postcards from the Edge.*) Of his *Graduate* days, he says: "Los Angeles was there to be caught! Those were the days: [Production designer] Dick Sylbert and I spent six months looking and preparing. We were obsessive. We'd ask each other questions like 'What would you see from a helicopter?' Answer: You'd see a pool behind every house. That means the line of the bathing suit strap has to be just right, because these are people who spend a lot of time by their pools."

Nichols was asked to recall his first day directing, and his laugh was mysterious. Somehow you feel you are not in on the joke. Then, abruptly, he lets you in. "My first memory is of Redford in *Barefoot in the Park*. There were altogether six days of rehearsal because this was summer stock. So my direction consisted of saying, 'You stand here, Bob,' and, 'You go over there, honey,' and, 'Your arm is exposed.' I was meticulous in a superficial way. Did I see a larger career for myself? No. Then one day Redford did something."

Nichols stood up and mock-flipped his collar to improvise a man wearing a topcoat, looking and sounding and feeling exhausted. "I remember telling Redford, 'The first thing to know is that being onstage is like being in battle, and the first thing to do is admit to being in battle.' Anyway, Redford and the other characters in the play have just come back from a Greek restaurant, and they've walked up five flights of stairs. And Bob is supposed to be beat. And Bob said something so smart. He said, 'What if I carried the mother-in-law up the stairs?' He was right, and it got an enormous laugh. Then I said to Bob, 'I think your character might have a head cold.' You don't have weighty discussions with a six-day rehearsal period. But Redford was such a good actor that he suddenly had a cold. I don't mean he went home for two days and worked out a head cold. I mean he got a cold then and there. I think at that moment I decided I loved what I was doing."

The joy (or power) came relatively late. Late, that is, if one subscribes to a Nichols' Theory of Life. The theory: "There are people to whom all good things happen in high school—and then there are the rest of us." Nichols, who admits he was not particularly happy in his first half, was a German immigrant who arrived in America by ship at the age of seven, accompanied only by his younger brother. (He spoke only two sentences: "I do not speak English" and "Do not kiss me.") The brothers' doctor father died only a few years later, leaving very little cash. It would seem a grim saga, but Nichols, as usual, is surprising. And, again, improvising. Moving around the Carlyle living room like a little boy—he did what Redford did: He actually became the immigrant child. He was suddenly remembering the *Bremen*, the German boat that brought the refugee brothers to America. By screwing up his face Nichols was seven years old. A very forbidding (and determined) seven-year-old.

"That little boy on the boat wasn't so unhappy," he said, improvising a Jack Nicholson grin. "I remember now looking for the prow of the boat, or was it the bow? I remember asking a fellow passenger, in German, where was the tip? I meant in which direction. He pointed to the tip of my nose. And I said, 'No, no, no, I mean the front of the boat! Don't kid around!' Well, he wasn't kidding around . . . And I was looking ahead, even then. And you know what?" Nichols was about to revise his theory. "I now think there are people who are happy as children, happy in high school, and happy straight through life. Isn't that depressing?"

CLUB RULE FIFTEEN

To succeed in the club, and last, you need more than one dimension.

Mike Nichols hides from the public, but onscreen he reveals a lot about himself. When he wanted Karen Black to wear strap-on breasts for *Carnal Knowledge*, her agent said Nichols was "screwy, and no thank you." Nichols went with Ann-Margret, whom he met at dinner one night at Sue Mengers'. (Sue put them together on purpose.) Nichols wasn't screwy, he knew *Carnal Knowledge*, he knew what *Carnal Knowledge* needed, and he made Ann-Margret an actress—and not just a star. By playing on her assets.

Ten years later he did exactly the same thing with Kurt Russell, in *Silkwood*. And Alec Baldwin, in *Working Girl*. If you study those two careers, the beefcake shots were turning points, so to speak. Within a year of working with Nichols, both men were movie stars.

Nichols undresses people. That's what made him a star director and not just a stand-up comedian. To succeed in the club, and last, you need more than one dimension.

7

Club Quarterback—
Jennings Lang

Jennings Lang did not get in because Walter Wanger shot him between the legs. Or because he had a thing with Wanger's wife, Joan Bennett. (Although he did.) Or because he had a thing with Joan Crawford. (He did that, too.) Jennings Lang got in because he practically created MCA-TV for Lew Wasserman, and it made them both rich. Joan Bennett did not get in because of her marriage to Walter Wanger, but because her sister Constance Bennett was practically the first bankable actress in the club. Constance Bennett got in because she made $30,000 a week in the Depression, and because she gambled on Sundays with the boys. Gambling, especially poker, is a bond in the club: David Selznick, Billy Wilder, Dean Martin, Si Weintraub, David Begelman, Dan Melnick, all played great poker. But nobody played like Jennings Lang. He gambled on Sunday the way he gambled all week long. You can't say that about anyone else in the club. Who's still alive.

People always blabber at parties about how New York ego is different from Hollywood ego. Hollywood shrinks talk seriously about "the New

York attitude" and "the New York edge," and they scowl when they say it. The thing they forget is that most Hollywood egomaniacs are former New Yorkers. Two former New Yorkers who *almost* went the distance at MCA are Jennings Lang, of the Golden Era, and Ned Tanen, of the modern era. Both were company men for two-decades-plus at the pre-Japanese MCA-Universal. Both men had club energy, which means they had stamina and style in a town which stopped valuing style. Ned still has both; Jennings, even after a stroke, has style—he can wheel himself into Chasen's looking like five million dollars. In the '50s Jennings was a bright young stud around town who understood Lew Wasserman, and wound up, after three decades, living two blocks away from him in a $9 million house. Ned was the Universal president, up from the ranks, from the music business, who only left when Paramount made him an offer he couldn't refuse.

How did these egos differ from a Mike Nichols? That's just what I decided to find out.

I did it more easily as the leg than you might think. The leg, because he is always underpaid, is never threatening to the moguls. Not really. Especially if your personality is unthreatening (translation: not pushy). And if the journalist truly listens. It's tricky to have the next young hot agent into your home, he might use you. But the journalist is pretty safe; he's only in awe of you. The thing is, nobody in Hollywood wants to be a journalist because if you are going to write—why not make $10,000 a week on *The Guiding Light*? But if you want to be a journalist—and people trust you—that's enough. They are rich and colorful and entertaining enough to compensate for what you lack. All you have to do is drool.

One of the first truly entertaining houses I went to was that of Monica and Jennings Lang, the outspoken producer and former agent who lost one ball (as in testicle) when Walter Wanger shot him in the crotch in 1951. Jennings Lang was the one man at Universal who knew where every body was buried; he was the best salesman at the studio and he was fearless—and he had this great-big just-what-you-expect used-brick Colonial house in Beverly Hills.

Before his stroke in 1985, I'd go in my Polo khakis for Saturday night dinners and screenings—with mid-sixtyish Jennings and his mid-fiftyish wife, singer Monica Lewis. What I liked about Jennings was his total recall. Did I sit at Jennings' feet? Of course. And did this former football star wear silk caftans? Yes. Did I want to move into the guest house, and be adopted? Yes, unconsciously.

Jennings was the one mouthy Universal survivor who had a kind of executive privilege—Lew trusted him, knew how much Jennings meant to the growth of MCA. Especially the syndication and distribution networks. Before the stroke, he gave up his executive stripes at Universal, after thirty-one years. But he announced his switch to independent production by calling himself the four-star general of MCA. They may have kicked him upstairs, but he was still in the Tower. He practically invented the profitable Universal TV stable of series—things like *The Virginian* and *Name of the Game*—so they were never going to throw him out.

The first time we met, Jennings was talking about having dinner the night before at Dominick's. He was sitting in the front passenger seat of his Cadillac being driven by a studio publicist who was paying close attention. Dominick's, on Beverly Boulevard, was the last true club-club hangout. A dozen tables, nothing fancy. You had to know "Dom" or Peggy to get in. If you were a journalist you needed *Chinatown* screenwriter Bob Towne to invite you, as he did the *Times* critic Sheila Benson, or you'd never get one of those dozen tables.

"So last night I walked into Dominick's," he said—as we rode in the studio car toward lunch at La Serre. (The Valley restaurant, now out of business, had a custom-made cane chair for Jennings.) "And just as I'm walking into Dominick's, Edie and Lew Wasserman walked out. Big hugs. Inside, I see [then–NBC chairman] Grant Tinker. Years ago I hired Grant at Universal. Big hugs. Grant says, 'Now that you're available, let's do business.' I turn around and there's [ex-Columbia president] Frank Price. I also hired him years ago at Universal. Big hugs. Frank says, 'Now that you've got this new independent setup, let's do business.'"

But it was the end of an era. Even though Jennings said things like "It's hard to leave home after thirty-one years unless you've been dumped on—and I wasn't." Or: "I sincerely believe the younger guys weren't out to get me. But, yes, things have changed. What was once a used-car dealer is now General Motors. There's less intimacy . . . and fewer movies. Word trickled down that I would be frustrated with curtailed activity."

What said Universal? "The danger in these announcements," said MCA president Sid Sheinberg, "is they tend to overstate. The truth is that the things Jennings is excited about are not always the things we're excited about. But this is not a golden handshake on the part of MCA." Carefully stated words.

Still, to do the executive shuffle at sixty-six took agility. Lang envisioned it working this way: "Let's say I want to do a remake of *Red River* with Clint Eastwood and Timothy Hutton. That's an $80 million grosser. But let's say Universal doesn't own the rights. Now I can put out the word to whoever does own the rights. They think, 'Gee, Jennings is very close to Clint.' The picture gets made. Universal will lose nothing but a piece of my time."

Lang, a lawyer at age twenty-one, was nothing else if not assured—always. His survival has hinged largely on candor and speed (in seventy-two hours he put together the deal for the Walter Matthau–Jack Lemmon–Billy Wilder *Front Page*). "My freedom in life came when I no longer had to calculate what I said," he said freely. "I spoke up and I never got fired. This company has been my umbrella. What was I going to do? Work out of a phone booth? I was never an officer of MCA; I was a vice-president only of Universal. I never saw a piece of profits—but what the hell? I got stock, a house, money, prestige, expense accounts, and friends. The Wassermans and Sheinbergs are family."

And at MCA it was Lang who watched the players play. "The structure of the company changed—Lew does things one way; Sid has his way. So did [the late MCA founder] Jules Stein. Always, I could disagree with them, and with [then–Universal president] Ned Tanen, too. Ned, maybe a little less; he was always so damn busy and pressured. But he knows, they all know, I'm an important part of the development of this company."

There's a double-edged reason. As one local wit put it: "Jennings could sell Ronald Reagan back to the movies. Then he'd handle Reagan with velvet gloves. It's a duality. He's both business and creative."

Lang says, "Anybody can make the best deal in town, but I'd rather make the best picture. That's why I didn't want to be on the MCA board. I wanted to be closer to the creative people. I'm looking for firsts and you don't find them in board rooms."

In the late '40s, Lang left the Jaffe Agency when his partner refused to set up the first TV distribution company. ("Six months later Elliot Hyman did it and made $10 million. I was looking ahead, and my partner was looking sideways.") Ahead were a few firsts; in 1951, he put on TV the first movie star, Joan Crawford; then came the first ninety-minute series (*The Virginian*) and the first long-form TV movies (*World Premieres*). Then (in 1975) there was *Earthquake* and SenSurround: "I'll never forget the first screening of *Earthquake*. Executives were running in from the next room. They'd never heard a worse reaction to anything . . . But these things are firsts . . . and nobody can take them from me."

What Lang is is a throwback. He's straight out of the showman era of gut instincts and grand gestures. Yet there's another side, a curious side. On the set of *Sting II*, he smartly told co-star Teri Garr: "Your hairstyle is pure '40s, but unflattering to you. We want you to look beautiful."

It's all part of being a producer, according to Lang. "Nowadays you are kidding when you use the word 'producer.' One guy here is producing three movies and he's never been behind a Moviola. Harry Cohn, whether he could read or write, knew every aspect of his pictures. He wasn't out buying Aspen or a Pepsi franchise. He was an Indian chief and he knew the reservation."

The reservation—Hollywood—has seen changes since Lang arrived in 1937. "Yes, but nothing really changes. *Private Benjamin* was a hit in the same way *Sergeant Bilko* was a hit. Audiences don't change so much. The only rule is that there are no rules. You just make your luck. I had a knack for backing into things. Like *The Sting.* If I had stalled three days, it would have gone to Metro. I had the bad luck to lose *Dirty Harry,* but I got Clint Eastwood for six pictures. Gave him his shot at directing. The battle was in convincing the boys Clint wasn't just a spaghetti Western star. But if you can't predict the stock market, how can you predict Hollywood?"

Hollywood, traditionally, has been a young town. And Lang has been adept at launching the young—from director Sydney Pollack to protégé Sid Sheinberg. What about today's young executives? "I credit them with revitalizing some of the old genres: sci-fi, serials, *Superman, Raiders.* But then I've had a serial sitting on my desk for three years. It's about a marine and a navy man searching for lost treasure. You'd see both parts in one night at theaters. A very bright man would not have given the go-ahead to *Star Wars.* Many bright men passed on it. It took a slighter intelligence to say yes. And a stronger sense of fun."

"Fun" is a favorite Lang concept. He thinks it's too much lacking today. "The new executives better learn all about fun. They'll make better pictures if they do. Otherwise they'll be punching up computers to come up with another *Four Seasons.* Better they go down to Panavision, ten minutes from here, and learn about the new anamorphic lens. And better they know what movies they want to make. If you don't know what you want, you live in fear."

Lang knew what he wanted early on. At twenty-one, he left Brooklyn and a newspaper job to drive west in a borrowed used car. He knew nobody but "a girlfriend of a girlfriend. I drove up to her house on Roxbury Drive and saw my first swimming pool. Brooklyn was behind me."

Ahead was an entrée to show business, through a new girlfriend, the niece of comic F. Hugh Herbert; Lang left a janitor's job at the Beverly Hills Thrifty Drug to become Herbert's agent. "I didn't know what an agent was. One day I got a call to go see [late producer] Walter Wanger. He wanted to hire Herbert. It was like going to see Louis B. Mayer. I wore my lawyer's suit and carried an empty briefcase. I said I wanted $5,000 a week for Herbert. He'd been getting $1,500 a week. I remember this because I was starving. Wanger said, 'Who the hell are you?' I wound up getting him $4,000 a week for five weeks' work. My commission was $2,000. I could live two years on that. So I married Herbert's niece, moved over to the Jaffe Agency, then became president. I stayed nine years and got close to people like Fritz Lang, Merle Oberon, and Joan Bennett."

Lang also got notorious. One afternoon he left a meeting with Joan Bennett to drive the actress home. Entering his car on Little Santa Monica Boulevard, he heard a verbal threat from Walter Wanger, who was then Bennett's (estranged) husband. The upshot: Lang suffered a gunshot wound in a sensitive spot—the thigh, he says now with a laugh.

"The press went wild. I mean, Hollywood is the largest fucking magnifying glass in the world. Jane Wyman came to my hospital room like Helen of Troy. I said, 'Wymie, relax . . .' All I know is it's the one incident that will be in my obituary."

The press didn't hurt. The day after Lang left the Jaffe office, he was approached by Lew Wasserman. MCA was then in the agency business, and Lang signed on. "I went with Lew and MCA for a reason. Lew elevated the status of agents. He resented the idea that agents were considered flesh peddlers. And he agreed with me that we had to make stars out of directors and writers."

Wasserman sent Lang to New York, to learn the new business called television. "We had only one show on the air, *Stars Over Hollywood*. I sold the second and third runs, and that was the beginning of syndication."

Returning to Hollywood, Lang went into live TV, sometimes directing and writing, and always selling. "I once went to New York with four pilots and sold them all. Overnight we went from nothing to number one. One show I sold only on the basis of a title, then forgot the title. I wrote the treatment for *Wagon Train* and it ran twelve years. Later, I sold *Name of the Game* by mistake. I was called crazy because of *Run for Your Life*. It ran five years. Now I want to do a sequel series called *Follow That Blonde*. The blonde is told she has six months to live—but she got the wrong X-rays. That way, it could run forever."

Lang's preference is for blue-serge pictures, genre pictures with a showman's twist. "For years I've wanted to make *Murder at the Movies*. With a live murderer in every theater. That you can't do at home, even with a satellite in your backyard."

If it sounds farfetched, it is. But so was SenSurround, and *Earthquake* remains among Universal's top dozen grossers. "There are very few firsts anymore," said Lang, his boom of a voice dropping a notch. "To survive, I had to be two things: creative and a manufacturer. I had to lead two lives, have two sets of friends. My life is a department store; I'm everywhere from furs to notions. My major goal is getting something done. It can be a nightclub act in Westwood or producing *Hamlet* in the nude. In the years I have left, I want to make things that will keep the audience in the middle of the storm."

Fourteen months later Jennings suffered the stroke, and the screenings stopped. It was then that Monica Lewis returned to singing, at a local club on Vine Street. I knew why she was doing it. It was Jennings' life-line. So what if Jennings had to be wheeled into Spago? He still got table No. 1. Sometimes.

CLUB RULE SIXTEEN

Club traditions are very deeply rooted, the way traditions were in the Old Country—and they must be paid attention to.

Example: Some people may not have liked Jennings Lang, particularly, but they knew he was a long-distance runner. And there's almost a reverence for certain long-distance runners. It's ancient wisdom that's revered by younger club people. In Ray Stark's living room, there's an engraved silver-framed photo of CAA partners Mike Ovitz and Ron Meyer, taken at a museum in Paris. It would be an invasion of privacy to reveal the inscription—but the intent is to pay respect to Stark. Younger tribesmen honoring their old master. Similarly, in agent Irving Lazar's den is a long shelf of small framed casual snapshots of everyone from bullfighter Luis Miguel Dominguin (Ava Gardner's longtime lover) to Gary Cooper. But there is also a gold mock-statue with a plaque that reads: "To Irving—from your student Mike Ovitz." The Ovitz plaque is the most prominently placed object in the room. Both Ray Stark and Irving Lazar pointed out to me their Ovitz talismans, each with obvious pride. Ovitz showed his respect to the *padrones*. And that's the way the baton gets passed.

8

Negativity and Illusion— Ned Tanen

Verna Fields got in because Ned Tanen liked not just her editing savvy—he liked her. Dawn Steel almost got the production presidency of Paramount because Ned Tanen liked her. Joel Schumacher became a movie director, after a career as a window dresser at Bendel's, because Ned Tanen liked him. Howard Rosenman (known in some quarters as Howard Rosenwoman) stayed in as a producer in spite of flops like Sparkle because Ned Tanen liked him. Ned Tanen would have become the president of MCA if Lew Wasserman hadn't been so loyal to Sid Sheinberg. Instead Ned became the oracle of Paramount. And very rich to boot. Ned Tanen is the only member of the club who wants to get out as much as he wants to stay in.

Ned Tanen really didn't want to be interviewed. He said no so many different ways I became determined—more determined than with anyone else—to "get" him. Ned Tanen is the most complex man in the club, excepting only David Geffen and Robert Evans, so I had to have him. Tanen is interesting because, like Evans, he's straight but has a strongly developed anima; Carl Jung would have been spellbound by Ned Tanen.

His female side is working, and he also likes and employs and dates women—one could almost say he favors them over men. Tanen has the best taste in clothes, in houses, in art, in movies—and he taps into women like nobody else in the club. He's also a brutal truth-teller.

Verna Fields (the godmother of George Lucas and Steven Spielberg) was his best friend and mentor, and he in turn tried to be best friend and mentor to Dawn Steel—but it didn't take. Sherry Lansing can talk rapturously about Tanen's talent in an editing room. About what he did for *Fatal Attraction*. It was Tanen who got Maxwell Anderson's writer-daughter Hesper Anderson to finally finish a screenplay (*Children of a Lesser God*) and then he got Paramount to approve Randa Haines to direct it.

Women. Ned Tanen and women. The one right-brained Hollywood executive survivor, twenty-seven years at MCA, sitting in the middle of the long table between Jules Stein and Lew Wasserman and Sid Sheinberg—Ned the mediator, probably the best man to succeed Lew (except for his temperament). Ned the smartest one.

Except maybe at home. His first wife died tragically. His second wife left him for a maintenance man; the second wife was Kitty Hawks, the prize catch, the well-bred beautiful daughter of the legendary Howard Hawks and the legendary Slim Keith. The Tanen house Kitty decorated was photographed in *House & Garden*, and soon after agent Jeff Berg bought it, Berg's own Hollywood luck soared. (It was the same year he became chairman of ICM.) Kitty decorated the I. M. Pei CAA offices, and moved back to New York. After Kitty, Ned seemed to drift. Executive women began to be acceptable to him as dates—businessman going out to dinner with businesswoman—talking business, it appeared. A casting director was his girlfriend in 1989; by 1990 it was somebody else.

But it was precisely because Tanen understood women so well that I wanted to meet him. No other club executive has the understanding of women Tanen has. In my friend Linda's avocado and pink living room, I harangued a Paramount publicist on the phone, a woman I'd known forever and liked a lot, into getting me Ned Tanen.

"I have to have him," I shrieked. It didn't do any good.

Finally I had to ask Howard Brandy, a publicist who subleased my office, one favor—to get me Ned Tanen. (I believe that in the club you can ask one favor of anyone, but not more than one. And you save it until you need it. And the higher up you go, the stingier you are about using up the favor. Because everyone keeps score all the time.)

Because of his friendship with Howard Brandy, Tanen said yes. One time only. Tanen and I had a long uninterrupted lunch on the patio of the Paramount commissary, and I learned something about loyalty (Ned's to Howard). And directness: "I like your shoes," Tanen said, as we parted. He was looking at my $58 dirty bucks from Church's in downtown Los Angeles. "I'll call your office with the address of the shop," I told him. "And we'll have lunch again soon," he responded. "With Howard." It was double-double sincere. But there were no more encounters for a very long time.

(A year later, lunching at Paramount, I bumped into Tanen. He asked me what I was working on, and I said a book on power in Hollywood. Before I could ask him to respond, he was already talking. The few words were Tanen-tense—typically. "Negativity and illusion," he said as we walked toward the commissary. "That's the theme of the book. The only words you need to know. Negativity and illusion. Especially negativity.")

But before Ned Tanen became typically cautionary, I asked him to walk me through his struggles on *Children of a Lesser God*. I wanted to know how it felt to see a seven-year dream come true. Tanen shepherded *Children* through two studios, tricky executive shuffles, Robert Redford, a dozen writers, several directors (and two score more directors who said no), and nobody knows what else. But there is a happy ending, aside from the movie's five Oscar nominations. And I wanted to know about it. I wanted to know just how Ned Tanen kept his movie *Children of a Lesser God* from dying. It was truly a club movie—which means it was a succés d'estime. You could talk about it at dinner parties.

"I've never before been to a Royal Premiere," said Tanen with some awe, "but Randa asked me to go. So I went to London for one day. Lady Di sat next to Randa, and I sat next to Prince Charles, with my daughter. And there was this moment. Randa and I looked at each other and started laughing, really laughing. Prince Charles said, 'Why are you laughing?' and we said, 'If you knew what we've been through to get here . . . We were dead in the water at least fifteen times.' And Prince Charles did, in fact, get it."

In the superstructure of the club, you have to get what Triad agent John Kimble calls a "take" on each executive: "The take on Ned is that he knows when to go the distance. He understands *Top Gun* but he also knows what projects to stay with, and he doesn't mind waiting. Like *American Graffiti* or *Children*." Normally Tanen—Hollywood's ultimate creative company man (thirty-three years at studios)—doesn't talk to the press. The reluctance is understandable: Ned Tanen taken out of context can sound like a hip, '90s Damon Runyon character, but with a self-effacing streak, as long as Wilshire Boulevard.

"The list of directors who didn't believe in *Children of a Lesser God* is the longest list I've ever seen," he deadpanned. "Twenty-five names is not too short a list." Tanen added he "didn't ever believe the nay-sayers were right. I guess I'm pretty stupid. I never believe anybody." But Tanen sees both sides, and more. Verna Fields used to say that "Ned could see three sides to every situation."

In fact everything about *Children* was a problem. The film's history is more checkered than a tablecloth at Elaine's. Tanen saw the Mark Medoff play at the Mark Taper Forum, as well as in New York, and "I tried to buy it when I was president of Universal. But the bidding was getting crazy. It got to $1.3 million. I got out because I didn't want to reach that high. Reluctantly I walked away. [*Children* co-producer] Burt Sugarman got the rights, but we kept calling each other."

One of those calls—in 1983, three years after *Children* closed on Broadway—led to Tanen putting *Children* into development at Universal, without a screenplay. "Then I retired," Tanen said as a joke, meaning he left executive ranks to become an independent producer at the studio. "Suddenly Burt and I were going to produce, with Mark Rydell [*On Golden Pond*] directing. But we still had no screenplay. So Mark went on to do *The River*, then *Children* went into limbo, and Randa came to see me. Randa understood what most other directors didn't."

Randa understood, but executives misunderstood. Especially at Universal where management changes were unusually (for MCA) unpleasant. Meaning Robert Rehme departed and Frank Price returned. And as Tanen puts it: "The project went into disfavor. Randa went into disfavor. And me? I'm always assuredly in disfavor. So I left Universal to come to Paramount. The first two things I did were say yes to *Top Gun* and try to get the rights to *Children*."

Here comes club politics at their murkiest. Club thinking had it that Tanen's Paramount contract included the rights to *Children*—that the project was a sweetener to get the executive to jump ship from MCA. "Not true," said Tanen categorically. "*Children* was not even discussed in the contract negotiations. When I came here, I had to buy the rights back."

What that meant exactly: "There was still no script. But I remember the day a check was messengered to Universal for $3 million. I mean, was that a lovely move?" That was the price Universal—which didn't want to make *Children*—made Tanen pay because Tanen *did* want to make *Children*. (The Spanish proverb "Take what you want but pay for it" comes to mind.) Tanen knew all along "this was not going to be *Raiders*, but once [screenwriter] Hesper Anderson was on the script, I knew we had a movie. Hesper had been with it at Universal, then left the project. We got her back at Paramount. We had to start from scratch, and did. Then we got lucky and got William Hurt."

Will lessons be learned from the success of *Children*? The movie's cost "all in" was $10.5 million; the U.S.-Canadian box office take was $38.8 million. "One lesson is that people say women can't direct difficult movies. Here's one who can. This was a difficult movie. But other lessons? No. The truth is, the game is the game. The club wants magic—but worse, it wants generalizations. And they never work."

But what magic kept Tanen hooked on *Children*? "To me this was a love story," said Tanen simply. "Any love story is about communication, or the lack of it. Always, love is about misunderstanding each other. But with hearing-impaired people it's difficult to get into the nonsense of relationships. Games don't really work with hearing-impaired people." Tanen took a breath and added, "That's the wonderful thing about this. It's a love story in black and white, so to speak."

Ned Tanen hasn't made a "personal" movie since *Children* in 1986. But in the club if you've done it once—you've done it.

His own ego was enough fulfilled: One *Children of a Lesser God* is trophy enough. Good for ten more years in the club. And when Tanen left Paramount, at the end of 1991, he left with no insecurity. So he didn't want to deal with another executive shuffle—the Brandon Tartikoff shuffle. So what? Maybe Ned Tanen is tired finally of all the negativity and illusion.

And maybe not.

CLUB RULE SEVENTEEN

Fuses always blow. The club operates with fusions—Ned Tanen and Sid Sheinberg were a fusion—and it was only a matter of time (twenty-three years) until the fuse blew. But fusion is essential in dealing with the club. As the journalist, you fuse into them, not the other way around. They are the players, so to get them to tell you their plans, or to tell you anything, you fuse. You listen. At lunch with Ned Tanen or Ted Mann or David Geffen, you barely say five words. What you have to say has almost no bearing on anything; what they have to say has heft, gravity.

The same is true with club stars. Image is ultimately all they have, so already they are nervous. The first time I did Gregory Peck, in 1975, I was afraid to ask about his son's suicide. Fourteen years later when I did

Jane Fonda, I was *un*afraid to ask about her mother's suicide. But it took those fourteen years to become brave enough.

In both cases there was fusion. It's just that Fonda has access to emotions I wasn't sure Peck had, or I had. Getting these people to open up means knowing how intensely to fuse. Rule to remember: Fuses always blow. So don't prolong the encounter.

9

Club Clothier— Edith Head

Costume designers are below-the-line people, and if they are in the club at all, they are in the costuming branch. On movie sets and on Oscar Night they are revered; otherwise, not. But a half dozen of them transcend—they have star quality. In the club, that always counts for something. Irene Sharaff got in because she was a star Broadway costume designer, and because she dressed Streisand as Fanny Brice in Funny Girl on film. Ann Roth got in because Mike Nichols won't do a movie unless she does the clothes. Theoni Aldredge got in because her costumes for The Great Gatsby won an Academy Award. Dorothy Jeakins stayed in because of class and style and because she costumed all the best John Huston movies. Bill Thomas got in because of brilliant designs, and he stayed in because he did Edie Goetz' personal wardrobe. All of these people were affected in one way or another by Edith Head, the first costume designer to win an Oscar, and the only person to win seven more. Edith Head was the club designer emeritus.

Another long-distance runner at Universal (along with Tanen and Lang and Hitchcock and Taft Schreiber and Sid Sheinberg—and of course

Lew Wasserman) was company woman extraordinaire Edith Head. She jeeped around the studio like the queen of the lot until the week she died. I was still the leg when I first met Edith Head, and she was no less nice then. (After all, I was still "the press," if only an assistant at a $1.50 an hour.)

Very early on, I learned not to bet against Edith Head. She knew Hollywood like a deck of marked cards. Out of the blue, she'd call. "It's Edith," the designer would say in that brisk, brusque voice. "I've just decided which actor will win the Oscar." You might disagree, privately of course, but you didn't dare publicly. Her instincts were better than Jimmy the Greek's. So you listened. She was convinced Richard Burton would win for *Equus*, and was devastated when he didn't.

If a reporter must know a community, then a reporter in Hollywood had to know Edith. She was almost my most invaluable source. Very green and in my early twenties, I got my first basic truth from her: "Do everything," she advised. "If you don't do everything in Hollywood, you aren't Hollywood. Learn to stand in back of people—like I did."

In back of the thousand-plus movies (and thirty-four Oscar nominations) stood the little dynamo. Either she liked you—or you didn't exist. "The people I don't like," she once admitted, "I turn off. They're just not there."

"There" was usually one of two places: either her office at Universal or Casa Ladera, her adobe hacienda in Coldwater Canyon. She scooted between them in a monogrammed jeep Hitchcock used to envy. Her bungalow at Universal was about the best on the lot. Spacious, it showed off her forty-odd miniature sewing machines—and the eight Oscars. Some were tarnishing (notably the one for *A Place in the Sun*), but Edith was too busy to notice.

Her companion at home, before his death in 1979, was her architect-husband Wiard (Bill) Ihnen. After his death, her companions included iguanas, deer, two skunks, several red foxes, seven cats, and four dogs. Every room in the house opened onto a noisy courtyard. In the '70s, and in her seventies, she discovered blue jeans, and wore them while feeding the animals and cooking. "In the next lifetime," she announced one night, "I'm going to be a chef . . . But I may not wait another lifetime." Quickly then, as always, the subject turned to Hollywood. She loved gossip, and reveled in a good feud, but refused to do put-downs.

Except about herself. "When you're not a beauty—and I'm not—you have to create a trademark. I have the bangs, the bun, and the glasses. The glasses are to see, the bun is for pencils, and the bangs I happen to like. The teeth, by the way, are from Barbara Stanwyck's dentist." She talked in quotes, the reporter's dream.

Drop a name, any name, and Edith had the answer. Mae West? "The only star you dress as herself. I inherited her." Marlon Brando? "He walked into my office one day stark naked." Natalie Wood? "I could not make her look unglamorous."

Oddly enough, Edith was never, as she put it, "chumsy" with actresses. Writing a profile, I could call her, get the right quotes, but never anything really personal. "I don't enter their private lives," she'd claim. Yet in times of trouble, she was there. Between marriages, Elizabeth Taylor nested at Casa Ladera. Another time, Anne Baxter holed up in the guest house and wrote her memoirs.

Edith, meanwhile, was either at Paramount or Universal, often working on five pictures at once. Probably only hairdresser Sydney Guilaroff can rival her for sheer number of starry film credits. By design, she was not always innovative: "I could draw a little," she said of the early years. (*She Done Him Wrong* in 1933 was her first movie credit.) "I could draw, but I could also borrow. So I survived. But never have I said I'm a great designer." A great politician was more like it. She could follow orders from the front office at the same time she was giving orders to movie stars to lose weight.

She dressed elephants and starlets and, on one occasion, members of the Coast Guard. Her great regret was turning down an offer from the Chicago Cubs. ("The studio wouldn't let me, and I never forgave them.")

Formerly a schoolteacher (with a master's from Stanford in Romance languages), Edith remained a teacher at heart. On the eve of Hollywood's seventy-fifth anniversary, I showed up at her bungalow with virtually no notice. She gave me a whole afternoon. But she wanted her pound of flesh.

"I insist you capture something," she bargained. "Capture how lucky we all are. Most lives are repetitive. Hollywood is fascinating because we don't repeat. It's been one explosion—from silents to color to TV to VCRs—after another."

And standing in back of it all was the outfitter emeritus. As she used to say, "Hollywood's a game of cards."

Shuffle the deck, Edith.

Edith wasn't an egomaniac, I don't think, but she did like being Numero Uno. Sound contradictory? Well, I was now beginning to understand how contradictory club wisdom could be. Here Edith was saying, "Do everything" while Neil Simon advised, "Do only one thing." Neither way is wrong, but it took me a long time to get that. When I met these two people, I was still starstruck. Not quite as much as during the Mike

Nichols encounter, but still a little. I still perspired. I wondered if I could ever synthesize all this wisdom. And then what would I do with it?

What I was just beginning to see is how these people—apart from being smart—are scared. Maybe more scared than the outsiders. Once you are in the club, so much is at stake. The most that can happen— that your membership won't be renewed—is pretty terrible. Edith Head watched that happen to people. But it never happened to her.

CLUB RULE EIGHTEEN

You must be Machiavellian while not seeming to be. Edith Head was, finally and foremost, a politician. The designing part never ever came first with Edith. Stardom was what interested her. She was the most political animal in the club. Mostly because she handled tough bosses like Hal Wallis and Barney Balaban, and simultaneously handled sensitive stars like Grace Kelly and Natalie Wood. Edith worked both sides of the street.

In the club you don't have to sleep your way to the top, you only have to play your way up. And make almost no mistakes. It also helps if you win eight Academy Awards.

10

The Duenna of the Piranhas—Club Hostess Edie Goetz

David O. Selznick did not get in because he married Louis B. Mayer's daughter, but it didn't hurt. Mervyn LeRoy got in because he married Sam Warner's daughter, but ultimately talent won out. Louis B. Mayer was a founder. His daughters, Irene and Edie, were club children at the very top, who took completely different paths. Irene married David Selznick, the club genius of the '40s who later collapsed (in every way) due mostly to Benzedrine and burnout. Irene left him and produced A Streetcar Named Desire in New York. While her sister, Edie, became the major Hollywood hostess of the '50s. Ross Hunter got in (for a solid decade at least) because Edie Goetz adored him and got him put in place at Universal—her husband Bill Goetz co-founded the studio. The Garson (Ruth Gordon) Kanins got back in, after years of exile in New York, because they met Natalie Wood at Edie Goetz' house, and Natalie let Ruth play her crazy mother in Inside Daisy Clover. Robert Redford got in because Natalie Wood had the box office clout to pick her leading men, and she picked Redford for Daisy Clover and This Property Is Condemned. Robert Redford didn't have to go to dinner at Edie Goetz' house to meet Natalie Wood, but he probably would have.

Miss Head wasn't the only Edith in the club. The other two Edies were Wasserman and Goetz. They ran the town, socially, as surely as Edith Head ran the costume branch of the Academy. Especially Edie Goetz, who came first.

Club bylaw: There is in any given era one hostess who dominates, one piranha who swims apart. In the '40s and early '50s Anita May was the duenna of the piranhas. (Her disciples included Edie Wasserman and Ann Douglas.) In the late '50s and early '60s the duenna was Edie Goetz. I only wrote about her two months after she died—in the summer of 1987—because nobody else did. It would probably sound surprising that the leg would want to write about the death of an eighty-three-year-old woman who never worked a day in her life. Who wasn't an actress or a writer or an executive or a pioneer. But Edie Goetz was the daughter of Louis B. Mayer, the founder of MGM, and that was almost enough. Forget that her Impressionist art collection not only prefigured all others in Hollywood and was recognized throughout the world. Forget that her screening room in Holmby Hills was the first great Hollywood screening room of its era—not to mention that the Goetz house itself represented an almost too grand style of life. The tented dinner parties for forty, the seating, the guests that spanned Chaplin to Streisand, the first editions . . .

The reason I decided to include Edie Goetz is because—maybe more than any other club hostess—she represented a fantasy. The girl who had everything.

Some of us grew up believing that life would be more fun if we lived in Hollywood and a character like Edie Goetz was in our world. Not for the fortune or the art so much as for the ease, the protection she represented. A founding family of the movie business; the ease that comes to founders—and the fun. Her rivalry with sibling, Irene Selznick, was probably Hollywood's one true sister cat feud. (The battle didn't end even when Irene Selznick staked New York as her turf, while Edie got Hollywood. Nor was it over when Mrs. Selznick published her memoirs, *A Private View*, in 1983.)

"Edie hadn't meant anything for years," one hostess said on the day she died. "But Edie meant everything for thirty-five years." Mrs. Goetz was a fashion plate who could be bitchy and funny, and whose snobbery at least gave Hollywood a patina, and a set of standards. She was Rosalind Russell's best friend and one of Merle Oberon's real intimates (versus the thousands she aimed to please). She was a contemporary of Norma Shearer and Irving Thalberg (they used to play volleyball at Santa Monica on Sundays, at her father's place). She was perhaps the ultimate wife, without aspirations to be anything else, and no apologies. She was also a little bit of a yenta.

When I encountered her in 1975, she helped me understand the role of a journalist. I was twenty-four and terrified. "Be a scribe, darling," she would say. "Swallow it all, especially the tiny details. Listen closely—and talk very little. Study eyes. Go into people's houses."

What a teacher Edie Goetz would have made! Instead she chose to play dowager on Delfern Drive on the best corner of one of the best blocks in town. I once watched her be fitted for a daytime dress by legendary Oscar-winning costume designer Bill Thomas, then be massaged by the famous Dona Freeman—and be interrupted by a secretary with social questions. Then be interrupted again, by two calls from Roz Russell—to whom she gave advice. Many thought her mean-spirited—and she had an edge—but, after all, she was playing a role. The daughter of the king of Metro-Goldwyn-Mayer. The Hollywood princess. ("Are THEY coming?" she once asked a club hostess when invited to a dinner; THEY were Harriet and Ardie Deutsch, with whom Edie was feuding. Edie was a lady, but she wasn't above fussing and fuming and feuding, or whining.)

Yet she rarely mentioned Irene Selznick, and never retaliated in public when her sister's scathing *Private View* was published by Knopf. Even her enemies thought Edie Goetz had a right to complain; Mrs. Selznick was unkind about the sibling rivalry. But Edie Goetz was publicly silent, as she had been for decades. That was her role.

That Irene produced *A Streetcar Named Desire* on Broadway seemed minor—their problems weren't about working. Mrs. Goetz never worked one day in her life. Instead she had two daughters, six grandchildren, and a long marriage to a man less famous than her father but more devoted. (Her husband, the late producer Bill Goetz, was a co-founder of 20th Century-Fox and Universal-International whose best film was *Sayonara*, with peak Brando and good direction by Joshua Logan.)

Also, she had memories. Irene (the single-name designer, not the sister) doing her clothes in the '30s, even the tennis dresses. David Selznick as a brother-in-law, the Thalbergs and the Zanucks as cronies, the Zukors as enemies—and a studio that could fulfill every fantasy. A sarong for a midsummer night's luau? Wardrobe whipped it right out.

"A luxury lady," her sister called her, "a woman with drive and ambition enough for two." At the time of her 1930 marriage Edie got even with her father for ignoring her as a child—and charged L. B. Mayer with one of the most expensive Hollywood weddings of all time. Her "dowry" was downright decadent: motorcars and a grand house and enough china to fill China.

But "she didn't do anything" is a line I heard a lot around the time

Edie Goetz died—and I resented it. Every aspect of her persona, every action, was done with an eye to impress. Some standards about being a hostess were set in Hollywood (and then in granite). And Edie Goetz helped set them. Had she done a book on entertaining (or snobbery)— move over, Miss Manners.

Walter Pidgeon—who had the best table manners in Hollywood—said Edie Goetz had the best tables because she had the best guests.

Will there ever be another club fixture like Edie Goetz? Don't bet on it.

Irony: Edie Goetz' daughter, Judy Shepherd, sent a note after I wrote about her mother, to say, "I thought I knew my mother, but you really knew her."

The irony: I only met Edie Goetz once, and briefly. She is the only character in this book, or in the club, I wanted to know but never got a chance to know—so I drove by her house a lot, and I imagined her life, and her art collection. At a party six months after her death I met Judy Shepherd, and told her I thought her mother's house should be sold to someone wonderful.

"At this point, I just wish it would sell," was her response. I realized then I was living in the '50s and Judy Goetz Shepherd was living in the '80s.

Six weeks later her mother's art collection went for $53.2 million at Sotheby's.

CLUB RULE NINETEEN

Homage must be paid to club father figures and mother figures. It's very costly, sometimes fatal, to cross them.

It's essential to know, first, that the duenna piranhas never get along with each other, ever. Especially when they're of different generations: Edie Goetz never acknowledged Edie Wasserman, and Edie Wasserman got even by ignoring Edie Goetz in her dotage. Edie Wasserman never paid proper homage to Edie Goetz, early on or later. The younger women who watched this—Janet Leigh, Judy Franciosa Quine, Polly Bergen— know better than to ignore Edie Wasserman. They made her godmother to their children, and they made the weekly calls just to check in. And Edie Wasserman never forgot. When Jamie Lee Curtis was hospitalized and near death, Edie Wasserman saw to it that her goddaughter got the best doctor in Los Angeles.

Paying obeisance pays off.

11

The Charity Game—
The Club Crankies

Ruth Berle was a noisy publicist who got in by marrying
Milton Berle and taming him. Ann Buydens was a European
publicist who got in by marrying Kirk Douglas, and not taming
him. Barbara Harris was a British publicist who got in by marrying Cary Grant, and then after that, living with Kirk Kerkorian. Veronique Passani was a French journalist who got in by
marrying Gregory Peck, even though it cost him a fortune to his
first wife. Felicia Farr was an actress who got in by marrying
Jack Lemmon, and giving up her career. Brenda Vaccaro is an
actress who got in, for a while, by living with Michael Douglas,
and grooming him, and spending weekends in Palm Springs
with Ann and Kirk Douglas. She got dropped when Michael
Douglas dropped her. Diandra Lukens was a Washington debutante who got in by marrying Michael Douglas, and using the
marriage. Lili Fini was a Carnation marketing executive from
Washington who got in by marrying Dick Zanuck, and finding
and producing Cocoon. All of these women (except Brenda
Vaccaro) are club wives.

"All social life is now Charity," complained club daughter Anjelica Huston one night at dinner at the Beverly Wilshire. "People don't give dinner parties anymore. People are no longer willing to spend their own money on dinner parties. I'm getting fifteen or twenty letters a week for everything from Yugoslavian dog illnesses to marathon diseases. It numbs you."

It doesn't numb some club wives who work as compulsively at Charity as their husbands do at studios. If Edie Goetz was a founding club wife, the women who followed in her wake wanted more out of life than giving dinner parties.

"We call ourselves Athos, Porthos, and d'Artagnan," explained the late Ruth Berle fingering a diamond pinky ring at a front table at the Hillcrest Country Club. She was talking about Mrs. Cary Grant and Judy Balaban Kanter Franciosa Quine, her co-chairs for the Princess Grace gala-gala. If the original Ma Maison is the truest modern setting of the club, Ruth Berle was probably the quintessential club mouth-wife of her day. I was practically the last person to talk to Ruth Berle—she called me from her deathbed at Cedars-Sinai to comment on an L.A. *Sunday Times* piece. Ruth Rosenthal Cosgrove Berle was a publicist with a reputation—a captain of the WACs in World War II who never stopped giving orders. She was known to go for fellas in a big way until she met the biggest of 'em all, Milton Berle, and married him in 1954. Their marriage spanned the best and last years of big-time lavish stay-up-late show business. In the '50s they were there at Mocambo and Ciro's; in the '60s it was Ruth Berle (almost as much as Peter Lawford) who understood and accommodated the Kennedys on their California stays. ("When Bobby died I went with him," she told me one day at the Polo Lounge.) Ruth Berle drew the line of how raucous you could be and how mouthy and still sit next to Cary Grant at dinner and be charming. She bridged more gaps than Alana Collins Hamilton Stewart—and she did it within one marriage that gave her clout in the '50s, and less clout after that, but always a presence. Also, she had enemies who were as loyal as her friends. I liked her because she wasn't masochistic in a town of masochistic wives—and her legs never gave out. She was the kind of woman who could sit up all night with Milton in Vegas, then fly home on two hours' sleep and the next day seat a banquet for 500 people.

She also understood that a good vanishing act may be a key to survival in show business. Knowing just what moment to be somewhere—the way Robert Redford knows which tributes to fly in for, and which to skip—is pivotal. Grace Kelly knew enough to fly in from Africa and the set of *Mogambo* to be at the 1952 wedding of her agent Jay Kanter to Judy Balaban—and she'd never met the bride. (Jay Kanter was then MCA's most powerful agent, and Judy Balaban was to become Grace Kelly's best friend. The three-day trip proved worthwhile.) In Hollywood things haven't changed much: A brief pivotal appearance can still take you a long way. The Hollywood charity game works this way: You have to know when to show up, and for whom—and when not to bother. The rampant rumor that Michael Jackson wanted to perform in honor of Cary Grant at the 1988 Princess Grace Foundation gala did not—repeat not—make much difference in ticket sales for the $1,000-a-plate evening at the Beverly Hilton. The crowd, which was very deluxe even by Hollywood standards, knew to turn out for Cary Grant and Grace Kelly. Nine days after the invitations were mailed, $675,000 in responses was deposited in New York's Chemical Bank.

What the club celebrates best, I discovered, is survival. A major fundraising gala is not going to honor Judy Garland after all, or any other Hollywood casualty. It's survival that gets the turnout that creates what Judy Balaban Quine calls "those wonderful little moments." The evenings that count are about the lasting pull of success. It's a royal pull, so to speak, and for those who can afford it, it's irresistible. But how does it come together? The list of those involved with the Princess Grace Foundation was heavier than a leaded silver tray—Barbara Sinatra, Edie Wasserman, Veronique (Mrs. Gregory) Peck, Gloria (Mrs. James) Stewart, Dina Merrill, Ginny (Mrs. Henry) Mancini. But this is essentially an evening put together by three people: Athos, Porthos, and d'Artagnan. "How do things get done in show business?" asks ultimate power-broker David Tebet, who survived five regimes over twenty-three years at NBC, and who helped coordinate the journal for the Princess Grace gala. "By two or three people sitting together in a room, and making decisions."

Paul Drehr, the Beverly Hilton catering manager, stood in the hotel lobby with Ruth Berle and Barbara Grant and Viki Loo, Judy Quine's assistant, waiting for Judy Quine. The second wine and food tasting for the September 1988 Princess Grace Foundation gala was to be at 12:30. The quartet looked a little anxious: Each day as the gala approaches the anxiety mounts. The group made small talk while waiting for Judy Quine.

"I first met Princess Grace at a dinner at Leona Helmsley's," said Ruth Berle nonchalantly. "It was after *Night of a Thousand Stars*. Or as I call it, 'Night of a Thousand Assholes.' " She put a cigarette into her ebony holder and looked impatient. "Thank God the money is coming in. You can smell it when the money doesn't come in. Do you know how small the group is that supports $1,000 dinners? I mean as opposed to $500 dinners? But this Princess Grace evening, I don't know . . . I just smell it delicious. I smell it sensational. Not that we don't kill ourselves."

"Our friends don't expect to hear from us for the entire week before," Barbara Grant said with some concern in her voice. She sounded like an archaeologist off on a remote dig, but confident.

"Milton expects me to be in Winnipeg with him the weekend before the gala," said Ruth Berle quietly, to an observer. "He's very understanding, and I understand when he wants me to be with him. So, I'll stay up late Sunday night and Monday night to do the seating. But do you know how hard it was for me to tell Judy that I'll be away for the weekend?"

When Judy Quine arrived at the hotel, the group went immediately to the Monte Carlo Room where a single table was set in the middle. This second tasting was to reaffirm the early choices, and try desserts for the first time. "Wheatey peach," replied Mrs. Grant when Mrs. Quine asked what color the tablecloths and napkins would be.

"Like the napkin you stole at the first testing," said Ruth Berle.

"That was dusky rose," corrected Mrs. Quine.

"Wheatey peach is the final name of the color," reported Mrs. Grant. "And we're using multiple napkin folds. Like this one." Mrs. Grant pointed to a crystal goblet with a perfectly pleated white napkin.

"Do they cost extra?" Mrs. Quine asked, and when Mrs. Berle shook her head no, Mrs. Quine looked puzzled. "Excuse me, Ruth, but why are you wearing two watches?"

"To remind myself that one of them needs to be fixed." As the first course of salmon mousse was served, there was a look of displeasure on Mrs. Berle's face. "Is this cucumber? So many people I know hate cucumbers."

"This time the salmon is oilier, Paul," Mrs. Grant said to Paul Drehr.

"I hate these rolls," Mrs. Berle said, pointing to a lazy Susan overloaded with dinner rolls. "They look so big, like lunch rolls."

"Before I met these ladies, I was twenty-seven years old," Paul Drehr said with a stab at humor.

"You have your nudges, Ruth, for Paul and I have mine," said Judy Quine.

"Paul—I think we want a moussier mousse. Like last time. This mousse infuriates me," said Mrs. Berle.

"Uhmm . . ." agreed Mrs. Grant. "But I love the salad dressing. It's mine, from home."

"I remember it from two Christmases ago," said Judy Quine.

"It's Paul Newman's!" said Barbara Grant, simultaneously making a note on her Cartier leather pad. "Burt Sugarman gave us a check for $15,000 this morning," she said matter-of-factly.

Judy Quine made a mental note to send a personal note to Burt Sugarman.

"Each check we get Viki deposits to our New York bank. Every buyer gets a note."

Events Unlimited, the party-planning firm, did the initial addressing of 1,300 invitations, but Quine herself does the personal notes.

"Events Unlimited could do the notes, too," the leg said timidly. "That seems simple."

"It seems expensive," said Barbara Grant.

"Ruth and Barbara and I are just not made that way," said Judy Quine. "It's characterological. Fine points are important to us."

"We try to look at it like a private party," said Barbara Grant. "As if we were entertaining in our own homes. Judy writes everyone a letter, as the checks arrive."

"I didn't get a letter," said Ruth Berle, coyly.

"You think I'd write you?" said Judy Quine. At Paul Drehr's request, the hotel wine steward poured a second selection, a chardonnay, once the Fumé Blanc had been approved by everyone at the table.

"I'm rhapsodic about the wine," Barbara Grant said.

"This is the first California wine I ever got attached to," Judy Quine said of the Mondavi Fume.

The main course, a chateaubriand with pommed potatoes and peas, arrived and Barbara Grant looked horrified. "I meant the peas to be shelled!"

"I didn't know that," said Paul Drehr, sounding contrite.

"Barbara, I didn't know either that you meant that," said Judy Quine.

"Barbara's British," said Mrs. Berle. "In Britain you pod the peas. But they look like succotash if you do."

The subject was switched to potatoes. "Last time," said Barbara Grant, "we let the potatoes sit while we talked because during the dinner the potatoes will be sitting there and they . . ."

"They don't sit well," said Ruth Berle. "This time they are smothered in salt," she says as she tucks her napkin under her chin.

"That's Mrs. Berle, all right," said Paul Drehr.

"Did you call Chasen's about the hobo steak?" Barbara Grant asked Paul Drehr, who hadn't. It's his job to be both diplomatic and defensive, if necessary. Hobo steak was not on his agenda, however. When the sharpness of the knives was questioned, he walked around the table once, then good-naturedly said: "These are the knives requested by Mr. Griffin [Merv Griffin, the hotel's owner]. If you don't like them, you bring the knives."

"What happened to the potatoes?" Judy Quine asked.

"They've gone back to the grease pit from whence they came," said Ruth Berle.

"Maybe an alternative, a safe alternative, would be new red potatoes. How small are they running this year?" asked Judy Quine.

"You mean running like grunion?" Ruth Berle wanted to know. "Is there a potato run?"

"No, they run different sizes in different times of the year."

"Excuse me, I don't get out much."

"Are there objections to hunks of beef?" Judy Quine wanted to know. "Or do we prefer slices as we had before?"

"Is that the royal we?" asked Ruth Berle.

"See I told you," said Judy Quine. "We don't have those kinds of ego problems internally that most groups have."

"Paul," said Barbara Grant. "Last time the Brie was wonderful, the size of the torte perfect, but it was just too sweet. How will we know . . . ?"

"Let's live with the realities," said Paul Drehr. "We are cooking for a thousand people. But the taste will be the same taste you taste today." Drehr immediately introduced pastry chef Mike Oldman, a new émigré from Atlantic City, who was followed into the room by a waiter with seven desserts.

"Let's taste the meringue swan first. It's the one we ordered," decided Ruth Berle. "Then we'll try all the others."

"Ruth, who doesn't drink, also doesn't eat dessert," said Judy Quine, dryly.

"The profiteroles," said Mike Oldman, "are made with bourbon and raspberry sauce."

"It's heavy as hell," said Barbara Grant. "I vote for the swan. *The Swan* was Princess Grace's last movie."

"Second to last," said Judy Quine, without any condescension.

"I say 'wrap it up' and I'll take it home," said Ruth Berle.

"There goes Mrs. Berle again," said Mike Oldman. The piña colada tart was followed by a pear William torte and crème of coconut mousse and crème brûlée and white chocolate mousse with three kinds of alcohol. "You have to appreciate that alcohol adds a lot of flavor," said Paul Drehr.

"Not too much flavor, or we won't be able to get into the dresses," said Ruth Berle.

Barbara Grant looked at the swan and wondered: "Can the wings be meringued?"

"Yes, everything but the head," said Mike Oldman. "The head is chocolate."

Barbara Grant looked as though she'd found a soulmate. "God damn it," she said appreciatively, "why don't *you* do the potatoes?"

"I'll do the dinner rolls," said Mike Oldman. "Because otherwise you'll get rolls in plastic bags. But as the pastry chef, if I go near the potatoes, the executive chef will . . ."

"But not an enormous round bulky roll, okay?" begged Ruth Berle. "So no one has to poke a fork into a mushy thing going around the table. Are we going to meet the man who does the potatoes?"

Paul Drehr vetoed that idea, and after "the torte problem" was solved by choosing "a San André, not runny, not too mature," Drehr finally took a seat at the table. "It's contract time," he said darkly.

"Now he pulls up a chair!" said Ruth Berle.

Details of timing and seating and pricing were discussed at length without any interruptions or flagging of energy or indecisiveness.

"Are we buying cocktails?" Judy Quine asked.

"Well, we can't start having them pay," reasoned Ruth Berle.

"No, but we have to know what the trade-offs are," said Judy Quine. The discussion moved on to lecterns, risers, lights, flowers, security. "We have Doug Collins for security," Ruth Berle said with great relief.

"The coat room," said Paul Drehr. "It's $75 if you let the guests tip."

"I think we let our guests tip," said Ruth Berle.

"We do have a sign that says, 'The hotel has taken care of your gratuity,' " said Paul Drehr.

"Don't put that up," said Ruth Berle.

"Okay. Do we collect the dinner tickets?"

"That's tacky as anything," said Barbara Grant.

"What about a drape to shield the cocktail reception from the rest of the room?"

"No drape, Paul. You said you'd grow something between our last meeting and now."

"It's up to you, Paul."

"Truly, Paul . . . rob something from the Presidential Suite if you have to," suggested Barbara Grant.

"Oh, candles!" said Judy Quine, sounding as if she'd been remiss. "Nine months ago I did an event, and used votive candles glued into the lip rim of the table base. An eighteen-inch mirror base."

The other women nodded in complete agreement.

"Will you charge us for phone calls?" asked Viki Loo innocently.

"You don't do it that way," said Ruth Berle testily. "You say, 'You will do the phones . . .' "

"For calls and installation I have to charge you, but I'm giving it to you at a flat rate," said Paul Drehr.

"Oh c'mon, Paul—you give it to everyone for that rate," said Barbara Grant.

"Well, Mr. Griffin has a big new home to pay for," Paul Drehr tried.

"Oh please, Paul, I drive by that house every day . . ."

"Do we get an office to use?" Judy Quine wanted to know.

"Parlor C—one room, one table, but we can supply whatever you need."

"When can we look at Parlor C?" asked Judy Quine, already halfway out the door. On the way to the elevator she said, "Ruth and Barbara and I all worked. I mean for money. So each of us is a one-man band in her own way, and each of us knows that about the other. Each of us knows that none of us could grandstand-play because it would be a mess. It's our secret."

"Uhmmm," agreed Barbara Grant, fixing a cuff on her navy Adolfo sweater jacket.

"When a $15,000 check comes in," said Judy Quine, "we feel such unleashed love we want to drive over and serve the benefactor breakfast in bed."

Barbara Grant seemed stunned at the idea.

"It's inappropriate for Barbara to call people for money," explained Ruth Berle of the widow of Cary Grant.

"What about the press?" asked Paul Drehr as the elevator arrived.

"They get zero," said Ruth Berle, without any compunction. The unspoken part: The press already are getting free tickets. There's ambivalence about the press in the charity game: The dependence for publicity is huge, but the intimacy can only extend so far. When Louella Parsons lived in the Beverly Hills flats, and Hedda Hopper lived north of Sunset Boulevard, the world was younger, and the club knew whom to trust. In other words, the press mingled as one with the industry it covered, and it can no longer afford to do that. In modern show business journalism, nobody can quite be sure how well a journalist listens. What if he or she writes the wrong thing? The line I said over dessert about Michelle Pfeiffer. In a self-conscious community the presence of "press" at intimate dinners is tricky. More than other company towns (like Washington, D.C., or Detroit) the press here is distanced from the community (with a handful of exceptions). The days are over when 20th Century-Fox bought Louella Parsons a house, and justified it by using Lolly's husband, Dr. Stewart (Docky-Wock) Martin, as house doctor.

And on the night of the Princess Grace Foundation gala, the press would know its place. The photographers and reporters' ball outside the Beverly Hilton would be for Barbra Streisand and Clint Eastwood and the handsome Prince Albert of Monaco and his sometimes troubled sisters and so on. But, Rule Number 1 for the press was firmly adhered to: Nobody could approach or ask questions of any member of the Royal Family.

In America only the paparazzi—and not the press—got a crack at the Grimaldis.

Them, and the club.

CLUB RULE TWENTY

Fiction is the truth in the club. Every rumor, every piece of club gossip, requires careful listening.

The one about Edie Wasserman having as much power as her husband is worth paying attention to. In the club, social symbiosis is common, even if commonly misunderstood. But the most powerful club wives derive their power from their men. *Still.* They are men's women, one way or another. And their impact is not to be underestimated. The Lew Wassermans operate almost as one person. The Jerry Weintraubs don't— but Weintraub himself believes otherwise. In public he says things like "I'm her, and she's me. We're the same person." Skeptics need not respond, and you must remember one thing here. You must believe any fiction any club member tells you. Fiction is the truth in the club.

LOVE

Sometimes late on a Saturday night, when charades are over, the diehards among us play a little game. Six or seven people sitting on the floor at 2 A.M. revved up as if we'd just been to a late show in Vegas in the '60s. The game we play is very basic: You have to say who you really wanted to be when you grew up. You have to tell the truth, even if it hurts, or embarrasses you. (What are charades, after all, but ways of embarrassing ourselves?) One night I admitted I once foolishly wanted to be Steven Spielberg. (Only a year earlier, I copped to wanting to be critic Walter Kerr.) One producer admitted he wanted to be Billy Rose, one actress opted for Joanne Woodward ("because she got it all"). Other role models, all show business, included Rhonda Fleming, Pauline Kael, and Ray Stark. With a little brandy, the names Lucie Arnaz and Sam Spiegel cropped up.

All of us sitting there that night admitted we got into this racket because of love. Not money, not really, though nobody minded having it. And everybody wanted it. It was nice to be able to buy a $200 pair of cowboy boots, and not worry about it. None of us was sexy enough to use sex to get in—unless you are a Travolta, or a Bruce Willis, you aren't sexy enough for the club. (Or unless you are a chiseled hustler or a perfect beauty—but that's another story.) Status mattered less to our under-forty generation than it did to the generation who came before us. No, we were too idealistic, too much a product of the *fuck-money* '60s. (Of course none of us is in the club.) We sat there on the floor and decided we were in it for love, finally.

So are most of the truly talented, creative people in the club. I'm not talking about the businessmen, or the climbers, or the starlets, the twinkies, or even the monsters. I'm talking here about the people who want to make something good and beautiful, with their own hands. Sometimes, like George Lucas, they get impossibly rich, and they distance themselves from the club. But money is sometimes beside the point. Most of the very rich people in show business didn't do it strictly for money. You really have to believe this. (It took me a while to believe it.)

Billy Wilder is one of these people. Formerly a newspaperman and a gigolo, Mr. Wilder is a millionaire many times over, but money wasn't why he came to Hollywood. The same is true of people as diverse as Sydney Pollack, who came out of the Midwest with a deep love of movies, and Sue Mengers, a secretary from Utica who loved both show and business.

And Steven Spielberg is definitely one of those people who got in it for love first, then money. You only have to know his movies to know how developed his fantasy life is. And that night at charades it was Spielberg's name that was hard to say aloud. Who was I to compare myself to Steven Spielberg? I can't take a snapshot without unfocusing it. So what if we were born the same year, in Ohio, to Jewish parents who are unalike, and who didn't belong in Ohio. So what? The truth is, we shared a certain dream about people in a community called Hollywood. And when I decided to buckle down and really learn about the club, I decided that Spielberg had to talk to me. He just had to.

And after two years of trying, he agreed. If he could talk with his friend, club director Sydney Pollack (*Tootsie, The Way We Were*). The two of them wanted to sit around and shmooze. Who would say no to that?

12

Club Kings—
Steven Spielberg
and Sydney Pollack

Steven Spielberg got in because he snuck on the Universal lot, and Sid Sheinberg liked him. Sid Sheinberg got in because of legal expertise and because Lew Wasserman needed a successor. (Lew had no son, and Universal has a policy of no nepotism.) Lorraine Gary got in because she married Sid Sheinberg. Steven Spielberg stayed in because he put Lorraine Gary in Jaws. Lorraine Gary stayed in in spite of giving the worst performance of the '80s in Jaws IV. Verna Fields got in because Steven Spielberg and George Lucas liked her. She stayed in because she was the voice of reason in an insanely emotional building, the Black Tower at MCA. She also stayed in because Ned Tanen was her best friend. Ned Tanen got in because of the music business, and because he could handle Jules Stein and Lew Wasserman and Taft Schreiber. Taft Schreiber dropped out when UCLA Medical Center gave him a bad blood transfusion, and he died. Jules Stein dropped out when he started caring more about his eye institute and his antiques than about the box office—and because Lew Wasserman could run the show better. Lew Wasserman stayed at the top because he worked harder than anyone in club history, until Jeffrey Katzenberg came along. Jules Stein got in because he could handle the boys in Chicago. Doris Stein

*stayed in because she gave beautiful parties in the best house in
Beverly Hills proper. Doris Stein dropped out when she began
falling asleep at dinner parties, at the table. Jules Stein's last
major club decision was to approve Steven Spielberg's $5 million
headquarters on the Universal lot. Steven Spielberg is a club
king, as powerful as Lew Wasserman (and more powerful than
Jules Stein, because Jules Stein had interests other than the
movie business). Sydney Pollack is a club king because he has
more sway over stars than anybody in the club, except Mike
Ovitz. Sydney Pollack got in because he could handle the politics
of TV at Universal and because Natalie Wood let him direct her
in* This Property Is Condemned.

What I discovered about Steven Spielberg is that he is shrouded by the
most protective group of people in the club. He wants it both ways—he
wants the creative stimulation of peers, yet he hires people who aren't his
peers, and they become his armor. It's the ultimate club dilemma: The
ego becomes so developed that you don't want anyone around who isn't
compatible.

Yet creative conflict is what makes movies great. *Jaws* was the ultimate
club movie, combining strong producers (Dick Zanuck and David Brown)
with real writing (Peter Benchley), real star power (Richard Dreyfuss,
hitting his stride, and Robert Shaw, in a last hurrah), plus the Oscar-
winning editing and love of club godmother Verna Fields. And then
there was Spielberg directing at the age of twenty-six.

The week that movie opened, in 1975, I interviewed Spielberg in his
corner office at Universal, a room where he made more political phone
calls every day than any director since William Wyler. You could feel
that day how satisfying those calls were, now that Spielberg had a blockbuster on his hands. Spielberg instinctively understood the club was really
a small Jewish community, a duchy, and he always wanted in—very
badly. He always wanted to be invited to Ray Stark's for dinner and a
movie. When I met him the first time, the week his movie was turning
into a phenomenon, he told me: "Let's call each other with gossip." I
knew that day it would never happen. And I knew why.

The thing is, I try to reinvent the wheel every time, for each of these
people. I don't want to exchange gossip, ever, with anyone. If I stay
completely off the gossip circuit, a subject won't hear negativity about
me when he checks me out ahead of time. For example, I never had a
lover in the Hollywood community, so no one could ever say, 'He was

so-and-so's lover.' I almost never bad-mouth (except Nancy Reagan, who deserves it) basing my behavior on Ann-Margret's, who survived thirty years in show business without ever making a known enemy. Or being mean. I always felt enemies could hurt you, and I didn't want to be famous.

So when I met Spielberg the first time, and he wanted a "relationship" with a journalist, I knew it would never happen. I didn't have it in me to shmooze or gossip—I had different kinds of energy, and was more internal. That's why I write. I don't like to talk.

So when I again met Spielberg, in the spring of 1989, I was a brand-new person to him. He might know the byline now (maybe) but that was it. There was nothing else for the dossier. (When Barbara Walters said, at the end of our interview, "Now turn off the tape recorder and tell me ten minutes about you," I refused. "There isn't ten minutes," I told her. She shot back, "Try me," and I tried her. But it was uncomfortable.) Journalists really do like playing *Zelig* and being chameleons. It's much more powerful to be anonymous.

Spielberg and I discussed two mutual friends, to give us a bonding of sorts—Verna Fields and Victoria Principal. He once called Victoria "a great mind trapped in a great body," which shows he does have a sense of humor. Of Verna, the Hollywood godmother, he said to me, "She was a channeler, I think, for a lot of us."

When Spielberg said that, I knew we were on the same frequency in one way. It's very hard to find horror stories (or humorous anecdotes) about him, either. And I, too, thought Verna was a trance medium.

At any rate, I like Steven best in his role as Hollywood seer. While the town scampered around trying to get the Sony-Guber-Peters story right—trying to figure out why Sony handpicked Guber-Peters to run Columbia Pictures—Spielberg returned from Hawaii and put it all in a Zen-like perspective. "Sony is giving the movie business a new checking account," he said the afternoon the news hit. "Sony isn't pretending to become involved in the creative parts. Sony knows it's Americans who know the movie business, and the fact of Guber-Peters doesn't personally bother me—but I'm wondering something: The Columbia logo is the lady with the torch. So will she become a geisha? . . . And I'm trying to imagine what a compact movie feels like. Does a compact movie get great gas mileage?"

Spielberg has been emerging from what observers call a prolonged adolescence—into a kind of mainstreamism. He is assuming a visible role in the community after years in the background. He wants to work less hard in the '90s than he did in the '80s. He wants to have the kinds of experiences he had in Paris when François Truffaut spent an afternoon taking him through the Cinémathèque Française, and they talked all day about movies. He wants to sit again on the beach in Hawaii with a friend like George Lucas, or cinematographer Vilmos Zsigmond, and make plans. He wants new vistas.

In April 1989, he looked as comfortable as a boulevardier at the American Cinematheque Moving Picture Ball; the evening honored Spielberg, and it reunited his entire family for the first time in years. It was also the last time Spielberg and his estranged wife, Amy Irving, would be seen together. Amy looked like she was in a straitjacket. It was the kind of club evening—Goldie Hawn and Richard Dreyfuss doing skits, the Bergmans doing inside jokes—Hollywood used to do best. Until TV award shows corrupted the form.

The staggering good fortune that came early to Spielberg is something he's wanted to share, primarily through Amblin, the production company where he's lent his name to younger talents like Bob Zemeckis (*Back to the Future*) and Kevin Reynolds (*Prince of Thieves*). It's at Amblin that Spielberg has experienced the greatest success in movie history: Seven of the top ten all-time films have his name on them. Simultaneously, at Amblin, he's taken the most flack. His die-hard fans want him to be mad as hell for not getting an Academy Award nomination for *The Color Purple* or *E.T.* And his detractors think he set up the campaign of outrage when he didn't get even a nomination. Spielberg may be too powerful to have enemies, but he is a topic of talk all over town, all the time.

"I've developed a pretty good sense of humor about it," said Spielberg one afternoon at Amblin. "I now have no resentment or malice. What else are people going to write about? I've gotten accustomed to people talking about me. They often project their own frustrations onto me, for whatever reason . . . I just feast on their comments."

But what about the day of reckoning when Steven Spielberg wins a Best Director Academy Award, when he is forgiven everything, even his billions? Can he do a creative visualization that far ahead? "I can see myself in a wheelchair, being rolled in to the Oscars, being totally gray and what's the word? Senile. So senile I won't really understand I've gotten one."

If it happens, it will probably be for a Spielberg Adult Movie, not an *E.T.*, which is where the Oscar controversy was: The windfall from the film hurt its "prestige." "People think we were greedy with *E.T.*, and I resent it," complained the director. "Seventy percent of the merchandising went to pirates. A lot of money was made, and we got blamed for it. We had thirty-three licenses, yet there were 150 products."

But Spielberg has other things on his mind now. He wants to be open again, and trusting. And if the '80s were a greed decade, with producers and agents and money people reemerging as stars—listening to Spielberg, you feel the '90s could bring a return of the Creatives. Spielberg sees Hollywood in terms of eras; there's a historian inside him oozing to get out. At most inner-studio offices, if you bring up names from even ten years ago, you draw blanks. But Spielberg, in a pair of discussions over several months, showed why he sits on top of a heap: He knows who his predecessors were. Tell him that Billy Wilder once said, "Twenty-five years ago I was Steven Spielberg," and he doesn't hyperventilate or pause. Or flinch. He just wonders, "Who am I going to say that about in thirty-five years? I hope there is someone . . . I hope someone comes along and rescues me. There are directors who need to do it until they drop, and nobody wants to grant them the opportunity. It's hard to imagine how hard it was for David Lean to get *Nostromo* off the ground."

Will Spielberg at eighty-one be as dogged as David Lean was? He doesn't think so. "I don't want to be David Lean at eighty on a sound stage in Mexico, though I admired him. I don't think my interests will hold out that long. I'm trying to think what else would distract me . . . But when you tally it up, I will have made more movies . . . no single one as good as David Lean's . . . but, I will have made more movies than David by the time I'm eighty. His movies average out to one every six and a half years. Maybe it kept David hungry." Spielberg paused. Sometimes you can feel how much he contains, and keeps to himself, even with his longtime loyal team of producers and associates, his protectors. Ask him about father figures, and he says: "David Lean is still the one I look to for most of my answers . . . I get answers from movies," said Spielberg quickly. "If you see a movie that's truly great, you just don't recover."

So a movie is more of a guru than a real guru. In person Spielberg has the same guru quality John Lennon used to share with journalists. Almost nothing he says is unquotable, yet he leaves much unspoken. "I'm a perfect example of the American dream," he said on a recent morning in a living room at Amblin, surrounded by Navajo rugs on the walls and the floors. He wants to sit around with actors—"Julia Roberts was here yesterday"—or cronies, like Truffaut told him they did at the Cinémathèque in Paris. It was in that vein that Spielberg talked one morning with Sydney Pollack. This is what they'd like Hollywood to be like—more of a creative center, with more shmoozing, less privacy, less business. As you listen carefully to these men, you hear something in their voices that's missing in businessmen's voices. Call it love. Obviously these men had to become rich before they could really be listened to as *artistes*—they had to make their bones—but their love of movies is deep. It came through loud in several hours of talking.

A generation apart (which means Pollack is more older brother than father), each is probably the preeminent director of his generation. Also, they're both Jewish Midwesterners—Spielberg born in Ohio, Pollack in Indiana—and together they give a new spin to the term Midwestern reach.

In a community as socially closed as Hollywood, insularity becomes a way of life. The club talks to each other—and only to each other, or so it sometimes seems. Spielberg thinks this reclusiveness is due in part to Hollywood protocol. "I want to call Sydney up sometimes, but I don't do it. I want to ask Sydney what was his experience like with Jessica Lange, who gave one of the best performances of her career in *Tootsie.*" Spielberg looked into Pollack's eyes: "How was it that your mojos were working so well at the same time? When everybody knew you had nine drafts of the screenplay. Nine screenplays, really; that's interesting stuff."

The image of '50s Sunday poker games (at Sam Spiegel's house) or of '70s Sunday brunches (at director Roman Polanski's) have been replaced. Hollywood's top operators are now family-oriented post-yuppies. Apart from their work, they have their children. Period. And you don't do the same business at Richard Dreyfuss' son's first birthday, as you do in Dan Melnick's sculpture garden. ("There's doing business—and then there's moving furniture," says William Morris agent Joan Hyler, who quietly is turning into one of the town's new hostesses; she mixes up producers and actors and writers on Sunday afternoons at Sea Colony. But CBS programming chief Jeff Sagansky brings his children. And no furniture gets moved.)

"I've done that a lot," said Spielberg about the notion of a creative round table. "Before our—what was our generation referred to as, the New Hollywood? Before that, George [Lucas] and I were . . ."

"The Rat Pack?"

"No, not rat. But literally myself and Marty Scorsese and Brian De Palma and George—about a dozen of us—we did hang out. We did go to each other's rough cuts," said Spielberg pointedly. "We did sit in screening rooms and solicit ideas from each other about how to make the cut better. We actually sat . . . I sat with Martin Scorsese at the Astoria Studios on Long Island, during the whole shootout on *Taxi Driver,* and I made suggestions with him and with Marcia Lucas, the editor."

Spielberg looked satisfied with that memory; it's from a time when he was less completely preoccupied with his own movies—and offshoots. So you try to keep him in that frame of mind, reminiscing.

"There was a geographic thing in *Taxi Driver* with Robert De Niro and I said to Marty, 'Gee—if you shoot that scene over his shoulder, you'll get full coverage on the scene.' And Brian De Palma was in my cutting room when we did *Close Encounters of the Third Kind.* When he said, 'I'm really confused about this movement . . .' " Spielberg paused. Then he corrected himself. "As a matter of fact, it was Brian De Palma who got me interested in using a Rosetta stone for the character's revelations . . . And for a mountain location Brian said, 'That mountain better be so unique and specific. We don't want them to think it's ten mountains in ten parts of the country.' "

Spielberg makes De Palma sound patriarchal, almost a fear figure. " 'You better find the most unique mountain,' Brian said. And I said, 'You know, Brian, you're so right.' I went out and found Doubles Tower, Wyoming, which is the most unique mountain in the country . . . That's the kind of creative stuff that I like, where your ego doesn't get in the way of accepting something from a close associate or peer."

But *Close Encounters* was 1975, and the *Big Chill* era seems remote now. Time and multiple Spielberg sequel movies make the clubbiness hard to come by. That's why Spielberg now seeks out Pollack. Sydney Pollack comes out of the rough-and-tumble time of early TV: He has a kind of sturdiness that reassures people. It wouldn't be surprising to see him playing one of the father figures in *Field of Dreams,* although he's barely sixty. "I was the last generation that came before film school," he said simply. "My film school was, I did twenty TV shows a year; it was another kind of film school. It wasn't theory, it was just pure trial and error. And you survived, because the quality level was so low that if you screwed up, they still gave you another chance. Half hour shows I'd do in two days. Chill Wills and Jimmy Dean in *Frontier Circus.* But, I learned about horses, I learned about tumbleweeds, I learned about gunfights—and how to stay the course."

Pollack, whose closest friend is director Mark Rydell (who also came out of early TV), had a harder, longer road to go than wunderkind Spielberg. He didn't have a Sid Sheinberg discover him. Remembers Pollack: "It was four *Ben Caseys* at a time: Prepare, shoot, prepare, shoot. Pure practical stuff. You try to put it together as well as a carpenter. And after four or five years of that, maybe somebody would give you a film to do. Some of us were able to do a little more, and some of us weren't. Some stayed in television, some faded away . . ."

Spielberg nodded knowingly. From the beginning he had a sense of politesse about how the club works. And his longing for camaraderie is almost palpable: "Don't you think that when Reagan and Gorbachev first met, one of the first things they wondered was what was in each other's refrigerators? Beyond any agenda, there's a curiosity about what's in the other guy's refrigerator. It's the same thing with filmmakers."

Yet Spielberg doesn't deny the privacy label: He admits to watching movies primarily in his screening room at Amblin, and often by himself. "When I have a couple of hours, and I can order up a film, I'll always run an old movie, some MGM classic. Because the difference in looking at *Mrs. Miniver* on videotape and looking at *Mrs. Miniver* on 35mm, good black-and-white film, is the difference between inspiration and observation."

Spielberg paused, and suddenly he seemed to be a teenager. "I can just sit in a screening room and see this movie and suddenly time stops. There is no distance between myself and that generation, of the '40s. I'm right there. That's the kinetics between the viewer and the screen. I'm talking about a large screen versus a little twenty-one-inch screen."

And yet Spielberg sees "almost everything" in a time when his film generation has dispersed, gotten lazy, and begun choosing restaurants over movies. (At a birthday dinner for a forty-year-old producer, each guest admitted to seeing "no more than six movies last year." And this was a movie industry group.) And that elicits the inevitable question: Is this or is this not a great period for movies?

Spielberg breathed deeply. "It's a very simple thing to say: The last great movie was *Godfather I*. That was my last great movie. And before that it was *Lawrence of Arabia*. I'm a real snob in that sense. Those were the two last great films."

So this isn't a great period?

"I think it's a transition period. *Godfather* was the last American classic, but I'm not saying that's the only great movie before or after. I'm just saying it's the last one in terms of a classic—of ranking right up there with *Grapes of Wrath*."

Spielberg feels "the transitioning" is to a potpourri, a bouillabaisse, presided over by bureaucrats. The director seems to have accepted the bureaucratization of America, of Hollywood. Ask him if he, of all people, couldn't fight the trend, and he thinks about it. "I've been fighting it. I did a couple of movies in a row that I thought fought it. *Color Purple* and *Empire of the Sun*. I did that on purpose," he said simply. "I made the movies for the selfish reason that I wanted to express the pleasure I had in experiencing those novels." Spielberg looked at Pollack. "*Out of Africa* is totally against the mainstream. And just because it made money, doesn't mean it copped out."

Africa also followed one very strict Sydney Pollack rule: It featured stars. Here is where Pollack has one up on Spielberg. "Sydney has directed Meryl Streep, Robert Redford, Dustin Hoffman, Natalie Wood, Barbra Streisand, Al Pacino, and on and on," said Spielberg with some awe. "I think to myself, 'I'm forty-one. Will I have the time to direct Robert De Niro or Barbra Streisand.'"

"I'm lazy," said Pollack in a kind of flip aside. "I read a picture and I see a movie star. Maybe if I started differently, I'd have developed differently. But the first movie I ever did had two stars in it [*Slender Thread* starred Anne Bancroft and Sidney Poitier.] To me, growing up in Indiana, everybody in the movies was a movie star. Debra Paget was a movie star in South Bend . . . But I keep saying I'm gonna do a movie with a nobody."

"I don't know that you should," said Spielberg. He has at moments a quality that could be called fixer-psychic—he sees you as you should be seen.

"Everybody beats the shit out of me," said Pollack, "for working with stars. So, I'm gonna do a nice little movie with nobodies before I die."

Spielberg gave Pollack an oh-sure look. Spielberg "had some bad experiences with TV stars when I was like twenty-one, twenty-two, twenty-three." Not Joan Crawford, by chance, whom he directed in a *Night Gallery* when he was twenty-one? "No, Joan was magnificent, on her best behavior. But after that there were some bad experiences." (Spielberg's TV works were *Duel*, starring Dennis Weaver, and an episodic drama with Roy Thinnes.) Even early on, Spielberg was the pragmatist: "At twenty-three, I was already saying, 'Life's too short to worry about the size of someone's trailer. Or the fact that they don't like the hairdresser because the hairdresser has coffee breath.' Little petty things used to make me crazy."

Like: "Actors not wanting to hit a mark, wanting to stage themselves, wanting to give themselves direction, not wanting to hear any of my ideas. I only had a few negative experiences in TV, but it kind of soured me along those lines." Thus the twenty years of not using stars—until *Hook* with Hoffman, Roberts, et al.

Hasn't Spielberg cut off his nose to spite his face? "But I've been okay without stars," he reasoned. He answers the question quickly but not defensively; he doesn't try to talk faster than everyone in a room—although he could. "The reason I didn't use stars before is that I liked people who bring very little baggage. It's very hard when you have an icon playing an ordinary person. My main drive since I began was not to use people who were on the cover of *Rolling Stone*."

And now? "At forty-one I'm starting to want to work with Meryl Streep." Spielberg has developed real passion and indeed readiness for stars. He sounds almost like an eastern executive who worries about the right table at Mortons. "I have a stomachache because I haven't worked with and directed Robert De Niro yet. I have a pain in my right side because I haven't worked with Barbra Streisand. I would love to do something with Tom Cruise." Could one reason be that Spielberg was the star of every Spielberg movie? That he was always the muscle? No confrontations, please, no star wars.

"That's a myth," Spielberg answered flatly. "You don't give up a single bit of control." Pollack picked up the cue: "I've done fourteen films, and none of them haven't had major stars. And I've never had anything but complete control. Even before I knew there was such a thing as control."

It's a myth, then, that movie stars control a project?

"It really is a myth," said Pollack. In most cases, movie stars hire themselves out because they trust and are seduced by the character they want to play. The idea of real luxury to intelligent movie stars—and most of them are intelligent—is to bury themselves in the part they are playing. It's an aberrant situation when you find an actor who wants to control the film."

And if that happens? "Then you are wrong chemically for each other, or you miscast the actor, or if the actor brought it to you, then he miscast you. I don't want to sound like a Pollyanna, and it doesn't mean you don't clash. But, I've worked with people who are supposed to be the toughest—going all the way back to Burt Lancaster, who had a fiendish reputation, and that was when I was a kid . . . Barbra, Pacino, Redford, Newman, Faye, Meryl . . . I've worked with people who have reputations. You think, 'Boy oh boy, you are gonna get into a big pissing contest.' It's just not true. Or it's not true unless something is wrong."

"Making movies is too practical," Spielberg added. "There's too little intimacy and too much immediacy about getting the shot, getting the day's work before the sun is covered. It really is work."

All work and no play? Spielberg has said that Time-Warner chairman Steve Ross is trying to teach him to relax. And he can become relaxed enough in the right setting. On a Sunday afternoon, from Pia Zadora's Trancas window, you might spot her next-door neighbor, Spielberg, walking the beach with his son, Max, or with one or two of weekend neighbor Goldie Hawn's kids (Dreyfuss and Hawn are probably Spielberg's two closest star friends; the three have been through various downs and ups, including parenthood). Spielberg sounds as relaxed as he probably gets when talking about a social evening, at his beach house in New York's Hamptons. But the anecdote, if you really hear it, is all about work.

"The abstract expressionist Willem de Kooning," began Spielberg, "was turning eighty. And we were having a little birthday party in Easthampton. Dustin [Hoffman] and myself and Steve [Ross] and his wife, Courtney, and Bill's wife, Elaine, who just died this year, and a few other people." Spielberg's truly private self is obvious here; he sounds slightly nervous.

He doesn't want to impress by name dropping, and on the other hand, this is the world he travels in. He doesn't sculpt and perfect anecdotes as actors do. A Jack Lemmon or James Stewart can become instantly intimate with an interviewer because it's part of their job. But Spielberg wanted to make a point here.

"We were sitting there, and Dustin was trying to express to Willem de Kooning how fortunate he is to be a painter. There is nothing between himself and his impulse and the canvas. There is nothing there but divine inspiration. And de Kooning wasn't understanding this. And Dustin said, 'Well, we make movies. We have a hundred people on the set all the time. And there are people hovering to fix your makeup, and the noise of pounding nails into wood all the time, and headaches from the noise. You can take as long as you want to finish a canvas, but we have pressure to finish a film.'

"Willem didn't understand. He was eighty years old, and he's really into his art. And Dustin said, 'Here's an example: There's a train track. Say Steven is standing on a train track, with a camera, and he's trying to get a shot in another direction, and the train is coming, and he's working to get the shot. The train is getting closer and closer. He's got the actors saying their lines as fast as they can. Just as he gets the shot, he cuts to the track—and the train passes.' And Willem looked at Dustin with great sincerity and said, 'Why does he make movies on railroad tracks?' "

It was a good memory, and Spielberg laughed out loud. Then he pointed at me to make sure I got it; I nodded. "Dustin was trying to show Willem the metaphor, the analogy . . . That we don't have time to think of ourselves as artists. Or to wax poetic. That all takes place when you're writing the screenplay, or when you're rehearsing. But, once you're making a movie . . ."

"It's crisis management," put in Pollack. "I always describe myself as a damage containment expert, and I'm only half joking. It's like a train wreck has happened," added Pollack, continuing the analogy, "and you want as few people injured as possible. The economics have made it impossible to do any real-time thinking. Movies are economically driven so badly that you are really now being a psychologist. Keeping everyone in good shape, keeping an atmosphere, getting the work done . . . When you go in at $30 million, that can go very fast to $40 million or $50 million, and overnight you can blow a studio."

Spielberg shuddered. In conversation his age—or rather his youth—keeps coming up. "I know I got started very young. I was discovered by Sid Sheinberg when I was a junior in college. I was within two months of my twenty-first birthday when I directed Joan Crawford. I was making movies since I was twelve; 8mm and 16mm when I was seventeen years old. So I feel a lot older than I actually am. I've been really serious about this as a career since I was twelve years old.

"They always write about me starting at twelve, but it's not apocryphal," said the press-wise director. He reads everything, and knows bylines. (At the New York opening of the *Lawrence of Arabia* rerelease, in which Spielberg accompanied Dawn Steel, he told a Hollywood journalist: "You're so much nicer than the things you write.") "I don't excuse those early years as a hobby—do you know what I'm saying? I really did start then."

And there really was a turning point. "I was fifteen and a half when I saw *Lawrence of Arabia*, and it turned me around. I really kicked into high gear, and thought, 'This I gotta do. I gotta make movies. I gotta really make movies.' But even before that, I was passionate about it, I had a lust for it. So, even though I'm in my early forties, I feel older in terms of my experience."

There is real nostalgia here: "You have to do everything yourself now. In the old days, you had editors who were like your right arm. Casting directors who were like your left arm. Producers who were real producers. Who shared your heart, and they were your alter egos. The producer was the person whose taste filtered down. And they had conscience. And, with that kind of teamwork, you can make more than one film a year."

Spielberg sounded defeatist when asked how such a hierarchy got so fractured (with lower-budget exceptions like Woody Allen). "It became every person for themselves. The business got too expensive. People say it's inflation."

Spielberg went into a businessman mode for a moment.

"Bette Davis probably would have been making the same money that Meryl Streep is making today, if you figure where the dollar was in the '30s, and where the dollar is in the '80s. But that's not true. In fact, Bette Davis' equivalent per picture is $350,000, where Meryl Streep's price is between $2 million and $3 million. I guess if Bette Davis had gotten $800,000, $900,000 for a picture, that would be the equivalent of $3 million today, but she didn't make that. Bette Davis made forty films in seven years, and Meryl Streep has done something like eleven. And she works more than anybody."

What Steven Spielberg sees all around him is "anxiety everywhere . . . a palpable tension. Careers begin or end based on one movie. There's no room for naïveté now. Everything has to succeed—or else. Your membership in the club is extended or denied based on one picture. I'm telling you it's viral. I shouldn't have anything to worry about," said the man whose personal fortune can only be guessed at. "I suppose people will always give me jobs, or I could go away and hide. But I still feel tension all around me, everywhere I look."

So what happened?

"It stopped being a family, Hollywood did. And started becoming independent acts of heroism. It stopped being a community. The director began to be thought of as no longer a collaborator, but as a kind of supreme being. I don't believe that, by the way. As a director I can make *Raiders of the Lost Ark*, but I can't be in it, like Harrison Ford. And I like that. I like it when somebody else does it for you."

CLUB RULE TWENTY-ONE

Know who the current club gods are; in other words, know the names of the star directors. Know a little something about the psyche of Mike Nichols or James Cameron or Garry Marshall. These real gods have more power than anyone in the club (except a few agents) because their name on a project is still the best guarantee of a blockbuster. And unconsciously or not, directors do see themselves as omnipotent.

Club director Mark Rydell says, "The role of God was taken, but we come next." On a movie set, in the editing room, at studio meetings—a bankable director *is* God. There aren't that many, maybe thirty altogether. Steven Spielberg and Sydney Pollack are true gods in this subculture. And you don't fuck with them. Tom Pollock doesn't fuck with them, even though he's the president of Universal, and Terry Semel doesn't fuck with them, even though he's president of Warner's. Even Lew never fucked with Steven.

To understand the club, know who the gods are. And take them at their myth.

13

Club Founder—
Billy Wilder

Billy Wilder got in because of Arthur Hornblow, Jr., and Ernst Lubitsch and Greta Garbo and (later) Ginger Rogers. Billy Wilder also got in because he had the razor-sharpest wit and a good sense of club politics. Billy Wilder stayed in after his partnership with Charles Brackett ended, because of talent. I.A.L. Diamond got in because he replaced Charlie Brackett as Billy Wilder's collaborator. Walter Matthau got in because of Billy Wilder and Carol Grace Saroyan. Carol Saroyan got in because of style and Oona Chaplin. Oona Chaplin got in because of marriage to Charlie Chaplin, and because she was smart. The Chaplins dropped out because they left America, and invited only the Matthaus to visit them in Switzerland. Carol Saroyan dropped out when she left William Saroyan for the second time. She got back in when she married Walter Matthau and he became a movie star, even after a heart attack seven weeks into filming his breakthrough movie The Fortune Cookie. (It was Carol who kept the pot boiling, and it was Billy Wilder who saw to it nobody replaced Walter.) Marilyn Monroe got back in because of Billy Wilder and Some Like It Hot. Fred MacMurray got in twice—for a few years at a time—because of Billy Wilder's Double Indemnity and The Apartment. In his

*seventies Billy Wilder went into limbo, sort of, because the club
didn't know what to do with him. In his eighties Billy Wilder is
the club wit emeritus.*

———————— ▬▬▬▬▬▬ ————————

"There are definite DMZ lines for the press," a producer told me one
night at a dinner party. "There are lines of demarcation which you cannot
cross. But you know that. That's why you're still doing it. You're perceived
as sympathetic."

I cringed, but in my heart I knew she was right. So the leg was a
political animal after all—avoiding enemies like crazy.

In a community this small you have to be sympathetic. I don't think
I'm rationalizing. One enemy and you never lose him: Roddy McDowall
claims I misquoted him at the American Film Institute dinner honoring
Jack Lemmon in 1987—and I suspect the great Hollywood historian
McDowall will never forget (or forgive). Because of him, after ten years
of covering AFI dinners, I stopped trying overnight to capture a true
Hollywood mood or evening. That's for a very young man. Ten AFI
evenings from Huston to Wilder to Lemmon to Peck to Stanwyck. But
it's the one night a year worth what Ali MacGraw calls "going in for."

Billy Wilder was worth coming to Hollywood for. The week I arrived
in the late '60s, I saw a row of buildings on Little Santa Monica Boulevard
in Beverly Hills. I began to fantasize about working there, in one of those
second-story rooms facing the railroad tracks and the flats of Beverly Hills.
Protected Beverly Hills! Ten years later, almost to the month, I got a call
that after two years my name came up on the waiting list—there was a
room available. The only other office on the floor with French windows
belonged to Billy Wilder. I would be down the hall from Billy Wilder.
Foolishly I believed I could now do anything, be completely unafraid of
life itself, slay my demons . . . My would-be office was $125 a month
(with annual $10 raises since then). It was padded like a cell and carpeted
like a whorehouse; it turned out to be a discreet Beverly Hills hideaway
for a game show millionaire named Chuck Barris who left after ten years
to acquire majority stock in a company called Guber-Peters. Anyway, I
got his room. It faces onto the corner of Rodeo Drive, of all unlikely (or
likely) places for a bordello. I tore out the thick bedroom carpeting, and
rearranged it so my desk faced the windows, which looked out to the
long-gone Hunter's Bookstore on Rodeo. Now a quasi-citizen of Beverly
Hills, I could even get a library card. My friend Mickey said the building
was the perfect setting for a detective novel, or a murder mystery. Then
a week into all this redecorating, Billy Wilder walked in. I showed him

my baby refrigerator, bottled water cooler, posters, and, of course, my view.

He scowled. "Are you a writer or a voyeur?" asked the greatest living movie writer-director.

I tried never to bother him, although I loved visiting his office; he had great pasteboard walls and (obviously) great art. But his desk did not face the French window. Soon mine didn't either.

The times I did bother him, he told me only great things. Like: The day after I sat through his movie *Fedora* twice, I couldn't wait to tell him. "Isn't twice too much?" said Mr. Wilder dryly. Or the day in 1980 when he got roasted by critics for his last movie *Buddy, Buddy*. Bellowing down the hall was Mr. Wilder's voice: "Don't cry for me, Argentina!"

That was the week he also told me to write on Saturday and Sunday as well as all week long. "Work seven days a week and you'll finish what you start."

Almost ten years after I moved into the Writers & Artists Building, Billy Wilder finally got the AFI Lifetime Achievement Award. Because of the attendant hoopla, he didn't want to do interviews in advance, in fact said no to our then-competition Aljean Harmetz of the *New York Times*. Finally he relented, and talked to her on the day of the event. But Mr. Wilder was good enough to see me before, at home in the staggering cozy Westwood apartment where "if you ask the doorman he'll wash your car" as Mr. Wilder told me. He told me more in forty-five minutes than anybody I ever met.

When I walked in the apartment, I discovered Mr. Wilder was having trouble finding a teaspoon, in his own kitchen yet. Finally, sheepishly, he curled a finger and led me to the Wilder dining room, the one decorated with Picassos and Klees. There the club's most mischievous immigrant borrowed a spoon from the impeccably set table. That night Audrey and Billy Wilder were entertaining for ten ("a nice little group of right-wing Democrats"). As Wilder swiped the spoon, he did a double take, making very sure his wife wasn't around. It's no accident that the Wilders' dinner parties are the closest thing Hollywood has to a salon. (Truman Capote's missing chapter on Hollywood in his opus *Answered Prayers* was called "And Audrey Wilder Got Up to Sing." There's a reason. The former Tommy Dorsey band singer still gets up to sing, but she also doubles as the club's most eclectic hostess.) "But today," complained Billy Wilder, "I wish I was on Sam Spiegel's yacht. In Sardinia. If I wanted all this media attention I'd have called myself Billy Windex." With that the writer-director-producer made instant coffee, answered another call, and took a seat.

The irony is that for all Wilder's bravura, and credits—*Sunset Boule-*

vard, Stalag 17, Sabrina, Seven Year Itch, Spirit of St. Louis, Some Like It Hot, and those are just the ones starting with S—Wilder is still very much the loner. For years he and his collaborator Iz Diamond spent five of every seven mornings (sans secretaries) at our building in Beverly Hills, working on screenplays. Wilder is always working, lately on his autobiography. So when the home phone rings, for autographs and interview requests—Wilder wears a mock look of being put upon.

The thing is, he doesn't mean it. Mr. Hyde and Mr. Hyde, as the late wit Harry Kurnitz called him, would never admit it, but he likes attention. To be fifty years at the top is no accident. In 1944 Alfred Hitchcock said it best: "The two most important words in the motion picture business are Billy Wilder." Hitchcock was talking about variety. To co-write *Ninotchka* for Garbo in 1937, then last long enough to be in Jerry Weintraub's temporary (like six months) kitchen cabinet at United Artists in 1987 is to go the distance. But unlike director-peers Hitchcock and John Huston, Wilder got the attention on his own terms, in his own private, chameleon-like way. No cameo roles for him, onscreen or off.

The Wilder wit—the sweet-and-sour cocktails he delivers on command, the lines like "slipping out of these wet clothes into a dry martini"—are always forthcoming. But Wilder, the man with the mind full of razor blades, is behind the scenes, never in front. One resists the temptation to ask Wilder if, like his quintessential Hollywood character Norma Desmond, he's ready for his close-up.

More to the point: What would the close-up reveal? How much of Billy Wilder is in Billy Wilder's movies? The silver-haired octogenarian rolled up the sleeves on his gray cashmere sweater, and agreed to give the question a whirl. In the '20s, after leaving Vienna to become a journalist in Berlin, in one morning he interviewed Sigmund Freud, Alfred Adler, Bertolt Brecht, and Max Ophuls. So the question-answer process is not unfamiliar.

"Isn't it pieces of yourself, of your life, that you inevitably use?" he asked rhetorically. "You suck art out of your finger in a way." In one way or another. Wilder was a gigolo in Mexico a thousand years ago, and a Mexican gigolo (played by Charles Boyer) turned up, rather impishly, in *Hold Back the Dawn.* "Or let's take *Sunset Boulevard,*" suggested Wilder. "Maybe you believe it when William Holden's car is repossessed. Because yes, it happened to me, it happened here in Hollywood, and it happened to work in that movie." On a more personal level, isn't Kirk Douglas' cynical reporter in *Ace in the Hole* more than a little bit of Wilder? Maybe and maybe not. "Anyone who knows me," he said slowly, "knows the cynicism hides my sentimentality." It's why Wilder's refugee-freshness about America slipped into Garbo's Russian in Paris in *Ninotchka*—or

James Cagney's outsider in Berlin in *One, Two, Three*. Before he was thirty Wilder had lived in Vienna, Berlin, Paris, Mexico, and Hollywood, and what he saw he used.

Clearly one could play twenty questions about Wilder's characters—Sefton in *Stalag 17*, Don Birnam in *Lost Weekend*, Walter Neff in *Double Indemnity*, Linus Larrabee in *Sabrina*—but clearly he'd rather talk about the casting. Wilder is canny enough to know the public is more interested in Gary Cooper and Humphrey Bogart than in the types they played, and so he deftly moves a conversation from characters to stars.

"Three times in my life I almost got to work with Cary Grant," remembered Wilder with both enthusiasm and disappointment. To realize that Billy Wilder never directed Cary Grant or Katharine Hepburn or Spencer Tracy is to be surprised, but not after listening to Wilder's explanation. "Every movie begins with the dream casting of Cary Grant and Katharine Hepburn. Then every movie faces the reality of casting Lyle Keller and Sadie Glutz. Cary [Grant] almost did *Ninotchka*, in the Melvyn Douglas role; imagine him opposite Garbo! The second time was *Sabrina*, and then at the last minute it was Bogart."

"The third one Cary almost did was *Love in the Afternoon*. Gary Cooper played it. Not that the replacements were so bad . . ." Wilder paused long enough that the dream pairing of Audrey Hepburn and Cary Grant in *Love in the Afternoon* could be seen in the mind's eye. *Afternoon* was the first writing partnership of Wilder and Diamond, and of course it was written with Grant in mind. "Cary was a good friend of mine, but maybe he was scared of me, I dunno," mused Wilder. "Cooper I think had not as much going for him in that role. Say the name Gary Cooper, and people think of a *High Noon* sheriff kind of guy, not a Ritz Hotel lover with gypsy music in the background who gets into one-night stands . . ."

The Hollywood one-night stand of all time, of course, is the one William Holden tripped into in *Sunset Boulevard*. It's still the best Hollywood movie of them all, which is why Andrew Lloyd Webber has spent years trying to turn it into a musical. And it's the film Wilder tends most often to talk about; mention it to him, and certain buttons are pressed. He visibly lights up. But again Wilder wants you to know how accidental the whole thing was.

"Mr. Montgomery Clift changed his mind," Wilder said, shaking his head at the very idiocy of such a move. "A week, maybe ten days before filming, Mr. Clift's New York agent sends word that maybe his client, the young actor Clift, should be gotten out of it. The feeling was that the younger man–older woman thing could actually ruin his career . . ." Wilder shook his head, sadly. "[Co-star] Gloria Swanson was fifty," he said, making it sound like fifteen. "Fifty is younger than Audrey Hepburn is now. Is fifty old? I think Mr. Clift was tortured. Can you imagine? Suddenly this change of heart I found very peculiar . . ."

But *Sunset Boulevard* was an inevitability. Budd Schulberg and Nathanael West and F. Scott Fitzgerald had already fictionalized Hollywood, but nobody had made the movie. Wilder and Brackett were already in place as the happiest professional couple in Hollywood, and ready to take more risks in exposing their adopted hometown. "Kaufman and Hart could write a terrible play, and close it in New Haven, before Broadway," said Wilder logically, "but in Hollywood we don't bury our dead. We finish the movies we start, then we find them turning up on TV in the middle of the night. That could be one explanation for an actor's fear." If Montgomery Clift had cold feet, Gloria Swanson, Erich von Stroheim, and Cecil B. DeMille did not, and the director was undaunted. And Wilder is the kind of realist who understands the Hollywood high wire. In other words, the show goes on, understudies emerge. "William Holden was a Paramount man, and he got a script at three P.M. on a Monday and said yes by five. No test, no reading, and he was, you know, perfect." (In her memoir *Swanson on Swanson*, the actress made the point that Holden was thirty-one, while the character Joe Gillis was twenty-six, and it was maybe *he* not she who should be "re-aged" with makeup, but the chemistry worked nevertheless.)

A Wilder trademark has been to get once-in-a-career performances from actors—Gloria Swanson, Fred MacMurray, Ray Milland. But again the director emphasizes serendipity. "It's because I know just how much was accidental. Swanson was not the first choice for Norma Desmond. As it turned out, it worked with her, and it would have collapsed without her. But Pola Negri is the one we thought of first, then we thought she hadn't really been in sound pictures. And then there was . . . can I tell you a story?" asked Wilder, with the kind of timing only actors and athletes know, then told it.

"I pitched *Sunset Boulevard* to Mary Pickford," he said, letting the scene emerge. "I went to Pickfair, to see Mary, with a script under my arm. Imagine me walking into that house with that churchy atmosphere. And then beginning to read *Sunset Boulevard* aloud to Mary Pickford. It hit me midway through that Mary Pickford was not going to play Norma Desmond. But what do I do? How do I get out of this one?" If you're Billy Wilder you think on your feet. "I suddenly stopped reading, and just said, 'You know, Mary, you can play anything. You really can. You can act rings around any actress. But Mary, I just realized this is not on your level. It's not up to your caliber.' "

Did Pickford buy it? Or did she want to play, as any actress would, Norma Desmond? "I'm not clear on the answer, because I never finished reading it to her. But you grasp what I mean about accidents."

And alchemy. "My father told me once nobody's an alchemist," said Wilder, with a wink. "But if I was, I'd make a thriller. There was never one kind of picture I made. I went from *Witness for the Prosecution* to *One, Two, Three.* Mr. Hitchcock, he made only thrillers, and magnificently. But you know what a thriller is to me? It's the movie where the boss chases the secretary around the desk . . . That's a thriller—and that's alchemy!"

Three nights later Billy Wilder received the AFI Life Achievement Award. It was probably the last truly era-spanning club event. Somewhere in the middle of the evening, the Hollywood clock stood still. Whoopi Goldberg was telling the room Billy Wilder stories, then within minutes Mr. Wilder was himself on stage thanking his mentor Ernst Lubitsch. Going from Lubitsch to Wilder to Whoopi Goldberg is more than a half-century time span, and nothing so simple as a mere time warp. As the AFI's George Stevens, Jr., put it, "The excellent becomes permanent." Not that the unpretentious Wilder would go for the line. "Thou Shalt Not Bore" is, after all, his creed. The six-time Oscar winner was anecdotal as ever: "One day I was walking on the Goldwyn lot, and I heard my name mentioned. I looked up, and Sam Goldwyn was standing there. 'You look depressed, Billy,' he said. I said, 'Well, my last picture went down the tubes.' And Goldwyn said, 'Listen Billy, you gotta take the bitter with the sour.' Well, tonight there is no bitter and there is no sour."

What there was, was a mix of power and magic that dazzled even the club nay-sayers who put everything down. Johnny and Joanna Carson making their first public appearances separately. Gregory Peck and James Stewart and Gene Kelly were there. Fox chairman Barry Diller and CBS Broadcast Group chief Gene Jankowski and then–NBC chairman Grant Tinker. Fred Zinnemann and Steven Spielberg. Ginger Rogers and Carol Burnett and Sally Field. The Kennedy Center's Rogers Stevens and the Brat Pack's Molly Ringwald, and every past and present AFI board chairman. When Jessica Lange and Sam Shepard are relegated to the second tier, you know the International Ballroom is beyond packed.

As Don Ameche put it, "Hollywood is a strange place. Forty-eight years ago I was in a picture Billy Wilder wrote called *Midnight,* and yet I'm not sure we've ever met until tonight." Imagine Jack Lemmon and Tony Curtis, looking like white-haired brothers, doing a takeoff of "I Enjoy Being a Girl," and you get an idea of the fun.

Walter Matthau—whose tribute speeches are always peerless and must be written by his wife, Carol—quoted Wilder: " 'Of course there are subtleties, just be sure you make them obvious.' . . . Billy also said there was no such thing as comedy," said Matthau, who became a movie star under Wilder's guidance. "It took me a long time to see that Billy doesn't just see the comedies or tragedies of life—he sees it all. He sees the best in the worst of us, and the worst in the best. And we owe him for it."

The best of Wilder—in clips that began with *Ninotchka* (1939) and ended with *The Apartment* (1960)—got unspooled with a kind of random finesse that held the audience. Garbo in love in Paris (*Ninotchka*). Hepburn in love in Paris (*Love in the Afternoon*). Gloria Swanson in love with herself (*Sunset Boulevard*).

Romance aside, there were the examples of what Charles Brackett called "the best dialogue in town." Like Jan Sterling telling Kirk Douglas, in Wilder's most cynical movie, *Ace in the Hole*: "I don't go to church. Kneeling bags my nylons." Or Fred MacMurray getting his comeuppance from Shirley MacLaine in *The Apartment*: "I guess that's the way it crumbles, cookie-wise. I'd spell it out for you, only I can't spell."

Wilder could spell and understand—and take his lumps. "You're as good as the best thing you've ever done," he once told Lemmon, during one of their seven collaborations. Jack Lemmon listened. But not even Lemmon could listen when outgoing AFI chairman Richard Brandt lectured one young scholarship winner. Said Brandt, pompously: "Go be a Billy Wilder."

It may be the silliest Hollywood line of all time. There aren't any more Billy Wilders.

CLUB RULE TWENTY-TWO

Get even for the early days. It's the only way to justify the hard work that it takes to *stay* in the club.

If you get even for being too short to play football by making a movie of *North Dallas Forty*, the work is worth it. People forget Billy Wilder was a journalist before he was a gigolo. Then he was an unemployed writer living with Peter Lorre in downtown Hollywood. Wilder was maybe the first club member to understand that getting even works. By leaping from writer to director, he leapt in club status at the same time. It happened not overnight, but over a decade. And it's emblematic. The club is made up of mostly self-made self-starters who struggled forever. It's not about overnight success. Barbra Streisand is a wunderkind exception to a world in which it took director Herb Ross twenty-five years to segue from chorus boy to esteemed movie director. With success, the director got outrageous. As he told Dolly Parton on the set of *Steel Magnolias*, "Why don't you take some acting lessons before your next film?"

Moral: You don't get mad for all the early battles—you get even. Take it out on somebody else. Before Kim Basinger was bankable, before *Batman*, executives told her her hands were ugly. Now they'll wait for her decision—they wait for her to say yes or no. Because if she nods in favor of a movie, the movie gets made. Her hands are no longer an issue. But her whim is.

14

An Enormous
Favor, Darling—
Sue Mengers

Sue Mengers *got in the door because she was the secretary in agent Charlie Baker's outer office, and Gore Vidal got a kick out of her. She stayed in because she would do anything—she would go out every night—and she listened to smart men like Billy Rose. She also got in because of a closeness with Joanne and Paul Newman that led to her being hired by David Begelman to run ICM's theater department. When she fused with Barbra Streisand—for a solid productive fifteen years—she went from agent to powerhouse. And she finally got in the club. When she moved to Hollywood she brought humor—which was missing in town, and which kept her in. She filled two voids with one move west—the humor void and the social void. Mike Nichols and Robert Evans went to Sue Mengers' little house above Pickfair, and soon Woody Allen was going and Frank Yablans was complaining about the food—but Barbra would be there and David Geffen, and Bob Fosse. Sue Mengers was damaged by a Holocaust mentality (her parents barely escaped, and her father later committed suicide). She got out of the club in 1986—for a long hiatus—and came back in 1987. With an impossible task ahead of her. She was given the title of worldwide senior VP, literary and motion pictures, at William Morris, and asked to step into*

Stan Kamen's shoes. The whole club was watching. By 1990, it was over, that job. But in the club you never bet against Sue Mengers. She may or may not be working, but she's permanently in the club. Because she only plays with members.

"Ali's got the biggest balls in the world."

Sue Mengers was complaining about her closest friend, Ali MacGraw.

"Imagine Ali calling me a female Billy Wilder! What *cajones!*"

Agents, whom I avoided, were finally unavoidable. Because they are the most insecure, appealing people in the club. Most are not at all like the image. Most are more honest than that, and more self-deprecating than the way they are played in the movies. (Even in *Breakfast at Tiffany's*, which is dead-on about people, the agent O. J. Berman is a caricature.) In real life, agents are the butt of their own jokes, and their own worst enemies. That way the client remains the Nice One, the star, the Bright One. Example: Sue Mengers saying, "My husband is a much nicer person that I am. We have different values."

That's about as self-aware as it gets, or as self-deprecating. The top agents are, as a group, much more sensitive than outsiders think. One night at a dinner party in Santa Monica a longtime powerhouse woman agent (not Mengers) told me she had to ask her boyfriend (also an agent) to pull over to the curb before parking in front of the house—so she could throw up. Panic attack for a little dinner party. A major star agent throwing up on the street. Generally the agent's acute sensitivity to talent goes unnoticed because agents must appear always confident—and they are expected to be funnier than Mae West.

Sue Mengers' sense of humor was compared to Mae West's when Barbra Streisand played an amalgam of both women in Gene Kelly's underrated *Hello, Dolly!* That was 1969, and it was the beginning of the Sue Mengers reputation—that performance by her client Barbra was based a lot on Sue's behavior at her own parties. The parties were cast like movies or wet dreams. Sue was a major force of the '70s—the first female heavyweight champion of the world, her boss Freddie Fields called her.

Sue and I had these long bicoastal sessions only after much prompting on my part; in 1987 she began an eighteen-month sabbatical from the business, sliding between Beverly Hills and New York and Europe and having, for the first time since she started working at seventeen, a ball. A hiatus is the best time to catch a club member. It's when they're the most relaxed and mouthy.

Sue didn't know it (and may still not) but there was a cosmic thread here. In 1975, she had asked me "an enormous favor, darling." I was still the leg. One of her female star clients had gone to Palm Springs to be with Sally Kellerman's husband, Rick Edelstein—but Sue wanted it not to be printed.

So I took care of it.

"I owe you one, darling."

I forgot about it.

Fifteen years later she let me probe her, endlessly. It was an unconscious payback.

Some junior and senior editors were sitting around an apostrophe-shaped table at a major publishing house, picking brains. The idea was to find the quintessential Hollywood book of the '70s, combining business and glamour and stardom. A coffee-table book, maybe, with photos from private lives. Or perhaps an oral history? Or simply a guide to power? Inevitably a bright young editor said the name "Sue Mengers." And the room stopped cold.

"Sue Mengers," shrieked one of the others. "Oh, but of course. She's the best Hollywood story of the last twenty years!"

One of the people in the room didn't know the name. (Only one, though, and he's no longer in publishing.) To fill him in, his colleagues began tripping over each other with all the name dropping. And the stories.

"Sue Mengers is pure Hollywood," said the wunderkind who thought of the idea. "She was the highest-profile agent in the business, man or woman. Streisand, Ryan and Tatum, and then Ryan and Farrah. Peter and Cybill, Candy and Ali, Cimino and De Palma, and Nichols and Lumet . . ."

"I know her a little," said one of the senior editors. "I met her in Italy. She stays with Gore. So bright. And she's kind of . . . bohemian. Has a bite of life. You know, adventurous. And funny—terribly, terribly funny . . ."

"She left the agency business last year," said one of the office gossips. "Saved her money. Sold her house at the right time. Never has to work again."

"Great house, top of Bel Air. She gave the best parties since the days of Frances Goldwyn. And she was funny like Sam Goldwyn. Maybe less printable, but . . ."

"Steve Sondheim and Tony Perkins based the Dyan Cannon role in *The Last of Sheila* on her."

"My favorite story is after the Sharon Tate murders, her reassuring a nervous client. 'Don't worry, honey, stars aren't being murdered. Only featured players.' "

"This sounds like the sequel to *The Best of Everything!*"

"No," said the man who had met Mengers in Italy. "She's more complex than that."

"But who is she really?"

There is a moment in any conversation with Sue Mengers when she reveals who she is really. Or almost. It's when she removes her glasses. What you see is someone who has a completely developed fantasy life—and a total sense of reality. In the last decade the fantasies have been changing. Pure ambition being replaced by a need for an inner life. Whatever the price, she will pay it, but the price won't be humor. Sitting in a garden at the Bel Air Hotel, posing for a photograph, Mengers will play any role you want.

"Is the long blonde hair flowing freely like waves around my shoulders?" she asks spontaneously, spewing the words like dialogue. "Do you want me to play Anita Ekberg in the fountain?" she wonders, referring to *La Dolce Vita*. "I could be lured into a room for a cheeseburger. 'C'mon, little girl . . . here's a cheeseburger.' I don't know how models do it. That's why I turned down the contract with Estée Lauder . . . This is the true sign of a person who's not narcissistic. I didn't bring a mirror."

"Sue opened doors," says Jeff Berg, chairman of ICM and the colleague who's worked the longest with Mengers (seventeen years). Berg, the youngest long-distance runner in the agency wing of the club, says that "Sue knows that at some point the carrier pilot must decide about making more night landings. She's tactical enough, and brave enough, to walk away from the day-to-day shorthand." Fox chairman Barry Diller called Mengers "a beacon to all—to all obsessive-compulsives who make up a large part of this industry—that a decision can be made to seek an alternative."

And the next alternative? There are those who will tell you that maybe Mengers *burned too many bridges, honey*. That the new players don't have relationships with her. But producer Ray Stark went right on the line: "She's finding out exactly what she's capable of. And I'll tell you, she's capable of being a head of production, and she's capable of being the head of a company. There are a lot of people eager to fill her shoes, but they can't. She has the two prerequisites of every great agent: vitality and humor—especially about herself."

Yet there is still about her what Ali MacGraw calls "armor. With Sue there are layers to be peeled away before there's trust. It's like when you meet Mike Nichols and the intelligence is so threatening. Then you see what's underneath. With Sue the armor is in direct proportion to the vulnerability." Then there's the wit—"I was so driven I would have signed Martin Bormann."

When Mengers calls herself "an aggressive smart piece of manpower," she means both right and left brain are working; nothing is wasted. Not the elocution lessons in Utica, not the Saturday movies in the Bronx, not the years of being a secretary. Of being so ambitious that it hurt. Of renting a mink coat and walking into Sardi's and offering David Merrick casting tips. ("Put Ginger Rogers into *Hello, Dolly!*") Of calling Sidney Lumet at midnight to sell him a client and being told, "If you're this pushy, I want you to be my agent."

"All of us who made it were outsiders who wanted to belong." Mengers says now, and you can just hear the outsider in 1963 making that first "You-don't-know-me-but-I'm-Sue Mengers" call. To would-be client Julie Harris. (The next day Mengers made the same call to the producer of *Bonanza*; "Miss Julie Harris would like to guest on *Bonanza*.") To make those calls—to sell past the resistance—took something less than identity and more than need. It took pure *I-would-have-done-anything* obsession.

Sue Mengers is now somebody in transition. She's reinventing midlife—kind of like a business version of Richard Dreyfuss or Bette Midler. One morning playing tennis at the Beverly Hills Hotel, Mengers was observed by Katharine Hepburn ("Backhand's not bad—serve's terrible!"). On that day Sue Mengers was probably the happiest person in Hollywood. To hear Hepburn critiquing her tennis was worth all the years of schlepping and dreaming and entertaining. Sue Mengers belonged now, if ever she was going to.

And in 1986 when the announcement came that Mengers was leaving ICM when her contract expired nobody much flinched. (The same thing happened in 1990, when she left the Morris office.) If she wanted time off, fine; from the very beginning, whether she knew it or not, the club wanted Sue Mengers to win—mostly because she wanted it so badly. Her friends—Barry Diller, producer Robert Evans, David Geffen, Helen Gurley Brown, Barbara Walters, and Ray Stark—are people who are too smart to be fooled by guile. Mengers goes beyond guile, and thus has their loyalty. And her enemies? "I don't know who they are," she said one afternoon fiddling with a finger sandwich at the Regency in New York. "You never know who they are."

"If she's hated and feared," says Gore Vidal, "it's because she has a sharp tongue. And a gift for self-mockery. In this great land of the free, we are all supposed to be creatures of compassion and caring—and Sue is that—but let's face it, she has a sharp tongue." Vidal remembers "in the late '50s she was in the outer office of my drama agent Charlie Baker. She was this pretty, mildly zoftic blonde, and she twinkled. She has this great smile . . . Once I was visiting Charlie, and I heard this laugh . . . I looked out the door, and there she was at the keyhole, eyes and ears both . . . Frankly I think she just wanted to have an adventurous life, and in the sense of having a complete life, she's now getting it all done." Or as producer Freddie Fields, Mengers' ICM boss, put it: "All her energy went into somebody else's Oscar. What Sue needs is a new view from the top."

In the late '80s the view was social. Suddenly Mengers—who shares apartments in Manhattan and L.A. with her writer husband, Jean-Claude Tramont (*Ash Wednesday*)—seemed to be everywhere: She guested in the South of France on the yacht chartered by the Leonard Goldbergs and the Sidney Poitiers; she house-guested in Ravello as she does every summer, with Gore Vidal; she livened up the Norman Mailer Halloween party in Manhattan and the Jerry Weintraub fiftieth birthday party in Malibu; she trekked to Israel. She taught a course on Hollywood at NYU, and she turned down all kinds of job offers—simply to do nothing. Then came the William Morris job.

With the sale of her showplace house in Bel Air came the luxury of never needing to work again—not that she's rich-rich. ("If the fantasy was about money, I'd have never stopped working. 'Cause I ain't wealthy.") At fifty, it was a sensible if surprising sabbatical. "After all, she's been on a roar for the last twenty years," is how Bob Evans puts it. Mengers also had not stopped working since 1955 when, at seventeen, she answered an MCA ad for "receptionist, theatrical agency."

What made her leave the business? She sat quietly in the Bel Air garden, thinking about it. "Hackman," she said abruptly, in the trademark throaty–baby girl voice. "I represented Gene Hackman. At one point he said to me, 'I don't want to work for a while,' And I said, 'Great, Gene, what's a while? Three months? Six months?' He said, 'I don't know, and if I give you a date then it's not open-ended. Then it's just a holiday.' I admired that. Gene had been doing pictures back to back, and he hadn't been happy with them, and he wanted a chance to renew himself, and just get away from the movie business. I said, 'Gene, I totally understand.' "

Six months later the understanding was harder to get. "Two scripts came up that they wanted Gene for, *True Confessions* and *The Great Santini*. Gene was tempted, especially by *Santini*. I said, 'Gene they'll wait for you. What do you want? Another three months? They'll wait three months. Maybe they'll even wait four months,' and Gene said— I'll never forget it—'If I give a date now—even if I do a picture in six months—every day when I wake up, I'll say to myself, okay, only X more days until I have to think about working.' He was not ready at that moment to commit."

My first question was, where did her drive come from? Gore Vidal says there's "a lot of Hamburg in that girl. Sometimes she just lapses into German. It's no accident that Germany is the most advanced country in Europe." In 1938, Mengers and her parents arrived from Germany, escaping the Nazis and speaking no English. What Mengers remembers most is a sense of exclusion, of being left out—and wanting to belong. "It's a wanting to experience in reality . . . the beautiful home, celebrated people, all the superficial accoutrements that you fantasize about." Could the fantasy have been about acting? Yes, until she went to acting class. "I looked around and saw everyone was more talented, more beautiful. And I thought, 'There goes that dream.' "

Was the dream to be part of a family? Mengers nodded. "I think my father's suicide probably, you know, made me feel guilty—made me want to be better," she said calmly one afternoon in New York. "I was fourteen when my father died, and because it was a small town, Utica, New York, everyone was aware. It's *Stella Dallas*, you know?" Mengers means that just like in the 1937 Barbara Stanwyck movie, it was mother and daughter against the world. Mengers' mother, then a bookkeeper, moved with her daughter to the Bronx.

The daughter of Stella Dallas didn't tackle the blue-tailed piranhas who inhabit agency board rooms, however—nor did virtually any other women pre-Mengers. Even her detractors admit she was the first female to play hardball in the club. And not only with movie star careers: Apart from actors, Mengers was negotiating with the careers and the lives of directors like Lumet and Nichols and De Palma, talents who know what they want—and are used to getting it. A ribald comic strip blonde would only satisfy those men in certain amusing ways. But handle their salaries? "She's much more than a cartoon," explained Vidal. "To people who have a false view of themselves, the wit and irony are off-putting. But reality was her only way of coping."

And for years clients gave Mengers her only sense of extended family. Representing Peter Bogdanovich and Cybill Shepherd, Paula Prentiss and Richard Benjamin, Jacqueline Bisset and Michael Sarrazin, Ryan and Tatum O'Neal—teams that were pieces of Hollywood mythology—gave Mengers security. Perhaps false security. "I thought no one would grow old," Mengers says now, analytically. "I thought everything would stay the same. So I said no to a lot of new people, because I thought it would always be like that. And of course it isn't, for anyone. Don't forget, I had no brothers or sisters, no cousins, for a long time no boyfriend, no husband. This was family."

Mike Wallace stood in his CBS office riffling through a fifteen-year-old transcript of his *60 Minutes* segment on Mengers. "Listen to this," said Wallace as he began reading aloud:

"I was a little pisher, a little nothing making $135 a week as a secretary for the William Morris Agency in New York. Well, I looked around and I admired the Morris office and their executives, and I thought: 'Gee, what they do isn't that hard, you know.' And I like the way they live, and I like those expense accounts, and I like the cars. And I used to stay late at the office, just like *All About Eve*, and I suddenly thought: 'That beats typing.'"

Wallace paused, "I mean c'mon, have you ever heard a better paragraph than that? It's perfect."

Because she played the secretary role for almost a decade—at MCA, at Baum-Neuborn, at William Morris—Mengers-as-typist has taken on something of mythic stature. To say you knew her then is like saying you knew Meryl Streep at Yale. David Geffen remembers being in the mail room at William Morris in 1965, "and I already knew the legend. It was bigger than life. I remember I wanted to get to know her, and then it was instant friendship." Producer Marvin Worth (*Lenny*) remembers taking Mengers "to the Paramount Theater in 1958 to see Joni James. She says now it was her first date. She was blonde and round and fun." Agent Tom Korman, who gave Mengers her first job as an agent, remembers her tenacity.

"Marty Baum [then partner at Baum-Neuborn, now senior agent at Creative Artists], must have fired her fifty times, fifty-two times. One day Sarah Marshall, an actress who was our client, was supposed to audition for *The World of Suzie Wong*, and nobody could find Sarah. Sue, only Sue, knew Sarah was having an affair with a married musician. She even called the rest home where Edna Best [Marshall's mother] lived. Then finally she called the musician at home, and a woman answered. Sue said, 'Sarah, you old sneak! I found you.' Well, of course, it was the musician's wife. And Marty Baum fired Sue."

Another time, MCA agent Maynard Morris punished Mengers after ordering her to sit by the phone all day and wait for a call from Tyrone Power. At 5 P.M. Power called hastily on his way to the airport, but Morris (who's remembered as impatient and fussy) was in the men's room. Mengers couldn't get the two of them together on the phone—and again Mengers got fired.

But how does a secretary finally play agent herself? At what point can you really do the job you dreamed about? In 1963, Mengers remembers "Tom Korman saying, 'I can't pay you more than a secretary, but at least you'll have a secretary.' And I became obsessed." The two of them set up shop, with two clients (Joan Bennett—"easy sale, huh"—and Claudia McNeill). Korman (now with Agency for the Performing Arts) says Mengers "was the guts of the office. We were known as the Relative Wrong Agency. In other words, if there was Marge and Gower Champion, we'd have Marge. If there was Jocelyn and Marlon Brando, we'd have Jocelyn."

And while Mengers was "relentless from the start," Korman also remembers "this whole other vulnerable side that nobody can break. The vulnerability is very real." Korman gave an example: "One night in 1983 she asked me to have dinner, just the two of us. At dinner she handed me a Tiffany box. It was a framed silver photo of us in the '60s walking into Danny's Hideaway with Tony Newley, a client of ours. There was a bubble over Sue's head that said, 'I WANT TO BE A STAR.' At dinner Sue looked at me and said, 'It's twenty years, Tom.' "

Freddie Fields, who with David Begelman is often credited with moving Mengers to Hollywood, added: "Oh, the vulnerability cries its eyes out. It's a bashfulness, really, that Sue protects pretty fiercely." As Korman put it, "It's what gave her a rapport with the gay community. And what also let her go out with ladies' men like Billy Rose, whom she actually dated. I remember her saying to me, 'If I could be reincarnated, I would come back as Marilyn Monroe.' Of course Marilyn Monroe was still alive then. But Sue's fantasy was always to be a movie star. And in a way she did become one."

Mengers got to the big time by understanding the strength of stardom: Unlike many agents, who prefer to nurture newcomers, Mengers right away sought out star power. One late afternoon, Gore Vidal stood on the patio of his bungalow at the Beverly Hills Hotel with his friend Howard Austen and mused about Mengers, circa 1965: "She was dying to meet Paul [Newman] and Joanne [Woodward]," said Vidal. "So we arranged an evening at Sardi's, just us, that special table," added Austen. "And David Begelman walked in. He was then head of CMA with Freddie Fields. Well, there were his two top clients sitting with this young blonde agent he'd been hearing about."

Mengers, too, remembers the Newmans as being pivotal early on: "Through Gore, I'd met them. And being an aggressive little girl I used to constantly make them crazy by telling them about all the wonderful theater they should be doing. And they'd call John Foreman, who was their movie agent at CMA, and say, 'This kid Sue Mengers is telling us about all these great plays.' And John said to Freddie and David, 'This

girl is on the right track. She's making me crazy with Paul and Joanne.
Hire her.' I'm not saying Paul and Joanne would have left their own agent
for this little agent . . . but I was making them question things. So Freddie
and David thought, 'Let's hire this kid. She's got a big mouth. She's cute.
We'll use her in New York. She'll be our theater department.' "

And so a Manhattan star was born, at $375 a week. But how? As Fields
says, "There's no book on how to become an agent." What was Mengers'
strong suit? "Holding," answered Fields. "Selling is not important if you
give a client sound career advice. Holding a client, keeping a client from
the wrong move, is a real strength. Careers curve, and Sue knew the
curves as well as anyone I ever met. In small critical moments she made
great moves."

But who was Mengers' mentor? It's not a comfortable question. Because
there were no female high-stakes agents, there were no role models.
Somebody had to catapult Mengers, that's the common thinking. And
the common answer is that Fields and Begelman took Sue from the
chorus (or the secretarial pool) and made her a star. In truth, she was
pretty much a self-creation.

"She's responsible for herself," says Fields now. "It was what she wanted
to be—and what David [Begelman] saw in her." Though Mengers dis-
counts "ambition" ("I always thought I'd stay a secretary"), publicist Lee
Solters remembers her in the late '50s calling him "every day at five or
six P.M. 'Lee, any screenings tonight? Any openings?' For her it was like
attending class. And she learned. And quick. I remember her telling me,
'I'm going to be the most important agent in the business.' And I believed
her."

Next stop—where else?—Hollywood. One afternoon Robert Evans
stood in the garden of his house that Mengers likens to "Gatsby's house
in West Egg" and recalled when he first met Mengers. "A night in 1969.
Mike Nichols said to me, 'There's this funny blonde agent I want you to
meet. Come up to her house with me for dinner.' I had so much fun I
had tears in my eyes. It was the beginning of an infatuation. And it was
just at the time of her legend beginning out here."

How Mengers got to Hollywood is a question with more facets than
the Krupp diamond. One notion is that bringing Mengers west was a
Freddie-and-David brainstorm. Unleash Mengers on Hollywood. "Go—
go off to the Garden of Eden," Fields is supposed to have told Mengers,
and the myth of David-and-Freddie "creating" Sue began. "Freddie and
David were stimulating guys to work for, when they were running,"
Mengers says now. "But they hired me because I was bright, and what
did they have to lose? Really, I came to Los Angeles because CMA
merged with GAC, and the GAC had a more established man running

the theater department. So there was no place for me in New York. And Dick Shepherd, who was running CMA's movie department, said, 'We'll take a shot with her out here.' I had never been to California. They leased me a little apartment on Fountain Avenue. What an adventure!"

Unlike gray-suited William Morris and MCA, CMA in the late '60s was a stable of rising stars—young agents included Mike Medavoy and Alan Ladd, Jr., and Guy McElwaine, each with his own style and stable. Mengers merged and meshed with the freewheeling CMA ways: "We felt agents could be stars, too, stars in a different galaxy," says Fields now. "People liked responding to a visible agent who connected emotionally with a client, with a cause. That was the social mix—and Sue became the focal point." Mengers found her place, fast, but she's careful to say, "No one gets credit for my career but Tom Korman and, to a degree, Barbra Streisand."

The Mengers-Streisand friendship has a Tom Sawyer–Huck Finn quality about it—it's a myth that seems deeper with time, and more logical the closer you look at their careers. It isn't just the similarities—both women had fathers who died young, both lived in outer boroughs of New York, living fantasy lives, touching big time very early, almost prematurely. It's that they had such rapport.

(In 1981, there was the professional split, after Streisand starred in *All Night Long*, directed by Frenchman Jean-Claude Tramont, Mengers' longtime husband. It wasn't the husband who caused the problem, it was the failure of the film. But, friendship has endured it. "She's an original," Streisand told me. "There's no one quite like her. She's funny, she's honest, and she's been a good friend for many years.")

In 1963, Mengers and Korman were handling (among very few others) Elliott Gould and Kay Medford. Gould was Streisand's husband; Medford was playing Streisand's mother on Broadway in *Funny Girl*. When Mengers went backstage to see Medford, she also looked in on Streisand. The two of them came to Hollywood almost simultaneously, and they soared.

Streisand's first films were agented by Begelman and Fields, but Mengers remembers "Barbra being separated from Elliott. Whenever she was invited anywhere, she would say, 'I want you to invite my friend Sue Mengers.' And so I got to know people here it would have otherwise taken me years to meet. Barbra made it clear to people that my opinion was of interest to her. I began to be recognized."

And responsible. David Geffen remembers Mengers putting him together with Streisand when it became clear that Streisand should be recording more contemporary music, circa *Stoney End* in 1969. Mengers wasn't acting as an agent, but she was looking out for Streisand. When Begelman and Fields left the agency business (to eventually become producers), Mengers officially became Streisand's agent. The package that put Mengers on the map was *What's Up, Doc?* Mengers had signed Peter Bogdanovich at the time of *The Last Picture Show*, then she persuaded Streisand and Ryan O'Neal (whom Mengers signed just before the release of *Love Story*) to take a look. Mengers became known for putting elements together.

"Barbra's great charm is that she always lets you take credit, too," Mengers says carefully. "She didn't agree with you all the time, but she was never offended by hearing an opinion. She never got angry or hurt or insulted. And that was a great aphrodisiac to be able to talk to someone with that kind of talent and know that they're listening."

Streisand gave Mengers confidence, then? She nodded, and then seemed to go inside herself. "Maybe too much confidence, because not everybody's like Barbra. With other people I think I became too argumentative at times. Too outspoken with talent. It's a danger most agents fall into, because clients can be very seductive. Tell me the truth, they say— but you have to be careful who means it and who doesn't. Barbra meant it."

Mengers' aggression was her strength at the start, but it became a weakness as she began playing for bigger rewards. She was the first major player who wasn't a man. And she could be so blunt as to wound egos. Former client Dyan Cannon remembers the agent telling her "to wash your face before you come to my dinner party. I want people to see what you look like." Cannon was offended, but "then I just didn't let her be my mother."

Does candor work in negotiating rooms? "That's very tough," replied Mengers evenly. "You have to sometimes hide your light under a bushel, especially if you are a woman. I think I fell short in that area. I have been accused of becoming rough, and I never wanted to be. But I guess I did stop being a woman a lot of times when I negotiated. Or when I fought for someone to get a role. And it's difficult in a negotiation because very seldom do both buyer and seller say, 'Boy, I got what I wanted!' And it's hard for a man to lose to a woman. And I empathized with that."

Does she still? "Sure. As a woman you suddenly become all the bad things they didn't like about their mother. Or they don't like about their wife. And you suddenly are there in their sacrosanct world of business. There is the disapproving mother, the negative mother, the seductive mother . . . and the son reacts."

But on the other hand, "Most of my success was because I was a woman," insisted Mengers. "If a woman becomes emotional, which I did very often, it was excused. And in the beginning men were very kind to me; I was this amusing, aggressive blonde. As I started to play for higher stakes, I think it became less amusing and a little more threatening."

Because men aren't allowed displays of emotion? "That's right. And men can call each other names, across a table, and that's okay. If a woman calls a guy a name, it's not okay. But there's another misconception here . . . most of my negotiating was done on the phone. I didn't usually walk into rooms and face groups of people. If you are dealing with someone smart, and most studio executives are smart, I don't see the need to schlep to Burbank. Or them schlepping to your office. And negotiations are one-on-one. If I negotiated with Orion, it would be with [executives] Eric Pleskow and Mike Medavoy, and it would be a conference call."

If it was producer Bob Evans, probably her closest Hollywood ally, it was no different. Legendary is their bickering, and Mengers' pushing her clients on Evans. "I was casting *Chinatown* and she was pressing for Faye Dunaway," Evans recalled. "We were talking $250,000 and Sue said, 'I need an answer by the end of the business day Friday. Because Faye is considering a picture with [director] Arthur Penn.' So I thought, 'I'll offer *Chinatown* to Jane Fonda.' Jane met with [director] Roman Polanski. So I said to Sue, 'I'll give Faye $75,000.' There were screams . . . Then I said, 'Okay, I'm going with Jane Fonda.' And she hung up."

One hour later Mengers called Evans, "Honey, I spoke to Faye and we'll take the $75,000."

The deal was done.

That night, Mengers again called Evans: "There was this glee in her voice . . . *tee-hee-hee* . . . 'Honey, guess what? There was no picture with Arthur Penn! I made it up!' So I said, 'Guess what? Jane Fonda turned us down!' All this game playing, and Sue was my best friend!"

Evans' assessment a decade later: "It was good agenting and bad agenting, but mostly good agenting. Because Faye next did *Network* for $500,000, and took the Oscar. But the thing is how much Sue enjoyed the game. She couldn't wait to tell me! She doesn't know that much about numbers, but she was paid more than any agent in town. What she has is a specific singular charm, and it operates at the highest level of human relations. Sue is somebody people enjoy. You don't enjoy somebody because of his money or power . . . in fact you enjoy very few people in life. A lot of guys resent her, but when she's good, there's nobody better."

With time away from the business, Mengers could look back in both anger and relief. She's not shy about admitting mistakes, and some of them are true object lessons in how to play in the club.

"I would have to say I began my career out here when I started representing Rod Steiger," she reflected. "One of my greatest failures was not getting *Hospital* for Rod. I thought it would be a renaissance role, and I learned a valuable lesson. [Writer] Paddy Chayefsky and Rod had a stormy history from *Marty* and Paddy absolutely vetoed Rod. And I didn't let up. There wasn't a day I didn't call Paddy, [director] Arthur Hiller, the executives at United Artists. I knew George C. Scott had turned it down, and I went in hard for Rod. Telling Paddy not to be unfair . . . being cocky because George C. Scott said no.

"They were starting the picture in like two weeks, and we were in negotiations for Rod. And we were apart let's say $50,000, and I knew they were desperate. The UA executive said, 'Sue, close the deal.' One day I decided to hold firm for the extra $50,000 because Rod got it on his last picture. That day Paddy Chayefsky got on a plane to Spain, where George C. Scott was making a picture; Scott agreed to do *Hospital*, and I blew the deal. If I had closed that day, Rod would have had the picture. Rod was a gentleman, but I learned the lesson. Never ever blow a deal on money."

The power ascribed to agents, to Mengers and a handful of others, has limits. To not know those limits as an agent, is not to know one's strengths. In the end, the talent is the true power, and the top agents know that.

Example: Tuesday Weld, a Mengers client, was "the first person offered *Norma Rae*," recalled Mengers. "For whatever reason, Tuesday turned it down, whether she simply didn't want to work at that time or whatever. Had Tuesday done *Norma Rae*, it would have made her totally mainstream. I mean, Sally Field became a movie star with that movie, she won the Oscar! But some actors aren't calculating. Tuesday would work when the day would come where she'd wake up and say, 'Okay, I want to go to work.' If something came around that she liked, fine. But she wouldn't calculate, 'Oh, it's not a good career move.' I'm not saying she's right, by the way. But her private life was always very important to her."

Mengers feels that, like soap operas and trade papers, "There will never be anything new in the agency business. Which doesn't mean I wouldn't enjoy it again. But I don't feel something is happening I haven't done before. You do the same thing for the new crop of stars you did for the other crop. You try to get them the best roles with the best directors for the best money. Only the names change. Suddenly you know who Charlie Sheen is. Then you know who Tom Hanks is. So he's where Ryan [O'Neal] was seventeen years ago."

So is it simply evolution? "That's right. If Myron Selznick were alive today, he wouldn't have any big adjustment. If Irving Thalberg were alive, he would have a big adjustment. Because he'd no longer be able to tell the creative people what to do. If you want to keep Steven Spielberg happy, you don't have him tied up for the next five years. You give him autonomy."

Would Mengers like to have been Selznick—or Charles Feldman, the stylish powerful agent she's most often compared to? She doesn't think so. "Feldman did nothing [CAA boss] Mike Ovitz isn't doing today, that [ICM boss] Jeff Berg isn't doing, that I didn't do. The names are different, that's all. If Charlie Feldman and Myron Selznick came back to earth today, all they'd need is a telephone."

Mengers is still by her telephone, still swapping trade lines with David Geffen early in the morning. (In the club, exchanged compliments are known as "TLs," or trade lines.) But the difference now is that she isn't entertaining as lavishly as before. "But great business was also done at those dinners," remembered Ali MacGraw, who's been both client and friend to Mengers since 1969. "Burt Reynolds met [director] Alan Pakula at Sue's dinner table, and got *Starting Over*. Ann-Margret met Mike Nichols and got *Carnal Knowledge*. Lauren Hutton met [writer-director] Paul Schrader and got *American Gigolo*. It was the closest thing to a salon I've ever seen in this country or Europe."

MacGraw went on: "The parties were impeccably cast, and fun, and if you were an actress it was the one moment you wanted to walk in knowing your hair was right, your weight was right. That you had on the right dress. You wanted to be what Sue wanted you to be. When I was on the cover of *Time* magazine, it made Sue happier than it made me. Candy [Bergen] and I were her pain-free WASP princesses—that's how she saw us for a long time . . . But it was fun to be a movie star in Sue's time, because Sue was a star, too. I think now, through twenty years of ups and downs, if I thought anyone was going to hurt Sue on any level, in any way, I would personally break their legs. She inspires more loyalty than anyone I've ever met."

MacGraw and Mengers are also a good example of the peaks and valleys of a client-agent relationship. They met on the Gulf & Western plane to New York for the premiere of *On a Clear Day You Can See Forever*. Mengers was there for Streisand; MacGraw was there for her new husband, Paramount's then–production chief, Bob Evans. "Sue had on a brown T-shirt and pants, this is many pounds ago, and I fell instantly into her spell," recalled MacGraw. "More than anyone else, Sue believed in the myth of Ali MacGraw as movie star. And she believed in the myth of Bob-and-Ali. And when it was over, she took it very hard. So when people say Sue can be negative, I say it's not negativity. It's disenchantment. Because Sue Mengers is about enchantment."

And when Bob-and-Ali came apart—and when Ali wanted not to work during her marriage to Steve McQueen—Mengers did take it personally.

"There were times in my marriage to Steve that I was so angry at Sue . . . angry really at myself . . . but the anger was because she was right. For example, I didn't want to do [director Sidney Lumet's] *Just Tell Me What You Want*. Sue said to me on the phone, 'This call isn't even a question, or a conversation. This call is to say, you are getting on the plane to New York—the ticket is paid—and you are going to see Sidney Lumet.' She didn't know it would be the best work I ever did. But she knew I had to get on the plane. She says things to you like, 'Don't spend money on such-and-such, I don't want you worrying about money in your sixties and seventies.' Who thinks about those things for other people?"

One day Mengers decided to deal with the issue of being the hostess, the proprietress of the salon on Bel Air Road. Social cachet in the '70s was critical in a way that no longer exists; Mike Ovitz and Jeff Berg, the agents who work with the biggest players, can almost certainly be dubbed antisocial, especially in contrast to Mengers.

"If I'm remembered for anything," Mengers said one afternoon in New York, "it will probably be the parties." She didn't seem ecstatic about that legacy. "If I had to give a dinner, it was never about the people I loved, and whom I wanted to see. It was always 'Who can help in business?' It was totally calculated. As a woman, when I went out there, I felt I needed something to put me on the map."

The two Mengers houses on the map were very different, and offer perfect Hollywood metaphors for levels of success. "The little house on DawnRidge was where we had the most fun," remembers MacGraw, of the modern unpretentious view house near Pickfair where Julie Christie met Princess Margaret, where John Travolta met Laurence Olivier. Then in 1977, Mengers and Tramont bought the seven-bathroom French Normandy chateau owned by Zsa Zsa Gabor atop Bel Air, and the Mengers salon had an extravagant home base.

"Our house became like a restaurant," she mused one day. "At first I'd be grateful to look around the living room and see these glorified people. I mean I was chasing after Rita Hayworth, just to meet her, and I was already in my thirties, folks! But the celebrities hadn't come because they wanted to see me or my husband; they wanted to see each other. I was never the star at my own parties. I was the catalyst to bring creative people together. I was the concierge. No one said, 'Let's listen to Sue's bon mots.' I was tolerated. I don't know any agents who entertain that way today. Or any that need to."

Was there ever one moment where the dream matched reality? A moment of realizing *I made it!* She thought less than a minute, and then took off the tinted, wire-rimmed glasses—a pose that had to once have frightened executives. Then she nodded and seemed almost to coo:

"The day we moved into the house in Bel Air. That was the moment. The first night we slept there, that was it. I grew up sharing a bathroom with three other people. So that house symbolized having made it. And the fact that I was able to chuck it, showed, I think, that my values had become more down to earth . . . It's like, 'Okay, that was one period of my life. Now let's get on to growing up a little.' I don't need a huge house anymore to proclaim what I am. Does that make sense?"

Gore Vidal remembers, "In 1963, I was sitting on a set at Columbia Pictures with Hank Fonda, and I got this call from a Miss Mengers. I honestly didn't remember the name. Then I remembered she was the blonde we'd had up to the house on the Hudson. So I'd known her socially—I mean she's the best company in the world, riotously funny, and yet I didn't remember the name . . . and suddenly on the phone she said, 'I want you to send a telegram saying you want Jack Klugman to play so-and-so in the movie *The Best Man*.' And I said, 'But I don't want to!' And Sue said, 'I don't care if you want him or not, I just want you to send the telegram. I want to sign him as a client.' "

Upshot? "I sent the telegram. Klugman didn't get the part. But Sue got the client."

"I don't remember that story," said Mengers. "But there are so many stories, some of them must be true. I do remember we put Klugman in *Gypsy* with Ethel Merman."

In terms of a Jack Klugman, the transition for an actor from smaller parts to bigger is usually achieved only with several agents, from small-time to big-time.

"That is my one talent," she admitted one day. "It's an instinct, really, something you can't define. I think what's very hard for an agent to do is to know that moment when you go for the bigger money. For Timothy Hutton, for example, there was no money before *Ordinary People*. It was whatever the part was, what do you want to pay? I didn't start representing Timothy until after *Taps*. But whoever got him from *Ordinary People* to *Taps* had to know how to take him to the next level . . . I could always smell when the moment of heat was."

Example: "Ryan [O'Neal] made barely above scale for *Love Story* and just after that was the moment to go for bigger money, and I wasn't afraid to." She took the actor from $22,500 for *Love Story* to $300,000 for *What's Up, Doc?*

It's a marketplace savvy that begins with imagination and instinct, and winds up showing itself in the numbers. Though Mengers-watchers will say figures weren't her strong suit, she might not agree.

"I remember calling Goldie Hawn after *Private Benjamin* opened, to congratulate her. She was represented by another agency and she was as hot as anyone in the business as a result of that picture. And she said to me, 'Listen, what do you think I can get now? My current agent feels I should get $2.1 million.' And I said, 'Why should you get less than an actor who is getting $3.5 million?' And Goldie said, 'Don't be ridiculous. I can't get that.' I said, 'Tell your agent you won't work for less.' And that's what she did . . .

"See, I know what heat is," said Sue simply. "It's a killer instinct, to know that. Jeff Berg has it, Ovitz has it, [CAA president] Ron Meyer has it. Only a handful. It's knowing the right price. And the right price is never an unfair price."

Mengers' client Streisand got $4.5 million, plus percentages, for twenty-seven days' work on *All Night Long*. Mengers, before unfolding the details, marveled a moment: "This was 1979. I don't think there's a richer deal for that time period. I especially needed to make a strong deal because it was my husband's picture," Mengers began, not ducking. She knows the talk—the notion that Streisand left Mengers because of the movie's failure, and that somehow like Topsy the disenchantment grew—leading Mengers to ultimately leave the business. In fact, if it was a movie that caused the split, it was *Yentl* and not *All Night Long*.

"I had never been the biggest believer in *Yentl*," Mengers acknowledged, "although I beg you to put this in, because I mean it from my heart—I thought the picture was brilliant. But I think it caused a problem then between Barbra and me. She always wanted to do the picture, and I was always negative about it and after a while I became a little too dogmatic, and then . . ."

And then there was Jon Peters, Streisand's companion and adviser until 1981. "Jon and I had trouble communicating, and Jon was very much in her professional life then. But mostly I think it had just run its course by then, with Barbra. Barbra was like my little sister, and how in the world was she going to direct this difficult picture and play a boy? To my chagrin, I was wrong. I never had enough belief. I remember going to see it—at the time we weren't speaking—and crying, and saying, 'Thank God she didn't listen to me!' Right after that I called her, and we are friends again."

But did the loss of Streisand cost Mengers clients? The answer is shaded. "What was costly was my reaction," replied Mengers. "The industry is used to people losing clients. Steve McQueen left [agent] Stan Kamen, who'd nurtured his career from the beginning—and I can take much less credit for Barbra Streisand's career than Stan could take for Steve's. But I overreacted. I felt my whole identity was tied up in being

Barbra Streisand's agent. It took me years to realize it wasn't, and this was totally my problem."

The question is, did the problem affect other working relationships? "It didn't affect my work, it affected my trust factor. Nobody said, 'I'm leaving because of Barbra Streisand.' Clients leave, that's a part of the game. Good agents accept that, but I was like a walking wound. In my mind, I no longer had this shield. So I lost some of this joie de vivre. I became even more Jewish-mother negative, as in 'You should lose some weight' or 'You're doing too many pictures.' I guess I never believed in myself, only in myself as the agent to these important people. I realize now the strength was in me. It was me."

After months of traveling, and just thinking, Mengers has come to some conclusions. "I realized something about people in the club," she said. "I'm not saying they liked me. But they took me seriously. People who didn't like my style, I don't think they'd like me more today. But I really would like to believe I was respected. Nobody said, 'She didn't work hard.' I was tough, I was inflexible, I was fair. I was rough on lawyers . . . because there's competitiveness. *Who do you love more, honey, me or the lawyer?* I got maternal, I got possessive, and in looking over my career, I see negativity as probably my major fault.

"But this is what's true about being an agent: You get second-guessed all the time. It's also the most stimulating nontalent branch of show business. But being an agent is taking the veil. And I'm not ready yet."

When Gore Vidal was asked what he thought of Mengers' sabbatical from show business, he offered a novel thought: "She discovered the Great Books of the World. Howard [Austen] said, 'It's too bad she didn't do that thirty years ago.' And I said, 'Oh no. Thank God! She would have been the head of Hunter College English Department, and the world would have lost Sue Mengers.' "

CLUB RULE TWENTY-THREE

Emotional reflexes are the ultimate club tool. Which is why when a woman finally makes it in the club, she has the edge over almost any male.

Sue Mengers and Sherry Lansing are the two club women who emerged in the '70s who were still being talked about in the '90s. What they have in common is an emotionality that has nothing to do with being female— and everything to do with being in show business. So they're emotional? The fact is, the club reacts viscerally, quickly, and emotionally all at once. The reaction of one person can make the difference in the ultimate pattern of a movie's release.

Example: "Sherry cried," was the reaction hoped for when Sherry Lansing was production president at 20th Century-Fox. If Sherry cried, the picture got the right ad budget, the right distribution.

True club power shows itself in emotional reactions.

SEX

The leg wasn't just a simple nickname. It had other meanings, symbolic ones. Like any one-legged person, I was pretty much asexual—or let's say sex didn't come easily. The myth about journalists being warm and cozy with stars, the snuggling up you hear about, is just a myth. You never spend the night. I never got any closer than a Jacuzzi with a movie star, and even that alarmed me. For years I had this one deep (silly) belief that I didn't want anyone to be able to say that I was so-and-so's boyfriend. It was crippling enough to be the leg. I didn't want to be a kept leg, or the boy who slept his way up. And since the club really isn't as sexy as people think, it was easy to stay asexual. Sex gets in the way of ambition. It uses up your endocrines. And it's threatening and messy. "The greatest orgasm in the world is the moment you make the right deal," is how Robert Evans put it a hundred years ago. Evans, the ultimate ladies' man, knew the greater thrill was to score in business, not in bed. Name half a dozen club members, and you'll also name at least five sexually disinterested people.

Every rule has an exception, obviously. In the club the exceptions to the asexual rule are the stars, the movie stars. That's what got them in the club. Sex. (*No wonder* I never made a pass at a movie star. Who could match that voltage?) To be blunt about it, every movie star in the club—and there aren't that many—is in the club because of sex. Period.

Without sexuality you aren't a movie star, not for long, anyway. "You have to retain sexuality and it's a big bore," Jane Fonda told me one morning while packing for a trip east in her bedroom in Santa Monica.

The maintenance of sex appeal is the maintenance of stardom itself. The moment Robert Redford's looks go, he will be venerated, but he won't be box office. (Look at the box office of *Havana*.) The club won't take him as seriously now; he's probably fucked out. When Al Pacino stops making women drool, he will be the best character actor in the business, and maybe the richest, but he won't be a star. Debra Winger is an intellectual movie star, one of the only ones, and she survives without box office hits—but it's sex that put her over. Remember her riding the bull in *Urban Cowboy*? Or the hot love scenes with Richard Gere in *An Officer and a Gentleman*? Jane Fonda became a star before she became an actress—but when she took off her clothes as Barbarella, she became a household name. Think of a successful Fonda performance without sexuality (excepting only *Julia*) and you come up blank.

There are only two generations of full-scale blue-chip first-class movie stars. Call them the Fonda-Redford generation, and the Pacino-Winger generation. Skip the Ally Sheedy–Michael J. Fox generation. (They're five-minute stars, not long-distance runners.)

"I'd like to find out," Jane Fonda went on that morning in Santa Monica, "if I still need to be sexy in my fifties." That week she'd been to Frederick's of Hollywood to pick out part of her trousseau for her marriage to Ted Turner—a publicity ploy, no doubt, to retain sexuality. Such good copy. "You can't name me a movie star who kept it without staying sexual," Fonda insisted.

Katharine Hepburn? I said to Fonda.

"Hepburn is the exception that proves the rule," said Fast Jane. "And besides, she did stay sexy."

Stardom equals sex is an equation understood, painfully, by women like Elizabeth Taylor and Sophia Loren. They had it, and then with age, some of it goes, and so does some of the star power. Harvard professor John Hallowell's observation that Marilyn Monroe "was lucky to die when she did" rings true. Monroe at sixty-five—as what?

It's this fear of age that can ruin movie careers; think of Julie Andrews or Doris Day, not sexpots but clearly sexual movie figures of their day. Think of their movie careers in the '80s and '90s. It's the fear of aging that terrifies people like Cher and Warren Beatty. Cher talks about it (endlessly), while Warren spends untold hours in steam rooms with ice packs on his eyes murmuring things like "Oh to be forty-three again . . ."

To explore the sexual side of stardom, I went first after Fonda. Mostly because she seems so determined to play out the myth. At fifty-one Jane

Fonda was still trying to play virginal, in *The Old Gringo*, and it nearly killed her movie career; the same year she tried to play a thirtyish widow in *Stanley and Iris* with De Niro no less, and nobody went. Suddenly she was like Jack Nicholson after *Heartburn*, a star without a comfortable image. So I started with Jane.

All four of these stars—Fonda, Redford, Pacino, and Winger—are club members. They are part of the club machinery, the public part. All four have in common a sense of their sexuality. Pacino is as dark and complicated and neurotic as Redford isn't. Redford, who preceded Pacino as a sex icon to women, has enjoyed the kind of long-distance career that gives him hall of fame club status. So I sniffed after him like a bulldog. Pacino I wanted to meet only because I sensed he was the touchstone of dark: No matter how black your mood got, Pacino got darker. I spent a long Christmas week with him, until he took off on the Warner's jet for Jamaica, and I took off for the outpatient clinic at Camarillo. It took almost until Valentine's Day to get over Pacino.

Winger came to me, and I came with twelve blank ninety-minute tapes, and we still ran out.

Jane Fonda was a different story. Just look at the unpredictability of her life: She may be one of the few modern stars who can't be pinned down—she's as apt to be hiking in the Santa Rosa Mountains as she is to be presenting a Golden Globe in a sequin bustier. But she likes flying high, and always has. I decided the only game to play with Jane Fonda was the truth game.

15

Ultimate
Club Child—
Jane Fonda

Jane Fonda got in because of bloodlines, and stayed in because of compulsion. Shirlee Fonda got in because she married Henry Fonda, and after his death was escorted by Douglas Cramer. Peter Fonda got in because of bloodlines and Dennis Hopper, and dropped out because of fragility and disinterest. Henry Fonda got in because of talent and Margaret Sullavan, whom he married, and Leland Hayward—who also married Margaret Sullavan. Leland Hayward got in because of style. Brooke Hayward Hopper got in because of bloodlines and style and Dan Melnick, and her marriage to Dennis Hopper. Dennis Hopper got in because of George Stevens and Henry Hathaway. Dennis Hopper is the perennial club dark horse; don't bet against him in the long run. Brooke Hopper, even though she remained Jane Fonda's oldest friend, dropped out after she moved back to New York and married Peter Duchin. (Peter Duchin doesn't mean anything in the club.) Donald Sutherland got in because of Jane Fonda. Alan Pakula got in as a director because of Jane Fonda and Liza Minnelli. He got in as a producer because of Robert Mulligan. Robert Mulligan dropped out because he was replaced on Rich and Famous by George Cukor, of all people, and the movie still failed. Jackie Bisset dropped out because of Rich and

Famous, *which she co-produced, and because she used people unmercifully. (Especially the venerated ICM elder club agent Ben Benjamin.) Candy Bergen did not drop out after* Rich and Famous *because she's better bred than Jackie Bisset, and a better sport. Ultimately Jackie Bisset dropped out because her heart was in the wrong place—she wanted a money career. In the club, money counts—but not for everything. That's why even though Shirley MacLaine and Jane Fonda were financially set for life in their early thirties, they went on to be star-stars—the really-reals, as Natalie Wood called them. Jane Fonda is the club child who's lasted the longest as a movie star.*

This is what people were saying about Jane Fonda when I caught up with her.

Her second husband, Tom Hayden, dumped her for a younger woman.

Her daughter's boyfriend was arrested for heroin possession.

Her son was in some kind of trouble. (Later he was arrested for vandalism.)

Her movie *The Old Gringo* would go into the crapper.

Her next movie *Stanley and Iris* was in trouble.

She's facing her fifties.

Her mother checked out when she was forty-two.

These were the variables floating around in my head that day. Also I was reading *Haywire* the night before publicist Pat Newcomb called to offer me Fonda. *Haywire* was the book that revealed how Fonda found out about her mother's suicide. When the call came from Newcomb, I knew we'd have to discuss the suicide.

Synchronicity?

But what intrigued me about Fonda was her early vulnerability—her emulation of Kim Stanley and need for guru-ing from a succession of father figures (Russian, American, French). I always thought Hollywood children (daughters especially) were interesting for their needs, which often were larger than life. (An example would be Mia Farrow's needs for different playmates—from Frank Sinatra and Eddie Fisher to André Previn and Woody Allen.)

No other female star—except Shirley MacLaine—has lasted as long in the club as Fonda has. And Fonda, for all her privilege, had the toughest odds going in. Her outside was pure thoroughbred, but inside she's forever trembling. The way you play the truth game with Jane Fonda is you say a word and she gets to define it.

Hollywood?

"A business wrapping its mouth around an art form."

Power?

"Using whatever weapons you have at the time."

Survival?

"Genetics, willpower, strength, foolhardiness."

There is a Hollywood axiom that an actress is a little bit more than a woman and an actor, a little bit less than a man. And this seemed the right time to confront Fonda with it. Her much-postponed $31 million *Old Gringo*—the "first bicultural big Hollywood movie," as Fonda calls it—opened and closed after eight years and four suites of executive shuffles. Some people say she needed to make the movie about the flowering of a repressed woman in order to have the guts to leave Tom Hayden. (What a price to pay.) Could Jane Fonda be hurt professionally by whatever might (or might not) happen with one movie? Is she woman enough to take any consequences? Would this be her last star vehicle?

She stretched the Fonda legs over a brass coffee table in a Westwood office, and thought about it. "Can I be hurt professionally?" she asked. "No . . . If it doesn't do well, it just makes you sit down and think, 'What did I do wrong?' But I feel the same way about *Old Gringo* as people feel about *Out of Africa*. When it was all over with—all the talk—you only had to look at the international grosses. It went into profit. It's so hard to do a movie you can't put into one sentence. *Old Gringo* I did because it's a movie about a woman who takes responsibility. It says you have to own yourself, your own power. The woman I played—this spinster, this virgin—doesn't do that at the start of the film. If you don't own yourself, it doesn't count. I also learned that to make a movie like this, you have to be fired up."

You have to be Jane Fonda. One of the "understoods" in Hollywood is that (à la Clint Eastwood) nobody at a studio interferes with Fonda, ever. Say it, and she shoots back a look of disbelief. "It's not true. It's their job to interfere. One of the real tenets of Hollywood now is that it's big business and high art and Coca-Cola and Wall Street and major multinational companies. It's important to understand those dynamics and demands. It's part of the pressure of the movie business to understand the amalgam, and if you don't—then get out of the business. I resent people who are negative and bitter about corporate demands. Work within the system or be quiet. Modern life is about corporate pressure. And you know what?" she added, thirty years (and forty movies) of her stardom showing. "Corporate pressure has always been part of the game. The only people who moan are the people who can't play."

The players here are like a cast of characters from an updated *The Bad and the Beautiful.* Who else but Fonda will hurdle a picture through four studio regimes? Maybe Streisand, but not Jessica Lange surely. Nor Madonna. Explains Fonda: "On all of the [five] films I've produced, I've never been the actual producer. That would be acting like God, and I can't do it. But if I'm needed," she added, "I can do both. After thirty years at this, I am going to speak up."

And be listened to?

"Yup. I can wear different hats, and I can switch gears—whoosh! zam! zap! But somebody else is doing a lot of what I seem to be doing. One example is my workout business, which somebody else runs. I'm only paying attention to it between movies." Somebody else runs, and ran, Columbia Pictures, too, through all the regimes in which *The Old Gringo* survived. The one reason *Gringo* is interesting is that it's a case study: The perception is that *Gringo* is the only major picture to have lived through both the David Puttnam and Dawn Steel eras at Columbia—based solely on Fonda's strength as a star. And the studio's craving for relationship with stars. But *Gringo* in fact is older than that.

"It goes back to Frank Price! Before Frank Price!" Fonda said the name of the Columbia president like it was a blast from the past. In Hollywood, if you are out of circulation as long as Price was, the muscle tone goes out of the name. (Price, who was also formerly Universal's president, is club sprinter emeritus. After five dark years as an independent producer, he became in 1990 president of Columbia Pictures. Again. By '91 the exit rumors were already flying.) By then *Gringo* was history—Frank Price had washed his hands of it. The eleven-year struggle was all Fonda's.

Fonda was just turning forty when the Carlos Fuentes book (then called *Frontiers*) appeared. The big worry about turning Four-O was hitting her. She sees the timing as "synchronicity, which is something I've had almost my whole career. *Golden Pond* appeared at the time I wanted to do something with my father; *China Syndrome* . . . Three Mile Island." Fonda can go into stream of consciousness and it works because her movies tend to jibe with the headlines, almost like clockwork. So the fact of *Coming Home* taking five years to develop, or *Dollmaker* taking eight years, doesn't throw her.

Gringo didn't throw Frank Price either because as Fonda puts it, "He could conceive of this as a very small art film. The thinking was, 'We'll let her develop it. It's not gonna cost a lot of money.' "

Flash forward two years. Price was out, and Guy McElwaine was in. (He's the agent who's now again an agent, back at ICM—club members do like to replay old roles.) It's in such executive shuffles that movies die quiet (or loud) deaths; new regimes don't want old ideas. It's a moment in which a studio cleans house. Fonda is a pragmatist, and understands this. She also knows her value as a star to a Guy McElwaine, or a Frank Price; it's not for nothing that it's Fonda, and not some other actress, who's developing the remake of *All About Eve* with herself in the role of the quintessential star Margo Channing. (And her niece Bridget Fonda as Eve?)

"Guy wanted me to do *Agnes of God*," Fonda said without any emotion. "So I said, 'Okay, Guy, I'll do *Agnes of God*. But in return I want to hire a new writer for *Old Gringo*."

She paused purposely. "It was a semi–quid pro quo."

Were they indulging Fonda, these men?

"Absolutely. But I don't care what their motivation is. My former partner Bruce Gilbert and I spent the first five years of *Dollmaker* trying to get it made as a feature. Then we saw *Roots* on TV and changed our minds overnight. *Dollmaker* was right for TV. You have to learn to shift gears."

Quickly. Ripeness is all. "The day after I won my second Academy Award, I went to see [ABC then-president] Tony Thomopolous about *Dollmaker*. How was he going to say no to me? This is how you get projects made. In little increments. You don't go straight ahead, you go in toeholds. It's like climbing a mountain. You never look straight up."

You also don't look away, ever. By the time Fonda finished *Agnes*, McElwaine left Columbia, and Englishman David Puttnam arrived. The switch was fortuitous for Fonda. "The day I pitched *Gringo* to Puttnam, I knew he was the right person for the movie. It was his kind of story. He liked the idea." Puttnam lasted a rocky eighteen months in Hollywood, and most of his movies were written off by Columbia as bad judgment calls. In 1987 he was replaced by Dawn Steel. "We were relatively pregnant with this movie when Dawn came on," remembered Fonda. "Sets were being built. Dawn could have ended it. She's extremely strong. She said, 'Okay, go ahead, but you get this amount of money and this amount of time. And don't come back for more.' "

Yet rumors persist that Fonda went back, and back again. "Oh, yes, well we needed three more days. So in that case I got on the phone with Dawn and she agreed. She talks tough and straight. The fact that she's tight about money and scheduling is healthy. It forces you not to be indulgent. She flatly said no to an extra week of hacienda shots we wanted. But when she came to the set, people still cheered, and came up to her thanking her for those extra days. And it wasn't an easy trek to get to that location."

Fonda has other gripes, though, in a larger sense about "certain personalities in our community being somewhat cavalier in terms of accounting. There doesn't seem to be any logic when you look at how much movies cost, and how often they go way over budget. It's totally incomprehensible to outsiders."

Example: Fonda's workout business. "It's a small service business and the woman who runs it is from a nonentertainment area. If you asked her, she would say that some people in Hollywood are out of control and irrational. Because we also went into the video business—and because I am who I am—this woman from the outside gets to see inside. I think what she sees is that very often we are making movies over the backs of a bunch of dinosaurs."

Fonda wasn't finished. "Can you hear the hysteria in my voice?" she wanted to know. "Look, I don't chafe at corporate involvement with movies. The new employers are people with their asses on the line from major multinational companies, and I owe them a certain kind of responsibility. Because I'm strong I can handle that. But to say that the business is totally corrupted is silly."

Play the truth game again and say two words to Fonda: the business.

"A strange amalgam of art and commerce. People behind the money are dealing with people who are artists. It's a different gestalt. Dennis Hopper and Peter Fonda come along with a movie called *Easy Rider* and it makes a fortune. So some young filmmakers who are not Dennis Hopper and Peter Fonda come along and get a chance. And nothing happens. You can't feed it to a computer."

But all the therapy and all the side ventures and video income and political controversy—all the staying power—don't mean you don't remain vulnerable to early issues. With all her power she seems frightened still. That's what's so startling about Fonda: Tell her about reading *Haywire*, the memoir by her childhood friend Brooke Hayward, and she doesn't back off. She knows the Jane Fonda quote you're talking about: "The one about those two women—Margaret Sullavan and my mother—committing suicide. All that bottled-up rage inside you with nowhere to go." So the rage doesn't go away? Her look says no—the rage can be triggered by a mere glance. Both Margaret Sullavan and her mother were married to Henry Fonda; Brooke Hayward's sister, Bridget, killed herself, and her brother, Bill, was hospitalized for mental illness. And at Vassar it was Brooke Hayward, not Jane Fonda, everyone expected to become the movie star. (Hayward made the cover of *Life* on her sixteenth birthday; it took Fonda a little longer.) "Life experience teaches you finally the survival is in yourself," Fonda said firmly. She played with the buttons on her red linen blazer. "I've got a third of my life left, and it's mine. To act out those early family dynamics takes so much out of you."

The early memories she's most famous for are the Tomboy Memories, the climbing and hiking around Tigertail Road in Brentwood, her father being the gentleman farmer and Sunday painter and also a club movie star. "I was always racing around the hills, either being a cowboy or an Indian. One or the other. It was sort of schizophrenic." And scary? "Maybe. But maybe if you are not scared, it's not interesting . . . In Mexico, on the set [of *The Old Gringo*], I was sitting at [co-star] Greg Peck's feet asking him why we put ourselves through this. And he said something that made so much sense: He said Walter Matthau is happiest when he's gambled everything, and lost it. It's something akin to bases loaded, in the ninth inning . . . Again this is a contradiction in me, because neither of my parents was that open or that much of a gambler."

The mother-father memories are worth bringing up, because Fonda isn't used to being asked about them—because of her mother's suicide, it's a taboo. So, you ask her to go to a specific memory.

"Them getting ready to go to a party, and me being awfully young, watching them get dressed. My mother wore clothes beautifully. She . . . cared greatly about her hair, and her appearance, and her jewelry, and the effect could be extraordinary. And I remember my father standing there in his tuxedo . . ."

And didn't young Lady Jane (as Barbara Stanwyck called her) want to wear her mother's clothes, like every other little girl? Her face spoke volumes. "I wore his clothes," she said like it was the most natural thing. If the Fonda power drive that fascinates the club (and the country) comes from her mother's death—and the unappealing way she found out, years later, at boarding school, while reading a movie magazine!—she could care less.

"It may never absolutely go away, that memory," she said, "and it may not be necessary that it go away. You aim for forgiveness. Some people go under and remain damaged—not that I don't believe I'm damaged. I'm not pretending I'm not damaged." The subtext here is "Deny the hysteria, deny the stardom." The actresses who accept their contradictions at the core (Meryl Streep, Mia Farrow, Bette Midler) are the ones the public connects to. Fonda said if she weren't acting, she'd "probably be institutionalized." Mia Farrow and Meryl Streep have used the same word. Club shrinks talk to you about these women being "borderline personalities," which is why they are such a horror show on a movie set. Half vulnerable and half iron is a Hollywood recipe that goes back to Loretta Young in her prime. It's the actresses who deny their contradictions (Jill Clayburgh, Kathleen Turner) who tend to lose bankability (and movie fans) very fast. Clayburgh by playing only her neuroses—and never her light side—and Turner by underplaying the dark side, or maybe even denying it completely. The gossamer thread that connects all actresses is their voltage, their strength. It's here that Fonda, compliments of good Midwestern genetics, has the edge.

"I'm extremely strong," Fonda reminded, lest anyone forgot. "Which is not necessarily good. I have tremendous will. I am not going to be destroyed. I'm going to survive. I'm not my image; people who have these superwoman images are not that way at all. I'm stubborn, but the people who are close to me know that my main characteristic is that I'm open—which is a contradiction. But if you want to grow up, or change, badly enough, the idea of change can penetrate your being. I have a strange lack of rigidity. For the last nine months I've been free-falling through space."

Remind Fonda that in 1964 she was voted at Harvard the human being most likely to become a "Thing," and she laughs. She's been called a lot of things, after all. "A whole lot of goddamn blonde hair" is how she once described herself. But now she's facing those fifties and the marriage to Ted Turner *and she's not a bankable movie star at the moment.* How will that be?

"If a marriage is working," she said carefully, "then a movie or two movies can be a strain. But movies don't break a working marriage."

So no regrets? She shook the head full of blonde hair in a way that said no. "I guess I'm comfortable being a movie star." She shrugged the Fonda shoulders.

What about directing? "I'm not comfortable with the idea of ever directing. I like to be directed. I still get frightened working, I still get cramps a lot. I can make decisions and choices, but I never want to be the buck-stops-here person."

What about writing about Hollywood?

"Writing about it?" she said like it was a terrible idea. "I have enough trouble talking about Hollywood. Because I never know what's true and what isn't."

CLUB RULE TWENTY-FOUR

Sex is a subject not a verb. Sex is largely talked about rather than performed. Stars use sex onscreen, and other club members use libidinous energy at lunch, or in meetings with people from New York, or late at night when they often coddle their stars on long, long phone calls.

After Joe Roth coddles Julia Roberts late at night on the phone—
usually about the day's rushes—how sexy is Joe Roth going to be? Conversely, Jane Fonda talks endlessly about sexuality because, for all her
zeitgeistness, she's an old-fashioned star. Her training tells her movie stars
should look like they want to fuck each other, like Joan Crawford looked
onscreen (and off) with Clark Gable. Fonda had this bred into her bones.
(Remember how her father was onscreen with his big love Margaret
Sullavan?) But in real life, real club life, sexual activity is probably ninth
or tenth on a member's priority list. Even (or especially) in the Gay Mafia.

Example: It is a given that Meryl Streep is celibate while making a
picture. That's partly where her creative range came from, from the
bottled-up sexuality. If your husband is a sculptor, as hers is, the husband
will understand if, for fifteen weeks, you're incommunicado. People
speculated about Streep's flings with Jack Nicholson and Ed Begley, Jr.
They went so far as to create bizarre scenarios. But if you want to pin a
word on Meryl Streep when she's working—it's *celibate*.

16

Club Star-Star— Robert Redford

No *two leading men got in by the same route. But all leading men share traces of rumors. He was a male hustler in Harvard Square, or other suggestions, equally lurid. The truth is that each leading man in the club is an exception. Clint Eastwood got in not because of spaghetti Westerns, but because Jennings Lang convinced Ned Tanen and Lew Wasserman to let Clint direct; Clint did six pictures for Jennings. Paul Newman got in because of star quality—and beauty. Paul Newman at thirty (or forty) was the handsomest actor alive. Robert De Niro got in because Brian De Palma and Martin Scorsese saw him as a role model. Jack Nicholson got in because Dennis Hopper put him in a star-making role in* Easy Rider. *Warren Beatty got in because of William Inge and Tennessee Williams—who wrote his first two movies—and Natalie Wood. Robert Redford got in because of Mike Nichols and Natalie Wood and because he had more charisma than any other blond in the movies. Robert Redford is the club star-star.*

When I asked Robert Redford why he didn't have stronger leading ladies, he didn't even stop for a beat.

"Jane's strong," he said of his co-star in *The Electric Horseman* and *Barefoot in the Park* (the movie that made him a star). Then he pointed to Patricia Newcomb, his and Fonda's mutual publicist, and said shyly, "Pat's strong." Both Newcomb and Redford blushed simultaneously.

Pat Newcomb is the publicist a producer meant when he asked me, "Are you putting a publicist in your book? They're the ones with power now."

Pat Newcomb is probably the most intelligent seductive member of the club—not just because she was Marilyn Monroe's best friend. Newcomb is a petite creature with true largesse—she's political. Every grown-up Kennedy adored this blonde beige daughter of a psychiatric social worker. It was Robert Kennedy who appointed her to head the U.S. Information Agency. When working in the Hollywood publicity firm Rogers and Cowan in the early '80s, Newcomb did it completely her own way—she worked at her own pace, her own hours, yet she worked within the corporate maze that is Rogers and Cowan until she left to become a VP at MGM where she ultimately was a victim of bad timing, not judgment. It was because of Pat Newcomb I met Robert Redford.

It was because of Pat Newcomb I understood the real Robert Redford. In the middle of our meeting in his Fifth Avenue office, Newcomb uncharacteristically swooped in—almost Loretta Young–like, but she looked startled. Or terrified.

The conversation stopped. Redford listened very closely while Newcomb explained she'd mistakenly left her leather Filofax—"my whole life"—in a taxicab. The world stopped for a few minutes; Pat Newcomb's friend Bob knew there was nothing reassuring to say or do. He was just very gentle, until the call came from Yellow Taxi in Queens that Miss Patricia Newcomb's Filofax was found.

Had he willed it?

Had he that much power?

Recently, an agent told me that the movie business is star-driven. As if he was telling me something new. Well, that day on Fifth Avenue I knew what was meant by star-driven. But Redford may be the last movie star who still operates this way—which is to say, solo. There is no battery of assistants, no entourage—in short, nobody else is making the decisions. So he can actually hear what Pat Newcomb is saying. (He's no Eddie Murphy, who's oblivious to his underlings.) The people in Redford's professional life have been there for years—but he doesn't lean on them. If anything, it's the other way around.

As Redford loped into his Manhattan office, twenty-two floors above

Rockefeller Center, he simultaneously grinned and apologized (for tardiness) and explained why he'd been in three states in the previous thirty-six hours—and why the life of Robert Redford is complicated.

Redford removed a navy baseball jacket and wire-rim glasses and settled into a straight-backed chair with a tumbler of ice water. His smile—boyish even at close to fifty—was ironic. And right up close he looks like Robert Redford.

He is either restless or relentless. In the span of a long weekend, he was in California, Utah, Connecticut, and New York (where, except for California, he has homes). Not that Redford needs a reason to be peripatetic. "I don't live too much by program," he said lightly, "and it drives my friends crazy!" (That Redford is attentive to his friendships is both well known and surprising: Star movie actors are more often than not in search of new best friends. Redford clings comfortably to the old ones.)

That sense of being housebroken, comfortable at any cost, extends to his New York headquarters. There is no outer office, no name on any door and almost no mark of stardom in the inner office. Furnished with a slouchable love seat and a couple of chairs, the undersized room would hardly seem to be designed for a megastar-director-producer. One wall is completely framed with family photos, some fuzzy and unfocused, but none of them without real sentiment. (The only "star" photo in the room is a still from *The Way We Were*, with Redford and Barbra Streisand.)

Another wall offers random yellowing *New Yorker* cartoons, bits and pieces of wisdom one wouldn't dare to quote, let alone read. The books (authors range from Peter Benchley to Oriana Fallaci) and scripts (*The River*, *The Verdict*) reveal an eclectic taste. It's the size of the office (barely nine by twelve) that's startling—startling, that is, until one remembers that Redford has 7,000 of the best acres in Utah. When one has that kind of acreage, a small corner office in midtown Manhattan is perfectly suitable. Redford only hangs his hat here, not his identity.

When Redford asked a secretary on the floor for "two glasses of water, please," she responded, "Perrier?" Redford nodded, gesturing in a way that said, "We have guests." The surprise was that Redford—the man who's never done a talk show—would sit for hours in a straight-backed chair and never flinch from a question. No prior list of questions was requested, and there was no issue that could or couldn't be discussed. No star trips, in other words, unless you count the waiting.

Waiting for Redford, though, is instructive—one realizes that it would be useless to try to see him in other, more revealing, surroundings. In public, there would be no getting close to him, no getting him to open up. While waiting, one question kept surfacing. How can Robert Redford the man of action, the downhill racer and amateur mountain climber, be reconciled with Redford the reclusive sketch artist, the eager movie director who personally storyboarded every shot of his debut film, *Ordinary People*? Is he the jock or the introvert? Or is his energy so unsquandered, even after twenty-five years at the top, that he's both brawn and brain?

"I'm schizophrenic," he responded, flashing his deadpan glance from *The Sting*. "I'm also Irish," he added gravely. "I recently decided that two words hit me when I think of being Irish: selfish and loyal." Redford's pause is intended to allow for a point: Being both selfish and loyal implies the kind of contradiction that's not at all unstarlike. Redford's father, a former Los Angeles milkman, calls his son "a combination of Tom Swift and Attila the Hun." Paul Newman calls Redford "a barracuda pussycat." Barbra Streisand says Redford "doesn't act the way he looks," a statement that cuts to the core of Redford—and he knows it. It's his duality that has allowed him to orchestrate a durable star career on his own terms. If Redford disappears from the screen for years at a time, he also returns to the screen usually in the right year. And in so doing he has made the films that addressed his own personal obsessions (*Downhill Racer, The Candidate, All the President's Men*).

Age, at this point, would not seem to be one of Redford's obsessions. And if anybody's wondering how Redford is aging, the answer on close examination is that he seems not to be aging. Onscreen, in *Havana*, he aged; off screen he looks ten years younger—or fifteen. Okay, he slouches a little, after three hours in one chair. And, yes, the eyes can crinkle, but they rarely do. The point about him isn't that he's above and beyond the demands of stardom—but rather that he would simply prefer privacy. That's what got him the stardom in the first place: his sense of observation. Anyone who's hitchhiked cross-country twenty times, as Redford has, is an observer. Anyone who's walked eighteen Manhattan blocks in pajamas in daylight, as Redford has (once), is an observer. Anyone who's lodged himself in a Manhattan trash can (once) is an observer. "And you cannot observe the world by looking at yourself too much," said the star who gets looked at as much as any man alive. So much for a career (or a life) based on blond-on-blond good looks.

"Right from the beginning, I had a problem with my looks," Redford admitted, again crossing his legs, a little self-consciously. "I haven't talked about this much, but I always saw myself as dark haired. There is this thing about blond people being more privileged; at least I've been told that." Redford's smile became shy, disbelieving. "People tell me I somehow suggest a highly educated person, when I'm really someone from Van Nuys who left college to bum around Europe and had no real education. What kind of person I am has nothing to do with my . . . appearance. The same thing holds true about age.

"To play twenty now," Redford said slowly, "means showing the innocent part of yourself. I work from the inside out, and so it's a case of getting rid of a lot of emotional weight you carry around. I am never really going to pass for twenty now, but to try means . . . a lot of help from your cinematographer. I think it's your vanity that likes to think you can do it. I believe people should bear aging. Women get a nice look when they start to experience things, and so do men."

Experience brings consequences, though. Even Redford confessed to a dark side. ("Call up any of my friends," he suggested, looking out at the Manhattan skyline, "and they'll talk at length about my dark side . . .") But, simultaneously, he claimed never to have had, or needed, a role model. "I always had a sense of my own instincts. They were undeveloped, maybe, but they were there. When you are younger, you wear them like a badge, but always you have to trust them. Mine came largely from sports."

With Redford, more than instincts were sharpened in sports. Very early on he devised, and seems glad to discuss, a kind of code. It's a code he adheres to regardless of how popular or unpopular it is—or he is. And it came from sports. "In athletics, right away, I learned that life did not exemplify the Boy Scout maxims. I learned that life wasn't about how you played the game. It was about winning. Winning is what we celebrate." Redford leaned forward, illustrating his point with hands outstretched as though holding a globe of the world.

"We are all given these instructions as kids, these do's and don'ts, which seem to be written as if on tablets. But what they have to say just isn't true. About how good wins the day, and so forth. Maybe, in fact, those things were true then, but not later. Yet most of us operate from these truths, until we learn somewhere that life is not fair. Adult life then becomes a matter of putting one foot in front of the other; it means you rethink. I hope I don't sound pretentious . . . but what you begin to see is that life finally is about winning."

And, Redford conceded, winning may mean not always being the Nice Guy. "But what does un-nice mean?" he asked. Clearly, he's in a profession where being liked is critical, yet in private life he doesn't do a please-like-me routine. "I have no real interest in false humility," he confessed, adding, "To be loved, to be a nice guy, is not necessarily a goal. I would never conceive of going on a talk show, for example. And yet I may be hypocritical because here I am talking to you."

The subject of the media is the subject that rivets Redford. His "personal" movies—*The Candidate, The Electric Horseman*—examine what the media (read "fame") does to people. In reality Redford is underexposed. If his peers—Dustin Hoffman, Jane Fonda, Paul Newman—are written about more often than Redford, he couldn't care less. His reluctance began in the '70s, and it's never vanished. That was the time of *The Great Gatsby, The Way We Were, The Sting,* and (in reaction) the covers of *Newsweek* and *Life.*

"Those cover stories, at that time, well . . . I had real mixed feelings about them," he said, nodding at the paradox. "You felt that something in you was going to be lost, on the one hand. Or that there was going to be a real cost. On the other hand, you are only human, and it's exciting to see yourself on the cover of *Life. Gatsby* was such a bar of soap, a product sold to the public, and I felt a part of that, and yet not a part of it. Even then I had strong feelings about the environment and Watergate and I probably tried to use the press to express those views. But you see yourself on those covers and what you think you have created is An Image. A separate thing."

Does one then make a separate peace with that thing, that image? "You never get comfortable with it," he claimed, "but you maybe get more accepting."

From the moment Redford entered his office, he had on his mind the dilemma that doesn't go away; the dilemma of how to remain an observer. The best actors, people like George C. Scott and Robert Duvall, talk endlessly about the problem. About how they grew up watching people (while usually being ignored themselves) and how the reverse is now true. Redford, the man who spent his twentieth year in Europe doing nothing but watching people and sketching them, is even more of a media victim. "But how can you complain?" he asked rhetorically. "When you know without doubt that people would gladly change places with you. It's like complaining about having money."

And so Redford isn't complaining. Taking a break for a phone call from his daughter, he left the room, returned twenty minutes later, and did something one doesn't expect even from a friend (even a close friend). He picked up the conversation at precisely the point it left off. "Oh, I never had a problem with concentration," he said casually. Reminding him that Robert De Niro, for one, can on occasion take a role home with him, in terms of living with a character twenty-four hours a day, Redford demurred. "For me, carrying over a role into private life would be a little much. There isn't one right way to act. There are only different ways of working, and one major way is physical." (George Roy Hill, who directed Redford in three movies, once remarked that "Redford never intellectualizes.")

This physical way of working is something Redford likes to illustrate. "Let's do walks," he suggested, standing up and reworking his immaculately lean body into that of a motorcyclist. "The movie is *Little Fauss and Big Halsy*, okay? And I'm playing a low-grade biker, a man with a . . . swagger." He straightened up, momentarily. "Now, it's *Electric Horseman*, and my character is somebody whose lower back is out; that's how I pictured him." Again Redford illustrated, with the grace of a pantomimist. "Bob Woodward [in *All the President's Men*] had an absolutely linear, straight-ahead walk. He doesn't waver." Neither does Redford; nor does he spend hours "conceptualizing." "Too much talk that goes on too long and begins to sound alike makes me spin." (A true Californian.)

Yet Redford has a real grasp on the Image, on why it grew and on how it's maintained. His appeal goes beyond looks, and has more to do with a kind of endless soothing adolescence, tempered by an erotic promise. And Redford is smart about this. He turned down *The Graduate*, saying "nobody will believe I am a twenty-one-year-old college student who never got laid." He turned down *Superman*, saying he was uncomfortable in capes. He turned down *Kramer vs. Kramer* because "I was too obvious a choice, and I may have been wrong about that." He accepted *A Bridge Too Far* (at $500,000 a week) because it was "stars on parade" and it couldn't really hurt his career. When he and Paul Newman became *Butch Cassidy and the Sundance Kid*, they also became the movie couple of that decade, sex symbols in a time when there almost weren't any.

But the real Redford movies are the "personal" ones that address his own obsessions. It was Redford who convinced Bob Woodward and Carl Bernstein to write the book *All the President's Men*. (The Watergate reporters had instead intended to write a biography of former attorney general John Mitchell.) What intrigued Redford was "the way journalists can catch lightning," the way they can grasp a story in an instant. Redford wanted to produce and not star in *President's Men*, but the studio insisted. With *The Candidate*, he wanted only to co-star (as the campaign manager, instead of the candidate). "But I found I had to sacrifice the role to the plot, in various movies," he said. Making those kinds of choices, that's how a star career is maintained.

Choosing to play Jay Gatsby is how a star actor stretches, against opposition and against type, and for better or worse. In person, Redford would seem more Hemingway than Fitzgerald, more about outdoor angst than indoor. Not that Redford would agree.

"Why I insisted on doing *Gatsby*," he explained, "was I had seen how money alters people, and it didn't always feel good. I didn't grow up in houses like Gatsby's, so I was fascinated with how people grow up in those houses. And the degree to which people will go to achieve certain lengths. Again the resistance, at the beginning, was about how I looked."

The opposite was true with *The Way We Were*. It just may be the quintessential romance movie of the '70s—the favorite sexual chemistry movie—and, as Redford put it, "It seems to grow in people's minds, becoming more popular with time." Why this leading man can't find other leading ladies for movie romances is a real question. "The answer," Redford said, "is that today all barriers to romance are down. So what do you write a love story about? Since *John and Mary* around 1970, we've had movie romances lodged in psychoanalysis. But *The Way We Were*, obviously, was set in another time period. What was timeless about it was the subject: two people who try to love each other, and can't. It was also about a man who tried for success and stumbled."

"So much was expected of this man," he said empathetically. "He looked wonderful in everybody's eyes. But what if the early promise wasn't there? I understand this notion of constant expectations. And I felt, for him, it might not be so bad to be a TV writer."

But not for Redford. From the beginning, he was not marked for a career in a TV series, and he not only knew it, he acted on what he knew. Slowly, then with punch, like a storyteller, Redford recalled that "in 1963, I was offered a lot of money to do a TV series. I had no money, and a young family. I was the breadwinner, and it felt real good to have an offer of security. And I said no. Then they raised the offer to a figure that was ridiculous. To the point where my agent said, 'If you still say no, I don't think we can go on representing you.' I remember now slipping into that zone where you think, 'Gee, I could move my family out of Hollywood . . .' And then one morning I walked on the beach, one of those walks, and I said to myself, 'No.' I just couldn't imagine living with a TV series."

Redford paused before adding, "Naturally they came back with even more money. But by then it was easy to say no. Two weeks later, I was in Bucks County [Pennsylvania] trying out a new comedy for Broadway called *Barefoot in the Park* with a first-time director named Mike Nichols."

Turning down TV in favor of Bucks County is one indication of how Redford operates so differently. In Paris, at twenty, he wore a beret and became such a convincing sidewalk painter that one American tourist snapped thirty-four poses, until even Redford had enough. He simply pointed to his argyle socks, as if pointing to his American heritage, and the embarrassed tourist vanished.

When Redford tells this anecdote, or another, it's with the eye of a painter, or maybe a movie director. That he won an Academy Award for

Ordinary People is less the point than the fact that the ballplayer from Van Nuys chose as his directorial debut a movie primarily about behavior. "There had never been a good movie about the middle class," he said during filming. At that time, the worry was how would Redford, the Californian, capture the stifled life of the Midwest. That he'd hitchhiked through the territory didn't seem enough preparation. But Redford's preparation was actually emotional; his dark side surfaced with *Ordinary People*. "Look, at fifteen I wanted out of Los Angeles and I've never really wanted to go back. Even now, when I get on the Ventura Freeway I feel this great huge hand smothering me, and I get sweaty from the moment I arrive."

What directing gave Redford was a new sense of trust, both of himself and others. "When I think of [director] Sydney Pollack, I realize we've known each other thirty-five years, and all of our trust is now part of who I am. I might argue with Sydney—we've done eight films together—but I'd also do something his way if he wanted me to. Because of the friendship, he has some sense of me that even I don't have."

Redford might have been defining friendship, but considering the warmth registered in his voice, he was also examining himself. "At one point I began to look at my own work, as an actor, and I saw that what was emerging onscreen was a cold person. This wasn't by design, and it isn't who I am." Redford cleared his throat, because the talk was coming to a close. "Let's just say, I like to shadowbox with success."

CLUB RULE TWENTY-FIVE

There's always a gutter, even in the club where people are forever nice on the surface. Even the most threatening language isn't taboo, in certain situations.

Robert Redford is operating from experience when he talks about not being able to tolerate Hollywood. He stays so removed that even his studio secretaries, employees of his for years, have never met him. Redford distances himself from the club because he knows one basic club truth: These people can turn very mean, very quickly. The undercurrent is always there. Power in the club, remember, is never really inherited— nobody gives it to you. You "acquire" it. Some members know how to talk street talk *if they have to.* (Nobody wants to, and everybody avoids it, but sometimes there are grudges.)

Example: During the 1988 writers' strike, at the American Cinematheque tribute to Bette Midler, Chevy Chase was forced to rely on his own material. When he looked at Disney chairman Michael Eisner and said, "I'd like to piss in your mouth," there was complete silence. What could Chevy have against Michael? There are twenty different answers, but the point is that the remark was mean.

Another example: One jealous trade paper columnist asked how a publicist got a Lamborghini six months after getting her job. "For eating Kim Basinger's cunt" was the answer. Meanness lurks everywhere. Most people avoid this language. But you have to know they've heard it before. And they know how to use it.

17

Club Comeback— Al Pacino

Al Pacino got in because of Marty Bregman, who sponsored him. He stayed in because of Jill Clayburgh, who groomed him. Jill Clayburgh got in because of a screen test she made to play Carole Lombard. She dropped out when the movie Gable & Lombard bombed. She got back in because Paul Mazursky gave her the leading lady role in An Unmarried Woman. She dropped out again because she played one too many unmarried women. She got back in by marrying club writer David Rabe, whose movie Casualties of War was a club favorite because different club branches—directors, executives, producers—fought for its survival. And because Pauline Kael loved it. Then it bombed, and was no longer a club favorite. Al Pacino dropped out for a while in the mid-'80s when he stopped working and people stopped talking about him. He got back in because of Pauline Kael's review of Sea of Love, and because of his Vanity Fair cover—and because of Diane Keaton, who further groomed him. Diane Keaton got in because of Woody Allen and TV commercials and Stan Kamen. She stayed in because of Warren Beatty and great cheekbones and deep conflicts. Al Pacino and Diane Keaton were the neurotic club couple not because of their talent, *or their survival—but because of their keeping a distance from Hollywood.*

The club's favorite actor is probably Michael Caine, because he never ever says no to anything they offer him. A Michael Caine retrospective would probably last three weeks. If you could sit through it. Because socially he's fun (and so is his wife, Shakira, on occasion), nobody holds the B pictures against him. Not that the club requires an actor to be social. Actually it can be hurtful. (Because of an aggressive wife, Michael York goes to so many parties he seems too "available." So the club invites him but doesn't take him seriously. Ditto Kirk Douglas. The opposite is true of Burt Lancaster, who retains mystique, before and after his stroke.)

Michael Caine uses the power of saying yes, and Debra Winger uses the power of saying no, and Marlon Brando uses the power of saying maybe. All three strategies appeal to the club's sense of game playing. Saying "maybe" kept Richard Gere in the movie business long after his bankability seemed gone. (Gere also had a loyal pusher in agent Ed Limato, whose club status zoomed when client Michelle Pfeiffer got very hot, and stayed loyal.) But the master of "maybe" is Al Pacino. Nobody else but Brando comes close, and Brando is an icon (and perennially troubled) and not a player.

The thing is, the club wants what it doesn't have—period. So for years it was De Niro and Pacino, those "goddamn brilliant outcast actors from Little Italy," as one producer called them. Dustin Hoffman played tennis at Robert Evans' house—but not Pacino and De Niro. Nobody could get them to their dinner table, nobody except maybe Margo Winkler. (In the club, if you can be had, or bought, you're boring. What really whets Hollywood's appetite are the people who have the nerve to live in New York, like Woody Allen and Arthur Krim and Paul Mazursky.)

At some point in the late '80s Robert De Niro became boring. "He did *Midnight Run*, for God's sakes, and *Jacknife*," a producer said to me, with disgust. "He started doing package pictures for the money." Then De Niro started doing interviews, finally, when he bought his studio in TriBeCa—and that was the moment the mystique started to fade. Too many photo layouts. Al Pacino was the reverse: He got in just under the wire—at the tail end of the '80s, with the comeback of the decade. His thriller *Sea of Love* did $10 million in its opening weekend in late September. And Pacino, who hadn't had a hit in ten years—not since *And Justice for All . . .*—was back as a star. Once again Al Pacino could "open" a movie. Even after all the seclusion and silence and aging and saying no.

Pacino was so intense on the December morning we met, I felt like a psychoanalyst. He pointed to the oversized Christmas tree that dominated the living room of his suite at the Beverly Wilshire, and said quietly, "Marlon brought me this." The tree was decorated with silver bells and silver strawberries, and Pacino looked like a leprechaun as he fiddled with the lights. Then he began to pace the room with a drowsy, heavy-footed walk. "Why am I walking this way?" the actor asked himself. "I put on a necktie and suddenly I'm walking like a grandfather." The tie would come off later that morning, and Pacino would appear in a Navy peacoat, then a silk sport jacket, and finally—for a long afternoon of talk—a Brando-torn T-shirt. (I myself even went home at lunchtime to change clothes. My switching from Shetland cardigan to sweatshirt seemed to appeal to Pacino; he got chummier.)

Pacino at almost fifty still wears many hats, and shirts, and identities. As Marthe Keller, a former flame and co-star (*Bobby Deerfield*), put it, "He plays so many parts every day." And not necessarily onscreen, or onstage. The actor was only visible in three films in the '80s—*Scarface* and *Revolution* and finally *Sea of Love*. But nobody ever questions what Pacino is up to: He's just being Pacino.

The star has always moved in his own circuitous, complicated way, not unlike a restless chameleon. Playing *Richard III* on Broadway, he was known to eat a box of doughnuts a day, and walk alone for hours after performances. After *Serpico* was over, he tried arresting people on the streets of New York. After *Scarecrow*, he wore the character's prison shoes for months. But the off-stage part Pacino seems most often to play is prince of darkness.

"Do you think I'm intense?" he asked, without any apparent guile. "I've been told that." Don't people tell Pacino to lighten up? "It depends. Lighten up about what? And why and when? You mean at a dinner party? When you are making a movie, you are intent on getting to the other side, and that's your sanity. Period. So when you are working, and walking through a hotel lobby, you're thinking about the movie. And so people think you are intense. That comes with being in this position and coping with this stimuli." The "position" means Pacino, six times nominated for an Oscar, is a $5 million player. ("His salary for *Revolution* was seven figures," acknowledged producer Irwin Winkler. "But lower seven figures than Sly Stallone or Bob Redford. His salary for *Godfather III* was $5 million.")

But money is beside the point. "You bend your psyche if you are an actor," admits the actor, "and it really is a relief when it's over. Weeks after *Richard III* closed, around eight o'clock at night I'd find myself walking with a limp. The body doesn't know a role is over until the mind tells it." Pacino's body on this particular day was a victim of jet lag, and a nap was suggested.

"Me nap? How do you spell that? K-n-a-p? I've never napped. Maybe one day . . ."

Instead, for what he said was the first time in his life, Pacino put a "Do Not Disturb" sign on the door, and buckled down to serious discussion. When a hotel maid knocked anyway, Pacino saw the irony, and grinned. Most probably, the maid wanted to see a movie star right up close.

"Do you mind if I smoke?" Pacino asked, then never lit up. Similarly, he ordered room service but never bothered with the milk shake. He poured coffee without drinking it, preferring to concentrate instead. (As he once put it: "There is no such thing as happiness. There is only concentration.") Fame is just one of the ambivalent cards that Pacino plays with. "I've been adjusting to fame for fifteen years," he said matter-of-factly. "I know the ups and downs, right?" Wrong. "I still have ambivalent feelings. At one point in my life, there was suddenly this sense that I was going to become a commercially popular and successful actor. It became a given. I don't know even now how right that was for me. Commercial movies are not where you learn and experience, not that I'm complaining. But maybe I've neglected another part of my work life, or my personal life."

Pacino claimed to have only lately discovered what fame means to him. "See, in the old days, when I met somebody there would be a natural evolution. Two people meet, and there's something there or not. You took the time to find out. Now, people just know you right away. Maybe fame is not an easy thing to understand unless you've experienced it. People just think they automatically know you."

Unlike George C. Scott or Spencer Tracy, who thought it wasn't a man's job, Pacino is much taken with the notion of the actor as Everyman. "From childhood, I would go to the movies with my mother, and come home and playact all the parts. In acting you could find some peace, you could get away from the loneliness. It was important."

Especially if home was one room in East Harlem. Pacino's parents were divorced when their son was two, and it was the actor's maternal grandmother who became his audience of one. "I would do Ray Milland looking for the lost bottle in *The Lost Weekend*. I would do it in various ways. That was my favorite, that and doing Al Jolson. I would do these scenes alone, and then my father would take me to visit his family and I would do the scenes again, and they would start laughing. Everyone in that house was quiet because my aunt was deaf, and I think that's how I learned mimicry, my sensitivity to it. I remember saying, 'Why are you all laughing? This guy can't find the bottle!' I remember that picture having a lasting effect on me. We had no TV, and I'd get so involved I'd lose track of time."

It's not accidental that, early in his career, Pacino primarily played junkies. Two of his closest friends died of drug overdoses, and Pacino now admits he "used to drink and do all that stuff. There was a lot of stimuli around, and the more sensitive you are, the more you think you need to dull your senses with drugs or alcohol. Slowly you realize what you could become if you stopped. I stopped slowly. And things got a little clearer. But I mean just a little . . ."

And not overnight. Not until he was twenty-eight did Pacino seize his power, in an off-Broadway play by Israel Horovitz called *The Indian Wants the Bronx*, which won him the Obie. (The year before, Pacino had been a janitor at Horovitz's apartment building.) Previously, he'd worked with the Living Theater and Actors Studio, and was developing the kind of underground reputation that let him borrow from the studio's James Dean Memorial Fund. In Boston, at the Charles Playhouse, he was the talk of the Hub in plays like *America Hurrah* and *Awake and Sing*. It was there he made the pivotal decision not to do small parts, ever.

"God, Boston," recalled Pacino, his eyes moving around like busy marbles. "I borrowed money to get there, and lived on the floor once I did. That's where I met [future roommate] Jill Clayburgh. I weighed 125 pounds, and when I walked in they handed me a script of *Caucasian Chalk Circle*, and offered me a small part at $50 a week. All my belongings were in a paper bag. But I said no, because I wouldn't do small parts. I'd been working already. It's funny. In those years, I was always working. I knew how to get from job to job real fast."

By 1970, the Pacino reputation was coming up from underground. "It's very tricky. You want to be anonymous, yet the work doesn't have any value if nobody knows. Not to have recognition and, worse, not to have work—those things are harder than fame. To be recognized and appreciated takes luck and timing, but there's something else," said Pacino, as though posing a question, or testing his listener. "Whatever it is, you recognize it. Some club singers have it. Bobby De Niro young had it, and the young Dustin Hoffman. I think it's need," he said after pausing a very long time. "I think it comes down to one thing: If it doesn't happen, you'll die."

Pacino admits his movie career blossomed originally "because Marty Bregman made it happen. He saw me onstage, and said, 'I'll sponsor you.' He became my personal manager. He got me to work more, and he absolutely made *Serpico* and *Dog Day* happen. But then, you know, it became a different relationship."

In other words Bregman became a producer, and not just a father figure. "In some ways now, it's less complicated," Pacino said. "I'm less the kid now, less the boy. But it always takes two. I don't want to get into 'He did this to me,' because it implies 'I did that to him.' And I'm not completely over those feelings." But enough over them that Pacino teamed again with Bregman on *Sea of Love.*

By 1990 he was in *Godfather III* and back into his ongoing relationship with Diane Keaton. Together again for the umpteenth time. Clearly she's been part of his search for a private life. "It's good to go home to other people who bring you their problems," he said, almost convincingly. Pacino's private life is protected by more than publicists and bodyguards. He avoids hangouts like Elio's and Elaine's, where he might be photographed outside. And he avoids any discussion of the women in his life, past or present. It was the only subject he up front asked not to discuss. Yet he didn't shy away when the topic turned to marriage.

"It's possible. I think about it sometimes. It could be an actress, or maybe not. I haven't known many women who weren't actresses. It's the world I travel in. With actresses, the work can pull you apart for unnaturally long periods of time. But if you can afford it, there are ways to get together." (Pacino's most visible liaisons, long-distance or otherwise, have been with half a dozen of the most interesting actresses imaginable: Jill Clayburgh, Marthe Keller, Tuesday Weld, Susan Tyrrell, Kathleen Quinlan, and Debra Winger.)

"It's very attractive to me now to see a love relationship in which you are also friends. I think when I want to have a family, I will have one. So far, there must be a reason why not. But I'll tell you, it's very appealing. A good relationship makes you feel whole, I guess. Alone, I don't think you ever feel whole."

Finally Pacino, after hours on end, seemed to be fading. He got up and circled the room service table that had remained untouched. "To endure is everything," he said knowingly. "But how do I keep doing this? I'm a little out of it, so you probably wonder how come I'm still here doing this?" He looked away long enough that it almost got embarrassing. "Luck," he said finally, trying to explain his staying power. "It's luck, and I like the game. I like the involvement. It's some place to put the self."

This is the kind of thinking the club hates—loathes, in fact. Because their identities are largely fixed *socially*, members can't understand the agonies of an actor, the endless search for identity. The intensity may look aimless, but it's usually very focused—on the role they're playing. Where the club really wants Pacino is on a movie set, not at a dinner table. His role as a social zero made me sad for him. Poor little rich boy. I think I wanted Marlon Brando to have brought him the Christmas tree, not an unemployed actor named Marlon Smith.

Yet it's ironic. Because of his indelible Michael Corleones in the *Godfathers*, Al Pacino has club hall of fame status.

CLUB RULE TWENTY-SIX

The club wants what it can't have. Especially the *attention* of certain stars.

The Pacinos and De Niros are the most sought-after dinner guests mostly because they almost always refuse. (Except when Irwin Winkler invites them.) The club understands that stars are worth coveting for a reason: No stars are accidental, not even spacey ones like Pacino. You can calculate their effect in terms of *aftershock*. Real stars haunt you— emotionally, sexually—long after the original encounter. Again, it's the sexuality: Sophia Loren gave me blue balls, Robert Redford made me want a blonde, and Pacino. . . . well, Pacino had such an effect, I cried all of Christmas . . .

Even in the club, stars shine brightest. (Especially when they take off their toupees. There are no good toupees in the club, which is why Barry Diller looks real and most of the toupee wearers don't.)

18

Club Holdout— Debra Winger

*D*ebra *Winger got in because of Jim Bridges, and in spite of Robert Evans not wanting her for* Urban Cowboy. *Debra Winger stayed in because of Larry Mark and* An Officer and a Gentleman *and Jim Brooks. And in spite of Richard Gere not wanting to do love scenes with her. Polly Platt stayed in because of Jim Brooks. Polly Platt got in because of Orson Welles and Peter Bogdanovich. Orson Welles stayed in because of Peter Bogdanovich and Cybill Shepherd. Cybill Shepherd got in because of Peter Bogdanovich, and she got back in because of Bruce Willis. Bruce Willis got in because of club agent Arnold Rifkin, and stayed in because of* Die Hard. *Cybill Shepherd and Peter Bogdanovich tried to get back in with the sequel to* The Last Picture Show. *Polly Platt got further in because of* The War of the Roses. *Cameron Crowe got in because of Polly Platt and Jim Bridges and before that, Art Linson. Art Linson got in because of Ned Tanen. Ned Tanen got in because he could handle Jules Stein and Lew Wasserman and Taft Schreiber. Kitty Hawks got in by birth and got back in by marriage, to Ned Tanen. Penny Marshall got in because of Jim Brooks. She did not get in because of her brother Garry Marshall, but she got in the door. Garry Marshall got in because he's funny and* *he hosts the most exclusive Saturday morning basketball games in the club. And because he directed* Pretty Woman, *he stays in for the rest of his life. Anjelica Huston got in by birth, and she got back in because Penny Marshall gave her day work on La-verne and Shirley. She also stayed in because she was the adjunct to Jack Nicholson before she was a star. Jack Nicholson got in because of Dennis Hopper and Peter Fonda. Debra Winger got educated in the club by Jack Nicholson and Penny Marshall. Debra Winger stays in, in spite of box office duds, because she's the girl who almost always says no.*

"You're just like Debra Winger," one of her co-stars, Shirley MacLaine, told me on the way home from dinner at La Scala at the beach. I looked at her with a wrinkled face. What did that mean?

"You go through all this inner trauma, and then you go into a trance. And the work always comes out of that."

Neurotic. Ohio. Jewish. Good things to have in common.

Except that I'm a homebody and Winger is a vagabond. You have to move very fast to keep up with Debra Winger.

"I'm in the middle of moving my entire life to New York," she told me in 1988 while she was in the middle of selling her house at Point Dume, just beyond Malibu. There was a time in the '70s when Winger lived in a single room at the Chateau Marmont that you could nicely describe as cluttered. People who don't tune in closely think Winger is cluttered, too—but actually she's the brainiest of actresses. She's the modern Natalie Wood: Both women got offered everything good, usually said no, and exuded a dark Russian sexuality both on the screen and in the club. Their conflicts made them stars, along with their sexuality.

Winger now—because she has a half dozen years on Meryl Streep—is alone at the top of a heap. She is offered nearly every woman's role, in spite of commercial failures like Arthur Miller's *Everybody Wins* and Bertolucci's *Sheltering Sky*. She hit the target twice (*An Officer and a Gentleman* and *Terms of Endearment*), so she's covered, in terms of bankability. Winger is also the only performer in the club I didn't once want to be. I never saw *Urban Cowboy*, never saw her magic at all really until *Terms of Endearment*. At the end of that movie I turned to a friend and said, "Which actress will win the Oscar? That's the only question." For me Debra Winger became a star in the 137 minutes of that movie.

And when I met her I was just glad I had (for once) brought a tape recorder, and umpteen tapes. Of modern actresses only Kim Basinger goes off on more tangents than Debra Winger. (And for years they had the same agent, CAA's Rick Nicita, who also handles Bette Midler and Margot Kidder.)

All my years of fusion with a dramatic savvy actress-archetype mother paid off, once I realized that a star gives an interviewer the best two hours of her life. All you have to do is take it from them. And find that piece of them you identify with. With Winger it was Ohio-neurotic-Jewish; with Jane Fonda it was the fragile desperate mother; with Kim Basinger it was being told you were good-looking by the wrong people. All you have to do with a star is find that place.

And stay out of their way.

And listen.

And empathize.

And don't disagree.

You can't win a disagreement with an actress.

Unless she's not a star.

Because stars with real power have always known how to use it. When Marilyn Monroe walked off the bandstand after an umpteenth take on *Some Like It Hot*, she scowled at director Billy Wilder. "Put a black rinse on the blonde in the third row," she said coldly. MM was so conscious of her image as a star that she let nobody compete—there were no other blondes. Power, however, has little to do with identity, which even the best film stars admit can be a problem. (It's why they play roles.) An identity crisis is why Monroe left Hollywood at her peak, in 1955, to study acting in New York. She wanted to be more than powerful, she wanted to act, to find herself.

Debra Winger—who's always moving her life somewhere or other— also has an identity that might be called fluid. Like Monroe, she operates from intuition not intellect. And the Hollywood community can't figure her out. She is one of the handful of Hollywood's Yes People—her yes gets a movie made—but Winger is more apt to say no. To *Broadcast News*, to *Nuts*, to *Peggy Sue Got Married*, to *Marie*, to *Crimes of the Heart*, to *Raiders of the Lost Ark*, to *Arthur*, and others. Her movies aren't always career moves—and that's one reason why Hollywood is so taken with her. She makes decisions they don't understand. (Example: She chose to do *Black Widow* and not to do *Bull Durham*.) And she doesn't mingle. "I certainly tried to live like a movie star," said the girl who never dreamed of becoming one. "But it didn't work for me."

Winger's star behavior is different from Monroe's; it's not about glamour, or maintaining an image. Like Streep (her only real competition) Winger has a career that doesn't rely on looks. And yet almost every

Winger movie features backstage trauma stories. On a set in Alberta filming Costa-Gavras' *Betrayed*, Winger one day stopped a take midway through. She didn't like the approach to a scene with Tom Berenger, who plays a widowed Midwestern farmer who marries her and then reveals himself as a white supremacist. Winger had known all along that Michelle Pfeiffer and Melanie Griffith—Winger calls them "young blondes with wheat-colored hair"—were first choices to play the undercover FBI agent who falls hard for Berenger.

Within certain limits Winger can do anything, but she can't play blonde.

Winger remembers during shooting when she shot Costa-Gavras a look, then asked him: "How would Michelle do it?" Her whine was from Cleveland, and so was the insecurity.

The director's response: "You worry too much. You remind me of Simone Signoret."

The idea of a list with the names Debra Winger and Michelle Pfeiffer and Melanie Griffith sounds off. Griffith was merely last decade's blonde who got rediscovered by Mike Nichols. As an actress, Pfeiffer for all her acclaim still isn't Winger; it has taken her ten years and seven movies to do what Winger did overnight in *Urban Cowboy*—become a star. But putting Winger on any list seems off; ultimately she's a chameleon. Wandering the halls at the 1984 Academy Awards, on the arm of Barry Diller, Winger went almost unrecognized even by insiders—and she was a nominee that year for Best Actress. In short, a Winger is not anybody's idea of a sandwich at the Stage Deli.

Her major strength as a star—"my only real power" as she put it—is her ability to say no. "I can't remember a time when I couldn't say no. Or walk away. Because I weigh it against my life every time. You have to have standards you won't lower. To be able to say there are things you won't do, and know what they are. For me that's not hard. It's like being in a family that's too poor to buy things. It's easy to say no. But then I learned real fast about this town."

Winger's laugh is that of a fourteen-year-old who's tasted whiskey. "I say 'This town . . .' like I was Barbara Stanwyck or somebody. 'Honey, in this town . . .' "

The company town can't control Winger, or predict her moves. Either she fuses with directors (Jim Brooks, Jim Bridges) or she rubs them the wrong way (Taylor Hackford, Ivan Reitman). Bridges made her a star with *Urban Cowboy*, then wrote *Mike's Murder* for her. Brooks directed her in *Terms*, then wrote *Broadcast News* for her—but Winger got pregnant (with Noah, her son by Timothy Hutton, from whom she's divorced) and said no. In the '80s, how many directors wrote movies for actresses and got them made? Not many. In the '90s it's almost a fantasy to write a movie for a specific actress.

Winger didn't work for almost two years after finishing *Betrayed*; she waited for John Malkovich to be ready to film *Sheltering Sky*, the Bertolucci movie of the Paul Bowles novel. But she's a case study in club power because of how she plays the game: In 1986 Winger was the first star to leave CAA after being unhappy about being packaged with Robert Redford in the $39 million unfunny comedy *Legal Eagles*. (Redford and Winger were promised that it was to be an updated *Adam's Rib*, but it wasn't. Winger was vocal about the movie being edited by a chainsaw.)

Even without an agent—and in spite of Costa-Gavras wanting wheat hair for *Betrayed*—a very pregnant Winger convinced the director that she was right. Costa-Gavras sat in Winger's backyard at Point Dume and decided on the spot. Winger got an early look at the script because her attorney Barry Hirsch also represented the screenwriter Joe Eszterhas; the casting was a matter of timing. Then in late 1988 another Winger jolt hit the town: The actress returned to CAA—or, more specifically, to CAA agent Rick Nicita. Insiders felt it was like a KGB defector coming home.

Ask Winger if she ever fantasized about stardom, and she looks at you like you are crazy. In person, curled up on a sofa in a West Hollywood office, Winger seems so open as to be almost naked. Wearing a black T-shirt dress and no makeup, smoking unfiltered Camels, she takes an observer on an uninterrupted all-day trip. The way to keep up with her is simply to listen very closely. Director Jim Brooks likens her to the smartest girl in class, the one you want to study with for final exams. As coffee was delivered in Styrofoam cups, she demurred: "I don't want to be a prima donna, but could I have a mug or a real cup? White Styrofoam cups remind me of movie sets."

The cracks-and-plaster voice has more octaves than Yma Sumac's. (For *E.T.*, Steven Spielberg used a mix of Winger's voice with the voice of an older woman in Sausalito.) But Winger is too intense to be *E.T.*-like. Not that intensity means she's actressy. She isn't. "See, I don't want to be an actress at any cost," she says easily. "I only want to act if I can do it great."

Whether it's her public relationship with Nebraska governor Robert Kerry or her private problems with co-star Richard Gere (on *An Officer and a Gentleman*), Winger is controversial. She'd rather talk about D. H. Lawrence than Hollywood agents—but she's savvy enough to know what questions are coming. She might even verge on psychic. "One reporter and I were discussing quantum physics . . . and I knew any minute we'd be onto the CAA question. I could feel it coming."

Winger acted without an agent for her first three films. "So it wasn't like I thought I couldn't exist without an agent. Then after *An Officer and a Gentleman*, I went with Rick [Nicita]." Just after *Betrayed*, Winger returned to Nicita, but on different terms. The name Debra Winger is not now mentioned aloud in CAA corridors. When the agent sends the star a script, it's in a plain white envelope. If a note is attached, it's on plain white paper—no agency logo.

"I don't see it as going back," Winger said edgily, tired of the question but not ducking it. "I've strummed up a different relationship with Rick. I believe in championing the individual, and so does he. Being with an agent brings in something . . . the social atmosphere of the business. So you stay in contact more; you're not as isolated, and waiting for things to come to you. It's a dangerous thing to wait for things to come to you. It's Newton's First Law of Motion that a body in rest will stay that way."

What Winger missed during the hiatus from CAA was contact. The Timothy Hutton household at Point Dume was a long way from town, and Winger tends to her son without a nanny. "You won't have very many friends at the end of the week if you only talk about work," Winger says. "See, I have an old-fashioned idea of talking to an agent every day about work. It's old-fashioned because even if an agent's personality is that way, the business isn't. The business is more package-oriented . . . But my idea of an agent is someone who knows you so well—what you are going through in your life—that he can say, 'Do this.' It's Peter Brook directing, and it will take in everything you are going through."

Winger has an even more old-fashioned sense of being paid to work. She knows the club would be happy if she would set up Debra Winger Productions; she also knows that on some level it would wreck her. She is notorious for not having three films in development, for working full out on one film at a time. She spent two years working with Penny Marshall on *A League of Their Own*, and wound up being replaced ten days before shooting by Geena Davis.

"If a studio gives me money, I need to go to work," Winger says simply. "There are a lot of people in Hollywood who spin plates. Remember the guy on *Ed Sullivan* who kept seven plates spinning at once? Well, I can't spin plates. People collect money here without doing anything, and I'm politically opposed to it. It's a middle-class Ohio Jewish work habit that I have . . . so I don't fit into this hype-and-jive category. So I don't really benefit from this modern way of dealing . . . Maybe my mistake was in pointing my finger at CAA. They're doing their thing, they're doing it very well. It's a modern thing, and maybe I'm just not up to modern times."

Or maybe it's just this community. Winger's disappointment at the nonnurturing nature of Hollywood is almost naive, almost like an echo of Monroe. "I'm heading for New York because I'm not finding things I want to work on here. I'm not finding material. I feel maybe it happens more in theater. People coming together to work for natural, organic, artistic reasons.

"That sounds maybe too blunt, but it's the way great things happen. Now you are going to get people who disagree with me, who say New York theater is dead. But my sense is that there are people there who aren't afraid to sit down in a room and read plays. I may be naive and get my face slapped."

On the other hand it won't be surprising if Winger becomes a stage actress—the way Julie Harris went back to Broadway after *East of Eden*. That prospect doesn't scare her. "I get weak knees at certain points. But I never turn back. I'm the kind of person, if I forget something at home, I keep driving. I don't go back for it. I figure I gotta keep going forward, not looking down, not looking at the sides. It's like when I left CAA. At times it did become scary. But I just forged through it. That's the only courageous aspect. Because the decision was my choice."

Smart people in the movie business inevitably say that they think they'd "like" Winger if they knew her—but haven't met her. Partly what they like about Winger are her choices. They are fascinated that she would say no to Steven Spielberg (on *Raiders of the Lost Ark*) or to the very sought-after *Good Mother*, which ultimately went to Diane Keaton, and ultimately bombed out. Saying no—especially in a sparse era in terms of "go" screenplays—is seen as strength.

"It's part of my creative strength, yeah," she agreed. "I get transformed every time I make a movie. That's the big argument with agents. 'Say you like a project now,' they say. 'Don't be afraid of it.' But who knows how I'll feel when the time comes? Saying no is your only real bargaining power. I need time for my life. I don't have the stuff to go from one film to another. That's like lining up your life, and it doesn't work. If you know what you are going to do next year, you become that."

Winger learned about star leverage even before she had it. "*Urban Cowboy* was the first real deal I ever made, and I learned real fast." Winger was maybe the 200th actress to read for the part of Sissy (for which Sissy Spacek was first choice). "The shit was hitting the fan, 'cause it was like Scarlett O'Hara Wars. They were flying actresses in and out of Houston. [Director] Jim Bridges really wanted me, but the powers-that-were at Paramount didn't."

Winger paused to light a cigarette, then walked to an unopened window, opened it, and exhaled. "At one point I said to Bridges, 'No more.' I told him, 'Either I do it or I don't.' Because at that point I was starting to feel bad about myself. And nothing was worth that. So even when you have no leverage . . ."

But still you have competition: There are only so many *Terms of Endearments* or *Bull Durhams* in a given year. But Winger doesn't see herself as competing. "You always know there's the next young starlet coming along. There's already another actress right next to you. There's always another blonde. I can remember being in waiting rooms to audition for commercials, being a little overweight. There would be every possible choice for beauty, and then there's me. You feel awkward. You have to give up the awkwardness."

Early on Winger was unspectacular, unpromising, and hardly a candidate for stardom. George Cukor, as a favor to her father (who had installed Cukor's burglar alarm system), saw Mary Debra Winger when she was fourteen; Cukor saw no particular promise. After leaving home (and trying Israel briefly), Winger did TV things like *Police Woman* and *Wonder Woman* (playing Lynda Carter's kid sister). Then came the kind of corner-turner (or career-maker) that Hollywood novels are made of.

On New Year's Eve 1973 she fell out of a truck at Magic Mountain. The cerebral hemorrhage and temporary blindness gave her resolve—to become not just another actress but a star. Suddenly there was chutzpah: Winger's grandfather had been the first Ohioan to ride a Harley-Davidson to California, so there was spirit in the family. But not until Debra Winger fell off a truck did she have any real ambition. Or enough to go from playing a troll at Magic Mountain to doing a studio picture for Jim Bridges and producer Robert Evans. "In the hospital I decided I'd become the first blind actress"—she means star—"with speed bumps onstage."

The bumps are off stage, of course. Winger's career looks like a game of chance at almost every point. Spacek was only one of many wanted for *Urban Cowboy* but the chemistry with John Travolta was off; Raquel Welch was fired from *Cannery Row*; Bill Murray was wanted for Winger's attorney role in *Legal Eagles*.

She laughed about the castings. "I followed in everybody's dust for a while." Now people follow in her dust. It was Winger who turned down *Marie* before Spacek got it. "Yeah. Now sometimes I turn around and say, 'Wow! She took that and I turned it down.' Like Susan [Sarandon] was meant to do *Bull Durham*. It became clear to me when I saw it. If I had done it, it wouldn't have been the same movie."

Hanging on a wall in the office was a poster from *Crimes of the Heart*. An '80s women's picture, with three sought-after roles, and truly Winger was sought after for one of the three sisters. Wasn't she? "I read that," she said, "but I couldn't have been in that . . ."

She halted, to make sure she was getting through: Star power is made up of protocol, too—respect for peers, and their positions. "I think they knew who they wanted [Spacek, Keaton, Jessica Lange]. And that was that. I might have liked to have done it, but I didn't even go that far to think about it. I wouldn't take that from any of them. If there was something I had to do, and didn't get it—I don't know what I'd do. But I've never been in that situation."

Twelve movies, twelve years, no disappointments?

"I believe you get in when you are supposed to. If you believe in something more than anyone else . . . they'd be a fool not to hire you."

Winger is at a tricky age for an actress. The desperation about age crops up later, closer to forty. It's what writer-director Joe Mankiewicz calls "the Four-O syndrome. Fortyish. The bitterly sad point of no return for an actress. A kind of professional menopause. The jokes may be funny but don't laugh." Winger isn't yet worried, but she knows what happens to actresses as they curve in on forty.

"An actor's greatest gift is to know what she looks like at any given time. Faye Dunaway has always been good about that. In acting class, twenty-year-olds want to play old, it's an actor's disease. To know what's right for you at your time of life is a gift. I always want someone to catch me before I do something stupid, and say, 'No, Debra you are too old.' I'll take that very well, by the way. Even though I'll probably feel like I'm nineteen."

She can do a perfect impression of an aging Bette Davis dolled up for a talk show, then dithering on the air. Somehow she makes you see an absurdly made-up harridan giving orders to a makeup woman. "But if you dish it out—and God knows I can dish—you gotta take it, too. Taking it is a prerequisite to dishing it out." Okay, then, her looks—what does Winger think of them? Is she smart about her own looks? Her eyes became the size of black agates.

"I don't know if I'm smart but I try to pay attention. It's definitely something I think about. I'm always worrying because I feel older than I am . . . Once you're a mother, man, once you've carried this kid around, and given birth to it, you pretty much never feel the same."

Looking at Winger and knowing the wild-youth stories about her, you wonder something: Why doesn't she look beat up? Why doesn't the emotional torture show physically? Off the record Winger co-workers will tell you what she puts herself through on a set. The *I-can't live-through-this* torture one associates with a wunderkind composer—and the question becomes: Why doesn't the torture show physically?

"Some roles use your sexual energy, and some passion inside of you. You know what happens when you fall in love? You change. It's a life force that comes up in you." And it's temperament, too; that's been there in every female movie star from Bette Davis to Betty Hutton. Davis said Winger was the one actress with enough temperament to inherit her mantle. "When you work with nice," as Jim Brooks puts it, "what you get is nice. When you work with fire, you get smoke on the screen."

To be clear, Winger does not storm off movie sets like scenes from cliché Hollywood movies. She is more apt to be overbearing—not in a star-ego sense but in terms of the work. On *Urban Cowboy* she stayed up all night before the cemetery scene, then got Jim Bridges to stay up all the next night to rewrite it. ("I thought I was going to go insane," Bridges said at the time.) For *Cannery Row* she moved into her trailer on the MGM lot, and went all-night bowling and carousing in Culver City with (co-star) Nick Nolte. For the noir-cult film *Mike's Murder,* she moved into the Westwood Marquis to get the sense of the simple Brentwood girl who falls in love. (To prepare for a crying scene she listened to tapes of her mother talking.)

Winger's cabin in New Mexico was her hideaway mostly before her marriage. One doesn't sense she's very rural; the mind is always working. "But for an actor to be good, you have to get your stuff, you know. You have to refill the well. It's not a bottomless pit. I think you can name the actors who probably thought it was." Words like "revitalize," "nurture," and "fed" come up. "I spent a lot of years trashing myself when I worked, then recovering when I didn't. I can't do that anymore."

Winger curled her finger like a schoolteacher who's caught you telling a fib. "Your mistake," she said lightly, "was you thought I took care of myself when I worked, and trashed myself the rest of the time. The truth," she added, laughing hoarsely, "is that I've learned how to trash myself when I'm not working. I've learned how to do it in my time off. By trashing, by the way, I mean emotional badgering of myself—not physical."

Good ole girl or good ole boy? Winger more than any actress of her generation is compared to men—to actors like Robert De Niro and Jack Nicholson. (Nicholson has said, "She's a lot like me.") She says the comparison to male stars "helps me . . . it makes me feel more coura-geous. The female stuff I got genetically, right? So I like having a little macho in there."

Or is it intensity? Winger tucked her legs under herself, and responded: "We're talking about intensity, yes. Women often shy away from intensity. What actresses—as great as you think they are—how many of them would you call intense? Not very many. Intensity means present tense, full of life. Human development doesn't care about gender."

One of the girls who's one of the boys. There are those who would have predicted the burnout of Debra Winger by now. Possibly in a James Dean sort of way. As Jim Brooks put it, "There's no second gear with Debra. She goes all out."

"It's the chance you take," Winger answered about burning out. "Henry Miller trashed himself every day until he was eighty-five. He said we wake up daily, only to slaughter our best instincts. Me, I would die before I burned out. See, to me, intensity is the opposite of burnout —I get ignited . . . It's not like fizzling out. Physical trashing will burn you out. But I'm talking about sticking it to yourself. Am I being honest here?

"Sometimes I worry that in this media age we just talk at each other, meaninglessly. People aren't listening—they're just thinking of the next thing to say. It's a *National Enquirer* mentality where we talk about a woman who ate a dog to survive. We have become a lot about garbage and fiction."

Hollywood money is something Winger was forced to understand early. To play in the club you have to understand money. "You have to know something about business. Otherwise a studio will make you think they're doing everything for you. And you find out they've sold your film down the river. So you have to know enough to find out if they're lying."

You have to pay attention. "Yeah. I have to earn it a little bit, at this point. When your life becomes somewhat privileged, you have to earn it. You also have to be brave." But how did Wonder Woman's little sister make the leap to playing Travolta's love interest? Wasn't she frightened ever? "I don't believe in fear that way. You don't go out and have an affair in order to have the guts to leave your wife. So I didn't go out and find out if I could have a film career before I quit TV— I just quit. It didn't work for me. I couldn't do it. I wasn't going to secure something because I'm not that kind of person. You just go out into the void."

Because there's so much money involved, no star today can afford to be dumb about studio politics or producer's policies or power in general.

"I think if I ever lost my soul," Winger said cavalierly, "I'd go to work for a studio. I could do it pretty good. Not to say that every studio executive is soulless by any means . . . but having a soul is not a prerequisite for the job."

Why does Winger say no so much? "One wrong movie—it's amazing the mileage the bad taste leaves in your mouth. You know how long it stays there?" Her look says forever. "So it's better not to work than it is to get squashed. Because that takes a chunk out of you that takes a long time to repair."

She continued: "It takes a long time to recover from *An Officer and a Gentleman*. I don't know how to say that and be political about it, or diplomatic. Yes, I was nominated [for an Academy Award, as she was for *Terms*]. I was thankful. But I'm embarrassed about it. I'm physically wounded from it. That doesn't mean I'm afraid to work with directors I don't know, by the way. It's not like I'm afraid to go into unknown situations. Unknown is fine—but if I already sense something bad . . . One rule of this business is that it doesn't get better—it gets worse. It festers."

Where did she learn so much? "From being on movie sets. Everything's so peak when you are working. You are probably more receptive then than with any other learning experience; all the nerve endings are alive, everything. So whatever information goes in stays in. And hopefully you get that way about other things that you need to learn in your life. I'm talking about your spiritual development—your way to work through life.'

Maybe Winger was best understood by Ray Bellamy, her location driver in Nebraska on *Terms of Endearment*. Said the driver: "She's a nice girl who's very ambitious."

In the club that takes you the distance.

CLUB RULE TWENTY-SEVEN

You have to be a sucker for real talent. You have to grovel, if necessary, or pay exorbitantly one way or the other. You have to put up with the Debra Wingers of this world.

When club director Jim Bridges first saw Winger's screen test, for *Urban Cowboy*, he realized what she had. And he made her a star. This kind of unconditional, asexual love affair happens all the time in the club. (Liza Minnelli and Fred Ebb. Whitney Houston and Clive Davis.) And not just because an artist can make money for a businessman. The fact is, club members have the best eyes and ears. When David Geffen first heard a tape of Laura Nyro singing, before she was anybody, he cried for a weekend.

Time Warner chairman Steve Ross is as vulnerable to Barbra Streisand as he is to his children. Edie and Lew Wasserman are as worshipful toward Gene Kelly as if he were family. It was Gene Kelly who taught Edie and Lew Wasserman how to relax—and to survive.

STATUS

Club status is conferred largely on rituals. Ma Maison in its heyday had status, as did the Robert Evans tennis court. (The new Ma Maison lacks status because going there isn't a ritual—the time of Ma Maison is long past.) The Evans court still has status, in spite of Evans' hard luck, because it's the best East-West court in town. The Beverly Hills Hotel retains club status, in spite of new arrivals, because it's legendary and old and has a dowager quality. And the club lacks for dowagers these days. Liz Smith and Barbara Walters aren't dowagers, or rituals—rather they are club archetypes. The Gossip Columnist and the Insider. (In another era, Walter Winchell played both roles.)

But as the leg got more comfortable in the community, he began to wonder how did club members unwind?

Hollywood was still a semblance of a swinging town when I decided to write about the outer boroughs—Malibu, Palm Springs, and Santa Barbara. The dazed romantic sense of these communities—the promise—somehow always added up to a complete fantasy life: the house in town, the house at the beach, the place in the desert. Again I felt *you have to go into the houses*. So up and down the coast I went, looking up and in, finding big welcomes. And making discoveries.

Gradually I could give my own tour of the houses, I knew them so well. I knew which beach house was Jackie Bisset's, with Michael Sarrazin; which one Rex Reed rented the summer he was the most sought-after journalist in Hollywood. Rex's avocado rental was an upside-down two-story converted railroad car. I knew the Doris Day house had been remodeled by David Geffen, who had lived there since 1973. I discovered many things about people in my explorations of their houses.

I discovered the truly monstrous women in Hollywood are the stars' wives. Don't tangle with them. They never forget anything ever. And then they ghostwrite their husband's autobiographies, and get even with everyone their husbands slept with, or got rejected by. They are the Greek chorus that speaks the truth—because they are protected by layers of club agents, attorneys, managers, business managers, maids, masseurs, manicurists, dress designers, and so on. You know who I'm talking about. Or if you don't, here's an example: I called Robert Mitchum one day in Santa Barbara, and he picked up the phone himself. "I want to do a story on how the club really gets away, unwinds, and why Santa Barbara is where they go," I told him. "Mike Nichols, Ray Stark, Mel Ferrer . . . and since you live there, I thought—"

"Sure," said Mitchum, who had no clue if I was or wasn't legitimate. "When do you want to come by for a drink?"

He didn't ask who else I was talking to, he didn't ask if we could do it on the phone, he didn't refuse to be photographed, he didn't state ground rules. So Mitchum became my star centerpiece, and I headed to Santa Barbara confidently. After an interlude in Ojai, I called Mitchum, and this time his wife, Dorothy, answered.

"He isn't here. He doesn't want to talk . . . You can't come here."

Then would he meet me for a drink?

"No, he won't meet you for a drink. Call the agent in Hollywood."

The agent in Hollywood, a woman named Nicole David, is a woman who's so cheery her trademark blouse is a short-sleeved Peter Pan number with red cherries on it . . . I like her a lot, but that day she wouldn't take my call. So—no Mitchum. Dorothy Mitchum's rejection gave me pause enough to forget about exploring Santa Barbara any further.

Instead I headed one Christmas week for the pool at the Racquet Club in Palm Springs. Club cosmetic surgeon Dr. Harry Glassman and I had once decided it would be remembered as one of the few icon places in club mythology—that wonderful little poolside bar at the Racquet Club. The place where Marilyn Monroe got discovered for the first time.

19

Club Getaways

Palm Springs was the first club getaway, founded because Ralph Bellamy and Charlie Farrell wanted to get away somewhere warm where there were no Jews. Palm Springs was also the club getaway best equipped for getting discovered: Marilyn Monroe played starlet by the pool at the Racquet Club, and got her first studio contract. Santa Barbara was the most private club getaway, mostly because it had the biggest ranches. Santa Ynez was the spin-off of Santa Barbara that became the club getaway in the '80s when Ray Stark and Mike Nichols established thoroughbred horse ranches there. From the '40s on, Laguna was the gay getaway (male) and Santa Fe was the gay getaway (female). Aspen is the club's Christmas getaway, unless you go to the Kahala Hilton on Oahu. Connecticut is the East Coast club getaway with the most prestige: Mike Nichols and Ron Howard and Jay Presson Allen hide away there, but it's Dustin Hoffman who has the killer club getaway house, in Roxbury.

One day I arrived at the pool of the Racquet Club and ran into the longtime semiresident novelist Sidney Sheldon, who told me about the time producer Sam Spiegel was working the pool. It was the afternoon of a New Year's Eve, almost 1958, and around the pool sat half a dozen of the world's highest-paid celebrities. Spencer Tracy, who loved the desert and occasionally stayed at the Kirk Douglas house on Via Lola (next door to the Sheldons) was around—and so were names like Niven and Huston and Oberon. And around three in the afternoon, the Oscar-winning producer Spiegel—host of the club's starriest yacht trips in the '50s— began working the pool. Within an hour, Spiegel had collected twenty people for a New Year's Eve supper.

"But Mr. Spiegel!" worried Fred, the Racquet Club maître d'. "We are totally booked. I have a table for two for you, but that's the best I can do . . ."

Sam Spiegel shouldn't be underestimated. That night, by himself, he simply began working a new turf—the Racquet Club dining room. Some of the names had changed: Fairbanks Jr., Capote, Slim and Leland Hayward. But the star wattage remained the same. "And Sam managed to connect, willy-nilly, all these tables for two," Sidney Sheldon recalled. "That's what the desert was like in those days. Everyone from Garbo to Dali seemed to be there, to belong."

Belong to what? To the other Hollywood, that cluster of communities (Palm Springs, Palm Desert, Rancho Mirage, Cathedral City) known as the desert. This second Hollywood may also be the most idealized small town in America. It's where people who got themselves discovered as stars go to rediscover themselves as people—and just live simply. (Well, sort of.) It's where Frank Sinatra cooks pasta with what Robert Wagner calls "the ease of a chef." It's where Marlon Brando is spotted in a jeep, fiddling with a CB radio and wearing a bandanna headband. It's where Joel McCrea could be seen carrying his own luggage (and that of his wife, Frances Dee) to his rustic room at the secluded Two Bunch Palms, looking every inch a star.

It's where TV stardom means almost nothing, and youth even less: When Donna Mills, the tough blonde cookie of *Knots Landing*, went to unwind at Ingleside Inn, almost nobody around the hotel's pool knew who she was. ("She's so young looking for forty-nine," one woman from Akron remarked at poolside.) It's where Al Capone came in 1929 when the Miami Beach police gave him twenty-four hours to get out of town. It's also where Mia Farrow got so lost in the wilds of Hermits Canyon that it took a search party—led by Ruth Gordon and Garson Kanin— four hours to find her.

"Palm Springs is like a small town at the turn of the century," explained R. J. (Robert) Wagner, who's been a self-styled "desert rat" since his teens. "There are enough famous people in the desert that it's no longer about being famous." Added Ann (Mrs. Kirk) Douglas: "Here stars are no longer stars. The differences fade. When Claudette Colbert would come to paint watercolors, and I would go to visit her, I would sit in the room and feel no difference between us. Obviously, I know there is a difference. But the desert is about simplicity."

Even if the simplicity is expensive—and theatrical. Stars may not be stars here—but still there are more entourages than in Hollywood, nearly as many private screening rooms, though not quite as many distractions. "The appeal is that there are very few choices, or decisions," explained the late entertainment attorney Joe Peckerman (his clients included Mel Gibson and novelist William Kennedy). "There are no true snob restaurants, no race tracks or casinos, and no places to spend big money. And that appeals to the rich."

"And yet there's this ironic contrast," reminded writer-director Joel Schumacher (*Flatliners*). "The fact that Palm Springs is built on an Indian burial ground isn't lost on the natives. There's definitely this sense of destiny, or mortality, that pulls all these people here. Five minutes from the most lavish estates anywhere are odd mobile homes and homesteaders living on the edge. When you first see Palm Springs, it seems mystic, magical, exotic, sultry . . . but it's a strange oasis."

And it isn't understood all at once. In the mid-'50s, Kirk Douglas, between pictures, packed up his new wife, European publicist Ann Buydens, and their young son, Peter. "He told us we were going to the desert," recalled Ann Douglas, now a kind of den mother of social Palm Springs. (Her houseguests span Robert Kennedy, who left the Douglases a bust of himself, and Henry Kissinger, who comes regularly every other winter.) "In the movies, when you hear the word 'desert,' you think of the Sahara. Then you fly over Palm Springs, and you see all those patches of blue and green, which are swimming pools." (Note: There is one private pool for every four desert residents, and about 400 private tennis courts and there are only 85,000 residents).

And future den mother Douglas was captivated from the first: "Within two hours of arriving, Kirk and I rented bicycles, and we've never left . . . For twenty years, I didn't have a single dress in the closet here, only slacks. But now, of course, on Christmas Eve you go to the house of Marvin Davis, and they have snow brought in from the studio." Ann Douglas sniffed ever so slightly. "So you get dressed up. Yes, the desert changed but, no, not that much. So now I keep one dress in the desert. So?"

Ann Douglas, petite and kind of all-over beige from the sun, is like a lot of desert regulars: She doesn't waste words, or time. Her desert days are as regimented as an army sergeant's: up at sunrise, tennis early, lunch with houseguests, a nap, bicycling, a 7 P.M. movie, dinner out, and maybe an ice cream cone. It's a desert way of life, but not the only one. "You see a place from different angles," she said knowingly. "It just depends on who shows them to you."

That a former President (be it Ford or Ike, who also loved Palm Springs) can mill around a shopping center almost undisturbed says much about the Palm Springs pattern. In Los Angeles Kirk Douglas would not be caught dead waiting for a table at the popular Billy Reed's club. But he does it in the desert. It's very clear here that pulling rank (or ego) just for the sake of it is silly.

Bette Midler talks about a "physical release" that happens on the drive to the desert. She does a lot of time at the 600-calorie-a-day Palms. "I feel the tension leaving my jaw around Colton," said Helen Rose, the MGM Golden Era costume designer who was a confirmed desert dweller for a dozen years. "From then on, I just let go. It's kind of like the Whitman poem 'Snowbound.' I feel I don't have to do anything I don't want to do. Ever."

"It's not the fast lane," reminded veteran producer Hal Wallis (*Becket, Dark Victory*), standing in a portico of the adobe house he shared with wife Martha Hyer that faces the Rancho Mirage home of Barbara and Frank Sinatra. Wallis had been coming to the desert since the '30s, when he headed production for Warner Brothers. Though Wallis wouldn't deny the oft-told tale of Jack Warner buying movie rights to *My Fair Lady* (for a then-record $5.5 million) from Irving Lazar in the sauna of the Spa Hotel, he pooh-poohs the notion of Hollywood business dominating Palm Springs.

"But I'll tell you something illogical," said Wallis. "Over the years I've maybe gotten more done in the desert—more reading of scripts and books, and more concentrated work—than I have in town. When we did the Elvis Presley pictures, for example, Presley and I and [Presley manager] Colonel [Tom] Parker would meet here at the house and think out the movies. Now, even though I keep an office in town, I find I spend more time here. I play golf three times a week. I'm very active."

"Time stretches in the desert," said TV producer Michelle Rappaport, whose series *Paper Dolls* was concocted during a brainstorming Palm Springs weekend with friends sharing a rented condominium. Rappaport, though, is as apt to be playing Scrabble as she is to be coming up with TV ideas—or doing any business at all. "Don't tell my accountant that," she deadpanned, "but as an example, let's take one Thanksgiving weekend. I got down here, I got to Jurgensen's, I got the turkey, I got the keys to the condo, I got my friends together, and we never left all weekend. We watched eight hours of *The Honeymooners*, and it was the best TV

I've seen in years. Also, I won $75 at gin rummy, and while that might not sound like much, at three cents a point, it's a lot."

"Let's get it straight," corrected ICM agent Michael Black (clients: Jamie Lee Curtis, Liza Minnelli, among others). "Michelle lost $75, to me. Not vice versa. The point is, we weren't there to be sociable or to do business. The hardest work we did was to barbecue in our bathrobes. Frankly, I go to the desert to get tan. I spend an hour putting the oil on . . . I mean, catch me at fifty—you may just find me in the desert, looking like an old Bass Weejun."

The unwinding, for those who in town overwork or overworry, would seem to be in the area of mental relaxation. It's simple pleasures versus sybaritic (à la Las Vegas) ones.

The creativity is the real appeal for some desert fanatics: In spite of the jokes about Palm Springs being "God's waiting room" and in spite of the reputation for the early retirement of its citizenry, facts are facts. The following pieces of work were actually completed—not dreamed up, not fantasized about—but completed in the desert:

Mario Puzo's first draft of *The Godfather,* Neil Simon's screenplay of *The Sunshine Boys,* much of composer Frederick Loewe's score for *Camelot,* all of the Leslie Bricusse score for *Dr. Dolittle,* the first jazz album of Barry Manilow, the three published (in *Esquire*) chapters from Truman Capote's *Answered Prayers,* the last three chapters of Steve Shagan's novel *City of Angels,* the location work on Frank Capra's original *Lost Horizon,* and the autobiographies of President Gerald Ford and wife Betty, among other things. Palm Springs is also where Henry Kissinger came to organize the notes that made up his first volume of memoirs, and it's where fledgling (and not so fledgling) screenwriters come to find their elusive muses. Usually at the secluded La Siesta Villas.

Victoria Principal, who finished her first exercise book at her Palm Springs condominium, was discovered one recent afternoon on her way to a favorite delicatessen, where she permits herself one chocolate chip cookie per weekend. "Recovering from something, anything, I always by rote brought myself down here. I've been doing that for twenty years now. How fancy my lodgings were depended on the state of my career. But I always know that ten days by myself here will mean I'll review my life, and I'll bounce back. If I get lonely, I call my friends, and they come down."

(Principal's first time in California, in fact, was a New Year's Eve in Palm Springs, just three days before her twenty-first birthday. "Somehow I had come for a party, yet I remember knowing literally nobody in California. I wound up going to several parties that night. And I remember being intimidated by the sophistication, the fame . . . and yet the people who were the most famous were the most thoughtful and gentle. And these people reflected a certain serenity and knowingness I envied. And that night I saw a reason for me to stay in California. I was eager, and naive, but no longer scared. I only envied their sense of belonging. And I wanted to belong too.")

The businessmen are here, too, of course. "It's a swell place to continue the week's business," says William Morris agent Norman Brokaw, who represents his Rancho Mirage neighbors President and Mrs. Ford, as well as Bill Cosby and Loretta Young. Brokaw's condominium complex now also houses some of his William Morris colleagues. (One can spot them on a Sunday morning, strolling down Palm Canyon Drive.) "I've been coming for so many years," said Brokaw enthusiastically, "but when I began to know the Fords, I came more often. Not that I haven't always loved it down here. I mean, after all, Johnny Hyde was my cousin!"

The late agent Johnny Hyde was also the man who discovered (or rediscovered) Marilyn Monroe in 1948, after she'd been dropped as a starlet by 20th Century-Fox. The setting was the Racquet Club pool, the occasion a sitting of photographs for the famed Bernard of Hollywood. Monroe's discovery by Hyde became mythic for one reason: It implied to the community that Palm Springs was where one could be discovered (for any number of things, but mostly for stardom). Yet aside from Monroe, almost no other examples of star discoveries exist.

"My career was, let us say, helped by the people I met at the Racquet Club," acknowledged Robert Wagner, who lived here for a time on Crestview Drive, with Natalie Wood. "I met the world in the bar at the Racquet Club, meaning I met the Zanucks and the Goldwyns and Cary Grant and everyone. The most vivid memory is of the way the men's jackets hung, and how well the slacks were tailored. I'm not talking about labels, I'm talking about style. I mean, I would see Greta Garbo window-shopping. I was a very young, very aspiring actor, and I think what Palm Springs gave me was a glimpse of belonging. It was a very generous time."

Belonging, certainly, but what about doing business? "More business is probably done now than in the old days," argued Hal Wallis. Countered attorney Peckerman: "The action is not why people come. If business gets done, it's just happenstance. As it would be anywhere. There is not the smell of negotiation one finds in town."

To illustrate: Peckerman spent a long weekend around the grotto of a pool at Two Bunch Palms with maybe half a dozen attorneys (coincidentally) present. (Also present that day: Fox chairman Barry Diller, Lauren Hutton, screenwriter Tom Hedley, and Peckerman's law partner, Barry Haldeman.) "I thought Haldeman and I would talk business, right? Well, we never talked business all weekend. And the other lawyers from other law firms just happened to be there . . . but none of them were talking shop either. Does it hurt business to be in Palm Springs? No. But is that why you go down there? No. It's not why this generation goes, anyway."

Successful Hollywood people in their thirties are not going to Palm Springs to make contacts, keep up appearances, or climb a mythical social ladder. Without exception, the younger desert devotees all have the same reason for going: to simply relax. Maybe get stoned. Hopefully unwind. From talking with agents, attorneys, actors, and others, a kind of *Big Chill* image emerged. It's a world where club singles can revel in the loose camaraderie. And get very stoned for a long weekend. As for the younger, more energized born-to-run crowd, they do a kind of nightly mating dance.

But, is the desert sexy? "Well, let's put it this way," says Victoria Principal: "I wouldn't advise going to the desert with somebody you don't like."

Adds den mother Douglas: "I don't think you meet somebody here, but I think if you invite somebody for the weekend . . . it is most likely a success."

Adds Joel Schumacher: "Hot winds, that onyx sky, suntans, and aromatic nights . . . I do think some people find each other here. Whether they find each other for a lifetime? That I don't know."

"People who are married to other people," explained one wizened desert watcher, "plan secretly to meet in Palm Springs. They drive down separately, stay secluded, and why not?"

It's not always so complicated, of course. Yes, Howard Hughes and Ava Gardner did check into the Ingleside Inn using the pseudonyms "Earl Martyn and Mrs. Clark," but that was the '40s. Yes, John Gilbert did build a hideaway house here for Garbo, but that was a long time ago. And, yes, Clark Gable and Carole Lombard did honeymoon at the Ingleside Inn, but that was no secret. Palm Springs may be more Hollywood than Hollywood itself.

Example: "The H is still on the wrought-iron gate of the house Barbara Hutton built for Cary Grant," remembered Bob Wagner, somewhat of a desert historian (he's been going since adolescence). "The bars are still on Elvis' windows. On the street where we lived, when I was married to Marion [Wagner's second wife, also formerly the wife of director Stanley Donen], also lived at one time or another Rudolf Valentino, King Gillette, and Zane Grey." Added Wagner: "Do people know that Salvador Dali visited Palm Springs, and loved it?"

Would people care? Yes and no. There is a curious laissez-faire attitude about almost everything that goes on in the desert. Tell natives that Al

Capone headquartered in a stone cottage at Two Bunch Palms in Desert Hot Springs for years, and the response is still a shrug. Tell people how Debbie Reynolds planned her own fiftieth birthday party at the Ingleside, only later to discover that Eddie Fisher tried to book a room for the same weekend, and the response is minimal.

More importantly, tell people about anti-Semitism in Palm Springs in the '30s and '40s and nobody denies it, or much seems to care. "Right here at my hotel," said Ingleside Inn's current owner Mel Haber, "I discovered a dossier on every guest, with labels like 'J' (for Jewish) next to the name Goldwyn."

It's a nice bit of irony that Haber is Jewish, from New York, and a former manufacturer of angora dice. He bought the place when it was ramshackle, and returned it to former glory. (Frank and Barbara Sinatra had their prewedding dinner here.) "Frank can come and stand at the bar and never be bothered," boasted Haber, making a point about Palm Springs. "Nobody wants to look like a tourist here, so nobody gawks."

Of course, nowhere else in the world would a best-selling author (Truman Capote) set up his maid in the catering business, only to find that the experiment worked. "Food is important here," said den mother Douglas. "Fritz [Frederick] Loewe always had the best chefs . . . and when Moss Hart lived here, he and [wife] Kitty Carlisle entertained lavishly. Every night they dressed for dinner."

As years went by, the gala charity parties at $25,000 a couple really weren't mythical—they became very real. And the sensation of waking up rich is also no fable. "Go out to Palm Desert," suggested Bob Hope. "There's so much loot there they could give Texas food stamps!" Yet Hope denies any responsibility for the moneyed influx: "I don't really sell Palm Springs to people. Some years ago at the White House, I remember I started to talk up the desert, and Nancy looked at me and said, 'Don't! We've already got enough people!' "

After a week I had desert fever—I was ready for the beach. For Malibu. Sometimes-manager Jeff Wald, who's flamboyant, told me that he and Jerry Weintraub, who's also flamboyant, took daily horseback rides together along Old Malibu Road. This I had to see. Wald and Weintraub in tandem on horseback—that would be a real moment. At five minutes before noon one Tuesday, Jerry Weintraub arrived at the back door of the Wald house—on horseback. Exactly as planned. I watched from the house next door, with binoculars.

Wald's back door happens to strategically face the Pacific: In 1985, he paid Robert Redford an even $2 million for the former Bing Crosby house. Weintraub (who rides a Tennessee walker) and Wald (who prefers a thoroughbred buckskin) are unlikely nature boys. (Producer Weintraub [*The Karate Kid*] also managed and promoted the concerts and careers of Frank Sinatra, Neil Diamond, and John Denver, among others, and is a major fund-raiser for Republican causes—even though his Weintraub Entertainment Group went bankrupt. Wald, a Democratic money-raiser, promoted then-wife Helen Reddy into a star in the '70s, and has "calmed down" at Malibu after a much publicized battle with cocaine.)

Now Weintraub was "parking" his horse at Wald's TV satellite dish; the newly converted equestrians were trotting over for lunch at La Scala Malibu. Were they talking business? No, that's not done here. "This isn't Deal Beach," explains Wald dryly, "and there are no telephones on a horse."

Elsewhere in Malibu, they get off their horses and walk like everybody else. Sort of. It's only a half mile wide and twenty-seven miles long, but maybe nowhere in the world is there such a concentration of wealth and stardom. "The industry lives here," says Dyan Cannon. Residents range from rock megastars (Bob Dylan, Joni Mitchell, Mick Fleetwood) to TV stalwarts (Johnny Carson, Dinah Shore) to movie legends (Jennifer Jones, Steven Spielberg, Barbra Streisand). They're packed sometimes like olives into hundreds of houses spread through five beaches and six canyons. And most of them are role playing like nobody's business. Do you want to be in a movie? Come to Malibu in July. It's like a real-life movie—cast with more all-stars than there are in heaven and hell. Or at least in Hollywood.

Imagine Larry Hagman arriving seaside for a lunch with Carroll O'Connor, the two of them arriving at Beau Rivage in twin Rolls-Royces. Imagine seeing Hagman in a caftan on his weekly day of silence, a tradition he's honored since arriving at Malibu in the early '60s. Imagine Ali MacGraw riding a Styrofoam surfboard on the edge of Trancas Beach, landing smack in front of her startled agent and friend, Sue Mengers. (Recalls MacGraw, "Poor Sue thought I was a beach bimbo!") Imagine Ned Beatty being mistaken for a box boy at the Market Basket—and good-naturedly going along with the mistaken identity. Now, whenever he's in the grocery, Beatty takes out the bags for friends and favored shoppers. Imagine several Sinatras strolling Trancas Beach on the fifth of July with Eydie Gormé and Steve Lawrence, and being undisturbed. Or Cheech (of Cheech and Chong) removing all the "Public Access" signs from the street where he lives, with grinning highway patrolmen looking on. Or Pia Zadora stopping Tony Curtis on Pacific Coast Highway to ask him the exact color of his Mercedes. ("Lapis," said Curtis.)

At Malibu, if you look and listen, you will see and hear the most colorful locals in the club. You need only tunnel vision and a map:

Focus primarily on three beaches—Carbón, Malibu Colony, and Broad Beach—and prick up your ears. They will tell you how two of Colette's boudoirs have been transplanted from France piece by piece to the Irving Thalbergs' Normandy castle that sits (for sale) behind the local Hughes market. They will tell you how Johnny Carson became involved with his much publicized fourth wife, Alex Maas, just because she donned a bikini, strolled by—and got invited in. (In other words, Malibu is wide open, if only one is ready.)

They will tell you mostly about houses. About how Barbra Streisand's compound in Ramírez Canyon is really this generation's San Simeon, replete with a pink-and-green Art Deco house that has never been slept in. They will tell you how Burt Reynolds became so enamored of Malibu that he impulsively bought Freddie Fields' beach house after a Sunday brunch and a quick look-see, without even checking out the upstairs.

They will tell you how the late Merle Oberon's house had the finest antique furniture in Southern California—and how a dying Oberon was paid regular convalescent calls by a babushka-wearing Nancy Reagan. Or, a thousand years ago, how the late Gloria Swanson posed in a bathing suit at Malibu, thus inventing cheesecake. It's no wonder Frank Lloyd Wright built his last, and most personal dream house here, in the hills. Where better for dreams to come true?

"There's a sense of acknowledged anonymity," explains Mrs. William Wyler, widow of the Oscar-winning club director (*Best Years of Our Lives*). Talli Wyler summered at Malibu Colony from 1949 until her death in 1990—and Talli knew. As Ali MacGraw, a fifteen-year resident, elaborated: "Nobody expects to see Neil Diamond on the public beach, so when he goes there, which he does with his son, he's not bothered. It's part of Malibu etiquette to acknowledge but also to ignore celebrities. And with residents like Neil and Dylan and Streisand—do you think any of the rest of us are bothered?"

Still at Carbón Beach (renamed Deal Beach years ago by producer Larry Gordon), and at almost any other beach, business is being done, consciously or inconspicuously. And ideas are born. In 1963, the Broadway musical *Mame* was conceived by playwrights Jerome Lawrence and Robert E. Lee over eggs Benedict at the late, lamented Santa Ynez Inn. In 1964, the rock group Crosby, Stills, Nash & Young was a midnight inspiration from David Geffen on the Colony deck of his partner, Elliott Roberts.

Not only is business done, but news of it travels fastest here. The word about Larry Gordon's 1984 appointment as president of production at 20th Century-Fox hit the beach a full week before it hit the streets of Hollywood. Joe Wizan, the outgoing president, was spotted early one morning walking his dog on Old Malibu Road. (A rival executive confides: "Joe had a big smile on his face. Whether he was walking toward Larry Gordon's house I don't know . . .")

"It's really *Gilligan's Island*," sums up Tom Hedley, after the success of *Flashdance* one of the industry's hotter screenwriters, who became a converted Malibuite before moving to Ojai up the coast. Hedley likes to apply a writer's slightly tragic edge. Late one Fourth of July, he surveyed Latigo Cove and explained: "Malibu is best understood by knowing the old has-been actor joke. A studio executive asks, 'Whatever happened to that guy?' And the answer, almost always, is, 'Oh, he's out at the beach . . .' And when they say 'out at the beach,' they don't mean it kindly. It's a form of dismissal." Surveying the fireworks from a prime spot on the deck of a friend, Hedley pointed skyward. "My favorite metaphor for Malibu," he says slowly, "is the airplane flying across the ocean. The planes flying in bring all the new talent. And the planes flying out cart away all the old talent."

"Do you think Malibu is swinging?" asks novelist Mickey Ziffren (*A Political Affair*). "I think Malibu is tranquil . . . I think the Valley is swinging." Ziffren reacts with the appropriate I-told-you-so look, then takes the umbrella table outdoors. "We're really creatures of unreality here. Then whammo! Malibu gets hit with storms or fires or gales and we're faced with reality, harshly. And like creatures in shock, we come together as a community. Suddenly descending from the hills are these remarkable residents with sandbags and sincerity and grit. And we get through the disasters, the closings of the roads and so on, precisely for that reason: Because this is a community."

It's a community of rituals and myths, spoken and unspoken. First in order is privacy. Nothing on the beach matters more. "True Malibu," says Jay Allen, the man who invented book publicity on the West Coast, "operates with hand signals." The game works this way: You spot an acquaintance on the beach. You can wave, as an acknowledgment. Or you can wave the person up to your deck, by cupping your hand. Or if the person is someone you don't want to see—you simply don't see them. As Jeff Wald puts it: "I've been [personal manager] Elliott Roberts' friend since grade school. Now he lives right up the beach. But I wouldn't dream of walking up to his house unannounced."

Similarly, it's "kamikaze," to stop a club executive on the beach only to discuss business. "The executive may never forget you did that," says David Geffen. "And for a very good reason. People are here to unload their protective armor. One learns to spot a business encounter on the beach twenty miles away." How? "The little hairs on the executive's back curl up."

If you have the *From Here to Eternity* fantasy—Deborah Kerr and Burt Lancaster lustily embracing on the beach—expect disappointment. Malibu is not a romantic playground. Yes, Ryan O'Neal lived for more than a decade on Malibu Beach, with all his pre-Farrah romances— Anouk Aimée, Barbra Streisand, Ursula Andress, etc. But hardly a one got *launched* at Malibu. "Well, is flotsam sexy?" wonders one O'Neal-watcher. "The sand may be hot but the atmosphere isn't. Movie people find their romances on movie sets, where there's more intensity." Malibu's movie couples—including in the '70s Jacqueline Bisset and Michael Sarrazin and in the '80s Rachel Ward and Bryan Brown—did indeed find each other setside, not seaside. "Two famous directors who live down the road are living very much alone," Dyan Cannon observes. "I don't think the beach is about love-in-bloom."

Jane Morgan Weintraub was standing on the farthermost point of a bluff at Paradise Cove on the fifth of July, describing her own dream of Malibu: "I always wanted a blue stucco house facing the blue sea, with a blue sky above. That's why we've called our house Blue Heaven." House isn't quite the right term for Blue Heaven—"Malibu's grandest estate" might be more to the point. Replete with stables and stable boys, a tennis court, an Olympic-size swimming pool, a screening room, and ten zillion manicured acres. Blue Heaven has not gone bankrupt. Blue Heaven awaits visitors—and maybe even buyers atop the best (and last available) land at Paradise Cove. "My husband is like eighteen dynamos," understates the former recording star ("Fascination"), "and I wanted a retreat for him. A house complete unto itself. This spot when I first stood on it, grabbed me. It faces south, so it's always balmy. Anyway, I bought the land three years ago, and we moved in with a crib and two beds and a baby nurse and Abbey Rents furniture and ourselves . . ."

Blue Heaven would seem to be built on stronger foundations than mere luck. It's a kind of hybrid mix of Cape Cod, the Deep South, and Old Hollywood. If Malibu's social life is in minor disrepute, the Weintraubs haven't heard about it. Charity galas go on into the night here, and so do children's birthday parties (the Weintraubs between them have several children, and extravagant theme parties are the norm). The kids' galas are like nothing since the '40s extravaganzas given for Hollywood children like Candy Bergen and Liza Minnelli, where clowns were really movie stars.

The adult galas, especially the one for President and Mrs. Bush in 1991, are as stuffy as it gets. The "A" turnout for the Weintraubs— in spite of his business flopping—proves that upward failure exists in Hollywood—still.

"Frankly," says Jane Morgan Weintraub, "my husband doesn't really slow down, ever. But here is where he almost slows down."

We were now upstairs, and she was beaming. "This is where I cook for him late at night," she said, pointing to a miniature kitchen just off the master bedroom of the beach house.

"We love our neuroses," I shot back. Suddenly the only thing I could remember about Jane Morgan was Rex Reed's line, about her singing, in the late '60s: "The only way to stop Jane Morgan is to drive a stake through her heart."

But here she was in her bedroom, in a pair of camel slacks and matching cashmere crew neck, looking very loved. Rex was wrong, I thought, about Jane's heart. I mean the woman is in her sixties and mothering a trio of adopted Vietnamese daughters. And maintaining a marriage to Jerry Weintraub. (The producer calls himself "President Bush's best friend," and is also the club's screamer emeritus.)

"Having the kitchen here, it's like—it's like Vegas!" she said, lighting up like the "Hallelujah Hollywood" marquee at the old MGM Grand. "Yeah, it's just like Vegas," she murmured. "I mean . . . Vegas during Elvis. I cooked for Jerry every night in Vegas in those days." She sounded like she missed it. "The Dunes even put in a private kitchen in the bungalow, and a tennis court, so Jerry could play. After late suppers. That was 1962," she said and paused. "Christ, we had fun."

CLUB RULE TWENTY-EIGHT

You must know how to relax in style. Exhausted workophiles bore the club. You must have "another life out at the beach," as Ray Stark puts it—or in the desert.

The club getaways are real getaways. Otherwise they're bogus, and don't last. Club novelist Sidney Sheldon and his late wife, Jorga, lived next door to Ann and Kirk Douglas in Palm Springs for a thousand years, down the street from Don the Beachcomber on Via Lola. The Sheldons got so unwound in Palm Springs they would often sunbathe nude—until one day when they got trapped outside the walled gate of their single-story lemon-and-ivory house. In 115-degree heat. And Ann and Kirk were back in town, in L.A. And the Sheldons didn't even have a towel between them. So Jorga had to walk for fifteen minutes before she found a cop. And they lived to tell, and laugh, about it. And dine out on it, for years.

If you think Sidney Sheldon could have done that at home in Holmby Hills—you don't understand the club. The point is, club members really do let loose—when they feel safe. Check out Gstaad some January when Julie Andrews sings torch songs at the bar of Chalet Marz. She's as naked as Sidney Sheldon was in Palm Springs: But like Sidney, she was hiding out.

20

Sunday Club Tennis

Greg Bautzer was the first attorney in the club because he dated Joan Crawford and befriended Howard Hughes. Sidney Korshak was the ultimate club attorney because he operated by his own rules—and he was the only one who really did. Ed Hookstratten was the first star attorney who crossed over from show business to sports, and made many enemies. Norman Garey was the first club attorney to understand and communicate with both Ilya Salkind and Marlon Brando, not to mention Bob Daly and Barry Diller. The two protégés of Norman Garey who reinvented entertainment law in the club were Barry Haldeman and Joe Peckerman—they combined style with detail and (after Norman's suicide) corralled everyone from Mel Gibson to Gene Hackman. Jake Bloom is the club attorney at the absolute top, and so is his partner Alan Hergott. Eric Weissmann is the club lawyer the directors gravitated to. Eric Weissmann is also the attorney with the best backhand in the club.

Las Vegas wasn't the only tennis court where Jane and Jerry Weintraub had fun. In fact they're never without a tennis court. On Foothill Drive, at the house five doors from Edie and Lew Wasserman's, the Weintraubs had not one but two courts. There were also courts at Blue Heaven and at Kennebunkport, where Jane met Jerry when he was a road manager for Connie Francis, and she sang in her brother's road house for room and board. That's where they still summer, and where Jane became Barbara Bush's best friend (for real, not for show).

Often Washington meets Hollywood most comfortably on a tennis court. Teddy Kennedy is a tennis star in Hollywood. He plays mostly at Dinah Shore's court. Casey Ribicoff plays on the Jeannie Martin court. George Hamilton and Janet Leigh play on the Berry Gordy court. If I was going to write about tennis in the club, though, I decided to stay away from stars. Because all a star has, ultimately, is image. That's why every Paul Newman interview sounds like every other Paul Newman interview.

Attorneys, however, don't have public images. So when I asked entertainment attorney Eric Weissmann to let me observe his famous weekly Sunday tennis match—such characters! A female judge. The movie director Mark Rydell. The Oscar-winning set designer Terry Marsh. Eric leapt at the idea. It was less dangerous than letting me sit in on his 200 phone calls a day—and Eric Weissmann loves being written about. Naively I thought I was getting a Hollywood ritual, Sunday tennis. The attorney knew he was getting some free publicity. Which he could control. Surely all the guests were coached on how to behave in front of the journalist.

I imagined the conversation:

"Remember he's poor, he's a reporter."

"Power without money."

"So dress down."

"Don't drive the Mercedes."

"We'll serve Fritos and hot dogs."

"He's nice—he'll take good care of us."

"Is the photographer doing color?"

"Yes."

"Then that means it's the cover."

"Let's decide who wears what."

It was a cover. They all wore white.

I haven't picked up a tennis racquet since that day. Writing about these kinds of rituals is like doing one-night stands. You write about the Polo Lounge, and you never want to go back. Especially once you see how labyrinthine even sports are in Hollywood. And how seriously they're taken.

Each Sunday morning for years Gilda Radner and Gene Wilder would face the same decision: Where to play tennis? The choice was between two very different games—social and competitive. "Mel Brooks is a competitor," explained Wilder, "and he has been since he was fourteen. So Mel may throw a racquet. But Anne [Bancroft, his wife] discovered something. She now gives him someone else's racquet, and he releases the week's frustrations. The Weissmann court is the only court where Mel would not throw a racquet."

Lawyer Weissman, one of the club's half dozen most powerful entertainment attorneys, has a client list loaded with club directors—including Paul Mazursky, Robert Altman, and Alan Pakula, among others. He also happens to be the best organized of tennis hosts. For his thrice-weekly games, he works from typed lists of privately ranked club players. (The guarded lists involve a ritual all their own.) During a pregame luncheon one Sunday, Weissmann told why the club prefers fun tennis to money tennis. "No pressure," he said simply.

He was stretched out by his Encino pool that adjoins the court. "[Club director] Arthur Penn was once playing here. He served, rolled on the ground, and tore a muscle. I was then head of legal affairs at Warner's, and Arthur was doing a film [*Night Moves*] there. The day after tennis, Arthur was naturally in a glum mood. We were in a meeting with Ted Ashley [Warner Brothers' then-chairman]. Ted took me aside." The upshot? "Ted handed me a list. He said, 'These are directors who have projects here . . . Don't invite them to tennis.' "

Director Mark Rydell (*On Golden Pond*) interrupted Weissmann only long enough to make a point: "If I beat you today," worried Rydell, "I won't get a picture to direct until the year 2000."

Is the game that important? Yes and no. A perfect example of club tennis importance is Barbra Streisand. With customary single-mindedness, Streisand took up the game in the late '60s—with a vengeance. "Barbra had to learn form," recalls actress Adrian Aron, one of the club's favorite pros. "But if you play with her, you notice something. She never makes the same mistake twice." That bit of logic is typical of club players. Watch closely. Usually—unlike at the office—they are harder on themselves than on others. Unless, of course, they're negotiating deals instead of playing tennis.

"Tennis is useful for business," explains producer's representative Leon Roth. "But it's bad form to discuss business. It's unspoken." Mostly that's true. But exceptions also are common. Jerry Weintraub once conceived—and sold—a Dorothy Hamill special while lobbing with ABC chairman Elton Rule. (Weintraub celebrated by dispensing Cuban cigars—another ritual until the bankruptcy. He also served chilled Cristal champagne.)

Even more important than the game is the court. Club TV producer Quinn Martin moved his entire seventeen-acre Beverly Hills estate when local ordinances forbade his building a tennis court. Buddy Hackett got around the ordinances by building his court below street level; Hackett has room for 205 spectators.

"Look, we're all competitive," admits Gene Wilder. "It's why we got into this business in the first place. And the need shows itself on the court. It's difficult in this city to find players who aren't connected to the industry in some way. But when business is being done, it gets very obvious. A business conversation is almost amplified on a court. I stay away from those courts."

"Jennings Lang," said Mark Rydell, "always used the line 'What are friends for?' That line applies to business, to tennis, to this town in general. It also applies in Detroit. But a more important line is this: 'Who can you get on the phone?' You can play tennis at someone's house, and bring a script to a producer, but can you get him on the phone the next day? That's the question. A lot of tennis wizards are very accessible on Sunday, but not on Monday. A lot of them fail on the phone."

CLUB RULE TWENTY-NINE

Act like you are from old money—and know that in the club it's never about money. So concentrate on the social graces money buys, and not money itself.

Example: Club director Richard Brooks was probably the best tennis player in the history of the club. And he wasn't a bad courtside observer, either. When Mrs. Y, a much married movie star of the late '70s, called the leg to tell him she had just "fallen in love with the tennis pro at the Weintraub house—I'm like delirious," I got excited. I called Richard Brooks to tell him about it. "She isn't the first nympho movie star to discover sex on the court," he snapped back. "The really good players aren't in it for money, they're in it for the sex—the rush, the narcissistic win." It's why Teddy Kennedy is worth watching on a court, and Merv Griffin isn't.

In the club it's almost never about money. Because once you are in the club, money is a given. Money is something you have access to. What you want, as David Geffen puts it, "is to get laid a lot."

21

Passion and Loyalty— Robert Evans

The newest club game in the '90s is also one of the oldest. It's called "My dick is bigger than your dick." It's played mostly by producers, who are now reclaiming their power from the agents and attorneys. This is how it's played: Guber-Peters is bought by Sony for so many millions that the ante is raised for everybody else. So, too, are everyone's egos inflated. Jon Peters decides on a whim to buy San Ysidro Ranch near Santa Barbara, where Jackie and Jack Kennedy honeymooned. (So did Vivien Leigh and Laurence Olivier.) Sony vetoes Peters. But largesse is back in style. Suddenly Simpson-Bruckheimer announces an unprecedented deal with Paramount that gives them so much power and freedom that producer Don Simpson even gets to co-star in their movies. And Simpson-Bruckheimer's control is so complete now that they only have to meet Paramount "at the theater" with a final print of the movie. So what if the deal disintegrates? The stakes were still up. At Warner's, Joel Silver begins to believe in his power so completely he has a harem now everywhere he goes— women following him, who tie his shoes, who draw his Jacuzzi, who sublimate their whims to his. Silver's alter ego, Larry Gordon, formerly president of 20th Century-Fox, is back, too. Largo is the name he gives to the company that has several hundred *million dollars in Japanese financing. Suddenly Sandy Gallin is seeing to it that column mentions are forthcoming about Sandollar, the company he runs with Dolly Parton; Sandy Gallin wants to play with the other producer players in the club. He pays Michael Douglas $13 million to star in* Shining Through. *To keep the old guard alive, Dan Melnick partners with Ray Stark, for a while. David Begelman is rumored to be signing an extraordinary deal with Orion—which just may be bought by John Kluge or Marvin Davis, or may go bankrupt. Dawn Steel—the first woman star studio president since Sherry Lansing—leaves executive ranks to do what Sherry did: become a producer. Disney wants Dawn so badly they agree to day-care centers on the lot—anything. Simultaneously, Sherry and her partner, Stanley Jaffe, sign a new, lucrative Paramount deal. Before Stanley becomes chairman of Paramount. And then the smartest one of them all—excepting maybe only Mike Ovitz and Barry Diller—tops everybody. David Geffen becomes the next Lew Wasserman by selling his record company to MCA in a deal that gives him more stock than—yes—more even than Lew himself! Then Geffen buys the Jack Warner house in Beverly Hills—for $47.5 million. Then Matsushita pays Geffen $710 million for his MCA stock, and he becomes the club's first authentic billionaire. All of these producers are in the club, of course. But there's one producer who's separate and apart from the others. All of them know all about him. But none of them know why he has so much mystique. Not that they envy him. Still, none of them understand why—even without money—his dick is as big as their dicks. His name is Robert Evans.*

Long before *Shampoo* in 1975, the tennis court was already the prime sexual status symbol of the club. If Henry Kissinger played on your court, it was an A court. Or if Robert Wagner played, or Streisand. Or if Alan Bergman did, or Janet Leigh. There were only half a dozen A courts in those days—the Newleys', the Wagners', the Richard (Jean Simmons) Brookses', the Weintraubs', and of course, the Robert Evans' court. That was the starriest one of them all.

My first time there, in 1975, I was a spy. I felt like a male Sabrina in the Billy Wilder movie, spying from the sycamore tree over the tennis court at the fabled sixteen-room French Normandy house, the one that had been photographed by Alfred Eisenstadt for *Life*. ("The others you can contest," one agent told me, "but Robert Evans' house, darling, that was a star house.") More deals were put together in Evans' house and projection room—and on the tennis court—than at any studio; it was where Marlon Brando was thought of for *The Godfather*, and where *Shampoo* was conceived.

Basically, I was a tennis bum at Evans' house; he lived around the corner from my boss Joyce Haber, so I'd go over occasionally. (It's where I saw Teddy Kennedy play doubles with Dinah Shore and John Tunney and Evans himself.) Evans' butler David (who later became the butler to David Geffen) was obliging—and so was Evans.

But this particular party—this one I had become obsessive about. It was for Time Inc.'s editor-in-chief Hedley Donovan, his first show business dinner party. There was never a way I could be invited, so I decided to sneak in, and I decided where I'd perch. And it worked. Only because of the 400-year-old sycamore in Evans' backyard that shades everything.

"Aren't these fabulous trees?" I heard Goldie Hawn murmur.

"These trees are one tree," said Natalie Wood.

Never had so much glamour sat under one tree. Maybe not even at the Goldwyns', up the road.

I heard *Time*'s then–assistant managing editor Murray Gart tell Robert Wagner, "I haven't seen a party like this since Hedley and I were entertained by the Shah of Iran."

Everything was black and white and beautiful, the chili was from Chasen's, and the circular pool was so perfectly lit that Roman Polanski told Donovan, "Maybe we should throw you in so you'll really remember tonight."

I felt like I was in Camelot, T. H. White's Camelot.

Raquel. Candy. Marisa. Alana. Dyan. Michelle. Diana (pregnant but skinny). The directors went from Nichols and Wilder to Frankenheimer and Penn. The Matthaus, the Ziffrens, the Zanucks, the Wassermans, even George Hamilton! Even Clint Eastwood, who told somebody it was his first private Hollywood dinner party in ten years. ("Maybe I've been missing something," Clint added.)

I took down every word when Evans toasted the editor of *Time* by admitting, "There are many bigger businesses than ours; we hardly ever make *Fortune*. We're in the back of the book at *Time*. Still, six of the ten of the top-selling *Time* covers in the last five years have been show business covers, which proves that the movies may not be the biggest business, but they're everybody's business. That's why people in our industry are so sensitive to the press. We're personalities, not utilities. A hundred bad lines written about you aren't worth one good line."

Then Warren Beatty toasted Evans—Warren and then "fiancée" Michelle Phillips stayed over a day for the party, before leaving for Bali for what everyone said would be their honeymoon. It wasn't. But how could they—even *Warren*—top this evening at Evans'?

I knew then I'd one day write about Evans—and ten years almost to the month, it happened. I went to New York to see how his ill-fated *Cotton Club* was going. On arrival I got a call from Evans. I remember barely being able to pick up the phone. "I may have to wear pajamas," I told him sheepishly, from my room at the St. Moritz. "My right knee just locked."

"Then we'll have dinner in the bedroom and watch TV," Evans responded, not missing a beat. The producer was living in a rented East Side brownstone he couldn't afford, in the middle of shooting the very troubled movie. This most seductive of all Hollywood players would ironically that night give his last interview for half a dozen years. This man who loves being profiled went into exile after his cocaine arrest in 1980. *Cotton Club*, or *Cotton*, as Joan Didion dubbed it, was almost his undoing. But on this freezing day in November the producer was full of beans. Into the phone he said, "Hello old chap, it's Evans."

He sounded just like you want Jay Gatsby to sound. Or maybe Jake Barnes.

But it took a lot of years.

The first time Ernest Hemingway met Robert Evans, he didn't like him. It was 1957 and Evans, then a pants manufacturer, was playing the Hemingway bullfighter Pedro Romero in *The Sun Also Rises*. A pants manufacturer was playing Pedro Romero. Hemingway tracked down Darryl Zanuck, demanding Evans be fired. Zanuck, then chief at 20th Century-Fox, arrived in Mexico, instructed Evans to get into his suit of lights, then to appear in the bullring. Ten minutes later, over a loudspeaker, Zanuck bellowed, "The kid stays in the picture. And anybody who doesn't like it can leave."

Nobody left—but a pattern was established. For the next thirty-five years Robert Evans would make almost nonstop news. Whether as Hollywood's handsomest bachelor or husband (four marriages, to Sharon Hugueny, Camilla Sparv, Ali MacGraw, and Phyllis George). Or as Hollywood's top host: One would not be surprised to find both Teddy Kennedy and Henry Kissinger and Ambassador Henry Grunwald houseguesting. Evans also made news through his movies (*Chinatown*) and his ten years of trouble, starting with the 1980 cocaine bust.

For a very long time, Evans endured in the movie business—as an actor, then studio executive, finally as an independent producer. In the '80s nothing happened, but the kid still stayed in the picture. Such a climb, even in Hollywood, has a cost, and the cost is what makes Evans so intriguing. So what if he was involved tangentially in a murder trial? His tenure as Paramount's production chief lasted longer (seven years) than most of his rivals—or his marriages combined (six years). His output of hits is rivaled only by his flops. Evans has various identities, but overshadowing them is a cloak of mystery. He's childlike in a way that's much misunderstood: Evans is incapable of simply retelling an anecdote—rather he must elaborate it with an actor's demand for attention. He's obsessive, primarily about work, but also loyal to those who are no longer in fashion. A legendary womanizer, Evans is not a legend at playing Hollywood politics. He's been too much the lone wolf all his life. What he operates with, finally, is a kind of electric charm. That the switch could go off—that the charm could be withdrawn at any instant— is what (on a personal level) both fascinates and frightens people.

There aren't ten stars in today's Hollywood that have his mystique. And there are those who resent Robert Evans for just that reason. It's a situation understood by his friend Warren Beatty, who's suffered similar Hollywood envy. Beatty once wanted to buy film rights to *The Great Gatsby* and star Evans in the title role. Both men still think the idea was sound; both have taken their raps for being handsome. After Beatty's *Reds* failed to sweep the Oscars (although Beatty won Best Director), Beatty turned to Evans and said, "You and I will never get the sympathy vote."

On the top floor of his rented three-story town house, Evans was serving late supper himself. Sturgeon and smoked salmon sandwiches and, for dressing, a kind of nostalgia. Watching him, the years fell away.

"Nobody believes I don't dye my hair," confided Evans, then fifty, fiddling as he often does with various pairs of eyeglasses. "I won $7,000 last week, proving I don't. I let my beard grow seven days. In seven days, your beard either goes white or not. It didn't go white, so I won $7,000."

"Would you like to see the cassette?" Evans asked abruptly, as supper was removed from the room. The cassette is a reenactment of *The Robert Evans Story*, produced by his sister Alice for his fiftieth birthday and featuring an astonishing cast: Henry Kissinger playing Evans' high school teacher; agent Sue Mengers playing Norma Shearer, the actress who in 1956 "discovered" Evans poolside at the Beverly Hills Hotel; playing himself is the much-discussed but elusive Hollywood attorney Sidney Korshak. Two ex-wives appear, as do the late Natalie Wood, the late Paramount founder Adolph Zukor, the late Gulf & Western chairman Charles Bluhdorn, Dustin Hoffman, Raquel Welch, and Helen Gurley Brown.

With friends like these, how could Evans ever be in trouble?

"Let's say a person has twenty people in his life, maximum," Evans proposed. "In my life, of those twenty people, sixteen would be women and four would be men. I haven't in my time found that much loyalty from men, and I've helped men. Liv Ullmann heard about the troubles on *Cotton Club*, and sent me a check for $400,000. She said, 'This is my savings, but you need it.' I framed the check and returned the framed check to Liv. Cheryl Tiegs offered me help and others have offered. Okay, yes, it is pride that won't allow me to accept. But it's more than pride, too. These people are my friends for one reason. I'm a total romantic. A total romantic, a loyalist and . . . a terrible businessman."

There's the rub. The combination of romantic and loyalist is not unattractive to women and to the media—but it doesn't play well in Hollywood business circles, in the club. If Evans hasn't found loyalty from the club, the reason is apparent. It wasn't his track record that was ever in dispute, it was his style.

In 1975, Evans was the man who had everything—the sixteen-room French Regency house with the Renoirs and Degases, the stars as dinner guests, the loyalty of a critical handful of mentors, men such as Bluhdorn and Korshak. One could almost smell the envy outside the gates on Woodland Drive.

"And, remember," Evans reminded, "my gates were always closed, except to my friends. Of course my image is so diametrically opposed to my real life . . . Thanksgiving, for example, I'll be in bed alone. Also, probably, Christmas and New Year's Eve. But my theory is that when you go out, you go out."

It's that sense of occasion that works both for and against Evans. Though there are executives who categorize him as naive, it was never that simple. Nobody who becomes a millionaire in the garment business before age thirty is naive. Rather it's the combination of naïveté and fiber that led Beatty to see Evans as Gatsby. Ironically, it would be Evans who bought the film rights to the book, to star then-bride Ali MacGraw, with a Capote screenplay. (It wound up with Mia Farrow as Daisy and Francis Coppola as screenwriter.)

It was the partnership with MacGraw that probably horrified Hollywood most. Here they were, the perfectly constructed, supremely successful couple of 1970. God and goddess. She was on the cover of *Time*, and he had the key to New York City. Together they had a darkly handsome baby named Joshua, and an all-time blockbuster movie, *Love Story*. And there would, by necessity, be a price. By 1973 MacGraw was married to Steve McQueen, and living in seclusion outside Malibu. Scrubbing the toilets herself, at McQueen's insistence. In 1978, when MacGraw was no longer a star, loyalist Evans starred her in his forgettable tennis movie, *Players.*

"Let's talk about being set up," Evans said, suggesting some dark club forces at work. "Let's talk about the first screening of *Players* in New York, and how some people liked it . . . except a few of the audience who were instructed to laugh at Ali's line readings. That kind of mean laughter spread to other screenings. I'm not saying it was a great film, but I'm saying we were set up. And it's not the only time."

In July of 1980, Evans pleaded guilty in a plea bargain in U.S. Federal Court to possession of five ounces of cocaine. (Similar pleas were entered by Evans' realtor-brother Charles, and their brother-in-law, Michael Shure.) The plea bargaining resulted from an investigation in which two women were indicted on charges of conspiring to distribute cocaine. A federal judge offered Evans a chance to expunge the conviction by using his "extraordinary creative talents" in an antidrug campaign. It resulted in a starry NBC special, *Get High on Yourself*, that drew much press coverage and no ratings.

The cocaine charge made Evans press-shy for the first time. "I don't feel I did something that wrong," he said evenly. "Mine was a victimless crime. Yet it sticks with you; people love to make dents in a high profile. Look, I'm guilty of usage. But so are fourteen out of fourteen people I know. My usage has been at three or four in the morning, say in the editing room. I don't like cocaine socially; it's bad for sex. It also ruins your tennis game, and I like playing well."

Again he feels the cocaine arrest was another setup: "My brother Charles was set up in Manhattan. I was 3,000 miles away, in California, on my way to Malta, when I picked up a phone. I was asked, by a female voice, 'Since your brother made a good score, aren't you interested?' Clearly, I was set up."

And from that day forward, Evans claimed, his career has been on hold: "I spent a year and a half on that TV special, and all I was required by law to do was to produce a simple TV commercial. And three weeks before it aired, [NBC chairman] Grant Tinker got a call saying that Bob Evans was going to be set up again. At that point, at my own expense, I spent $1,800 a day on guards. I couldn't go to Pink's for a hot dog alone, or go to the bathroom alone—or even have groceries delivered to my house. But then when we actually did the show, it was such a turn-on."

Evans went on: "I'm not saying I'm the Virgin Mary. I'm guilty of a lot of things in my life, but . . . let me tell you that cocaine is more of a problem in Detroit than in Hollywood. The main reason Japanese cars are outselling American cars is that our auto workers are on cocaine." Evans believes his reasoning is sound. "Actors, frankly, are too narcissistic about their bodies to do too many drugs. I've done cocaine, sure, but not at parties. I don't do marijuana, and I've never done 'ludes [Quaaludes]."

Evans has at the ready a perfect example of America's current drug problem. "I gave an $11,000 party at my house to raise Texas money for *Cotton Club*. I had like eleven hostesses, women I knew, Ali [MacGraw] being one of them. And I told the women, 'Under no circumstances are you to offer even an aspirin if someone asks. Not a pain pill, not anything.' And you know what? The girls weren't asked for anything—but they were offered every drug you could think of."

On the cold Sunday afternoon after our long night, Evans led a visitor into his two-story living room. Jack Nicholson was dropping by and then they were going to a movie. The evening was to be one of Evans' rare nights out. Nicholson took off his navy cashmere topcoat, and lit a hand-rolled cigarette.

"I gave Jack his first commercial film," recalled Evans with some pride. "Before *Easy Rider* made him a star, I put him in *On a Clear Day You Can See Forever* as Barbra Streisand's half brother."

Nicholson looked like a kid who's been discovered shoplifting. "I remember how we haggled. Jack wanted $12,500 and I would only pay him $10,000. He needed the extra $2,500 for alimony."

They bantered for a few minutes like the characters in *Carnal Knowledge*:

"Neither of us are jock heads," Nicholson offered. "Both of us like women. I can beat Bob at tennis, and Dustin can't."

"Before *Chinatown* did you ever play a romantic lead? C'mon, tell me!" Evans urged.

"No, Bob, unless you count *Carnal Knowledge*. The romantic lead thing began I guess with *Chinatown*. Did you know Bob and I were supposed to play the two Jakes in the sequel?"

The sequel to *Chinatown*, *The Two Jakes*, written by Robert Towne, who won an Oscar for the original, was the most awaited film of 1986. But watching these two survivors together, you wonder, maybe they should have played the two Jakes? (In fact they almost did: One week into playing the role of Jake Berman, in 1986, Evans was removed, and the picture was temporarily shelved).

Said Evans tightly: "The idea was for me to go back to being an actor to reclaim my success."

The success started early.

Evans is from Manhattan's tony Riverside Drive; his father, a dentist, didn't object when his eleven-year-old son became a radio star. Some 300 broadcasts, regular appearances on *The Right to Happiness* and *Young Henry Aldrich* convinced him to be in show business. By his middle twenties, Evans (with his brother) was making and selling pants. (The company, Evan-Picone, was in 1958 sold to Revlon, netting Evans "a couple of million dollars.")

At twenty-five, he was minding what he says was his own business when then-retired Norma Shearer, the widow of Irving Thalberg, spotted him; Shearer had approval over who would play Thalberg, the Hollywood Boy Wonder, in *Man of a Thousand Faces*, the Lon Chaney biography to star James Cagney. Shearer approved of Evans in a big way.

Six months later, "I reluctantly went to El Morocco, very late one night, wearing the same clothes I had on all day—and Darryl Zanuck spotted me. 'Kid, are you an actor?' he asked me. And I said I wasn't, but also I was. That I'd done this role of Thalberg. He asked did I want to be in a movie with Ava Gardner . . ." Evans startled himself at the recollection. "People really can't believe how long I've been around. I mean, in the '50s, I actually dated and fucked Ava Gardner and Lana Turner."

Also, Evans got tabbed by Zanuck as "the hottest young man since Valentino." *Time* magazine said of Evans' film debut, *Thousand Faces*, that he had a "fierce intensity." It got him two other movies, the title role in *The Fiend Who Walked the West* and something smaller in *The Best of Everything*. Then, after losing *The Roman Spring of Mrs. Stone* to Warren Beatty and *The Light in the Piazza* to George Hamilton, Evans retired from acting.

"I was never a good actor," Evans admitted, "but God knows I was more prepared for it than I was for what did happen." What did happen was the kind of serendipity that's usually reserved for Jackie Collins novels. Gulf & Western's Bluhdorn read a *New York Times* article describing Evans' knack, even as an untested producer, to get new material. What he had was the "couple of million dollars," a desk at 20th Century-Fox, and a pipeline to *Publishers Weekly*, from whence he discovered manuscripts. And he had his foot in the Hollywood door.

Ten months after setting up shop at Fox, Evans became vice-president in charge of production at Paramount. Hollywood was shocked—not that a pants manufacturer was playing Pedro Romero—but that a failed actor was running a studio. Bluhdorn's Folly, they called him. Within six months *Daily Variety* printed reports of his imminent demise. "I tracked down Charlie Bluhdorn in Switzerland," Evans remembered, "and he said words to me I will never forget. I said, 'Charlie, they say I'm finished.' And Charlie said, 'You will be on the job longer than they will be in Hollywood.' "

As if to show everyone, Evans began what would become his ritual: the seven-day work week, featuring eighteen-hour days and over-too-

quick romances and much visibility—and success on his own, very delib-
erate terms. In a pivotal eleven-page spread in *Life* magazine (photographed by Alfred Eisenstadt), Evans revealed secrets. "I just worked
harder, I put in the time and in the long run that counts," he said. "Also
I'm selfish. And a gambler. And I can hold my own in any jungle."

The results for Paramount: an endlessly chronicled rise in revenue and
prestige. Early hits (*Rosemary's Baby, The Odd Couple*) contrasted with
early flops (*Darling Lili, Catch-22*). By the early '70s, Evans was en-
trenched. He bought a treatment from Mario Puzo called *The Mafia* for
$5,000 down, and thus began *The Godfather*. When Erich Segal pre-
sented Evans with a screenplay called *Love Story*, Evans suggested that
Segal also write a novel based on the film. For the first time in American
pop culture, a book and movie were simultaneous hits. Also a star (Mac-
Graw) was born, and a movie that cost $2.1 million became one of the
all-time top twenty hits.

By the middle '70s, Evans was much more than Charlie Bluhdorn's
Boy Wonder. He was making a lot of other people rich, and finding out
that he had an understanding of film. Of a score of people interviewed
about Evans, almost nobody failed to mention his editing contributions
on films like *Goodbye, Columbus* and *The Godfather*. Plagued with a
recurring sciatica condition, Evans would often be at Paramount, in a
hospital bed, wearing elegant black-tasseled slippers, and supervising final
touches on films that would make other people's reputations. And other
people's fortunes. He would be there into the night.

"I remained salaried," Evans explained, "and well salaried, but nevertheless . . . I could never pay my taxes, nor did I ever have a chance to
see my son."

In 1974 the timing was right for Evans to make a move. Sidney Korshak, who'd negotiated six previous Evans-Paramount contracts in three
years, spent three months clinching a deal for Evans to become an
independent producer at the studio.

The weather at Paramount changed in 1975. Within a seven-week
period, Barry Diller had arrived as board chairman and Frank Yablans
had departed as studio president. Evans was given a new deal: He was
expected to become Paramount's top independent producer; the studio's
chief supplier. During eight years he had to deliver no fewer than twenty-
four films. Such deals are never as rich in reality as they are in announcement, though Evans' did have extraordinary terms. In the ensuing eight
years, he produced for Paramount only five films. *Chinatown*, was a '70s
benchmark, but *Marathon Man* and *Black Sunday* were off the expected
mark at the box office. *Players* was a disaster, and *Popeye* was notable
primarily for friction on the set. "My offices stayed at Paramount for ten

years afterward," Evans will say now, "and my relationship with Barry Diller has been much maligned, and wrongly characterized. I was there for seventeen years. That says it." (In 1991 he went back, with a solid five-year deal.)

"I think people see me as this slick operator," Evans once told me. "And sometimes I wish I was more of an operator." He was sitting at his home in the projection room where Warren Beatty had his mock bar mitzvah. The room, and the host, are a throwback to plusher times.

Evans reflected: "I've had a high profile, and I've paid for it." He told about how a houseguest, a club member out from New York, invited friends over to screen some films. "I didn't join them," Evans related. "I was tired and I stayed in my bedroom. Later I heard that a Paramount executive—who was not even there that night—told people he had been to Bob Evans' house and there had been vials of cocaine passed around . . . Look, he wasn't there and I wasn't there, but you see what I'm talking about."

Evans paused to let the story register. "I think there's one thing, one word, that matters," he added, carefully. "Loyalty. That may be my personal priority in life."

Then Evans surveyed the room, and the memories and the framed movie star photos and the cost, and finally looked his age. "Whatever happened to loyalty?" he said to nobody in particular.

CLUB RULE THIRTY

People in the club have short attention spans and long memories. You can't buy these people.

You can't buy Jack Nicholson flying to Monte Carlo for forty-eight hours to save your house for you. He did it in 1989 for Robert Evans. Nicholson in a day in France managed to undo a two-week emergency escrow on a $5 million deal that would have cost Evans his house. This kind of loyalty, or leverage, is given, freely. It's never taken forcefully. People in the club give each other everything from gifts to dreams. But they know the difference between gifts and business.

22

Club Headquarters— The Beverly Hills Hotel

The Garden of Allah was the first club headquarters because it drew wits like Robert Benchley and stars like Paulette Goddard. The Chateau Marmont was the favored hangout of the '60s because employees looked the other way about drugs and sex. And because Tuesday Weld held great salons there. And directors like Bob Rafelson and Dennis Hopper put deals together there. The Beverly Wilshire was the hideaway in the '70s because Warren Beatty lived there, in the penthouse, all by himself. The Hotel Bel Air was the club headquarters of the '70s because it was timeless, and foreign money liked staying there. But it's the Beverly Hills Hotel that remained true club headquarters, because in 1912 when it was built—there was no Beverly Hills. It hadn't been incorporated as a city yet. But there was the Beverly Hills Hotel.

Practically around the corner from Evans and Haber, a few blocks away, was the other great tennis center of Beverly Hills, the Beverly Hills Hotel. It was the only court Katharine Hepburn ever played at. The hotel was not the only club headquarters, but it was the most accessible. You wandered around the lobby and ran into people like Bob Fosse, and Johnny Carson, and Doris Day, who bicycled from her house a block away.

Why this hotel?

The David Begelman check-forging scandal of 1978 is an example of why. The scandal meant a lot of extra business for the hotel. New York executives from Columbia Pictures, Begelman's then-employer, held many of their top-secret meetings in the hotel bungalows. The fate of Begelman was decided in Bungalow 3. (Bungalow activity got so intense at one point that Columbia's then-chairman Alan Hirschfield moved to L'Hermitage, a hotel in lower Beverly Hills, to escape media glare.)

"I decided then to gut a few of the bungalows," said Muriel Slatkin, the hotel's co-owner from 1954 to 1984. "I figured if so much business was being conducted in the bungalows, an extra bathroom might be in order. A powder room, so to speak. I mean, a lot of business is conducted in those bungalows."

Monkey business and serious business. Former Fox owner Marvin Davis lived in Denver, Manhattan, Palm Springs—and Bungalow 1 of the Beverly Hills Hotel, for years. (His personal bill at the hotel was an annual $300,000.) In 1987, when Coca-Cola began takeover talks with Columbia the talks were held in one of the twenty bungalows. In the '60s, when Charles Bluhdorn acquired Paramount Pictures for Gulf & Western, the deal was opened and closed in the hotel's famed Polo Lounge.

Not all machinations are about club business, of course. H. R. Haldeman learned of the failure of the Watergate break-in while he was a hotel guest. Howard Hughes once personally negotiated a $250 million loan for TWA in his suite of rooms. (At one point in the '40s, Hughes had twenty-one rooms; he liked to summon his executives, place them in rooms—and make them wait. Former Litton Industries executive Charles [Tex] Thornton reportedly left Hughes over just such a tactic.) Hughes also liked to keep girls waiting in specific rooms, mostly Bungalow 4. Oddly, the late Aristotle Onassis spent most of World War II in Bungalow 4.

The Beverly Hills Hotel is "a cubist ocean liner," as one novelist put it. It's also the center of its own little world. To grasp how that world operates, a half-week of watching seemed in order. Any hotel that housed both Greta Garbo and Howard Hughes deserved a closer look. It began, of course, with history.

Monday: The hotel pool may be the most exclusive spot in Los Angeles.

And size may be the reason why. With only nineteen cabanas (and 185 chaise lounges) admittance is tighter than a drum. The seventy-five-foot pool sits smack in the middle of the Sand and Pool Club. (Obviously there's no sand.) The pool is the source of legends and myths. They imbue the area—the snack bar, the high diving board, the rows of hyacinths—with the aura of possibility. Legend says that composer Leonard Bernstein conceived *West Side Story* by the pool. ("I offered him my own cabana," remembered Muriel Slatkin, "and I was kind of hurt when he didn't accept. Later I found out he couldn't work with the piped-in music . . . We no longer have the music.") The show Bernstein was composing was originally to be about a Jewish-Irish love affair. Sitting by the pool, Bernstein observed very few Jewish-Irish romances. And he got a brainstorm of an idea. The love affair, he suddenly decided, would not be Jewish-Irish but Puerto Rican–Caucasian. Thus was *West Side Story* born in Beverly Hills.

Tuesday: "The coffee shop is where it happens," confided Edie (Mrs. Lew) Wasserman. What could happen in a twenty-seat coffee shop? Plenty. When game show millionaire Chuck Barris was named *Cosmopolitan* magazine's Bachelor of the Month, the magazine listed the hotel coffee shop as Barris' mailing address. About 400 to 500 letters—per week—arrived there for him. So did a few prospective dates.

"Neil Diamond breakfasts here almost every day," said a somewhat shy Muriel Slatkin. "But for years he and I only nodded in passing, as regulars at a restaurant would. He just happens to be my favorite singer. So one day I walked up to him and said, 'You don't bring me flowers.' That was all I said. Now remember, I had never met the man . . . That afternoon, when I got home [Slatkin lives directly behind the hotel], I found a dozen white roses, from Neil Diamond."

She pointed at the glass wall: "That's where Peter Finch died," she said abruptly. "Peter Finch keeled over and died, right there. He was on his way in here to have breakfast with Sidney Lumet."

The breakfast actually was to be held in the Polo Lounge, a 120-seat restaurant so celebrated it has been mentioned as a title for both novels and feature films. One producer even optioned the title—without so much as a writer or concept. (That was 1976. The movie never got made, nor has the real novel been written.) In fact, it would take two volumes to get it right.

The bar's name came from the game of polo—and the men in the '20s who favored it: Darryl Zanuck, Will Rogers, Spencer Tracy. They would often play on weekends, stopping by the hotel afterward to cool off in the bar. When one of the local polo teams won a match, the silver bowl, the prize, was presented by the players to the bartender: The name Polo Lounge was born.

But has the Polo Lounge diminished? Some outsiders refer to it today as the Polio Lounge, but almost everybody in Hollywood does time there. It remains almost the only central mingling spot for publishers and agents, New York producers and agents and stargazers and agents, and club members are made to feel comfortable.

"I could operate out of that room, like an office," claims writer Jay Presson Allen. "And sometimes I have operated there."

Wednesday: A day spent watching the hotel operation. Hollis Polodna, the longtime reservations wizard, set up what may be the most elite reference system since the Social Register. It's the hotel guest file. Each guest has a card—or several cards. (All are kept under lock and key.) On the cards are the following tips: guests' preference for liquors, type of mattresses, favorite room service items, flowers. Also, any peculiarities, past problems, special needs (Elizabeth Taylor likes white pistachios waiting in her bungalow).

"The cards are catalogued by color, then fed to a computer," explained a staffer. "White cards are for first-timers; blue cards are for very special regulars—what you call club people. People in between get a pink card." What would be on such a card? "Lord Snowdon likes Gauloises cigarettes," explained the staffer, "so that goes on the card. When he arrives, we make sure the drugstore has those cigarettes. For years you couldn't find them in Los Angeles. We found them."

One especially spoiled guest was the late NBC founder David Sarnoff. "David was a personal friend," said Muriel Slatkin. "And he liked everything in Room 486 to be just so. I once gutted that room, fixed it up for his arrival with only hours to spare. Well, he was rather ill that visit. And some things went wrong. Let's face it, things go wrong at every hotel. Anyway, his freezer didn't work, a window wouldn't open. He was furious, and we were supposed to have dinner his first evening here. That night I called his wife and said, 'Meet us in the lobby, not in the restaurant.' "

Flash forward twenty minutes: The foursome met in the lobby. Slatkin, character that she is, "got on my hands and knees and crawled around behind David Sarnoff. I said, 'David, I know you love me. And you know your room has been attended to. Now you can kiss me.' I didn't tell him to kiss my behind; I just asked him to kiss me . . . David adored it."

And then there was the time when the late John Belushi played samurai in the hotel lobby with Paul Simon—at 4 A.M. Or the famous game of musical bungalows played by Yves Montand and Marilyn Monroe during the filming of *Let's Make Love*. Or the Oscar night when Sidney Poitier ran barefoot through the lobby after winning; or the night Faye Dunaway and Terry O'Neill rabble-roused until dawn, Faye never letting go of the Oscar she won the night before. And Terry never letting go of Faye.

"Face it," summed up Muriel Slatkin, "the hotel is a star."

CLUB RULE THIRTY-ONE

Be authentic in terms of following your own path. Get your bearings down about how you want to be perceived.

Example: Living inside the town is dangerous. To be at the Polo Lounge too often is to be too insular. The place seems to weave, like a ship of fools, after a while. Staying exclusively at clubhouses becomes both claustrophobic and addictive. Example: the business-breakfast-lunch-dinner syndrome that made Los Angeles a restaurant town in the '80s. (Even Joel Silver did deals at Le Dome. And thus added to the addictive behavior.) To miss a piece of gossip was to feel you'd slipped. So you dare not miss a breakfast-lunch-dinner.

There are two ways for club residents to handle this:

"Sometimes I handle it by going out every night," says producer Allan Carr.

"I handle it by almost never going out," says Bette Midler. "I mean, why?"

To go out when you are really "inside" (as in introspective) is to ask for trouble. The social ramble just ain't restful, as Satchel Paige of baseball fame put it. Best not to zigzag. Best to follow your path.

23

Club Watering Holes

Chasen's was the first club watering hole because Dave Chasen was a vaudevillian who told great stories for the amusement of movie stars—and served the world's best chili. (Elizabeth Taylor had the chili flown to the set of Cleopatra on a weekly basis. She still has it delivered regularly to the house in Bel Air.) La Scala was the club's early '60s hangout because it was beautifully lit, and because owner Jean Leon understood Italian food and Hollywood people. Matteo's was the club hangout on Sunday night in the '60s and '70s because Frank Sinatra and Jeannie and Dean Martin went there, and so did Lucy and Gary Morton. The Daisy was the club lunch place in the '60s because Jack Hanson invented Jax—the slacks to wear in Beverly Hills—and he invented the first patio on Rodeo Drive, for the Daisy. And he named salads after stars. The Brown Derby stopped being a club hangout in the '50s, when the Cobb salad, which it invented, was improved upon by the Polo Lounge's McCarthy salad. The Polo Lounge became a club hangout because Darryl Zanuck liked going there after playing polo. And Sam Goldwyn would drop by after croquet matches. The Bistro became the clubhouse of the '60s because Billy Wilder had his

*art director re-create a true Paris bistro—and the upstairs be-
came Club Heaven. (It's where Audrey Wilder got up to sing.)
The Bistro lasted the longest except for Chasen's; Spago will
wind up the long-distance runner because it has club energy—
every night. Jimmy's will last as a club dining room because it's
beautiful, and because Jimmy was a headwaiter at the Bistro
for 500 years. Not every clubhouse lasts that long. And every
clubhouse owner knows that.*

The Beverly Hills Hotel had only one rival—or colleague, for almost a
decade. And it wasn't even another hotel. It was a patio made of plastic
chairs and staples. When New Yorkers like Liza Minnelli flew to Los
Angeles, it meant two things: They stayed at the Beverly Hills Hotel (even
though Liza's father lived across the street), and they ate dinner at Ma
Maison. Or they had lunch there. Or both.

Shirley MacLaine thought I was kidding when I stopped her in the
parking lot of Ma Maison and told her something lucky happened every
time we met. We'd been meeting for almost a decade. "Lucky, like
what?" she asked me—Shirley is known in some quarters as the Question
Machine. So I told her about one encounter, late one Monday afternoon
in 1983, for an interview for her first psychic-spiritual book, *Out on a
Limb*. And how I drove from her beach apartment to the newspaper and
got offered my *Los Angeles Times* staff job. Fourteen years after I began
to work for Joyce Haber, I was being offered a real job.

I told all this to Shirley while we walked into Ma Maison. As Shirley
slipped into the star corner table with director Andrei Konchalavsky,
former flame on the brink of a movie career in America (*Runaway
Train*)—I kissed her on the cheek. Three hours later I won a local press
club award. One day after our next encounter, also at Ma Maison, I fell
in love for the first time in years.

The restaurant where all this happened was the last true club haunt—
its popularity hasn't been duplicated, replicated, or re-created. The chef
went on to open Spago—but in post World War II Hollywood, there was
only one Ma Maison. The first night I walked in, in 1976, the magic was
already in force. Joan Didion and John Gregory Dunne were so busy
watching they hardly spoke to each other, or even bothered to eat.

"I'm leaving for Tahiti in half an hour," owner host Patrick Terrail
told me. Boldly, from some undeveloped place maybe Jung would understand, I said, "Why don't you take a journalist along?"

Somehow Patrick picked up my cue. "Yvette Mimieux and Stanley Donen just canceled," said the Frenchman, with some annoyance in his voice. "Be at the airport in two and a half hours."

I was. With an expired passport—but who cared. Patrick Terrail knew the owner of UTA Airlines; I was in.

On the all-night flight Steve Jaffe, manager-husband to Susie Blakeley, told me if I wrote about the trip in any way not to mention them. Since Susie was the only "star" aboard, I had nothing to write anyway. I told Steve not to worry, but I felt like a pariah.

I slept for most of the trip. I slept all day, and stayed awake alone every night. I smoked and read Gavin Lambert's books, and paced around the beautiful straw hut for hours. I never could adjust to the time zone. The other nine people I hardly got to know. The last morning in Papeete, beauty Camilla Sparv told me, "We're not bringing you anymore—you're no fun."

Camilla was right.

Patrick Terrail was also right about opening and closing Ma Maison within a decade.

But, oh, while it lasted . . . I mean, only in Hollywood could Lauren Hutton saunter into a restaurant, properly late for lunch, and hand the proprietor a switchblade. "Would you oil this for me?" Hutton asked Patrick, as fifty lunchers looked on. He smiled slightly, and pointed what was then perhaps the most intimidating finger in Los Angeles. A moment later, the blade was oiled.

A pretty photographer, sitting nearby, asked Terrail to pose with Hutton. "Absolutely not," he replied. "I cannot ask Lauren to pose. I threw her out of here once."

It wouldn't happen in Washington, where protocol still reigns, or New York, where photographers rarely sit lens distance from stars (except at charity things). In Hollywood, at Ma Maison as at no place else, the elite met not only to eat but also to be strategically seated, and seen, and to devour one another. The restaurant remained, for its nine-year reign, one of the two or three sure stamps of club validation.

To discover why, I decided to spend a week just Ma Maison watching. Not so much for the place itself, but for the community that gathered outside on the fabled patio. The names you already know, from the Nivens (David Sr. and David Jr.) to the Bergens (Frances and Candice). From Neil Simon to Meryl Streep, Greg Bautzer to Rod Stewart, Billy Wilder to Wendy Goldberg. Were the patio wired, the community would be in a permanent blush.

Witness Hutton, lunching at Table No. 2 with three attentive business-men. Her swivel neck missed not a nuance. Hutton spied fellow model-actress (and club tennis player) Ann Turkel at Table No. 3, with her lawyer. The beauties winked at each other.

"Tennis?" Turkel mouthed eagerly.

"When?" Hutton's lunch partner asked loudly. "I'll call Natalie and R.J. and Jackie. For an early morning."

"Jackie who?" Turkel wanted to know.

"Stop breaking tennis dates," Hutton piped in, "and we'll tell you."

The date was made, and Patrick Terrail breathed a sign of relief. "I am still in awe of these people," admitted the restaurateur, whose family owns France's Tour d'Argent. "Every morning I wonder if they will still show up."

They did, though, entering from Melrose Avenue—long before Melrose was chic—through a canopied walkway, under surveillance. Indoors, Terrail could scan guests with a tiny black-and-white TV, and welcome them via a microphone, or ignore them so coldly they needed several shrink dates to recover. Entrances could seem as orchestrated as in a mythical royal court. Contrary to rumor, Terrail did not lick anyone's fingers. Regulars simply got a kiss, hug, or handshake—and the right seat. Only eight tables inside, along with a three-stool bar. A small sign read "La maison ne fait pas crédit." "There was a nice sense of theater to it," remembered regular Fred Astaire.

Eight backers, led by Gene Kelly, put up the original $40,000 stash. It was Kelly's involvement that lured the other investors (Dan Melnick, David Begelman, Freddie Fields) and gave Ma Maison its sense of show business. (One evening, Terrail approached Kelly about buying him out; Gene Kelly looked like he'd been threatened with a death sentence. The conversation proved to be merely table talk.) The profit participation, for Terrail and partner-chef Wolfgang Puck, was slightly less than 10 percent. Though there were only thirty-eight tables, inside and out, a daily 150 lunches and 150 dinners were served. Waiters, mostly American, earned upward of $3,000 a month, mostly in tips.

And in its heyday the place took in $10,000 a day. "Would another $100,000 a year make us any happier?" Chef Puck asked one night. It was ironic when he said, "No . . . Ma Maison is not a gold mine." Ironic because Puck went on to become the most important (and probably richest) restaurateur in the club (and in Los Angeles).

But Ma Maison's patio, one could argue, was exactly that—a gold mine masquerading as a casual French garden party. The decor was Hollywood low-key chic: Chairs were plastic, the carpet was Astroturf, the setups were simple. "I keep it together with plastic and staples," Terrail used to half kid. "The restaurant, after all, is only the canvas. I hold the paintbrush, but the people are the color."

"It was not at all about food," explained Jackie Bisset. "Ma Maison was really a . . . clubhouse." To wit: When agent Sue Mengers needed Paris hotel reservations, she rang up Terrail. When Miss Lillian Carter visited Los Angeles, she stopped by, and not for the salmon crudité. When Tina Sinatra bought jeans at neighboring Fred Segal, they were delivered to Ma Maison, to the chagrin of Segal's clerks. ("I finally refused the deliveries," says longtime Segal's buyer Mara White. "That's not the way one walked into Ma Maison.")

Others were less enchanted with "the restaurant," as it was known to insiders. The nay sayers had their reasons. They got tired of seeing Orson Welles eating caviar all afternoon. "I was insulted," says one agent who prefers anonymity. "I was made to wait . . . And then they wouldn't let me go upstairs."

"Upstairs" was for regulars only. The suite of rooms resembled a French country house both in furnishings and behavior. More than one Hollywood liaison was launched up the narrow staircase. When Burt Reynolds and Catherine Deneuve filmed *Hustle*, they rehearsed by the second-floor fireplace. You could hear them downstairs. "Hollywood people need security blankets," regular Dinah Shore told me. "They have their Chasen's security blanket, their Bistro blanket, and their Ma Maison blanket. Some will borrow money to come twice a week. Or they'll borrow good-looking friends."

Though the kitchen action begins around nine, the real action starts an hour later. A crew from a local CBS show is setting up cameras upstairs. "The press and the patio made Ma Maison," decided one of the CBS writers. Host Pierre Groleau looked on, amused. Maybe what the writer didn't know was that the press made Ma Maison by default. At the beginning, Groleau and his wife, Aron, tennis wizards, corraled their pals on the courts—people like Diana Ross, Tony Newley, Jack Lemmon—and dragged them into "the restaurant." As Groleau confided, "For me, Michael Caine would come. Then he would permit me to call the top columnists. The columnists loved both the place and the backers. And the reputation got started."

Patrick Terrail remembered: "Ma Maison became a success during one weekend in 1975. It was the week we were in Paris doing that party for *That's Entertainment Part II* for Dan Melnick. That was the moment we felt our impact . . . the first year, we almost went bankrupt." Terrail, "the tall terror," grimaced at the memory. So did Groleau.

Downstairs maître d'-manager Claude Gourdal felt comfortable with his reservations book. Each name was listed meticulously, in multicolored felt pens. Each hour of the day commands a full page in the book, and there are gaps on every page. "I don't see people in relation to their power," said Terrail almost convincingly. "I have no power myself. I am a servant, and nobody wants to eat with the help. That's why I don't go to Hollywood parties. I must not compete with my clientele . . . Let's say I'm cognizant of the power I don't have."

"I'll tell you what's wonderful," said producer Lili Zanuck, who met her husband, Dick, through Pierre Groleau. "What's wonderful is that you can come here when you're young and talk to people who are old. It's a mingle of young and old in Hollywood." Mrs. Z. had a point. Surveying the six best tables, those that front the outside walkway, one noticed the rare juxtaposition of Hollywood youth and experience. The two could mingle, however briefly. Regular Walter Matthau would make shoptalk with then-young actor James Woods; game show millionaire Mark Goodson chatted with rising entertainment attorney Ken Ziffren; Patti Davis Reagan kisses one of her mother's friends. It's cozy, though not always.

One messy patio incident was a throwback to Hollywood's palmier days at Ciro's and Romanoff's. One slow afternoon the agent Bobby Littman was accosted by producer Sidney Beckerman—the agent was dating his daughter. The argument was private, but the near fistfight witnessed by a full patio was rowdier than expected. The agent was unaware that the producer had been a boxer in his youth.

"The agent we never saw again," recalled Pierre Groleau. "But Sidney is here three times a week. It used to be four, until Mortons opened."

"Let's face it," said Wolfgang Puck, "the movie business is boring. If we would have only people from the movie business coming, we would get broke." There was silence for a moment. "Because you make a great movie doesn't mean you are a great man," Puck went on. "You're not Dr. Salk or anything. I think the doctor from Pasadena who comes here is just as important as the movie people."

Puck then got a look from Terrail that said otherwise. "Why do you think the doctor from Pasadena comes here, Wolf?" the tall terror asked, smartly.

"To see movie stars," admitted the chef. Puck now says that little moment was a turning point. He says he knew he had to strike out on his own and start his own business. To separate. And in the best Eve Harrington story in modern Hollywood, Wolfgang became Margo Channing.

If Ma Maison was dinner—the fabled, long-lasting Nate 'n Al's is lunch. (The day in December 1991 when Al Mendelson died was a day of mourning in Beverly Hills.) As the major daytime clubhouse in Los Angeles, only Hillcrest Country Club rivals the one-room deli. The major thing to know about Nate 'n Al's is that it's the only place in the town you can always find Lew Wasserman on Saturday morning, always with his grandson Casey (ultimately the heir to his MCA-Matsushita fortune). The long-distance runner is not the Polo Lounge, not Le Dome, but this nothing little room on Beverly Drive that never changes. When Marvin Davis wanted to steal a favored waitress from Nate 'n Al's for his new Carnegie Deli down the street—practically the whole club became enraged, and boycotted the Carnegie for weeks. The club has loyalties, and Nate 'n Al's is one of them. Maybe it reminds members of their salad days. Or borscht days.

"May I sign my check?" asked David Begelman politely, after a recent breakfast at Nate 'n Al's.

"You can sign the check," answered Gussie Friedberg, Begelman's favorite waitress, "but I want my tip in cash."

The exchange became part of the morning Nate 'n Al's folklore—or apocrypha. It spans five decades, from a back room in the '40s where Fanny Brice held court, to the ritualistic Saturday breakfast visits of studio men like John Veitch and Frank Price. It's a true club ritual: Darryl Zanuck used to ask his executives, "What happened at Nate 'n Al's this morning?"

If it sounds like a private club, in some ways it is. The deli, if only in the morning, is really a fraternity. It's so exclusive that even "members" line up outside to get in. By 8 A.M. the twenty-eight tables are usually full. Since the room seats only 101 people, every chair counts.

The place may be famous, but it's not been franchised, remodeled (in seventeen years anyway), expanded, or cashed in on. Originally called Nate 'n Lou's, the deli was built in 1943. Fourteen months later, Al Mendelson and fellow Detroit deli man Nate Reimer became partners. After Reimer died in the '50s, Mendelson took over ownership. It's still family-owned (by son Barry Mendelson), and it's never without action. Beyond the food, there's a mystique. It's best grasped in terms of a local hangout. Be it Romanoff's in the '50s or the Luau in the '60s, Beverly Hills has by tradition needed a central watering hole where Spencer Tracy or Arnold Schwarzenegger can slip in at three in the afternoon to shmooze with their lawyers. On a given day, this clubhouse features bookies, George Burns, former beauty queens (like former Miss America Mary Ann Mobley), former somebodies, financiers, and (when she's in town) Doris Day. Only for her is a table reserved—but only in Beverly Hills does a lady breakfast with her dog. "Do sneaks her poodle in," reports a smitten counterman off the record. "We feed the little dog, but don't tell nobody."

That's about as racy as it gets in the clubhouse. And the owner wants it that way. The club is explosive enough all day long—here they should relax.

"I knew I liked Hollywood," reasoned Mendelson, "the day I got an offer involving every studio in town. They wanted to put up $30,000 apiece. Each of the studios was going to be partnered in the future of Nate 'n Al's. They wanted to buy me the corner of Wilshire Boulevard and Beverly Drive . . . But I wanted to be my own boss. I mean, why break it up?"

Mendelson, then in his eighties, and a man who'd taken one vacation in twelve years, squinted and looked back in time. "That corner would have been a real gold mine," he admitted.

"Here we have only a silver mine."

The New York branch of the club headquarters is the Russian Tea Room on 57th Street, next door to Carnegie Hall. It's such a haven for people from Hollywood that in 1990 the owner of the RTR, a former actress named Faith Stewart-Gordon, had decided to create an Oscar night party like the one Polly Bergen had in New York every year until she moved back to L.A. (Polly's was the party where Mia Farrow met Woody Allen.) Faith wanted to do what Polly did—create a New York equivalent of the Lazar Party, as Oscar night is known in the club.

But Faith needn't worry about the RTR remaining the East Coast club headquarters. The place is an unbreakable. One day I got on a plane to New York and decided to haunt the RTR, to understand the mystique. I never heard so many dropped names in one week in my whole life. I only had to listen. A banquette away was a woman I'll call the Mouth. I could hear the Mouth babbling on about Raquel Welch.

After Raquel Welch made her Broadway debut, replacing Lauren Bacall in *Woman of the Year*, she headed directly here. Not Sardi's, not Elaine's, but the RTR. She needed validation of her new status as a Broadway star. Such nerve she has. Saying to Faith, "Now that I've got Bacall's part, do I get her table, too?"

Of course, Raquel got the first (and best) banquette, the one on the right, in the main room. The lady, that season, was a Broadway star. And, Bacall was in London.

Certain New Yorkers like to call it the Polo Lounge East. Californians often call it the Commissary, because as a lunch room it services the New York executives of the major studios. Those in the know also know the importance—literally the significance, within the inner sanctums of the club—of being seen there. Being seen on a regular basis is even better; it signifies good fortune, and a sense of belonging.

Those names, or their helpers, begin calling for tables around 9 A.M. Many of the calls have a nervous edge. You can hear it, in the voices that clog the restaurant's two switchboards. The voices on the phones are worried about only one thing—getting the right table. For some of those voices it's the biggest worry of the day. One morning author Peter Maas (*Serpico*) was pretty worried: *People* magazine was interviewing Maas, and Maas needed Table No. 1 to impress the interviewer.

"I was sweating bullets over that one," confided Gregory Camillucci, the RTR vice-president who doubles as maître d'. "I got very lucky with Garson Kanin. He came and went early. Because Gar is almost seventy-five, I can put him in the first booth without anybody complaining. He was out of here by two and Peter was in the booth five minutes later." Even then the RTR host couldn't breathe easy: "I got a copy of Peter's latest book," confided Camillucci, "and I sent it over to the table to be autographed." The host winked. "Those are the little touches—the minor seductions—that keep the ship afloat."

The RTR might be better referred to as the oldest established permanent floating Russian gold mine in New York. It sits there on 57th Street, the Street of Dreams, like an oasis. Club members breathe easier knowing it's there.

"Often," says the very visible club publicist Bobby Zarem, "you don't have to even say the name aloud and someone will know what you mean. Take the Kirk Douglases. Last night, late, I ran into them at Elaine's. It was too late to talk, but I hadn't seen Ann and Kirk in ages, so we decided to lunch today. Without saying it, we knew that meant the RTR; it's unspoken. Now, tonight, late again, I'm meeting Michael and Shakira Caine. And tomorrow . . ."

It isn't all social. Deals do get done here, too. Directly and indirectly, formally and informally. Adjoining regular tables "belong" to agents Robbie Lantz (Anthony Hopkins, Peter Shaffer, Elizabeth Taylor) and Sam Cohn (Woody Allen, Mike Nichols). (The sense of "agent talk" at the RTR is captured almost perfectly in the Sydney Pollack–Dustin Hoffman scene in *Tootsie*.) Cohn, often rumpled and often late for lunch, will if necessary take a client upstairs to the Casino—for any hush-hush deal making, or just to create a scene.

The scenes make good dish.

Dancer Isadora Duncan once took an apartment across the street from the RTR—just to be nearby, to get her name in the columns. Like Duncan, the White Russians who emigrated to America in the '20s were seeking a haven, a spot to gather and commiserate about their homeland. The RTR is really like a long-running émigré Broadway musical comedy-drama grossing upward of $10 million a year. Every meal is a performance, choreographed by savvy reservations clerks (and chefs). If it takes fifteen minutes to get from lobby to chair, so what? You probably ran into Susan Sarandon, gossip columnist Suzy, agent Sue Mengers, or Susan Saint James. (Their hairdressers might be there, too, at other tables, but that's the Manhattan melting pot.) Interestingly, nobody fusses over anybody. Dustin Hoffman unselfconsciously displays pictures of his children to playwright Arthur Miller. "No guest, star or not, is to be tampered with by another guest," says the host. "Oddly enough, people really do behave. We only allow two people, Woody Allen and Rudolf Nureyev, to wear hats inside. Now you'd think that Woody Allen in a hat in a restaurant would cause a stir. Yes, people stare a little, but nobody dares bother anyone." Not even semiregular Jacqueline Onassis is pestered. JBO, as she's referred to around the premises, prefers the pelmney Siberian (meat dumplings), as does Mike Nichols—and the management is aware of such preferences. (JBO also likes the house caviar.)

Clubbiness at the RTR reaches new levels. Stacy Keach gets his mail here. Sam Cohn, the hardest man in America to get on the phone, can be reached through the RTR switchboard (assuming you know to tip the switchboard people). Several years ago, when entertainment lawyer Arnold Weissberger died, his friends gathered at the RTR for the Jewish ritual *shiva*. When impresario Sol Hurok died, the RTR kept his table set—and empty—for an entire evening. Regulars Jerry Stiller and Anne Meara swear that they proposed to each other at the RTR way back when. Jackie Bisset and Alexander Godunov fell in love. Upstairs. Van Cliburn raved about the food to Nikita Khrushchev.

"You go there, or you go to Elaine's," sums up Shirley MacLaine, who sometimes goes to the RTR directly from the airport. "The RTR is . . . lunch. There's something about it, the samovars or the Russianness, that says daytime. I also don't feel I'd mind going there alone, as a woman alone. In the daytime. Now Elaine's is another story—I can write all day, then walk into Elaine's at three in the morning for pasta and confidence. I'll sit and talk to Elaine until five . . . But these two places, the RTR and Elaine's, are where you go to plug into Manhattan. The two of them are it. You just have to know which times to go where."

You also have to know the company you're keeping. You really have to believe you belong.

Otherwise you feel like you're in Siberia.

CLUB RULE THIRTY-TWO

The club behaves totally in the moment. Don't expect the moments to add up to anything.

Ma Maison is now only a figment of some people's imaginations—a fun figment, but a figment nonetheless. That's because in the club, memories are very long and very short. "There are actually people here who don't know who Freddie Fields is," a producer said of producer Fields, who was the most powerful club agent of the '70s. The other producer went on, a sense of wonderment in his voice: "There are people here who don't understand the tentacles of Ray." He meant Stark, whose disciples and former employees run much of the club. Or want to. The tentacles of Ray are the tentacles you can't afford to not know about.

On the other hand, nobody professes to much remember what happened to the tentacles of Ray that got away—the ones that left the business for one reason or another. The phone sheets are already too long to add names on the fringe. And not that many people come back.

Exceptions: Guy McElwaine and Sue Mengers, who both returned to the agency business after years away. (Sue got smart, in 1991, and got out again. But who can predict her future?) The point is, these names immediately went on the right phone sheets.

24

Club Gossip—
Liz Smith

Liz Smith is a gossip columnist who isn't in the club, but is read religiously by the club. So she's kind of a "special" member. Ditto Army Archerd and George Christy, who write very different columns for Variety and The Hollywood Reporter. These are not the only columns the club reads. Journalists aren't in the club, with no exceptions. But journalists can get people like Marvin Davis into the club via publicity. Army Archerd got Rock Hudson back into the club at the very end by sympathetically scooping everyone else about the actor having AIDS. George Christy first got read by the club when he got invited to dinner by Betsy Bloomingdale and Lorena Nidorf. (Lorena the Czarina was the widow of Louis B. Mayer, and she gave glorious little dinners at the chicest apartment in Westwood.) Aljean Harmetz went skiing with the club, when she was still with the New York Times. Liz Smith goes junketeering with the club, because she writes about their social lives. More than anybody since Winchell, Liz Smith is the club mouth.

Liz is the columnist you'd always expect to find at the RTR or Elaine's. She's a modern Walter Lippmann in terms of being networked. But it's likelier you'd find her at home, writing. In sweat pants. Liz is the gossip queen who spends more time at her typewriter than any secretary. But she's the club mouthpiece.

"And she doesn't see people in the apartment," is how her more-smug-than-Clifton Webb assistant St. Clair Pugh put it. But who wanted to meet her in a hamburger joint? It's one thing if a movie star won't let you see her house, but you must meet the press at home. Liz Smith's one-bedroom Murray Hill apartment is so unremarkable, so cluttered (unlike her personality) that you don't wonder why it's off limits. Unopened crates of Cristal champagne and demonstration tapes from MCA and CBS vie for room with two desk chairs and unused sofas. No wonder Liz Smith doesn't see people at home. Glamorous it isn't. Another illusion shot.

The first morning I arrived she seemed unaware I was there for about an hour or so, which was heaven. All those dishy phone conversations: Barbara Walters ringing up with news about Ivana Trump. Dominick Dunne phoning in an item. Irving Lazar, full of publishing gossip. Liz plays a lot of roles on those five lines and occasionally St. Clair Pugh plays director. ("He can be a bastard," Liz said one day at lunch, "but he's my bastard.") I watched him field her calls like a White House press secretary.

Bette Davis' lawyer, Harold Schiff, was on Line 1. Liz Smith took the call. "Hello, honey. Please don't write me a letter. Listen, Harold, I have a report that Bette and her daughter B.D. have reconciled." Smith said this dubiously. "No? Definitely not? Well, my source was right for once in his life!" She beamed and hung up.

A terrified caterer was on Line 2. The day before one of Peter Lawford's children hosted a square dance in honor of Caroline Kennedy's marriage. Caroline's mother, Jacqueline Onassis, was livid that the menu was leaked to Liz Smith by (presumably) Glorious Foods, the caterer. A waiter would have to be sacrificially fired. Said the caterer to Liz Smith: "You can tell Mrs. Onassis we're not firing anyone. Our waiters don't talk." That one stopped Smith in her tracks. "I guess he doesn't expect to be hired by the Kennedys again," she said after hanging up. "Or maybe he'd rather have a mention in the column."

A WNBC-TV producer was on Line 3. That day on *Live at five,* Liz Smith would do two items on her broadcast, a three-minute segment she does three times a week on the WNBC popular afternoon talkathon. "We need graphics of Nancy Reagan and Jean Harris," Smith said. "Nancy got sixty-three red roses for her sixty-fifth birthday from a florists' association. I know she isn't sixty-three but she sure sticks to her guns . . . Yes, I know Nancy sold her book to Random House. [Agent] Mort Janklow told me Random House came to him. If Santa Claus comes to the chimney . . . Jean Harris we're using because of her book, *Stranger in Two Worlds.* My lead is, 'If you like to argue, simply say two words: Jean Harris.' Listen, I know it's not easy to get a good picture in jail . . . But try!"

Joe Armstrong, former publisher of *Rolling Stone,* was on Line 4. "I've never known a day so dull," Liz Smith told him, not kidding. "The city is so totally deserted they should give me a plaque for staying in town . . . Now, Joe, where would you hear that the attorney general called *Playboy* pornographic? Okay, kid, you little gold mine . . . No, I already told Bella I can't use her item. I can't write only about fund-raisers!"

Now it was Line 5. (There are only five lines.) This time it was Diane Sawyer. Only now Liz Smith was making herself coffee in the kitchen of the apartment. Liz Smith has only two hands, both at this moment ink-stained. She'd just typed a column on how the rich are different, and had one hour to finish a Sunday piece that she would devote to a first novel by a colleague. Her calls were being answered for her. But this was *Diane Sawyer* and Smith snatched up the phone.

"Hi, you gorgeous thing, how are you?" said Smith in the kind of Texas drawl that New Yorkers find so intimate. It's a semiliterary drawl that novelists like Dan Jenkins and anchors like Dan Rather use to great advantage, and so does Liz Smith. "I saw your ex-boss [60 *Minutes* executive producer] Don Hewitt on a boat over the weekend," Smith confided into the receiver. "He said, 'I always believed Diane would never leave me' . . . Jean [Mrs. Douglas] MacArthur was also on the boat. She said to me, 'Liz, honey, I promised the general if I ever talked' . . . I told her if she ever talked, it should be to Diane Sawyer! What do you mean [producer] Charles Evans will kill himself if you don't return his calls. Trust me, honey, Charlie won't kill himself. It ain't fitting."

Probably Diane Sawyer took the advice. Liz Smith is listened to. She has already outlasted any and all gossip column rivals in New York, and in Hollywood she has competition but no equivalent. (Smith is syndicated in about sixty papers by *New York Newsday,* but her turf—and her power base—is Manhattan.) As David McClintick put it in *Indecent Exposure,* Smith has "redefined gossip and elevated it to a new level of respectability." McClintick defines the Liz Smith column as a "new form of gossip journalism."

Example: It was Smith who first printed "the possibility," as she put it, "that Richard Pryor might have AIDS. The rumors were rampant, and not because of homosexuality," Smith explained. "I printed a list of reasons, praying it wasn't true. But the talk was everywhere. Richard had admittedly been an intravenous drug user, and he'd had a lot of blood transfusions . . . Well, I was laid to filth by my friend [former club executive] Dawn Steel, saying how could I do this? Studio heads see the column faster than anybody."

Smith has been right—it was she who "kept the drum fires burning" in the 1978 David Begelman check-forging scandal and convinced chief witness Cliff Robertson to break his silence in the case—but she has also been wrong. She predicted that Robert Redford would enter politics and that Elizabeth Taylor would not marry John Warner. But whatever else Liz Smith has been, she has been pivotal—and personal. As Frank Sinatra calls her, "The Extra Strength Tylenol of journalists." Or, as producer Ray Stark puts it: "Liz isn't always accurate but she is always fair." What she isn't—and it works to her advantage—is Hollywood-based. "I don't have enough integrity to live in Los Angeles and write a gossip column," Smith told me, half joking. "I spent one Christmas there and I saw the gifts that went to Hedda and Louella. I thought then I could never live there. Now there's no temptation, of course: I'm too old to be corrupted."

"Gwen Davis called from L.A. She'll be in town tomorrow and tomorrow night," said St. Clair Pugh.

"Good. That means I don't have to answer the phone tomorrow night," replied Liz Smith.

It's harder to write funny than it is to talk funny, and Liz Smith knows that. She loves to recall the broadcast about Joan Kennedy moving to Boston while Ted Kennedy remained in Virginia. "Rose Kennedy saw it and said: 'Who's Virginia?' " The story is funny every time Smith tells it. But one can't do four columns a week, two broadcasts a week, four (or more) parties a week, four sessions with a hairdresser a week—and still be Dorothy Parker.

What Liz Smith does in reality is so unglamorous it would send journalism students back to film school. In a robe or a T-shirt, she sits in a 9 × 12 room facing an unbeautiful one-window slice of Manhattan and she types, using an old Texas Instrument and an earphone and a stopwatch to time and hear herself. She chooses the items. She asks Pugh for credits. ("Did John Hurt play *The Naked Civil Servant*?" Yes.) She wonders what's on the record, and off, but then she just types it all up. And reads it aloud. Not waiting for perfection, or inspiration—but often while waiting for a cab—she snatches time, and writes columns. And three-minute TV scripts. And gets interrupted all day long by Pugh, by calls she can't refuse . . .

"Liz, it's Simon & Schuster time," said Pugh one morning while Smith was writing a column. Twenty years and they're still together. Pugh even worked with Smith when she ghosted the Cholly Knickerbocker column in the '50s. Neither uses kid gloves with each other, which saves time. Writing is a cranky business, after all.

"Simon & Schuster, Liz," repeated Pugh.

"Meaning what exactly?"

"Meaning Dick [Snyder, S&S president] and Joni [Evans, his former associate-wife who then headed her own S&S imprint, Linden Press] are I think in Splitsville."

"Get me Joni."

One and a half minutes later, Joni Evans was on Line 1.

Evans and Snyder (or "Dick and Joni" to the trade) had long been one of Manhattan's most public and powerful couples; their rise through the ranks of Simon & Schuster, and their romance, had long been perfect Manhattan media fodder.

"Hello, my darling," began Smith. "This is the divorce call. You are still living together on weekends? I think that's very intelligent myself. Couples can't be together all the time. You are going on vacation together next week? Oh. No, I don't want to quote you. You just trust me. Yes, I love you too. Bye."

Smith swiveled in her chair, and raised her eyebrows to indicate amusement. "They're living apart, but are together on weekends and vacations. And, no, we are not calling her husband." She said this as if the arrangement was the most natural in the world, or at least in New York.

If not Hollywood. Liz sometimes looks askance at the club town. "A lot of Hollywood people are dead at sixty-five and don't know it." Or: "I realize that in covering Hollywood you have to go along with their fictions, or they close ranks. I do know you can't attack people who live there because they don't live in a realistic world." Or: "Everything in Hollywood is work and myth."

Still, even in New York columnists do become celebrities, especially with regular TV exposure. Walk with Liz Smith from Rockefeller Center to her dentist's office on 50th Street and you discover what local fame is like. Asked for an autograph, she replies: "You must be hard up tonight, honey." Here, after all, is a woman in her sixties carrying two tote bags, slouching, wishing she'd seen her hairdresser that day. "People see in me a middle-aged woman who talks like Texas and knows that 99 percent of them will never get into Elaine's. I have just enough celebrity that it's amusing. Walter Winchell affected the stock market. I can't do that. And I can't make a star. If you can't make a star, you have no real power."

CLUB RULE THIRTY-THREE

Don't believe anything you read about the club ever. Unless it's written by a member. You can discount almost any Hollywood journalism as being the work of an outsider.

At the same time you must read every word of it, always remembering that the press knows very little about the inner workings: Hollywood is the opposite of Washington that way, or New York. In Hollywood the press largely prints what it's told to print. That's why the David Begelman check-forging scandal was never really documented at the time. The press is more *out* than *in*, in many ways.

Example: When Time Inc. chairman Hedley Donovan came to Hollywood, and the *Time* bureau wanted to give him a party, they budgeted $3,000. The party cost $70,000. Even *Time* magazine's Hollywood bureau doesn't know the cost of things in the club.

25

Club Voice— Barbara Walters

Barbara Walters got in because she grew up around the club, in her father's nightclub the Latin Quarter—and she knew how to play by the rules. Because of her breeding—and because she's on network television—she's the only journalist since Walter Winchell to really be admitted. Both Barbara Walters' marriages—to producers Lee Guber and Merv Adelson—helped her get and stay in the club, even though the marriages ended. Both men understood the players and the plays. Barbara Walters' friendships with Mrs. Ted Ashley and Sue Mengers also helped. Barbara Walters interviewing only all-stars made her an all-star, too. Barbara Walters also stayed in because she had show-place homes on both coasts, and a house in Aspen where she entertains with great style. Barbara Walters would stay in even if she wasn't on TV, at least for a while, and not just because her last husband was a founder of La Costa. Not that that hurts.

Sometimes it *is* who you know. "I love you because you love Sue Mengers," Barbara Walters said five minutes after we met. She didn't remember our first encounter. I don't blame her. It was eighteen years earlier by the pool at the Beverly Hills Hotel. Then she was plugging her ghost-written book *How to Talk to Practically Anyone About Practically Anything*. She wore an orange wool turtleneck and skirt, an odd poolside get-up. But she was just a journalist in those days, not an all-star. And I was the leg. With her was her best friend, a woman named Joyce Easton who went on to marry the ultrapowerful archetype agent Ted Ashley, only to divorce him years later and become a child psychologist in upstate New York. (Shades of *Tender Is the Night*.)

"Listen to her story," Barbara Walters counseled that day by the pool. "She's my best friend since childhood, so it will shed some light." Joyce Easton, it turned out, had found herself in 1961 just out of college with enough money to "do one of two things," as she put it. "Go to Europe for a summer or move into the Beverly Hills Hotel for six weeks." She chose California, this sly girl, "and within two months I met my future husband."

I thought what Joyce Easton did said a lot about Barbara Walters. It took Barbara Walters umpteen years to find her second husband, Merv Adelson, but she knows something about timing. So eighteen years later we reminisced about Easton; unintentionally a chord was struck.

What I was most taken with was her way of running her fingers through her streaked hair and turning it into a topknot. Mrs. Robinson in *The Graduate*. That seductive. When she stands alone in a corner outside her New York office, waving good-bye to a visitor, she seems as vulnerable as Anne Bancroft was to Dustin Hoffman at the top of the movie. It's little things like that, like the personal poems she writes for guests at her dinner parties, that draw people to her.

Like the time she showed up with her cousin Shirley at Sally Field's house in Tarzana, and she started making coffee. "Maybe that's the power of Barbara Walters," Sally Field told me later. "You reveal things while you are making coffee. It's in her nature to ask emotional questions, but because she's sympathetic, you go deeper. She identifies with you, this woman who's been courted by royalty. So you go beyond the fear threshold."

Walters drew the line—how far can you go with a star?—in 1975, on her first ABC special. Barbara Walters touched Jon Peters' knee in mid-interview. "Why don't you two get married?" she asked Peters and his then-companion Barbra Streisand. Edward R. Murrow didn't do that: Barbara Walters had drawn the new line. And she toes that line—between revealing a star and hurting a star—very carefully. "You know what Hollywood is like," she said. "It's this big." She curled a thumb and forefinger into a circle the size of a small doughnut. "If stars were really unhappy with the interviews—one would have said to the other: 'Don't do her.' It would have all dried up. No one is going to come back again if they are damaged and hurt on what is really a long interview. You can't be a hit-and-run driver."

In person Walters has what Truman Capote called *lift*. That means her co-workers never look tired because she never looks tired. "If she has limits, I haven't seen them yet," says Tom Clancy, the *20/20* segment producer who's worked most closely with Walters. "You have to run to keep up with her." *Lift* is a quality that draws people out, rather than turning them off.

"I keep thinking it's going to get quieter, and sometimes it does," Walters relented, fiddling with a club sandwich. There's an attention to detail even her friends gasp over. At her Christmas dinner in Aspen one year every guest got a small gift that applied to that person. Her former producer Phyllis McGrady remembers "how Barbara never has to stop tape in an interview, ever. In the middle of doing Richard Pryor, his wife and son came on—nobody knew he had a wife and a son at that point—and Barbara just went on with the interview. Nothing fazed her."

You don't get the whole Barbara Walters story in one visit. You get it by asking her to connect with her own past lives. She was a child of nightclubs who saw Sophie Tucker without makeup, and listened to Sophie Tucker's confidences about her son. "I saw the beautiful show girls without makeup, too. Broadway stars would be in the house. I knew they had problems." Curiously, neither of Walters' parents fit the saloon clichés: "My father looked like an accountant," Walters remembered, "and he was a voracious reader. This man who ran a nightclub collected first editions. He had no business sense at all. He was in the tradition of the Ziegfelds, where you do beautiful shows and you die broke. My mother—a woman who never drank, even a sherry—probably would have been happier marrying a doctor. The family always said, 'Why did you marry this man?' He was funny, sensitive, and a wonderful writer. It was tough, we moved all the time. But my life wasn't show business; the schools and my friends weren't show business. We just happened to have Thanksgiving at the Latin Quarter. Doesn't everybody?"

One subtle theme to this woman's saga might be how she became the club Cinderella: The transformation of Barbara Walters from unexceptional-looking video club journalist to blonded best-dressed cover girl—that's a story.

"Every time I go on the air and look good, I get all kinds of questions about when did I have my face done. When I don't look terribly good, people say, 'Why doesn't she have her face done?' " Walters leaned across the small round table that serves as her desk. "I think there are a lot of things I have learned. My hair is lighter. My hair is better. I now have the same makeup and hair person all the time. I never had that before, never thought about it.

"One day my second husband said to me, 'Your lighting is awful. Every Hollywood star always worries about their lighting.' I didn't and now I do. I now have my own lighting person all the time. I now have lighting from the floor. It shines up—she demonstrated with her hands— and it takes away all of this stuff which you can see when you are with me in person. I never knew about all this. I went to England a few years ago to do Barbara Cartland, and she came with her own lights."

Walters watched and learned. Seeing her over a period of a week is to see a lesson in wardrobing: a beige-sueded T-shirt with a Harris tweed skirt, with a double strand of pearls linked by extraordinary onyx pieces. It's not just lighting—it's costuming, too.

On TV "you don't see the circles and you don't see the lines," as Walters puts it—even if you do see the hair. "I used to do my own hair. I never used to have streaks. I'd color it myself, all one color, and it came out orange. I don't do that now. I don't want to spend all this time talking about my face. But, well, we did Teddy Pendergrass recently, and they lit it. And I said, 'Let me take a look.' I asked them to move some of the lighting. I never used to look at myself that way, never. I now know which side of my face looks best. So now I will be shot from the left side, unless the guest wants to be shot from the left side. And I'm older. I've been doing this a long time now." Barbara Walters sighed. There was wear and tear in her voice if not in her face.

"There's wear and tear in my heart," said Walters with a slight self-deprecation, "in my heart and soul."

I asked here a quintessential Barbara Walters question.

"Do you ever lose control?"

"Once. On the first special with Barbra Streisand."

Barbara gave Barbra final control.

"Barbra got to see the tape the night we did the interview," remembered Walters. "The same night! There on a sofa were Barbra and Jon Peters and Sue Mengers—my friend who got me Streisand—and manager Marty Erlichman, with everybody having an opinion . . . I never gave anyone else control again, ever."

Then Barbara Walters got up to go home, and get dressed for a club cocktail party welcoming Sue Mengers back to New York. She asked me to go with her, but I couldn't wait to get back to the hotel to start writing.

CLUB RULE THIRTY-FOUR

Members socially ignore nonmembers; social energy, like psychic energy, is finite—members never waste it.

That's why you shouldn't be fooled by Barbara Walters' access. If she were not in the club, she would not get the dish she gets. The truth is, members are bored by nonmembers. At dinner at Primi, a club executive talked with a club agent and her club executive husband. This little trio managed to ignore their fourth table mate (me) for over two hours. Even though I tried (for once) to talk. I grew to like at least two of these people, but they were testing me socially. That night, I failed.

The point is, in the club you pay your dues before you're visible. Members feel they have the right to ignore or not ignore you. Once, in Mary and Irving Lazar's entrance hall in Trousdale, Farrah Fawcett looked right through me for twelve minutes. We were the only two people standing there. Farrah is considered by some people to be the shrewdest woman in the club under fifty. But I thought she was simply rude. (She did the same thing to me at the funeral of her hairdresser's mother—but I respected her for showing up.)

The only sure places nonmembers won't get ignored is on a company jet, or private (as in "home") screening room. There you're worth talking to. Whoever you are.

FEAR

The house where I worked as the leg had the best bones of them all. It was a classic of the Spanish Colonial Revival period, circa 1910. No Hollywood house I would eventually get into had this history. (Excepting only the Jack Warner houses—the one on Angelo Drive that David Geffen bought for $48.5 million, and the one in Palm Springs where the Shagans live and the one on Malibu Road where the Ziffrens live. The Ziffrens' Sunday salons were the best in the club, nonpareil.)

But the house where I worked was the party house of the '40s, the quintessential club party house. Single-storied, stucco, rambling, and cozy, it had the best lawn for club croquet; it was Darryl Zanuck's favorite house. On the night Clifton Webb and his mother, Maybelle, entertained there for Cole Porter, the guests included the de rigueur Coopers and Stewarts and also a shaky Marilyn Monroe and a then-sturdy Judy Garland. At one point, a quivering Monroe walked up to Garland, in the marble foyer, and clutched her arm like a frightened child. "Stay by me," pleaded MM. "I'm insecure."

Garland was in the throes of a new happy marriage, and she looked rather invulnerably at Monroe. Judy was probably in her cups when she said, "We're all insecure, Marilyn. Leave me alone."

Forget that Garland sounded cruel. The truth is, she was expressing real Hollywood wisdom at its razor sharpest: Even in the club, they're all insecure (or, *especially* in the club). Fear is what binds club members to each other, what keeps them in cahoots with each other. It's the glue. For both the business community and the creative community, fear reigns and motivates. The money monsters are always frightened they'll be out of a job, and the creative people are always sure they'll never work again. So they dwell on past glory, a lot. At parties Jack Nicholson talks not about his latest picture, but about *Tommy* in 1975. ("Remember how beautiful I was in *Tommy*?" he says to a dinner partner.) In the living room of the Irving Lazars', Farrah Fawcett, still scared about money, haggles over payments for some jewelry that Irving has located for her in New York. ("Pay when you can," Lazar finally tells Farrah.) In Lee Strasberg's acting class, petrified club star Sally Field goes berserk after a scene. ("I'm no good, Lee, I'm just no good.") As refuge from fear, Dyan Cannon has her private primal-scream room.

Fear is the one connective between the vicious Peter Pans—the Blake Edwardses and Frank Yablans of this world—and those simpler souls, the addictive overachievers. People like Edwards' wife, Julie Andrews, and the true club child Dick Zanuck. The talented ones who usually hurt nobody but themselves with their self-flagellations. Or the smart ones who survived family horror stories. I decided to track these people down, to get to the root of all the anxiety in Hollywood. I met a nervous Chevy Chase for lunch at the Beverly Hilton, of all places, and found him on the verge of paranoia about absolutely nothing. ("Anything can tick me off—my wife overshopping, anything.") Julie Andrews I found in her Century City office barely touching a watercress finger sandwich, a skinny star terrified of gaining a pound. In the '70s Julie gave up a major career to be in Switzerland with a neurotic husband she loves. Out of fear, she left Hollywood at her peak, and I wanted to know why.

What I learned as the leg—to weed out the phonies—served me very well later on. Because you can spot a phony as clearly (or more clearly) when you are twenty than when you are thirty. And a reporter who can sniff out the phonies is ahead of the game. Because the phonies resurface periodically, you must be aware. Steven Seagall is a phony even though he's a club star—he was Mike Ovitz' personal trainer. He's a phony because he primps for women at gyms all over Hollywood. Norman Lear kisses his secretary on the lips every time she interrupts a meeting with a message—but Norman isn't a phony, he is merely precious. He feels he's earned that right. Club lyricist Sammy Cahn is a phony because he drops you when you are out of print; club lyricists Marilyn and Alan Bergman aren't phonies because they don't do that.

These judgments are always subjective, always based on experience. An awful lot of phonies in the club seem merely "special" when you first meet them. People like the well-bred Bert Schneider (who announced his engagement to Candy Bergen even before he proposed to her) and the well-bred Cornelia Guest (who pretends to be a star when she isn't even an actress). Is Peter Bogdanovich a phony because he snubs you in his own breakfast room mistaking you for a messenger? Or is he a snob? When you meet him a dozen years later, on a movie set, he couldn't be more charming. Is that phony? Or is it fear behavior? At the Golden Globes, Diana Ross' first husband trailed behind her, looking foolishly lost, until she turned around and blurted, "I told you to keep up with me." At twenty I thought Diana Ross was cruel, but twenty years later, I think she was just terrified.

And so is everyone else in the club. And that's why I became less frightened myself. No longer the leg, I was no longer drenched in perspiration at the thought of being in Elizabeth Taylor's kitchen in Bel Air. Gradually I stopped all that. I became less nervous. I only sweated for the first few minutes, not the whole evening. Not because I thought I belonged, but because the one thing I saw around me everywhere I went was fear. What I saw, right up close, was just how terrified everyone else is. And that freed me, on some level. Because *they* were all scared—of failure, mostly—I didn't have to be.

26

Anxiety in Hollywood— Self-Elected Torture

LuWanda Katzman is the club shrink and fixer. (She fixed
Ann-Margret, and managed to keep as patients Steve Martin
and Bernadette Peters—before, during, and after their relationship.) Harry Glassman is the club plastic surgeon. Leroy Perry
is the club chiropractor because he tells club members the truth
about their mechanics. Rex Kennamer is the club internist emeritus because of Elizabeth Taylor and Edie and Lew Wasserman.
(The Wasserman house is the one house Rex goes to for dinner.)
Rick Clark is the club trainer because he can handle Jerry Weintraub. Aida Thibiant is the club facialist because she went to
people's houses before she got them to invest in her own salon.
Now they come to her. Jeannie at CIA Coiffure has been the
club manicurist for a hundred years because she still goes to
the houses. Mike Silverman was the club realtor forever because he
was as handsome as a movie star and because he had a publicist,
and the best houses. Sammy Cahn was the club lyricist (and
parodist) until he was succeeded by Marilyn and Alan Bergman.
The Bergmans stayed in because they have larger concerns in the
community than just writing parodies. The Bergmans also stayed
in because they fused professionally with Barbra Streisand. Fusion is the club game. Jessica Lange fused with Charlie Bluhdorn

and Bob Fosse and Dino De Laurentiis, who gave her King
Kong, *when she was just a model. She fused with her hair and
makeup women, and has used them on every picture since 1980.
(Meryl Streep fused with her hair and makeup man and has
used him on every picture since 1980.) Barbra Streisand fused
first with Ray Stark, who decided she'd be a movie star, and
then with William Wyler, who made her one. Barbra Streisand
fused with publicist Lee Solters in 1962 and has kept the fusion
going ever since. Lee Solters and Pat Kingsley and Pat Newcomb
are the club publicists because they survived the club control
freaks. (You know the names.) Control is the other favorite club
game, ranking right up there with fusion. Tennis is the club
sport, if you play with a pro, and not an equal. (You don't really
play. You just hit balls. That way you have control.) Weekends
at Two Bunch Palms are the club release, and so are weekends
at Canyon Ranch. The club Christmas is spent at Aspen. But
Africa is the true club getaway, especially if you stay at Tom
Mankiewicz's place. The Hotel du Cap is the club retreat in
Europe. Alaska is the club cruise. Anxiety is the club addiction.*

––––––––––––

The people with the most access to their emotions were the ones I became
obsessed about, and decided to pursue: the Jim Aubreys, the Lucys, and
the Carsons. I thought the really-reals would give me the best perspective
on the club. The ones who had survived the monsters, or been monsters
themselves.

To better understand the monsters and nonmonsters, and what made
them so scared, I went one afternoon to see psychiatrist Dr. Irwin Ruben
of Beverly Hills.

"You have no idea," he said gravely, "the pressure on doctors from the
Hollywood community. It's not unusual to get a call from a producer or
agent saying, 'Doc, your patient writes all night long, but we need his
pages. Don't change him too much! We didn't invent him, Doc, we just
need him.' There's pressure to step outside normal bounds, to bend rules
for somebody talented. The talented patient himself may expect special
treatment. The great story is about the star patient who can't pay his bill,
who says, 'Just tell people you treat me, Doc. They'll be so impressed,
you'll get new business.'"

It's business as usual in Hollywood, and the real business, I discovered,
is anxiety. In a town divided in two parts—the business community and
the creative community—there seems to be no division when it comes

to anxiety. It's Topic A. Whether on the ski slopes of Park City or in the barrackslike residence halls of the Betty Ford Center, it's become a badge of honor to tell all. To not only have a bodyguard, but to talk about why. What once was the stuff of Hollywood novels (addiction, seclusion, insecurity) is now the stuff of media. When Elizabeth Taylor admitted she needed the painkiller Percodan to face a cocktail party, people for the first time in their lives identified with Elizabeth Taylor.

"Do you think there's more stress with success or with failure?" wondered director Herbert Ross, as he scanned a back dining room at Le Dome. The question was like those one asks a Gypsy; there are twenty different answers. Because everything is magnified in Hollywood, nothing is what it seems. In the span of a season, an actor can become financially furnished for life—or permanently damaged by drugs—and the accompanying anxiety will not go unnoticed. (Especially in the various dining rooms of Le Dome, or Mortons, or Apple Pan.)

"Us? Complicated?" Julie Andrews laughed out loud for what seemed like minutes. Blake Edwards, her writer-director husband, was down the hall in his office. "Frankly, I'm surprise Blackie and I have been together as long as we have." Married in 1969, at the end of a decade in which both scaled Hollywood peaks, they survived *Darling Lili*, the 1971 Edsel that almost bankrupted Paramount, and resurfaced only in the '80s (with *10* and *S.O.B.*). Even their detractors—and they have them—are awed by the team's survival.

"Therapy," replied Edwards, sticking his head in his wife's office. "It's our one-word answer for everything." For one five-year period Julie Andrews was in psychoanalysis five times a week; her husband has been going on and off most of his adult life, lately to Dr. Milton Wexler— who was Edwards' writing partner on *The Man Who Loved Women* and *That's Life.* (Wexler—a former student of the fabled Theodore Reik— presides over group therapy in Santa Monica, which Edwards attends, but Andrews doesn't. Jennifer Jones Simon goes and so does Sally Kellerman. He tends privately to Carol Matthau. At Wexler's office one afternoon, the soft-spoken doctor discussed not the Edwardses but the problem with therapy in Hollywood: "For the last ten years of his life, Freud spent an hour a day analyzing himself. The point was to know himself better. Out here, though, there are too many therapies, too much narcissism, too much social chat about it. The question becomes: Who is stable enough to be analyzed?")

On consecutive afternoons at their Century City offices, Julie and Blake Edwards were surprised to be told that Edwards had brought out Andrews' male side on screen—and not just in *Victor/Victoria*. They admitted that Edwards renovated Andrews' "image"—and removed what he once called "the violets between her legs." Their effect on each other is both clear and complicated.

Said Andrews, stretching out in the all-white office: "Once when we were filming Blake said 'Just be yourself.' And I was aghast. When actors say 'Who am I?' they usually mean it. I'm not an exception. Blake makes you dig, because he digs. What's happened to us as a couple borders on old-fashioned. You should see us at Gstaad." (The couple has a house at the Swiss ski village, the only place Andrews says she has ever felt "completely secure.")

"But Julie has become very good at taking care of the kid inside her."

"That's changed, darling, from knowing you," she said, looking into his eyes. "Because it had to change. And both of us getting help is why we've changed as a couple. Look"—Andrews said sharply—"there are such discrepancies in our personalities—we are such opposites—that we had to agree on an investigation of ourselves. My Blackie boy was known as complicated and talented. I was known as sweet and talented. Labels are much too easy."

Is this Julie Andrews talking?

"I'm ambitious," she said strongly, "and I've worked most of my life. But I'll tell you one thing I know for sure. Marriage is the hardest work ever." In terms of defending one's turf? Certainly this couple had different skills, not to mention different approaches. Mary Poppins meets Godzilla, *Playboy* described them. Whereas Andrews is primarily a pleaser, Edwards can be the opposite of gentle in business situations.

"It's not about defending your turf," answered Andrews. "It's about understanding you don't abandon each other. No matter what."

Here a dilemma emerged. The one about separation anxiety. In the last decade—and even in the late '60s—Andrews had worked primarily for Edwards. As a tactic for club survival? A way to be together? Or were those just the jobs being offered? No performer is going to say "those were the only offers," and nobody questions some of the Edwards-Andrews output. (In fact his films without her—apart from the *Pink Panthers*—are the most lambasted: *Blind Date*, *A Fine Mess*. He's the most erratic director in the club.)

Edwards kicked off a sneaker, and made a hard admission. "I adore this lady," he said cautiously, "but if given the choice between doing what I do and staying home and being a husband—it would not take three minutes to say I need the creative outlet more. If I had to stop working, I'd shrivel and die. Period."

Because Edwards is male must he work? And because Andrews is female can she take time to nurture children? Both husband and wife shook their heads no.

"Forget male," said Edwards. "I just need a creative outlet. For sanity. I still need to play cowboys and Indians. Take it away, and I'm no good to anybody. I would be destroyed if I had to live without this lady. But probably more destroyed if I couldn't be creative. Without success I'd have thought of myself as a zero."

Julie Andrews looked like a bomb had fallen.

"Well, darling," said her husband ambiguously, "we play various roles in life."

Consistency in Hollywood? "Don't look for it," advised producer Richard Zanuck (*Driving Miss Daisy, Jaws*). Yet Zanuck, mid-fiftyish, has lived in one house for all but twelve years of his life. He had one partner (David Brown) for twenty-seven years. And he played tennis every Saturday, "since 1814," with restaurateur Pierre Groleau. He's also run exactly five miles almost every morning since puberty. "I didn't miss a single morning all of last year," beamed Zanuck one afternoon at lunch at the Bistro Garden. "But I finally realized I live like someone from an Eastern family. I actually like traditions. The morning run I do whether I'm in Sun Valley or the South of France. Is running that much fun? No. But stress is your only real enemy in this town. So it sets the day up properly to run."

Especially if the stretch of beach at Santa Monica is where you grew up. Father Darryl was generally considered to be Hollywood's most popular last and brightest tycoon. In the '30s the tycoon's family moved to the swankiest beach front: Neighbors included Louis B. Mayer, David O. Selznick, Mervyn LeRoy, and Bing Crosby. The sons of the fathers grew up, according to Zanuck, "disinterested or inhibited by the movie industry. But for some reason I had no fear. I saw the movie industry as a giant adventure. I can remember growing up with Irving Thalberg, Jr., who became a professor somewhere. He wanted no part of Hollywood. I always wondered if it was because he was named 'Junior.' That's the hardest label to live with."

Zanuck and Alan Ladd, Jr., are the club's only two offspring who've maintained club status as producers and/or executives. (Sam Goldwyn, Jr., runs his own independent company but in a lesser league. And he seems not to care much about the club.) In other industries progeny like Edsel Ford and Joseph Kennedy, Jr., are groomed to succeed in the family business. But in the club, fathers compete with sons. "I wasn't groomed exactly," maintained "Dicky" Zanuck. On the patio, in direct sunlight and at Table No. 1, he managed to go completely undisturbed, and the contrast to his father's legendary flamboyance was apparent. Sometimes the son rises quietly, if quickly.

When Zanuck père was chief shareholder of 20th Century-Fox, he installed his son (still in his twenties) as president. Later the chairman would fire the president before being ousted himself. The saga is tailor-made for a Hollywood novel on fathers and sons. But temperamentally speaking, the gap between generations was enormous. "Dad had a very short fuse," said Zanuck easily. "But Dad didn't harbor anger for long. He could throw you for a minute, but if he trusted you, he trusted you. I learned early to speak up."

Zanuck also learned, right out of Stanford, what club nepotism felt like: At twenty-five he produced *Compulsion*, based on the Leopold-Loeb murders, and within a year he was the youngest Hollywood production chief since his neighbor Thalberg Sr. in the '30s. The stress came from internal studio politics, not family politics, and Zanuck can now remember "having to prove myself to a lot of people. People said, 'Your father put you there, kid. It's as simple as that. We know why you're behind the big desk.'"

That was the spur Zanuck needed. "It prodded me to get involved at a very basic and ongoing level. I did a lot of the engineering on pictures like *Butch Cassidy and the Sundance Kid* and *M*A*S*H*, involving myself way beyond what a studio executive would. I had to prove myself." It was an era when jobs lasted longer and meant more, "But you always learned the same pressure lesson. More money is made outside executive ranks. I could take the pressure, but didn't want to. In executive jobs, you don't pay much attention to the happiness quotient . . ."

Zanuck's formula for relieving stress is simple on the surface. "I systematically eliminate whatever irritates me. I avoid functions I don't like, and people I don't like, and I only worry about one thing—twenty years from now will I still be interested enough to want to read the trade papers? It's what's fascinating about men like Ray Stark in his seventies. Well beyond middle age he is still like a young stag, hungry and determined. I don't know if I'll be that way at that age. I have other interests than the movie business."

Yet, there are definitely movie ghosts at the Zanuck company headquarters, historic suites of offices that at various times have belonged to Burt Lancaster, Robert Evans, and Dino De Laurentiis. (Zanuck's office features what may be the neatest desk in town; the producer is famous for his impeccable personal memos, written with multicolored pens. Another feature at the Z/B offices is a private gym, where a trainer comes several times a week. The offices, like the occupants, seem stressless.)

"We get a big kick out of the word 'stress,' " said Zanuck's third wife, Lili Fini, who's known as both a compulsive worker and a constant companion. The couple haven't spent a night apart since 1977. (It was Lili who found the property *Cocoon*, and co-produced *Driving Miss Daisy* with her husband. Her directing debut was *Rush* in 1991.) "People think Dicky is stress-free," said Lili Zanuck, grinning slyly. "But you should see the table he kicked over after the Rams game last night . . ."

Very late on a Friday afternoon, Morgan Fairchild was sitting in Chair No. 1 at the salon of José Eber, about to have her hair cut. Fairchild is as busy as José, the man who cuts her blonde mane, and so they had to wait for each other. That day José had already done Joanna Carson, Jamie Lee Curtis, and Jackie Smith. Fairchild was wearing a vivid orange leotard under an all-purpose jacket, the uniform of a busy working actress. Fairchild is visible in a community where TV stardom means work and rest and exercise and eating celery and carrots at home (often alone).

"It's nervous breakdown week, every week," she said, putting a pale orange smock over her leotard. "I mean have you ever had a week where you haven't had two minutes to yourself? I mean not two minutes!"

"Every week, darling," said José, the stylist who redesigned the look of Elizabeth Taylor.

"I'll tell you how Hollywood stress is different from Detroit stress," said Fairchild off the top of her head. "Last week I was at Nautilus, minding my own business, doing my exercises. I look up and there are three producers I have worked for. And there were the inevitable questions always about is-she-working and how-does-she-look?"

Fairchild's way of coping?

"Last week I quit Nautilus! Really, this is a one-horse town. I mean I love it, but we are insular, aren't we?"

"Darling!" said José. "Us insular? Who's kidding who?"

CLUB RULE THIRTY-FIVE

If you plan to marry within the club, prepare for a shift in power somewhere. Julie and Blake and Lili and Dick are lucky couples because they are not actors married to each other. In the club, star members of equal status can marry, but something has to give.

The obvious example is Joanne Woodward, after her marriage to Paul Newman. Another example is Esther Williams, who was one of the two top female box office stars throughout the '40s—it was her and Ingrid Bergman. When Williams met and fell for Fernando Lamas, she told him: "Come back in ten years, you've got a lot of fucking to do."

He came back. He proposed. She said yes.

"You get it all," promised the swimming bride, who by now had retired. "But you don't get Esther Williams." Esther Williams left "Esther Williams" at the studio. Mr. and Mrs. Fernando Lamas were married twenty-four years, until his death in 1986.

Esther Williams Lamas never returned to the cameras (during or after) her marriage. At least she hasn't so far. Although she shows up at more events than Elizabeth Taylor.

27

Club Mystery Man— Jim Aubrey

Jim Aubrey got in because of Leonard Goldenson, and because TV was brand-new, and he had prodigious energy. Leonard Goldberg got in because of Leonard Goldenson and Marlo Thomas, and the hit show he put her in, That Girl. Marlo Thomas got in by birth, and because her father's agent was Uncle Abe Lastfogel, the smartest one of his day. Spencer Tracy and Katharine Hepburn managed to have complete privacy for twenty-six years because of Uncle Abe Lastfogel. Stan Kamen got in because of Abe Lastfogel. Stan Kamen stayed in because he had the best client list in the club. Jim Aubrey went out first because Bill Paley got tired of his fooling around with his wife, Babe. Jim Aubrey got back in because Kirk Kerkorian remembered his successes at CBS, when the rest of the club wrote him off. Kirk Kerkorian stayed in because Greg Bautzer was the club's second most powerful attorney, after Sidney Korshak, and Greg protected Kirk. Jim Aubrey stayed in, for a while, because of Greg Bautzer. Howard Hughes stayed in because of Greg Bautzer. Because of Kirk Kerkorian's willingness to sell Judy Garland's ruby slippers (and most of MGM's assets), Jim Aubrey became the club target. He also never tried *to win friends or influence people. So he became a club mystery.*

——————————————————

Fear has made some club careers, and broken others. Fear probably broke Jim Aubrey's career—but not his *own* fear. The fear of the people around him. The fear of Jim. The colleagues who quivered if he didn't smile at them, the bosses who worried what would Jim do next? Jungle Jim Aubrey was the Jay Gatsby of the '60s and '70s. Aubrey was the first man to become president of both a network (CBS) and a studio (MGM). That means he survived, sort of, both William Paley and Kirk Kerkorian. I met the elusive James T. Aubrey—five Hollywood novels were written about his mystique—through a friend of a friend in 1982, when he'd just turned sixty. We talked often over a period of months in a rather plain house in Hollywood; no props, nothing lavish but his military-green Jaguar. The house had almost no furniture. He never did let me into his Benedict Canyon bachelor pad—and I never pressed.

I came to respect Aubrey for his calmness. And I could see how seductive he must have been in his prime. And why people said he was the most alluring yet scary figure since Howard Hughes. His friend Sherry Lansing told me what intrigued her about Aubrey was his "never needing to be invited or included. It's a quality we all want, and won't admit to." I would go nervously to see him, and I would leave soothed. He was Jungle Jim, the powerhouse in a day when power meant something—when you could throw it around.

"I thought my days on the Red Eye were over," said Aubrey, dryly, the first day we met. His night flight from Houston had been grounded for three hours, and only days earlier he'd returned from Sri Lanka, of all places. But jet lag doesn't show on Jim Aubrey's face. This most reclusive man in show business (and once the most fearsome figure in broadcasting) has been out of executive suites since the '70s, but he's still nimble. There was no visible fatigue.

"No man in history ever had such a lock on such enormous audiences," is how *Life* magazine put it in 1965, after Aubrey took his fall from power at CBS. The man Lucille Ball called "the smartest one up there," and others called (at least privately) Jungle Jim, was no mere workaholic. "He was the fourth president of CBS as Caligula was the fourth of the twelve Caesars," is how writer Murray Kempton put it. "Each carried the logic of his imperial authority as far as it could go."

If "larger than life" is one of those outdated terms, like "showman," it's also too simple a description for Jim Aubrey. Aubrey was probably *larger* than larger than life. John Houseman's nickname for him was "The Smiling Cobra." Mention Aubrey's name to any Hollywood practitioner over forty, and the response—after the eyelids raise—is invariably the same: "Is he really talking to you?"

"I've never done this before," said Aubrey. Before and after he left CBS to become president of MGM—he was the most press-shy (if not the most written about) of modern club executives. Aubrey is the antihero of several pop novels (one of which, Jacqueline Susann's *The Love Machine*, he rather quietly cooperated with, by giving Susann the background on how TV worked in the '60s).

At first he would only stretch his very long legs in his very spartan office (no art, no Aubusson rugs, a Doberman his only companion) and say softly: "I'm not talking to you for the sizzle." The later—and lasting—impression is of the classic loner. Yet Aubrey in conversation is appealing in a way one expects a politician to be—or a performer. He talks directly into your eyes, and brain, and your response is to be stumped. Why would this man shun limelight when he takes so naturally to it? "Because Jim keeps his own counsel," was the answer given me by his longtime attorney Greg Bautzer. The room where Aubrey works is on the second floor of a Hollywood house very near to where Scott Fitzgerald wrote *The Last Tycoon*. And Aubrey at the edge of seventy could be cast as Fitzgerald's Monroe Stahr, forty years after the fact. By now one would have expected at least a volume of Aubrey memoirs. Sizzling or not.

The suggestion of sizzle brought a glint to his polar blue eyes, and then the kind of slow smile that promised an anecdote. "A few years ago when [CBS founder] Bill Paley published his autobiography, I happened to be in New York," Aubrey began. "I had lunch with Bill, and he asked me if I'd read the book."

Aubrey's pause was purposeful. It took a moment to realize that Aubrey might still lunch with the man who fired him unceremoniously in 1965.

"I said to Bill, 'Of course I didn't read your book. You know I don't read fiction.' "

Aubrey doesn't generally look back, but there's no other way to tell this saga than looking back. Aubrey was the man, the monarch, on the twentieth floor of CBS at a time in the early '60s when CBS could be compared to JFK's Camelot. ("It was Paley's company but Aubrey's network," is how David Susskind put it.) In those days Aubrey was as assured and, it seemed, as secure as JFK himself. "You have to understand something," recalled Susskind recently, "a mere smile from Aubrey could make an account executive's day, and an Aubrey frown could drive a man to martinis. Nothing at the network counted except pleasing Jim

Aubrey. And Jim knew it. As Aubrey used to say: 'They're not going to do anything to me. I made them $40 million last year!' "

In 1963 CBS under Aubrey had twelve of the top fifteen nighttime series and all twelve of the top twelve daytime series. Network revenue nearly doubled (from $25 million in 1959, when he became president, to $49 million in 1965). "No man in TV history made bigger profits—or more enemies," is how the *Washington Post* explained Aubrey's fiefdom. (When he departed, CBS stock dropped nine points. At Time-Life, boss Henry Luce reacted by personally deciding to have two reporters spend six months exploring Aubrey's reign. The result was a piece in *Life* that ran to 7,000 words.)

Aubrey was a kind of video Warhol, a showman who could gauge popular taste; the favored programs were either rural corny (*Green Acres*) or sexy exotic (*Daktari*) or starry (the Danny Kaye and Judy Garland variety hours). He tended to trust himself in a business where people trust only their superiors. His decisions were strictly his, made on hunches, and his shows were known as "Instant Pop." He put on *The Munsters* (against Paley's wishes) after watching eight minutes of the pilot; he removed Jack Benny from weekly TV, after decades on the air, with no trace of deference. (Garry Moore and Arthur Godfrey got similar, terrible treatment.)

Just as swiftly Aubrey signed the Smothers Brothers and Barbra Streisand (her ten-year, $5 million deal came just before Broadway stardom). He gave the green light to shows as diverse as *Route 66, Mr. Ed,* and *The Defenders* as well as the pivotal (because of its spinoffs) *Beverly Hillbillies.* As *Hillbillies* producer Martin Ransohoff put it, "People thought Aubrey had a divining rod in the middle of his desk. And he thought so, too."

The rod also apparently was used for self-flagellation. At his peak, in 1965, Aubrey was abruptly fired. (He was attending Jackie Gleason's forty-ninth birthday party in Miami Beach when he was summoned back to New York, and Paley's apartment at the Regency.) There are at least 13,000 theories on why he got the axe, some of them lurid, but none as obvious as the fact that CBS was starting to slip in the Nielsens. "And there was a basic dissatisfaction with me," as he put it.

If Aubrey understood ratings, and revenue, he also was no stranger to a kind of after-hours recklessness that mirrored the Camelot of its day. Nobody questions that Jungle Jim had a good time in the playgrounds of Manhattan and Hollywood.

"Jack Kennedy was a friend of mine," Aubrey mused late one night, his eyes almost exactly the shade of Kennedy's. "We used to talk about this whole thing of being 'ladies' men.' People thought we got away with a lot more than we really did . . . I'm certainly no example of clean living. But as I always said, 'If a man can be indicted for liking pretty girls, I'm guilty.' " And legendary. For years gossip columnists had to bite their tongues because the fodder on Aubrey was so tempting, but mostly unprintable. How much was hearsay, and how much was fiction, is not clear. Did Jim Aubrey really walk on girls' backs?

Harold Robbins doesn't admit he based *The Inheritors* on Aubrey, but Jackie Susann (Aubrey's neighbor in Manhattan) was open about *The Love Machine*'s womanizing executive Robin Stone being based almost completely on Aubrey. As she explained before her death in 1975, "Jim is one of those people who are born to run the works. A natural for a novel."

Why Aubrey left TV remains something of a mystery. Curiously, at the time, he didn't really bother about setting the record straight. "That's like reading the trade papers," he says now. "Why read other people's lies and believe them? I never understood people who devour the trades . . . but that's why I'm a problem for the press, and always have been. I tend to be candid, and too forthright. I've been misinterpreted, and then I haven't bothered to do anything about that. But I've still found being direct is the best way. I've no regrets."

Even when direct answers mean hurt feelings, or damaged reputations? "It's an ego-oriented business," understated Aubrey, "and people are emotional." Take writers. Earlier that day, screenwriter Chris Mankiewicz had dropped off a script to Aubrey, and Mankiewicz had been told politely by an aide that he'd have a fast reply. (Speed was always an Aubrey trademark. The late Charles Powell, who was head of marketing at MGM under Aubrey, recalled "handing him three marketing campaigns for one film, and getting an answer within thirty seconds. Nobody was ever faster.")

"If I was in the tire business," reasoned Aubrey, "I wouldn't be hurt if the customer didn't buy my tires. I'd think, 'So what?' But in my business, if I don't buy the script, then the writer kicks the dog and beats his wife. So you learn to pay attention to personal relationships. But that doesn't mean you lie to people. I've been the screwer and the screwee, and I know which is better. It's better to be the screwer, and it's very difficult to do that with honesty, but it's how I prefer to be treated. I don't want power now, or authority, so I suppose my candor can't hurt me."

Not that he ever slapped backs. In an age of affiliation, Aubrey is somewhat of an outsider. Sherry Lansing compares him to Howard Roark in *The Fountainhead*. He's complex, colorful, and a soloist—and the club is made up of team players.

Aubrey approached the subject of a club as if it were a new toy. "Am I hurt that I'm left out? That's a rather acute observation." Aubrey was wondering aloud, as though this subject had never arisen. "I never felt the doors were shut. I actually think I've been given every opportunity to be a member of the club. If I'm not a member, it's of my own choosing. I don't play the game, that's true, but that doesn't mean I'm right. Those who play do seem to get a lot of comfort from dealing with each other. If I don't, it's just that . . ."

A pause was long enough for a station identification; "I hesitate to use the word loner. When I am called upon to get along with people I do it reasonably well. I know people who can't be by themselves, but it doesn't bother me to be alone. The reverse is also true. On the other hand, I don't feel any necessity to have people around."

Thus one is operating from one's own rules, and if that can lead to megalomania, it can also teach lessons. Producer William Dozier (the *Batman* series) recalled Aubrey lecturing at one of Dozier's UCLA TV classes in the early '70s. "In the question-and-answer period he was asked, 'What prompted you to put on the air three new series in the same season without making a pilot of any?' Aubrey hesitated a moment and replied, 'Arrogance, I guess.' It was a remarkably honest answer, containing a clear indication of Jim Aubrey's having taken stock of himself."

The lessons were learned in hard ways. Eight years after entering broadcasting ("In 1950, I was hauling cable around KNXT"), Aubrey was president of CBS. The how and why are the kinds of questions one can't usually answer oneself, but Aubrey tried. "I could sense the mood, if you will, or the response of people who want to be entertained, even though the products aren't things I personally liked. And then I always fought with my bosses, whether it was Bill [Paley] or [CBS president] Frank Stanton or Kirk Kerkorian, I always fought. If somebody didn't agree with me about something I believed in—or something I didn't believe in, but thought the public would buy—I fought. I'd just go out there and fight relentlessly, until finally they'd say, 'Look, Jim, NO!' and then you give up, because it's Paley's candy store, or Kirk's, and I never questioned that. I would battle, but they had the right to the final decision, and you have to be very careful about that."

Two examples came to Aubrey's mind, one a victory and the other a loss: "When I first left CBS in 1956 to go to ABC, to head programming, people in New York said, 'Oh, gee, why ABC?' Because really at that time there was no ABC. The headquarters was an old riding stable. But I went because [ABC chairman] Leonard Goldenson in effect said, 'Look, I don't know that much about TV, I'm a lawyer.' And he let me have autonomy." Aubrey used it by scheduling "wild, sexy, lively stuff, things that had never been done before, like *77 Sunset Strip* and *Maverick*, to get us attention."

At CBS Aubrey became convinced *Beverly Hillbillies* was going to work. "Bill Paley wasn't convinced. Bill has this great sense of propriety. Putting aside the Sarnoffs and all the other great names of broadcasting, Paley stood head and shoulders above everyone else. He had this blasting genius of instinctively looking at a show and knowing if it should be on the air. He could also be ruthless and distant. We used to date the same girls, and send the same girls bouquets . . . But Bill was intuitive about both the business and creative sides of TV. And he genuinely disliked *Beverly Hillbillies.* I put it on the schedule anyway."

Against all odds. "But I was very convinced about *Beverly Hillbillies,*" Aubrey continued. "I said to Paley, 'Everybody in America thinks he's Abe Lincoln. Lincoln is the patron saint of the U.S.A., and all Americans think of themselves as log-splitters.' I sensed the public would still go for the idea of buying the big estate. It was an idea that had been worked, hard, but it would work again. I remember Bill and Frank Stanton saying, 'All right, Jim, but it's your ass if it fails. You put it on, you pay the price.' "

He began paying early on. Paley built CBS from his own $400,000 investment in 16 radio stations; Aubrey built himself to network president (at age forty) from nowhere. Certain qualities (aside from ambition) had to have emerged early. Aubrey put some thought into trying to explain what they were. A lot of Chicago boys make it to Princeton, after all, but not so many get to the presidential suites.

"The thing that separates the men from the boys, in my opinion, the one thing in terms of leadership that stands out, is not intelligence or ability. Those who operate most effectively, those I respect most, simply are not afraid. And most people are afraid, they're scared of decisions. Bill Paley could be ruthless, but he was not afraid of decisions. Everybody has a fear level, when you've gone as far as you can go, but you do have to go that far. Your modus operandi can't be, 'What if it doesn't work?' I never really analyzed this, but maybe it's why I've taken the blame for many things. I was willing to take that blame."

The same was true at MGM. Four years after exiting CBS (and developing projects that mostly didn't happen) Aubrey was the Comeback Kid. In 1969 he signed on as the first president of MGM under new owner Kerkorian. Aubrey took a salary of $4,000 a week, but wanted no contract. ("I wanted Kirk to be able to say, 'Get lost, Jim,' without obligation if it didn't work.") It worked, for a while: Kerkorian and Aubrey reduced MGM's $80 million bank debt to $22.5 million. The heat was turned off (literally) on the top floor of the Thalberg Building, 3,500 employees were fired and twelve projected films were canceled (including Fred Zinnemann's *Man's Fate,* just days before production was to begin).

Largely due to the success of the Grand Hotel in Las Vegas, MGM went back into the black before Aubrey left in 1973.

(The Aubrey-Kerkorian connection was due to Greg Bautzer, the attorney for both men—and Howard Hughes. In 1967 Bautzer put together a deal for Hughes to take over ABC, with Aubrey at the helm, but Hughes refused to appear in front of the FCC. As Aubrey said at the time, "There have been a lot of almosts in my life.")

There almost wasn't an MGM. What Aubrey found in Culver City was "total disarray. Until you were in a position to lift up the rug, there was no way to know how much disarray. The crown jewel of studios had become a shambles." The studio's valuable film library made the Kerkorian investment pay off, but "Kirk and I decided we'd get rid of everything else, and we did. The banks had extended credit to such a degree that we had to have a meeting to indicate our willingness to make good. We sold off acreage, European movie houses, whatever we could."

Otherwise, as Aubrey states now, "There would be no MGM today. But I was silhouetted against a garish horizon." In other words, Aubrey was once again newsworthy, if not hugely popular. This time it was the public who got angry at Aubrey, over the auctioning of MGM nostalgia. Clark Gable's *Mutiny on the Bounty* jackets went for a dollar. "The buck had to stop somewhere, and it was with me," Aubrey says now, without apparent regret. "Nostalgia runs strong out here, so we were criticized for selling Judy Garland's red shoes. To us they had no value, and they had no intrinsic value." (Clarence Darrow's suit from *Inherit the Wind*, which went for $5, later turned up on a district attorney in the Charles Manson trial.) Reiterates Aubrey: "In all honesty, I don't think anyone—Kirk, Greg, myself—knew just what it was going to take to save MGM. We really had to claw our way back."

Side effects included cuts and scratches and bleeding. At one point economy measures became rather macabre: Aubrey told one extraneous studio executive, "We are sending you to Nepal for three months to convert rupees to dollars." The man took the hint and quit.

"Hollywood was so different from New York," simplifies Aubrey. "The major difference about movie making is that everything here is manufactured from dreams. TV did not work that way. Movie producers and directors are told that every picture is going to be a smash, and get Academy nominations. The moment a movie begins shooting the dream machinery proclaims it a hit. I find that attitude unrealistic. Some movies are not going to turn out well. Yet very few directors will stand up and say, 'I did my best, but it didn't work.' So the executive becomes the heavy."

At the studio (as at CBS) Aubrey would become known for reading every script of every program the company produced, and making suggestions on every area from casting to set design. "I liked my work to the point of not taking a vacation ever, to the point of being at eight A.M. meetings and hanging around at night to haul cable. It was never my desire to direct or produce or even to make deals . . ."

Aubrey was asked if he ever considered performing; his concentration can be so powerful that a camera would take nicely to it. "Oh God no! I've been enough of a shit in my life without becoming a star, too!" he said, with a self-deprecating laugh. "There was no compulsion to be creative," he continued. "If you are going to be a writer, you are a writer, period. There is not a way to teach it. You support yourself waiting tables because that drive inside of you determines that's what you will do. Me? I wasn't wanting to produce or direct or write. I guess I was thinking about surviving."

CLUB RULE THIRTY-SIX

Words are more powerful than body language—and more dangerous. Temperament, and the acting out of it, is what can make or break club careers.

Jim Aubrey's bluntness got him his power, and his failure. At forty he could talk back to Bill Paley and Frank Stanton; at fifty he talked back to Kirk Kerkorian and Blake Edwards. But at sixty and seventy, nobody wanted to talk to him. Too blunt was he. Bluntness is more powerful than body language. In the club it's what you *say* that gets remembered, not how you posed. (Unless it was for Herb Ritts, or Annie Leibovitz, or Bruno of Hollywood.)

Example: On a stretcher on her way into the operating room at Cedars-Sinai, the late Joyce Selznick said, "Just don't let them cut my cock off." That they talked about.

Another example: Maureen Stapleton dined out forever on the crack she made at a screening of *Bye Bye Birdie*, the day the entire studio brass—all male—saw the film.

What she said to Ann-Margret—"I'm the only person in this room who doesn't want to fuck you"—got remembered and retold.

28

The First Girl
in the Club—
Lucy

Lucille Ball was the second most successful businesswoman in
the club, after Mary Pickford. Lucille Ball got in because Sam
Goldwyn hired her at the last minute for the chorus of Eddie
Cantor's Roman Scandals. She stayed in because she wasn't sufficiently stacked to be a standout chorus girl (though she had the
legs), so she became "background." Desi Arnaz got in because of
Lucille Ball. Desi Arnaz, Jr., was the most confused club child,
the baddest boy, but he still stayed in because he was handsome,
and because his stepfather, Gary Morton, is the best friend of
Marvin Davis, who got Desi Jr. a TV series. Marvin Davis got
in because of oil and publicity—and because he was larger than
life, in one way anyway. Marvin Davis stayed in because Veronique and Greg Peck and Barbara and Cary Grant came to his
parties in Denver, and because he could communicate with Gary
Morton and Leonard Goldberg. Gary Morton got in because he
could communicate with the first girl in the club, Lucille Ball.

When Jim Aubrey was fired from CBS, he packed up and headed for one
of Lucille Ball's guest houses on Roxbury Drive where he stayed for three

months. Lucy and Aubrey were soulmates; they had the same sorcerer's understanding of magic, and the same fear of losing it. They were both loners in the extreme. So they understood each other better as friends than they ever could have as lovers. It's not surprising that Lucy wound up with a club fortune, and Aubrey wound up without a job. They were just flip sides of the same club coin: In show business, to lose big is not so different from winning big. There's the same isolation. Both of them understood that. I spent a lot of time with both of them before I ever knew how connected they were. They had played the company town in their own individual ways. Lucy owned three Hollywood studios. At one time. This was after the divorce from Desi. Her company Desilu produced 20 percent of all prime-time programming. Lucille Ball was the original Aaron Spelling, but with talent. RKO, the Selznick studio, and Desilu-Cahuenga all belonged to the redhead at the same time she was doing her own show, *Here's Lucy.* And so they said she was tough. A monster with a voice that got deeper every year, they said.

At the top of Mulholland Drive one morning, at the point where Coldwater Canyon intersects, Lucy in her powder blue Rolls (the one Hedda Hopper left her) almost ran into my Mustang convertible. I saw such panic in her face, I knew then she was no monster. Tough, maybe, but human, too.

She was the first girl in the club who was both "creative" and "business." But Lucy was, she always claimed, an accidental tourist in the world of corporations. When Gulf & Western founder Charles Bluhdorn offered her $17.6 million in stock for her company, she escaped to Miami Beach and locked herself in a suite at the Fontainebleau, to make up her mind. In sixteen hours she decided to sell.

The journey from hat model to chorus girl to B supporting player to TV star to a woman poised on the verge of a nervous breakdown—that's a true trip.

I could barely get up the day I was to finally meet Lucille Ball. I was cranky, I was nervous, one more legend was going to disillusion itself in front of my face. I just knew it. Her house, that was the problem. Lucy's corner of Roxbury Drive is the most public movie star corner in Beverly Hills. (The Jimmy Stewarts are one lot away, and the Jack Bennys used to live next door.) I'd driven around that block for seventeen years; I knew which house Polly Bergen lived in with Freddie Fields, which one was Rosemary Clooney's with José Ferrer during all those pregnancies and breakdowns. Which backyard Ira Gershwin's sitting room faced onto. Now I was about to meet Lucille Ball at her house to see if we connected. An audition I was grateful for, but afraid of—another anticlimax.

When you make your guest a margarita and then stretch out on the living room floor and say "Where's your pencil? Let's go . . ." that's a star.

It was a flirtation that took sufficiently that I went back every day for a week. I thought that at seventy-five she was very lonesome, and very serious and very much a victim of whatever life decided to throw at her. With Lucy, life had been very much happenstance. She wasn't truly funny—or a star—until she was forty. I also thought she was still in love with Desi Arnaz.

As I left her house the last time I remembered a day on the set of *Mame*. The young Patrick Dennis had done his teary good-bye moment for the eleventh time—and from somewhere in the flies, high above the set, Lucy cracked: "I don't buy it."

That's how I felt about life after Desi for Lucy. The endless roles she played were only afterthoughts. After Lucy finally left Desi, something in her died. She was like Raymond Massey in *East of Eden*, after Jo Van Fleet left. Alive but not really living.

So the people who drive around Lucy's house, wishing they were her—that's a mistake. They may have this idea that the very loved Lucy was a happy lady.

But I don't buy it.

Right up close Big Lucy, as the family called her, was like a well-heeled pink-and-orange version of Willy Loman. Or Woody Allen. She still needed to make good. "Compulsion," as her son Desi Arnaz, Jr., told me, "sometimes led her to do things that were unnecessary." Curled up on the floor of her Beverly Hills sun room, a drink in hand, Lucy was resting her back against a backgammon table. Resting was really the wrong word. Lucy didn't rest. Actually, Lucy was a complete contradiction in terms. Except in one way. From the week she was fired from the third road company of *Rio Rita* until the week her last TV series died as abruptly as Elvis—the woman was a plugger.

If the history of stardom can be put into two words, *uphill battle*, then Lucy was a walking history. She had more longevity than any woman in the business (including Katharine Hepburn, who took more years away from working). A Chesterfield poster girl in the '30s, the Queen of the B-minus movies in the '40s, the Queen of TV in the '50s—but those are highlights. It's the battles that clung to Lucy like charms on a bracelet. It's the battles that propelled her and it's the battles, inevitably, she wanted to talk about.

"Don't do that," she said as I moved next to her on a chintz sofa. Later she relented. It's called propriety. No, she wouldn't be photographed without approving the photographs. But you don't win uphill battles without acquiring scars. Actually Lucy looked more interesting than the airbrushed photos would indicate; she looked like a seventy-five-year old determined redhead who was afraid of plastic surgery. When her husband, Gary Morton, entered a room she became sexual in a way not seen onscreen. But the private Lucy knew the public Lucy. "I looked like an actress, but I played a housewife," she said accurately. In the '50s, teaching students at her Desilu Workshop, she told them, "Let's see ourselves as others see us." The henna hair and pink-kewpie lips and turquoise shirts are garments, part of the imagery of a star groomed by RKO, a studio she would later own, and MGM, a studio she would never dominate. Others see her as a glamour clown, Lucy believes, not a hard-bitten ex-showgirl. "People shouldn't have to think about Lucy getting old. In a still photo, they examine every tiny line."

In the early '50s Lucy and Desi and Lucie and Desi Jr. moved overnight from Northridge to Beverly Hills after getting wind of a kidnap threat. Lucy lived in the same white Colonial house for the rest of her life, with bars on the windows. When gawkers were rude enough to come to the front door, they were usually told that Miss Ball was in Europe. But when Miss Ball was at home, she was really at home. On a tour of the house, Lucy was very domestic, taking you through every pool house (there are three), pointing out the framed family photos, worrying about the clutter in a guest house, explaining the sensibility of having a mock–beauty salon at home. One afternoon, Lucy tackled the subject of movie stardom, and how it eluded her. In 1937 she joined a curious quartet of actresses in the now-classic *Stage Door*. What's curious is that all of them stayed so functional so long—Katharine Hepburn, Ginger Rogers, Ann Miller, Eve Arden, and Lucy—and all were ultimately considered among show business's wealthiest women.

"Stardom?" Lucy said the word like it was pastry and she dare not take a bite. "Ginger was a star. I never dared dream about stardom. In the movies, I was . . . atmosphere. I admired Ginger and Katharine but I never thought I was in their league. For years I was watching these women, and being taught to dance and fence and not pester people too much. But stardom I didn't think much about."

A clue to understanding Lucy (and her eventual stardom) is to know that early on in Hollywood she took the jobs nobody wanted. "This is very important," she said abruptly, lighting a cigarette, a habit she battled for decades. "In a career, it's better to be a bad musician and a bad juggler and learn to play mouth organ—than to just be good at one thing. As a kid, I did *Charley's Aunt* in my dining room, playing every part. I sewed the curtain and printed up tickets and sold the tickets. Did everything."

Lucy's point was about doing whatever had to be done. When asked to define her early Hollywood identity, she took time to think about it.

"Let's just say I was a girl in the first line of the chorus who didn't want to get moved to the second line." She said the line slowly, so it would sink in. "I knew right away in show business there would always be another crop of girls along next year. I wanted to get myself a real job, not just a chorus job. So I went to Harry Cohn's place, Columbia [Pictures]. I had never seen $750, and now I was making that, a week. With overtime and weekend work. As a model, I made $125 a week."

Was Lucy lucky? "Well when Desi and I had our own show, it felt like we had the world." Lucy on Desi near the end was like a testimonial. Mention his name, and she would remove her dark glasses; she didn't shy off. All bitterness seemingly erased, Desi went back on a pedestal. Of all subjects, he was her favorite. "With Desi nothing was impossible," Lucy summed up. "He could do what hadn't been done. [CBS founder] Bill Paley said to me, 'We learned together, us three,' and he was right. But Desi and I had different ideas." As she explained: "I wrapped myself around the show and the children, and that was it. I didn't have anything else. But Desi . . . He didn't miss anything . . ." Here the tears appeared real. "I am not kidding you when I say I was working days at MGM and he was working nights with the band (or whomever) and we would literally meet in the tunnel at Sepulveda Blvd. At six in the morning! That's the real reason behind *I Love Lucy*. After nine years of marriage, I wanted my husband at home. I didn't want to be a wife on the road, not that Desi ever asked me to be on the road . . ."

Suddenly she began pacing the living room, as if she was angry at somebody. "I'm mad about this idea I'm a workaholic," she complained. Lucy, who loved word games and game shows, pointed to a dictionary in a corner of the living room. "I spent some time researching words like *workaholic* and *perfectionist*," she boasted. "Workaholic is not what people think. For God's sake, I always took long vacations, eight weeks at a time in Europe, with the kids, and I always had three-day weekends. I thought that time away could save the marriage to Desi."

In that moment it became clear that there are various Lucys—not just the TV versions of Lucy—but in real life, too. Relaxed like this, playing on the floor, she seemed primed and ready to be asked the hard question. The one about Lucy the businesswoman. In the '60s she owned and operated three studios, without Desi. The product included shows like *The Untouchables* and *Star Trek*. This, with her own series simultaneously running on CBS—and at times as many as twelve other Desilu series in various stages of production. The word *tough* had to emerge.

"You mean like ogre?" Lucy shot back. As her daughter, little Lucie, has put it, Lucy is not always tactful. But tough? "The people I work closely with don't say it," said Lucy. "When I had good people around me, I let them have their heads." The photos of Lucy in those years, at stockholder meetings particularly, showed the beginnings of deep strain in her face, and she doesn't deny it. "I hated those meetings and still don't know why they existed. I did not want to crowd my head with business, and I couldn't do everything. My show was the bulk of my empire. So I was very willing, grateful even, to delegate."

The solution, in 1967, was Charles Bluhdorn, the acquisitive chairman of Gulf & Western, who'd recently bought Paramount Pictures. The late tycoon made Lucy an offer that would eventually bring her untold millions in Gulf & Western stock. For her thirty-six sound stages and sixty-two acres Lucy received one and a half shares of Gulf & Western preferred stock for every ten of Desilu's 1.1 million shares. In other words her shares that had a market price of $3.63 suddenly had a value of $16 each.

Lucy can admit she never met Bluhdorn, yet sold him Desilu, then in the next breath follow up with a baffled look and a question. "What does *titular* mean?" she asked, stumbling over the word. "I was the titular head of three studios, but if you don't know what it means I won't use it again. It's like the word *overhead*. I always hated that word." Lucy was re-creating a personal turning point, the moment when she decided to walk away from her own presidency, titular or otherwise. "I knew I needed to get away to think about it. So I ran." To Florida. "Why Florida I do not know. I'm so emotional I just need to run sometimes. I locked myself up in a suite while the whole deal was cooking, and told my lawyer [who then was club attorney Mickey Rudin, who also represented Frank Sinatra] to call me. He did, and it was a very good price we got offered, so within a day I said yes. I don't honestly know what the price was. But I held on to my shares, and they've done very well." How well is a matter of much speculation. But Lucy on money was, well, simplistic: "Anyone who made money after taxes came in hasn't kept that much," she claimed. "Real money belongs to insurance companies, General Motors, and banks. I always poured my money back into my business."

"I missed out on a childhood," Lucy said one afternoon when almost everything else in her life had been touched upon. Her Jamestown, New York, childhood is spelled out (usually luridly) in unauthorized books she loathed but kept in an upstairs guest room. "One said I was a hooker, based on the fact that my mother let me go to New York at fifteen for acting classes. Me a hooker?" She hooted like Lucy Ricardo.

Lucy's living room is where to find out the real truth. One afternoon she sashayed around her sun room, not to show off, but to show how a show girl walked. "The modeling gave me the walk," she said matter-of-factly. "Here I was at seventeen modeling for Hattie Carnegie, the dressmaker, and one day I was walking down the runway and my legs gave out." Lucy said it, she didn't sell it. "I fell to the floor, it was a Wednesday in July, and it was hot. I felt like a knife cut my legs in half. I remember Hattie—who was nice but not particularly personal about it—saying, 'Get her a doctor.' I was nobody special there. But I was shivering. And I had $85 to my name. No money, no hospital." So Lucy was sent to a charity clinic in upstate New York. " 'Go see this man,' I was told. I told the doctor at the clinic I had no money. I remember him injecting me with something. And saying the symptoms were not good. He took my case because it was unusual, and he developed a serum from the urine of pregnant horses which is still registered at his clinic with my name on it. I had a variation of rheumatoid arthritis, and crutches and a cane and weights to lift. From seventeen to twenty I basically couldn't walk."

Is that why she later ran so fast, from Manhattan to Hollywood, from chorus lines to movies to TV? "I hadn't thought about it, but a lot of what people think of as my drive came from that period. From seventeen to twenty if you miss proms and dates, and I missed out completely, it changes you forever. No dances, no boyfriends. I'll tell you what that does," said Lucy soberly. "It makes you pretty serious. About everything."

Again the question was, was Lucy lucky? She waited a moment to think about that. "What's luck?" she asked aloud. "I wasn't a great beauty, I wasn't a flirt, I wasn't a great anything. But I watched other girls. Some show girls came out here with sugar daddies, some girls had drinking problems. But I knew enough to know you don't do that. You don't get yourself in trouble. Being a Goldwyn girl was the nicest introduction to Hollywood, so how can I complain? Or say how hard this town is? The industry welcomed me, and all I had to do was not do anything wrong. The grass was never greener anywhere else . . ."

CLUB RULE THIRTY-SEVEN

Stardom must be accompanied by financial success to achieve true club status.

To be blunt, the real reason Lucy interested the club was money. Until her TV series, she was just another redhead. But the real goal in the club, the potential, is to make money. That's when Lucy started to be intriguing, when the reruns started. The idea is not just to become rich, but rich-rich. One *Lucy* or one *Rocky* is more lucrative, and sometimes easier to launch, than a Trump Tower. But the gamble may be greater. That's why the club is tightly run. It's why *Life* magazine doesn't do layouts of club poker games. It's why you rarely saw photographs of Ma Maison's private second story. It's why the club doesn't like to be written about except in terms of its wisdom.

29

Club Recluse—
Johnny Carson

Johnny Carson got in because Dave Tebet of NBC saw him do a benefit at a golfing resort in North Carolina, and knew what was there. Dave Tebet got in because he understood both talent and the bosses, and because he lasted the longest of anyone at any network (twenty-three years). Robin Williams got in because of Johnny Carson, and stayed in because of Jeffrey Katzenberg. Joanne Carson got in because of Truman Capote and her marriage to Johnny Carson, and she dropped out because she was not socially ambitious enough for the club. Joanna Carson, her successor, stayed in in spite of her divorce from Johnny Carson, because some of the club wives liked her. Henry Bushkin dropped out as a club lawyer after he was dropped by Johnny Carson, because he couldn't communicate with anyone in the club, except Carson. Most of these people never got into the movie colony branch of the club—they're strictly television. To bridge both branches you have to truly perform in both—like Clint Eastwood, or Candy Bergen. Candy Bergen got in because of bloodlines and beauty, and she stayed in because of humor and talent. Johnny Carson stayed in because of pure staying power, and because he has no other interests. Johnny Carson is the ultimate club recluse.

Lucille Ball told me she never knew what to say to Johnny Carson, which I felt was a profound comment. Lucy didn't say it lightly; Carson is never taken lightly in Hollywood. He occupies a unique position in the club. In an era without a star-maker, without a Walter Winchell, Carson (for thirty years) filled in. In mid-'91 when he announced his retirement, something ended on TV: the era of the truly long-running star. (Only Bob Hope remained.) When Carson would show up at a dinner party, it mattered: his dinner partner might turn up on a broadcast. For a very long time he could make a star. And Carson is still a boy from Nebraska, so when he sits next to Kim Basinger, and is enchanted by her—it doesn't hurt. Not that Johnny Carson goes out that much—to the Billy Wilders', maybe, or to Mary and Irving Lazar's. But Carson is the club recluse— because he turned down movie stardom, and instead survived the ficklest medium of all for the longest time. Without courting anybody. Stars come and go but Carson goes on and on. The club loves recluses because they can relate—every member is in his or her little world.

To outsiders—and even the closer you get to him—Johnny Carson seems not very different from other people. He had one best friend he trusted implicitly—until Carson abruptly switched allegiance from one attorney (Henry Bushkin) to another (Ed Hookstratten). He has a beautiful wife he met by chance on the beach. He works out regularly, yet smokes excessively. He's dallied with alcohol, but not on the job. He can be mischievous. When his next-door neighbors threw a wedding several years ago, he took a broomstick and wrote FUCK YOU on the sand, to shock the helicopter pilots and the press. The bride and groom happened to be Madonna and Sean Penn—and Johnny Carson is obviously different from other people.

He opens the front door himself. The glass-walled Malibu house sits on a 200-foot cliff overlooking the world, and it's a little overwhelming, even for Johnny Carson. "Bob Newhart took one look and said, 'Where's the gift shop?' " Billy Wilder may have been more to the point: "Where's the desk?" There is no question that Johnny Carson could do *The Tonight Show* here, and that may be the unconscious intent. To create a living area that's an idealized, glamorized version of the work area. Mirrored tables on white area rugs, swivel chairs, and simple glass ashtrays. This has to be the ultimate sixteen-room, six-bathroom $11 million show business house. Ed Murrow, if only he knew about this house, would return to earth for a special segment of *Person to Person*. Overflowing with flora and fauna (but no framed photos) the living room seems higher and wider and deeper than the lobby of the Kahala Hilton.

It's no wonder that Carson bought the place almost on a whim, twenty-four hours after a first look. "I was in escrow on another house," he confided, "when I saw this. I said, 'Can I come back tomorrow?' And I did. Then I said, 'Can I come back tonight?' And I did. And then I bought the place." (The move was typically Carson: In the early '70s he bought Mervyn LeRoy's Bel Air house for $800,000—over dinner.) "My dad," said Carson, a little self-consciously, "would probably say to me, 'John, do you really need this house?' The answer, of course, is that I really don't."

Carson, wearing a Battaglia sweater and Reeboks, poured black coffee into simple white mugs—and began a tour of the greenery and grounds and grotto. He likens the setting to Carmel or Acapulco, and he likes to remind a visitor his tennis building across the road isn't anywhere near as splashy. Which is apparent. Because Carson—at a distance and right up close—is the opposite of splash. He's a master of energy, of using and saving it—and there's a conservatism about him that has nothing to do with politics. As he settled into a leather swivel chair, his posture was midshipman-perfect. When our talk stretched to nearly five hours, another session was suggested—and the posture hadn't changed. Johnny Carson apparently cannot slouch.

Sitting in his living room with a pack of unfiltered Pall Malls, Carson might just as well have been in a dressing room in Burbank. At home, as at NBC, he fiddles with pencils or cigarettes (smoking a full pack during the first two hours. His only stipulation about cigarettes: He didn't want to be photographed smoking). An extrovert when working, Carson is an introvert when he isn't. Barbra Streisand's definition of fame—"not being left alone"—doesn't apply here. There is no bodyguard, no entourage, no driver.

"Oh God no!" said Carson, outraged at the notion. "That's like having license plates that say BIG STAR. I drive myself to work. If somebody is going to get you, they are going to get you. I remember once in Vegas, sitting at Caesars Palace, hearing a hushed voice whisper, 'Frank's here!' Well, of course you knew he was there. Sinatra likes that; he likes being surrounded by people. I don't."

If four people were asked to pin an adjective on Carson, at least three of them would pick "private." The label sticks to him like "tough" sticks to Dustin Hoffman and "nonverbal" to Robert De Niro. Major stars seem to require such quickie identity fixes, perhaps so the public can understand them. When Mary Tyler Moore stopped really playing Mary Richards (as in "cute"), the public got confused about her. "Private" is the label that keeps the public from being confused about Johnny Carson.

"Isn't it really a catch-22 situation?" he asked rhetorically. "If you're out with a group of people, it's called an entourage, and they say you're making a big play. If you keep to yourself they say, 'He doesn't like people.' The truth is that I never was a social animal."

If Carson is more social lately—turning up at the Comedy Store to see the last appearance of his friend Buddy Rich on drums, or at the eight-hour premiere of *Nicholas Nickelby*—the outings are occasional. "Ninety-eight percent of the time I come home after the show," he insisted. "Even in the '50s I never went to premieres out here. I never did understand anybody who puts on a tie and tuxedo to go to a restaurant opening. It's jive to me. The continual thing to concentrate on is the energy level for the show."

It's been protected at all costs: "I wake up hard," Carson said in response to one of his standard lines from the '60s—"I don't trust anyone who's alert before eleven in the morning." *The Tonight Show* is taped at 5:30 in the afternoon, primarily because that's the best and latest time the program can be fed to New York. Still, the timing worked for Carson's own personal rhythms, too. "Is it biorhythms or circadian rhythms?" Carson wondered aloud. "I know men have similar cycles and emotional swings as women, though much about this is unknown. I know I have mood swings, big ones. I don't know a creative person who doesn't have them. I know that if we talked at NBC today, I would be tired for the show. Even if I have lunch in town, some of the best energy is gone. Same thing if I go to the office too early. So I get in the groove out here, in the morning, and start my notes." Yet Carson is simply not a morning person, and he broke into a big grin when he repeated the line, "I do wake up hard. My wife calls it grump hour."

Clearly Carson has an attitude about his four marriages; after all, he's been married for much of his adult life, close to thirty years altogether. Unexpectedly he turned serious on the subject. "If I had given as much to marriage as I gave to *The Tonight Show*," he confessed, "I'd probably have a hell of a marriage. But the fact is I haven't given that, and there you have the simple reason for the failure of my first three marriages. I put the energy into the show. I've said before that what's most important to a man, in general, is his work. What's most important to a woman, in general, is her relationship. And for me, what I do comes first. But look at the failure rate of marriages in Detroit, something near 50 percent. Why should a guy who's doing a TV show be different from a dentist? I'll tell you why. Because of the press. But I now look at it this way: You're in the paper, and you're out of the paper."

Whether Carson earned $5 or $7 or $99 million a year, nobody will say exactly. "More than $23 million" is a figure nobody disputes. (*The*

Tonight Show earns NBC about $100 million annually.) Contrary to rumor, Carson's negotiations were never very complicated: "What Johnny wanted is basically what NBC gave him," explained David Tebet, the man who in 1961 decided Carson would be the heir apparent to Jack Paar. Published lists of names like Gleason and Newhart and Griffin and Cavett were so much balderdash. "There was no list. Carson was the list."

Money is still a subject Carson has real problems talking about—at first. "I never knew what my father made," he said matter-of-factly. "And it never would have occurred to me to ask him, 'Dad, how much did you make last year?' Maybe it's my Midwestern upbringing. It's like when people come into this house and say, 'What did you pay for it?' I say, 'Why do you ask?' What I paid is the government's business and my business. I'm not sure it's anybody else's business."

Yet money is not a subject one can duck, and once started Carson didn't stop talking about it. Several times in conversations he would return the subject to the public's fascination with big finance. "Humphrey Bogart said it all years ago," said Carson. "He was asked, 'Isn't $25,000 a lot of money for a picture? Why you?' And Bogey said, 'Because I can get it . . .' So, am I worth what I make? Yes—because I can get it." Carson delivered the line with the slightest hint of defensiveness, like a Midwestern multimillionaire who reveres privacy, and expects it. Where Carson comes from—which is not Brooklyn where the boys on the block boast to each other—discretion rules. In that regard he's not unlike fellow Nebraskans Fonda and Astaire and Brando. "But isn't it all relative?" Carson wanted to know. "Sylvester Stallone gets $15 million for a movie about arm wrestling before the movie is even made." Implicit is the point that Carson works year-round, while a Stallone may work twelve weeks on a film, and be done with it. "It's no different than any other business. What is anybody worth?"

Carson wanted to play out the analogy, and play devil's advocate. "People say, 'The President only earns $200,000 a year.' And I say, so? Maybe NBC had a better year than the President. Look at rock stars. You hear figures like $5 million for five nights. Nothing can top that . . . I don't go to a psychotherapist over the fact of the money I earn, believe me."

But the tranquility has taken some time. "I believe in a slow build when it comes to a career," he explains. But does Carson believe he's gotten better with time? "Probably. Acceptance is everything. You just do the next thing, whatever that is, and hope you're getting better. I think what you learn is what you can get away with. People ask, 'Why did the show last and do so well?' And again it's a catch-22. If you say, 'Because it's the best,' people say you're an egomaniac. If you say, 'Gee, I dunno,' you sound dumb. I always tried to be honest and say I was doing a TV show. The TV set is in your living room, not mine." Carson at home, listening and talking, is a different creature from the TV version. Ed McMahon once said, "He has to become Johnny Carson every day," but it isn't that. It's that Carson in private doesn't use the extra layer, the patina of trying to please. He doesn't hide the ambivalence about fame. He smiles less often, but who wouldn't? He's more serious, yet simultaneously funnier. Pointing to the house next door, the site of Madonna's media wedding, he said, "Madonna and Sean Penn turned the place into Circus Vargas!" Carson off the record, without writers or jokes, is funny in a way most comedians are not. "He's funny without bitterness," said Stan Irwin. "But that's because he's basically loyal. Just don't cross him."

"Part of Johnny's appeal," Dave Tebet had said earlier, "is that he's vulnerable without being a victim. Very few comedians can you say that about. Think about it." Yet Carson is made of tempered steel: "You don't just walk in and do what I do," he said bluntly. "You have to put it on the griddle, and it's from night to night. It's about momentum. That's why when I quit I won't come back to the same format. It's not like Jack Nicklaus, coming back to win the Masters. Maybe Nicklaus could play a smashing game once in a while, but . . . Jack Paar came back. Nobody remembers it, but he did. He said, 'I shouldn't have come back.' *The Tonight Show* really is about momentum. I don't think anybody again will do it this long. Maybe, who knows, but . . ."

But he hates it when they joke about his vacations. "The fact is," Carson said privately "I haven't had more than four consecutive weeks off in twenty-four years . . . Once in New York when I was doing *Who Do You Trust?* I was getting out of a cab when the driver stopped me. 'You got it made,' he mumbled. 'You only work two hours a day, right?' 'Right,' I said. The guy is driving a hack from midnight to eight in the morning. So how else are you going to answer him? Naturally people don't see the work, and they shouldn't."

The point is that Carson is completely involved to the degree where vacations are almost misnomers. (He'd hardly ever visited Europe until his third wife, Joanna, hauled him to Cap d'Antibes and her native Italy. *Tonight* isn't seen abroad, thus Carson goes unrecognized.)

If the show is both all-consuming and a well-oiled piece of machinery, then how could Carson walk away? "It's not a national shrine," Carson said quietly in response to his exit. "They are not going to erect any statues. But I will say this: I remember when Jim Aubrey canned Jack

Benny—and I made sure that wouldn't happen, to me. I always said I'll know when the time has come. The people tell you."

As a diversion, a Carson career-planning session ensued. Realistically, what will Johnny Carson do without *The Tonight Show*? Various ideas emerged until one word grabbed Carson's attention. Movies. The primary piece of art in the waiting room of his NBC office is a one-sheet from *Looking for Love*, a 1964 pseudosequel to *Where the Boys Are* starring Connie Francis and guest-starring George Hamilton, Yvette Mimieux, and Johnny Carson. In the '60s and '70s it was a show business axiom that Johnny Carson would become a movie star. It was to be the natural next step.

"Robert De Niro came here to the house," Carson said, a little awe-struck but not meaning to show it. "He sat in this chair." Carson swiveled around, as he does on TV when he becomes Ronald Reagan or Art Fern, and he became De Niro. He lowered his chin onto his chest, and looked like a skinny Jake LaMotta. Then came the impression: "Uhm, ah, I'd like you to do this, uhm, movie *The King of Comedy* with me," said Carson doing De Niro doing LaMotta. (The film, of course, was based on Carson, a look at the living hell that goes with being the most famous talk show host in history. Jerry Lewis played the part opposite De Niro as the obsessed fan.)

Carson switched roles, playing himself trying to decipher what De Niro was saying. He bent down as if looking up at De Niro and trying to make contact. "I said to Bob, 'I'll do the movie if you'll do *The Tonight Show*.' Bob shook his head no and said, 'I don't know how you do what you do.' And I said, 'I don't know how you do what you do.' And that was the end of that."

Carson's last word on the subject said it all: "Nobody who has played himself on TV has ever gone on to a successful movie career. Nobody. Redford can play a baseball player, but I've been playing me. Every night. Actors, God knows, have been successful going from TV to film, guys like Lemmon and Jim Garner and McQueen. But they played characters on television. I'm playing me. It's hard to have that kind of identification with the public and then go on to become a movie star. And I'll tell you something else," said Carson knowingly. "I go watch actors work. I don't think it's much fun acting in a movie. George Scott enjoys sitting around with crew people playing poker, then doing a pickup shot fourteen times. I don't think I'd enjoy that."

Carson knows full well his own most pressing catch-22. "I'm an entertainer," he said with an edge in his voice, and some regret. "I don't have that other thing in my life that would be as much fun as what I do now. I have tennis, I just built a court, but it's not the same thing."

Role models for walking away were discussed, largely to get Carson off the subject of himself. Unwittingly, he can become repetitious, if forced to overanalyze himself. To retain Carson's attention one must grasp this fact quickly. Otherwise all hope is lost. Carson will be gone. The thing to remember is that he's TV pure, and thus he will not stay long on one subject. He will not avoid but also he will not dally.

"I'm not hedging," Carson said finally. "I'd like to quit like James Cagney. He did that movie for Billy Wilder [*One, Two, Three,* 1961] and then just stopped working. Classy. But Cagney had this farm on Martha's Vineyard, and he loved driving cross-country. I'm not sure I could do that. To switch gears is hard for me." And there's another point Carson wanted to make. A very long pause left him room to get to it. "Creative people are spooked when they're not working. And that scares me . . . Still, you have to know when to quit."

CLUB RULE THIRTY-EIGHT

The company you keep keeps you, and rubs off on you, and smudges, and dilutes—and sometimes vanishes. But in the club you are labeled early on by the members you knew at the beginning. If the Ziffrens liked you, or the Steins did, it gave you an aura.

The man who discovered Johnny Carson at a golfing resort in North Carolina is the same man who lasted the longest at any network, twenty-three years. He was in a job—head of talent—that didn't exist before, and no longer exists. It takes an unusual talent to bridge both the creative and business branches of the club, but David Tebet did it. He was the prototype for the William Holden character in Paddy Chayefsky's *Network*. Cary Grant and Jack Benny also called him "best friend." I asked Tebet to explain power in a community.

"Let's go to France for a moment. A very broke young man asks the Baron Elie de Rothschild for a loan. And the Baron refuses. But the Baron gives the young man a true definition of power. He says to the young man, 'Walk down the street with me.' (The street was the Champs-Elysées.) 'Notice how the bankers and the aristocrats spot us together. Then ask any of them for your loan. Once people see us together—you can go to any one of these people for a loan. They'll see you're someone with potential power, because you've been seen walking with a rich man. That's a better gift I'm giving you than if I lent you the money.' "

Ironically it's the young club executives who would best grasp this story. They tend to attach themselves to power figures, and the aura often rubs off.

Upshot: They fail up, but in style.

30

Club Outcast—
Frank Yablans

Charles Bluhdorn got in because Gulf & Western bought Paramount. Frank Yablans got in because he had a big mouth, knew how to open a movie, and could talk to Charlie Bluhdorn. Yablans stayed in because he and Robert Evans and Peter Bart ran Paramount successfully. Yablans dropped out because Barry Diller was smarter and sleeker and more appealing to Charlie Bluhdorn. Robert Evans got in through Darryl Zanuck and Charles Bluhdorn and Joyce Selznick. (It was Selznick who told Evans to tell Bluhdorn he was bilingual, thus getting Bluhdorn to hire him as Paramount's man in Europe.) Joyce Selznick didn't get in because she was a woman, and it killed her. Robert Evans stayed in, for a long time, because of Sidney Korshak. Korshak was a club founder. Frank Yablans stayed in after he left Paramount, for a while anyway, because Sidney Korshak took care of him. Throughout the '60s and '70s, Sidney Korshak and Frank Sinatra were the most powerful men in the club. Then Lew Wasserman became the most powerful man in the club. Then Steven Spielberg did. And then Mike Ovitz did.

One of the true clichés in the club is that you'll never work in this town again. Another true fear is that you won't get your price, that you'll be undervalued. People look at club has-been Tony Curtis on reruns of *Vega$*, and they tremble. The big fear: that you'll be an outcast, like poor Bo Polk, or the forgotten Mel Simon, or the deposed Frank Mancuso, or the repetitive Mel Brooks. Nobody wants to happen to them what happened to Frank Yablans. Of all the club members who came out of Paramount in the '70s and '80s—and there are a lot—Yablans is the most worth studying. He flew the highest, and dropped the furthest. And nobody cared enough, not even the Paramount gang, to bail him out.

Actually Hollywood in the '90s could be dubbed Son of Paramount. Practically every major club executive (with exceptions like Alan Ladd, Jr.) was groomed, weaned, not nurtured exactly but pummeled at Paramount in the '70s. Michael Eisner, Martin Davis, Barry Diller, Stanley Jaffe, Frank Mancuso, Jeffrey Katzenberg, Dawn Steel—all the real boys went to real school at Paramount, and apart from the Gulf & Western founder, Charles Bluhdorn (who died mysteriously on a plane bound for the Dominican Republic in 1975), each of these people is running something in the club. I wanted each of them to open up to me without knowing it, and without my betraying them—and there was only one route. Going slowly. The greatest difficulty for a journalist in Hollywood is gaining trust.

Joan Didion was being a good reporter when she quoted the real Celia Brady (the one in Fitzgerald's *Last Tycoon*) saying, "We don't go for outsiders here." After fifteen or twenty years these people who don't waste time to begin with—won't waste time with you either. They'll just talk directly, once there's trust. Or they won't talk at all. To circulate you must not circulate too much—not get too burnt out or (God forbid) overexposed. Always it's their moment; and you let Frank Mancuso have his moment—it's his lunch, his advice, his problems. You thus are merely a confidant of the moment. One of many, but still . . .

Ask vicious questions and you might as well wind up a professor somewhere. You don't go into a club to tear people apart. That's suicide and though I'm, God knows, dark, I'm still too intact to be suicidal.

Which brings us to Frank Yablans.

He's the Damon Runyon of the Paramount gang, the outcast, the merchant, the street guy, the one who got taught how to talk proper English, how to wear a suit, how to be polite—but ultimately not how to succeed. His Paramount presidency in the early '70s wasn't just the luck of the draw—Yablans was the first of the marketing men to run things. Frank Yablans paved the way for a Frank Mancuso, who became Paramount's chairman from a marketing background. Yablans had Robert

Evans as his senior production VP, and he had the good timing to get blockbusters like *Love Story* and *Godfather*, and respectful things like *Save the Tiger*. ("Not every movie has to make money," he would tell producers—when he felt he could trust them.)

Yablans, before he got "fixed"—before he learned how to dress or talk—was interesting. Maybe it was because he was the last street-talker *macher* who made it to the top. He may also have been the precursor of Marvin Davis, the billionaire Denver oil man, who also thought he could buy class. And for a little while made some other people believe it, too.

> *I don't think I've made more enemies than Cecil B. DeMille or Jack Warner or L. B. Mayer or Harry Cohn. Nor have I made any more friends than they made . . . I'm a lot more decent than some of the popular men. Because . . . I will give a fast no and a fast yes.*
> —**Frank Yablans**, 1974

Speed may be the essence of Frank Yablans. Three months after he made the above remarks, Yablans was out of his job as president and chief executive officer of Paramount. Yablans temporarily became a successful independent producer (*Silver Streak*) and co-screenwriter (*North Dallas Forty*) and a consistent (if seemingly reluctant) newsmaker, before disappearing to Neverland. "I haven't really opened up like this in seven years," he admitted one morning in his office at 20th Century-Fox. Our talk had been scheduled for forty minutes; it ran three hours. That's because Yablans has more sides to him than a centipede has legs.

"I should have played Gatsby," he said when Paramount released *The Great Gatsby* in 1974 starring Robert Redford. The line was a clue to his character: Yablans is the loner, always. Another Paramount film of the period, *The Apprenticeship of Duddy Kravitz*, was a better clue, however; around the studio, they called it *The Frank Yablans Story*. His life, however, isn't that simple.

A cab driver's son from the Williamsburg section of Brooklyn, he had risen from assistant general sales manager to studio president before he was thirty-five. The wiry Yablans (rhymes with "The Dons") reportedly was given elocution lessons—and a custom tailor (in London) to prepare him for executive life. That was like polishing a rough-hewn gem. Three years into his Paramount stint, he was fired. To grasp why, one needs to take a brief look at Hollywood history.

In 1971, Yablans signed an eight-year Paramount contract (at $250,000 per year, plus 1.5 percent of gross profits). There were hits (*The Godfather I* and *II*, *Paper Moon*, *Serpico*, and *Save the Tiger*) and flops (*Catch-22*,

The Little Prince, Day of the Locust) and (in one year) thirty-nine Oscar nominations. There also was controversy: Yablans' personal style—his quick answers, his mean streaks, his flamboyance—resulted in his ouster. In 1974 Gulf & Western chairman Charles Bluhdorn named Barry Diller Paramount board chairman; seven weeks later, Yablans was out.

"Paramount didn't get rid of Frank," fabled attorney Sidney Korshak told Joyce Haber writing in *Los Angeles* magazine. "Frank got rid of Paramount. I negotiated his resignation. Bluhdorn stayed in that building until 11:30 at night. He kept saying, 'This isn't what I want. I want to keep him.' . . . I told Frank he should stay, but he said, 'No way will I work for people like that!' "

Then, eight years later, the rumor arose that he would replace David Begelman at MGM-UA; he didn't. Would Yablans ever return to corporate duty? One of his various answers revealed a possible negotiating stance. "During the Begelman rumor, I was in a very vulnerable period of my life," he said, sitting straight-backed in his office at 20th Century-Fox. "But let's put it this way about the Begelman job: I wouldn't not have taken it. I just wasn't interested in three fast years, and out. Hollywood is going to have to look ahead—or down the road—for any kind of effective leadership. The graybeards are coming back into vogue; peach fuzzes going out of style."

That's what Yablans said. He meant that the baby moguls of the '70s were a fizzle. On the subject of studio power, he is a true observer. In a silk shirt, smoking unfiltered cigarettes, he held court—and never avoided a question. If at fiftyish, Yablans is already referring to "my younger days," it's understandable. Hollywood is what Baudelaire called "Banal Eldorado," a town of old young men. "The younger executives," Yablans said, scowling, "haven't cut their teeth yet. They're expected to bark like German shepherds. That's a lot to expect . . . When I was at Paramount, three people ran the company. Myself, [production chief] Robert Evans, and [production vice-president] Peter Bart. Less is more," added Yablans.

"The biggest lesson," he said harshly, "is that you cannot be all things to all people. You can be one thing to all people, though. That one thing could have to do with executive leadership." He was asked to be more specific. "Specifically, let's discuss meetings. I used to take twenty fifteen-minute meetings a day. Instead, I should have taken three two-hour meetings. Three meetings a day, and you can accomplish something." Why, then, did Yablans overload himself?

"I was in the rejection business. It's a very hard task to say no sensitively. I mean, running a studio is a major, major task."

Out of the blue, a line of Fitzgerald's was summoned: "Not half a dozen men have ever been able to keep the whole equation of pictures in their heads," Fitzgerald wrote in *The Last Tycoon*. Yablans listened to the line, then said: "I think Fitz exaggerated. There aren't six people who know what questions to ask—let alone the answers, or the equation. And then, too, things have changed. I cannot assign Warren Beatty to a picture the way Louis B. Mayer could assign Gable."

If the equation of picture making is an impossible one, Yablans at least has some insight—from experience. (And he has an ego larger than Pickfair's living room.) He knows the seating plans of practically every theater in America built before 1970. The reason: He worked those towns and cities as a film salesman for four different studios. ("I could have died in hotel rooms in those towns, Omaha or Des Moines, and nobody would have cared.") Distribution, marketing, advertising were among his pursuits before the creative urge hit. "Frank got creative when he went independent," reported *Daily Variety* in 1978.

"When I read the press, I smile a lot," Yablans confided, not exactly smiling. "I think the press—with a few exceptions—knows very little about how power really works. So I read and smile. The problem is, it's only 10 percent of any interview that gets remembered . . . Usually it's the wrong 10 percent."

Yablans laughed. It's the sort of Yablanism he covets. As in "*I don't want to be the next Sam Goldwyn. I want to be the first Frank Yablans.*" Or: "We must nurture writers. The problem is, there are thousands of writers, and only seven breasts."

Yablans talks like a man who would like another shot at what he calls the "heady gas" of club power. "He would kill his children to be back in the club," a producer told me. Yablans referred to his Paramount days, more than once, as having been "short-circuited . . . I had a dream, but I was rudely awakened from that dream." Doesn't Yablans want to even the score? After all, *Silver Streak* alone made him a rich man. Worldwide grosses hovered around $100 million. "Winston Churchill," he said evenly, "left politics for ten years and just painted. Then he came back. I had the desire to come back—at a studio. But that desire went away."

Why exactly? Frank answered the question with another frank question. "Do you ever think about Ned Tanen? When *E.T.* became such a major hit . . . that was a heady feeling for Ned, as the studio executive. I know that feeling. But our American system is such that you can only enjoy that success for a moment. Right away the corporate pressure was on Ned to top that success. And he couldn't. The banks in this country say things like, 'Last summer you did $380 million at the box office; this summer you only did $300 million. What's wrong? . . . It's madness, but it's America's way of corporate life."

In the club, that executive way of life—limousines, private projection rooms, studio-paid assistants, travel—isn't refused lightly. Today's independent producer (no matter how successful) has a far rougher go than the independent producer of the '80s. Interest rates are part of the problem—but only part. As Yablans put it, "There's no jet plane to success. If a picture of mine gets turned down by a studio . . . then I feel like I want to take over that studio. I guess I'm in a risk mentality."

Frank Yablans is always in a risk mentality—and so is Hollywood. And that's why the Yablanses of this world are more interesting than the Gubers or Peterses. Because in the club, failure is thought to be contagious. And that's why Yablans hasn't gotten back in.

CLUB RULE THIRTY-NINE

The more things change, the more they don't. Robert Evans went into power in 1966, out of power in 1975, completely out of power in 1981, and in 1991—he got back in. Once a player, almost always a player. Be very careful of how you treat *everybody*.

Frank Yablans didn't get this idea, and it cost him his role in the club. He wasn't respectful enough. And in the club, the more things change, the more they don't. Example: Since the '60s, the club godfather, Ray Stark, has been the mastermind behind Columbia Pictures. In the endless executive shuffles at Columbia, it's been Stark the players would go to for counsel; he helped David Begelman, and Guy McElwaine, and Dawn Steel, and Frank Price, and he had next to no use for David Puttnam. So Puttnam left. Stark is strictly behind the scenes. But he understands how much the game is always the same game. The 1990 Columbia leadership, Jon Peters and Peter Guber, didn't scare Stark. As 1990 began he said, "I started out with Harry Cohn. Now I'm back with Harry Cohn. Jon Peters is Harry Cohn."

As the French would say, *plus ça change*. Unfortunately, Frank Yablans doesn't speak French.

CODA

31

The Amputation

What's the real story?" producer Polly Platt asked me the day Dawn Steel abruptly canceled her party for a fellow *Vanity Fair* writer. Polly had been told by Dawn's office the same thing everyone else was told—that the guest of honor suddenly had to return to New York. Which of course was a lie. The guest of honor, a perky blonde with "self-promotion" written all over her, couldn't pull a crowd. There weren't enough A acceptances to make it worth Dawn's time. The Peter Gubers had accepted, and so had Pat and Mike Medavoy, but not Mike Ovitz, or Barry Diller, or David Geffen, or Ray Stark, or even one star. Except Anjelica Huston, who was only coming because her best friend also writes for the magazine.

"Oh, Polly," I said sheepishly, "you know the real story. Journalists aren't stars anymore. They don't . . . mean anything."

Polly murmured sympathetically. She knew I was right. (Once upon a time Polly was a journalist herself, sort of; when her then-husband Peter Bogdanovich was still writing for *Esquire*, Polly was his transcriber.) So Polly could still remember when it meant something to be a journalist. The days when Doris Day would come to dinner if you had Rex Reed, as long as you seated him next to her. The days when Merle Oberon gave a black-tie dinner for Suzy, because the columnist was visiting from New York. The days when Gene Kelly and Joyce Haber made such a drop-dead entrance at Liza Minnelli's marriage to Jack Haley, Jr., that the crowd at Ciro's swooned—it was like Ciro's in the '50s, Sammy Davis said. (Sammy paid for the wedding, although the invitations said that he was co-hosting with the father of the bride, Vincente Minnelli.) Haber devoted four full columns to the wedding.

"*Joyce Haber,*" whispered Polly, with real feeling. She said the name the way you say James Hoffa. "Whatever happened to her?"

I told Polly the whole story. About her being dumped by Gene Kelly, and my trying to help her pick up the pieces, however lamely. I laid it out like a Hollywood casualty. And I hated the way I came off, sounding like the good cop. "The point is she produced," I told Polly defensively. "And she wrote beautifully." I was wounded by the realization of how tired I was of being asked what happened to her. Of my identity being wrapped up in hers.

Polly seemed to understand, or be interested, which was something new for me. I wasn't used to club members listening to me. I was the one who was to do the listening, in any circumstances. Because that was a given, it never bothered me. "What you are studying," Barry Diller told me, "is the art of tending the circus. Remember that, and all you have to tell is the truth."

I was having lunch outside at Malibu, on a deck overlooking the ocean, when I realized how bored with it all I was. I didn't even care that Julia Roberts had just canceled her wedding to Keifer Sutherland. I didn't care that the town's biggest star had sent a seismic wave through the community when she abruptly called it off. It was probably going to be the biggest club event since Edie and Lew Wasserman's fiftieth anniversary on the Universal lot. Julia Roberts was a true Cinderella in a town that needed one, and the wedding on the Fox lot would (for one day anyway), "glue the community back together," as one studio chief told me.

I'd been invited, and it didn't mean anything. I knew Julia Roberts was a character of mythic proportions, maybe the biggest star born in the club since Barbra Streisand. And this was the first wedding anybody cared about since Karen Black's 5 A.M. July Fourth fireworks marriage at Franklin Canyon. Before that, it had been Lucille Ball's wedding for little Lucie, in the backyard. Three big weddings in fifteen years. That's how much the club has changed from the old days.

When it hit me that I had no interest in going, I knew I'd changed, too. Only a week before I'd been at the American Cinematheque dinner for Martin Scorsese, the one where Paramount chairman Frank Mancuso was refused admittance three days after he abruptly left the studio when Stanley Jaffe was brought in above him. I heard about Mancuso being frisked for his tickets, and suddenly I realized something awful. Had I covered the event, I wouldn't have reported this wonderful little power play. And it *should* have been reported. But my thinking now would be, *why stick a dagger in poor Frank?* Of course Frank should have known enough to stay in isolation for a while. But so what? And who cared anyway?

Even a year earlier this would have mattered. It mattered when I saw Don Simpson go berserk after he was refused admittance to a screening in Century City.

"Do you know who I am?" he asked the ticket-taker indignantly.

"I know who you are," I told him. He looked at me like I'd caught him in bed with somebody. I calmed him down by empathizing.

But that seemed a long time ago. In those days, when Mike Frankovich called me *buddy*, my week would be made. I was that shallow. But the week after Haber was fired, when the phone stopped ringing, something was over for me. Some belief. I think I stopped believing in Queen Mothers.

Gradually a real life started to be appealing. In the club, a real life means you are what Ray Stark calls "a hundred percent," or completely trustable. If you are a journalist, and you are "a hundred percent," the members will stand up for you. Ray will endorse you, Geffen and Diller will stand up for you, as they did for me with Ray when he thought I misquoted him in *Vanity Fair*. I'm not sure I'm a hundred percent in Ray's eyes anymore, but at least I understand how this game works.

I do know it's an unforgiving game. When Mrs. Jack Warner started seeing Eddie Albert on the side, Eddie Albert stopped working in Hollywood. This was a year after he almost won an Oscar for *Roman Holiday*. He was on the brink of bankability. But in the club, the winners have to munch shit. The members like to watch that happen. They enjoyed watching Jerry Weintraub eat shit, when his company went bankrupt, and they wait for Sid Sheinberg's turn, or Martin Davis'. It's a revolving door, and the worst part is everybody wants to be somebody else. (With a few exceptions, like Ted Ashley and David Geffen and maybe Jack Lemmon.) Joan Cohn Harvey wanted to be Edie Goetz more than she wanted to be a grandmother. Allan Carr wanted to be Mike Todd. The ones who didn't want to reinvent themselves wanted at least to get even.

I'd really spent twenty years trying to weed out the phonies. And it took almost that long to know who was who.

How I did it is not something I'm particularly proud of. But it worked. Very early on I realized narcissists see nothing outside of themselves. So I could be whoever these people wanted me to be. I found they bought— or trusted—my nice Jewish boy persona. The wide eyes, the willingness to work harder and longer than everybody else, the need to be loved.

That's how I got people to open up, by showing my best side. I was easy to project onto. By never ever asking the embarrassing question, I'd often get the embarrassing answer. I didn't bring up Dean Martin to Jerry Lewis, so Jerry talked about "my partner," and he cried real tears. I'm not sure my tears were real, but I cried along with him.

Passive-manipulative, probably, but the club prefers that to guile. Guile they see right through. So I carried Dinah Shore's groceries to her station wagon at Food King, but I did it knowing that Dinah Shore's best friend was married to the most powerful labor lawyer in California. A club journalist only has to remember his place, as a watcher, and he won't get in trouble.

For a lot of years, that's enough of a reward. To stay in print and out of trouble. Gradually you want more. The day I went alone to Louella Parsons' funeral at Good Shepherd in Beverly Hills I was still the leg. The amputation didn't happen until years later, but it did happen all right. Maybe it was the night I went to interview Maureen Stapleton at the Old World on Sunset. "So what do you want?" she said to me bluntly. "Do you want me to suck your cock?" Somehow this was not the kind of flirtation I'd imagined for my Hollywood years.

Or was it the day I was so personal with Anne Bancroft, after an interview, that I offered to walk her home? I thought we'd shared a moment. How foolish. She looked at me like I was a homeless person. *Walk me home!?!* Her big black eyes registered a kind of terror at the very idea. And I closed off—something was over for me. I never again asked to walk anyone home. I stopped worshipping and started listening more to little peccadilloes about these people. Like the thing about Bancroft's murky sexual past. Here I am writing these words down—the leg would have kept them to himself.

Is it self-destructive? Yes and no. As long as the journalist has a power base, the power base will attract those who want recognition. They will still talk to you—it's the famous Billy Wilder line about Marilyn Monroe. *I'll never use her again until I need her.* So I'm not worried about people talking to me for publication. As long as I have an outlet, they'll talk. Carefully, but . . . talk they will. And if I don't have an outlet, I won't want to talk to them anyway. If you are off somewhere writing a book, they aren't even talking *about* you. (The leg would have thought otherwise, and worried about it.)

So, no, I'm not worried about burning bridges. Hollywood is a very forgiving town, if you have any power at all. If you have no power, it's the most unforgiving town in the world. And anyway I'd had the best job in Hollywood, at the newspaper, for exactly twenty years.

And I'd gotten into the houses. And that was the goal. And after a zillion nervous dinner parties, I realized why I was always so uncomfortable. Because I would hear things I'd want to use. *How Michael Douglas made poor Brenda Vaccaro buy back his half of their house.* But I wouldn't use these things, so I kept being invited back. Club couples had become my obsession. Knowing Felicia Lemmon meant as much as knowing Jack. Being Jane Eisner's dinner partner was as intriguing as an interview at the studio with her husband. But club evenings were accompanied, always, by panic attacks and tranquilizers. Not that it was all bad. Audrey Hepburn cooking in Connie Wald's kitchen isn't a bad memory. I never found the club to be cold, the way people said. In Virginia Zanuck's breakfast room, I found the kind of warmth I never found in Ohio.

But finally I stopped going because it seemed more honest to me to keep my distance—if I was to remain a reporter. "The day you stop being a journalist," Dan Melnick told me, over brunch in his dining room, "is the day you get invited back to my house."

"But by then I expect to be writing books about Hollywood," I told him earnestly. "And I'll want to use everything I see and hear."

That didn't sit well with Melnick, and at any rate he never asked me back again. Which was fine with me. Who wants to be in a club where they don't trust you? Can't trust you? And who wants to be a *HeddaLouella* monster? And, anyway, the press in Hollywood has always been controlled by the studios. Everybody knows that.

"You know how to listen," club daughter Judy Quine told me one long afternoon at the Polo Lounge. "And everybody knows it."

What Judy knew, that most other club members don't, is that listening is expensive. It wears you out. The night Joanne Carson told me the real truth about how Truman Capote died in her arms, I couldn't breathe. I went to bed for three days, where I replayed the scene over and over.

"No wonder your nervous system is shot," a healer friend of Cher's told me. "You've tuned in to their neuroses . . . And your heart is broken."

Maybe unrequited love is the right term. Journalists always say not to love a newspaper because it can't ever love you back. I found that cliché not to be true. For twenty years my paper was a very good and faithful lover. But I don't think you should love the club too much—because I *know* it can't love you back. Not really. The members are too narcissistic. They *like* you, but who knows if they will stand by you?

The morning that club attorney Norman Garey killed himself, after our breakfast at the Bel Air Sands, I realized I was the last person to see him alive. This smooth, sensitive counselor to people as high-strung as Brando and Julia Phillips was a very old soul, and a very good friend. When Brando had his stomach pumped for eating too much ice cream,

Norman took the call. We had a quiet little breakfast at the hotel, and he went home and put a bullet through his brain. His protégés, Joe Peckerman and Barry Haldeman, were among my closest friends. We were Norman's boys, and some of the club knew it.

After Norman died we invented the nine o'clock club, as a way of keeping his spirit alive. Once a month at nine o'clock we would meet with like-minded friends. "This club is going to save my life," Joe decided one night over dinner. And our club did become our salvation, for a while. We got heavily into nicknames as a way of getting closer to each other.

"The leg sounds so phallic," a producer decided one night. We were sitting around worrying about our futures. "I want to know where the leg came from," she insisted.

"You are too young," I told her. Then I told her that it was like working for Louella Parsons, my days working for Joyce Haber. I told her how the club courted this woman as if she were a mogul. How she made and broke marriages and careers. How people woke up trembling, until they read the column. I told her how one day the leg went to the back door to find Rosalind Russell in a babushka offering homemade fudge because Miss Haber (or Mrs. Cramer as she liked to be called) had phlebitis. (She'd been divorced from Mr. Cramer by then, but the club likes to call women Mrs. Somebody. They think it makes them feel more like women.)

The nine o'clock club wanted to hear more. Someone fiddled with the dimmers in the living room to make it more theatrical.

"Once upon a time," I told them, "not very long ago, there was a reign of terror in Hollywood . . . And I survived it."

THE ROSTER

A Selective Who's Who
in the Club

Mea Culpa: This guide to membership is purposely incomplete—a complete roster is impossible, as it would need updating every few months. The roster is also subject to upheavals, job changes, deaths, and other departures. Omitted are the names of some members who have chapters devoted to them. Essentially this guide is for the reader who stumbles upon a name like Bert Fields or Freddie Fields and wonders who's who. (If you already know who's who, you can skip directly to your last name to see if you made the cut. And relax: Birth dates are omitted.)

Merv Adelson—Affable founder of La Costa, less driven than people think, in spite of the Mafia rumors. The second husband of Barbara Walters, and one of the club's best Jewish athletes.

Jay Presson Allen—Could write the ultimate screenplay about the club; prolific playwright-screenwriter married to Broadway producer Lewis Allen. Texas tough, and very funny. Unusual understanding—for a writer—of money. (Ask her agent Jeff Berg.) Wrote *Prime of Miss Jean Brodie* in three days; the first draft of *Cabaret*, in a week; also she created TV's *Family*.

Woody Allen—Club hero because he won't work or live or spend time in Hollywood. (See Rule Twenty-six: The club wants what it can't have.) Best movies: *Manhattan, Hannah and Her Sisters,* and *September.* The club considers his *Crimes and Misdemeanors* one of their favorite movies of the '80s because it plays into club emotions.

Ann-Margret—The most vulnerable person in Hollywood, and perhaps the best soul in the club. Completely antisocial—she has only been to three restaurants in thirty years. She has true mystique. (See Rule Twenty-six: The club wants what it can't have.) Best performances: *Carnal Knowledge* and *The Two Mrs. Grenvilles.*

Army Archerd—The club's most important—and along with George Christy best-liked—news columnist, he understands the community as well as any journalist ever has. When he retires from *Daily Variety,* replacing him will be harder than replacing Johnny Carson.

Ted Ashley—A club elder statesman, former agent, former chairman of Warner's who was handed the keys to the studio by Jack Warner himself. Retired—but not retired from giving advice to members.

Dan Aykroyd—Club survivor who got through the death of his partner and a series of flop movies before landing an Oscar nomination for *Driving Miss Daisy.*

Barney Balaban—An early club member, a president of Paramount in the '40s, one of the first major movie distributors, and father of favorite club daughter, writer-observer Judy Quine.

Alec Baldwin—The handsomest actor in Hollywood, and maybe the most intense. Best performance, so far: *Working Girl.*

Rona Barrett—The pioneer of the TV gossip column. She was told by the networks that she was too Jewish to become Barbara Walters. When she lost her jobs on *Good Morning America* and *The Today Show,* she lost some footing. (To stay in the club after you lose your power base, you have to be both liked and lucky.)

Marty Baum—An agent's agent, a father figure at the founding of CAA, the old hand who knows all the ropes. In a movie about the club, he'd be played by Jack Palance.

Gregson (Greg) Bautzer—Club stud *extraordinaire*, and the first entertainment attorney to go the distance. Handled Howard Hughes and Jim Aubrey and club divorcees in need of consoling. Privately, Joan Crawford called him her favorite lover.

Warren Beatty—If the club ran elections, he'd be the best candidate for president. Learned at the feet of club founder Sam Spiegel, and has made almost no club mistakes. (Not even *Ishtar*, which got blamed on Elaine May.) One of the half-dozen true club legends, and studs. His best movies: *Bonnie and Clyde* and *Shampoo*, were also among the best movies of their decades. His *Bugsy* is a true club performance.

Sidney Beckerman—Sometime producer, with strong ties to power outside show business. His main claim to fame came when he slugged agent Bobby Littman on the patio of Ma Maison, in full view of *le tout Hollywood*. Only decent credit: *The Other Side of Midnight*.

David Begelman—The club newsmaker of the '70s, cast in a garish light when his check-forging scandal became public. His victimless crime is committed every day in Hollywood; his larger crimes are the emotional kind. Simultaneously charming and countercharming. A better studio executive (he approved *Close Encounters of the Third Kind*) than producer (his major hit is *The Fabulous Baker Boys*).

Gladyce Begelman—The club wife of the '70s, social in the extreme; her good graces and talents smoothed the way for her husband's comeback. Her death, in the early '80s, actually elicited emotion (sadness) from the club. One of her best friends, Annabel Weston, later replaced her as the spouse of David Begelman—which nobody minded. What people minded was Annabel Begelman's telling people she married David for his money. People got a kick out of that one.

John Belushi—The modern club casualty who single-handedly turned the tide against drugs in Hollywood. His misadventuures at the Chateau Marmont did more good than a hundred "Just Say No" benefits. Best performance: *Animal House*.

Peter Benedek—Literate former attorney who became a literary agent on advice of his college roommate, writer-director Larry Kasdan. A player. His bright wife, Barbara, co-wrote the seminal *The Big Chill*.

Robert Benton—A favorite club filmmaker because he consistently makes classy pictures as a director (*Kramer vs. Kramer*) and a writer (*Bonnie and Clyde*). In the Sam Cohn branch of the club, and especially visible in the Hamptons.

Dick Berg—Writer-father of club biographer Scott Berg and club agent Jeff Berg.

Jeff Berg—One of the best-educated members in club history. Bright, fast, more savvy about film itself than probably any other agent. Club directors like Bernardo Bertolucci and Jim Brooks crave his insights and ability to go the distance. One of the true heroes of the club's favorite '80s success story—*Terms of Endearment*.

Polly Bergen—The quintessential club wife of the '60s, as Mrs. Freddie Fields. She gave her husband style, class, and social cachet. Could probably write the best novel about the club since Jackie Susann. Best performance: *The Helen Morgan Story*, on *Playhouse 90*.

Alan Bergman—The club lyricist, with his wife, Marilyn; also one of Hollywood's best tennis players and most decent people. Major player in the ACLU, Hollywood branch. And in the music branch of the Academy. Best song: "Pieces of Dreams." Most popular song: "The Way We Were."

Jacqueline Bisset—Club has-been who traded her beauty for a money career. Played power games with ICM elder, Ben Benjamin. She treated men the way men usually treat women. Best performance: A bit as a flirt in *Two for the Road*.

Michael Black—ICM club agent, particularly adept with complex second-generation actresses like Jamie Lee Curtis and Liza Minnelli.

Charles Bluhdorn—Brilliant Austrian tycoon who made Paramount the flagship of his Gulf & Western empire. A gambler who bet on Robert Evans and Barry Diller, when both were young and untried. His mysterious death in the company's corporate jet is never discussed.

Charles Brackett—Billy Wilder's first collaborator, who later became a producer; one of the true club wits of the '40s and '50s. Best credits: *Sunset Boulevard* and *Stalag 17*, which are both about Hollywood in different ways.

Bill Bradley—The club's favorite politico. Sydney Pollack grooms him for TV spots, Ovitz and Eisner throw him fund-raisers, and nobody underestimates his jock charisma. He may be from New Jersey, but he plays in Hollywood.

Marlon Brando—The actor the club most reveres. During *Last Tango*, he told a club member, "I'll never give this much again." And he hasn't. The club takes him at his word, and pays him his price. The first actor to make $1 million a week.

Howard Brandy—Ned Tanen's best friend. He's the publicist Madonna's manager calls "the nicest man in show business." Most interesting client: Aretha Franklin.

Marty Bregman—Of the old school of producers who nurture stars, namely Al Pacino. Too East Coast to truly succeed in the club, but determined anyway. Most successful movie: Alan Alda's *Four Seasons*, a movie the club hated because it reminded them of their own mortality.

Evie Bricusse—Club wife of the '60s who became a club hostess in the '70s, in the South of France. A sexy broad who's a faithful wife, a rare combination in the club. Was known as the Community Chest in her salad days. Played Sheila in *The Last of Sheila*.

Jim Bridges—A club director who lost some ground when he took over the ill-fated *Bright Lights, Big City*, but is still the director who made a star of Debra Winger, in *Urban Cowboy*.

Norman Brokaw—"A lifer" at William Morris, now running the show since the deaths of Lee Stevens and Abe Lastfogel. This walking history of Hollywood represents Bill Cosby and Loretta Young. His own memoirs would tell much about the club in its heyday. The company man of all time.

Jim Brooks—The club's favorite writer-director, because he made two of the best movies of the '80s—*Terms of Endearment* and *Broadcast News*—and because he almost never makes mistakes. One of the very few creative geniuses in the club.

Richard Brooks—Erudite, amusing club director of the '50s and beyond who knows Hollywood better than any living director. A raconteur, ladies' man, and great tennis player. Would be a character in any movie about the club. Best movies: *Blackboard Jungle* and *In Cold Blood*.

David Brown—The most decent man in the club, brilliant about "story" and a survivor with true dignity. Difficult to cast in a movie about the club, because he's almost too good to be true—only he isn't. Co-produced *Jaws, The Sting*. Writes monthly cover blurbs for his wife, Helen Gurley Brown's, *Cosmopolitan*.

Jerry Bruckheimer—The business half of the Simpson-Bruckheimer team, this likable executive keeps a lid on partner Don Simpson's extravagances—sort of. His skill is in marketing. Co-produced *Top Gun* and *Beverly Hills Cop*.

CAA—The three initials that have replaced CBS, MGM, NBC, ABC— or any others—as the preeminent show business abbreviation. Creative Artists Agency is the starriest, most dramatic agency ever, and most of its founders (Mike Ovitz, Ron Meyer, Bill Haber) are still in there giving the Horatio Alger myth (along with other myths) a whole new coloration.

John Calley—Classy, bright, iconoclastic Warner's executive of the '60s and '70s who left the club of his own accord to live in Europe. Came back to produce *Postcards from the Edge*, realized nothing had changed, and returned to Europe.

Mark Canton—If Jon Peters and Peter Guber conceived a child, he'd be called Mark Canton. One of the youngest top-drawer club executives.

Truman Capote—If only he'd behaved, the club would have made him a hero. Because he understood them, and amused them. His piece *Duke in His Domain* about Brando is the best profile ever written about an actor.

Allan Carr—Flamboyant, misunderstood producer of two of the biggest hit musicals ever—*Grease* (on film) and *La Cage Aux Folles* (on Broadway). Gave the best club parties of the '70s.

Charles Champlin—The classiest of the journalists who covered the club.

Chevy Chase—The anti-establishment wit of the '70s who unwittingly became Establishment himself in the '80s. Best performance: *Foul Play*, with Goldie Hawn.

Dave Chasen—The former vaudevillian who became the first club restaurateur. His chili was the club food years before (and after) designer pizza.

Paddy Chayefsky—Playwright-screenwriter who scared the club because of how much he knew about the members. They gave him the Oscar anyway, for *Network*.

Cher—The club borderline who makes a success of everything she puts her mind to, except relationships. Unflinchingly honest. Best performance: *Moonstruck*.

George Christy—The club's most important social columnist, in *The Hollywood Reporter*.

Michael Cimino—Troubled director who causes the club tsuris. Won an Oscar for *Deer Hunter*, but everything since then has turned to mush. Too cantankerous for the club in the scaled-down '90s. Prospects dim.

Harry Cohn—The legendary Columbia president who was a club founder, and a terror to work for. Exploited women and simultaneously made them movie stars of the first rank. Crude and frightening. His best piece of work: Kim Novak's five star vehicles from 1955 to 1957.

Sam Cohn—The last club bulwark in New York. The classic agent with classic clients (Mike Nichols, Woody Allen) was saved from extinction when CAA decided not to open a New York office.

Doug Collins—The club's favorite security man for club evenings. Well-wired and well-liked and (most of all) trusted.

Sean Connery—The aging club sex symbol, one of the few actors who club members would change places with. Best performances: The James Bond movies.

Francis Coppola—Visionary club bad boy, the all-time profligate spender. The club has already cast him as a latter-day Orson Welles. But so far he's surviving. His *Godfather* trilogy is the ultimate club movie-movie, for obvious reasons.

Kevin Costner—The club actor with the best timing—he appeared at a moment when a hero was desperately needed. The club gave him the big shoes of Jimmy Stewart and Gary Cooper—whether he fit them or not. He is what Harrison Ford pretends to be. Best-liked performance: *No Way Out*, because his behavior as an initiate in a company town reminded members of their own salad days.

Douglas S. Cramer—The club's art patron and collector *nonpareil*; former husband of club columnist Joyce Haber, and co-producer of *Dynasty*. Gives the club its only hayrides (at his art ranch in Santa Ynez).

Tom Cruise—The go-the-distance club star with the best odds of becoming what Paul Newman became—as in *durable*. Best performance: *Rain Man*.

George Cukor—Legendary club director who had no peer at handling actresses and actors. Gave the starriest club brunches, and was a superb club dinner guest. An intimate of Garbo, Hepburn, Maugham, and especially Frances Goldwyn. Only club director to do pictures from the '30s through the '80s. Best movies: *Camille, Philadelphia Story, My Fair Lady*.

Ames Cushing—The affable William Morris agent who's a good sport socially, turning up when needed for tributes, benefits, and award shows. Pretty and loyal. Clients include Tess Harper and Faith Ford.

Bob Daly—A third of the long-running trio—Terry Semel and Mark Canton are the other two—that ran Warner Brothers from the '80s until Mark Canton left, in 1991. The club sees him as a team player, and leader. His background is television. His most profitable product: The umpteen Clint Eastwood pictures.

Nicole David—Cheerful, bright, a top actor's agent at Triad. A loyalist with long-range plans for clients like Amy Irving and Julie Andrews.

Barbara Davis—The new social leader of the club, a woman with good values and a terrible hairdresser. People are too afraid of her to tell her that the shellac look is out—permanently.

Marvin Davis—The billionaire from Denver who went Hollywood in a very big way. Hungers to be a studio baron. Living proof that not everybody in the club has a personal trainer.

Doris Day—The club victim, of bad business management and bad marriages—she elicits true empathy from the club. They know how hard she worked, what a big star she was, and how little she wound up with. The club doesn't want what happened to her to happen to them. Due for a comeback. The club loves her performance as Ruth Etting in *Love Me or Leave Me*, and often runs it on the private screening circuit. The club also respects the way she handled Rock Hudson's death—by not milking it.

Dino De Laurentiis—His image is more "mob" than club, but he surfaces in Hollywood every decade or so, with newer, richer deals. His prime has probably passed, but don't bet on it. Goes from clinkers (*Dune*) to occasional hits (*Serpico*).

Suzanne de Passe—Go-go club producer who never misses a night out. Protégé of Motown's Berry Gordy, she used to be the most ambitious person in the club under fifty. Can work any room, anywhere. Balls the size of watermelons. Best credits: Co-writing *Lady Sings the Blues*, for Diana Ross, and co-producing *Lonesome Dove*, for TV.

Armand Deutsch—One of the club's favorite hosts of the '50s through the '70s. The heir to the Sears, Roebuck fortune, he had ambitions to produce—but the larger ambition was to live well. A modern-day Gerald Murphy without the artistic ability. No credits, but one hell of a good life.

I.A.L. Diamond—Billy Wilder's longtime collaborator, brittle and up-tight and very funny. In the case of Wilder and Diamond, it took two to make one. Best screenwriting credits: *Some Like It Hot* and *The Apartment*.

Angie Dickinson—Club good ole girl who still visits JFK's grave, and will take her own JFK stories to *her* grave. The most sought-after single woman for club dinner parties, because of her glamour and humor. The club would love to see her re-unite with former husband, Burt Bacharach, as they were truly a club couple at the very top.

The Didions—How the writing couple Joan Didion and John Gregory Dunne are known in the club. The club sees them as having expatriated to New York, and so the screenplay deals haven't been as forthcoming lately. She's still considered the best writer in America by many.

Barry Diller—The one true visionary in the club, and (along with David Geffen) the smartest member. A Hollywood child with the best grasp of the town of any executive in club history. The chairman of 20th Century-Fox, and formerly the chairman of Paramount, where he spawned a whole generation of moguls.

Stanley Donen—A rather sour former fixture in the club, with nowhere to ply his wares anymore. As Gene Kelly's ambitious assistant in the '50s, he began taking credit on musicals before directing a few great ones himself—*Seven Brides for Seven Brothers, Funny Face*. An antique now, but a crony of David Begelman and Walter Matthau. Probably has a great Hollywood book in him if he would write down what he saw. Best movie: *Two for the Road*.

Ann Douglas—A club wife of the '50s and beyond who went the distance. Salty, but much beloved.

Michael Douglas—The driven second-generation movie star who outsucceeded his father as a producer, if not as an actor. Privately conflicted, internationally bankable, he'll go the distance. Best performance: *Wall Street*.

William Dozier—A club-observer member who surveyed the town for seven decades. In a movie about the club, he'd be played by John Huston. Or Jack Nicholson. Also produced *Batman*, on TV, and married club favorite Ann Rutherford.

Paul Drehr—Club caterer, hotel branch, at the Beverly Hilton.

Richard Dreyfuss—Would play a mogul in any movie about the club—very savvy about how the town works, and doesn't. Best performance: *The Goodbye Girl*.

Faye Dunaway—Club neurotic who failed in Hollywood when she married British photographer Terry O'Neill. She never quite recovered club status. Her best performances—*Bonnie and Clyde, Chinatown*, and *Network*—are right up there. Not to be written off yet.

Dominick Dunne—The scribe who best understands the club workings. Could be the modern Proust if he chose to tell what he knows, but he's probably too smart. Produced *The Boys in the Band* and *Ash Wednesday*, before he wrote *The Two Mrs. Grenvilles*.

Robert Duvall—Club disappointment who didn't follow up after winning the Oscar for *Tender Mercies*. But the club reveres him for his performance as Tom Heggen in *The Godfather*.

Clint Eastwood—Club hall of fame because of a fifteen-year unbroken string of successes. In the early '80s, he was the only star with veto power over studio decisions. His flops—*White Hunter, Black Heart*—are outweighed by his hits—*Play Misty for Me*, and *Dirty Harry*. Has the club's best-liked business manager, Howard Bernstein.

José Eber—The most successful club hairdresser, probably in history. The only tycoon who still makes house calls. He's the man who made over Elizabeth Taylor, among many others.

Blake Edwards—Club survivor since the early '50s. Perhaps the most erratic director in the club, he goes from brilliant (*Breakfast at Tiffany's*) to boring (*Switch*). Has faced complex sexual rumors for three decades, and simultaneously managed a marriage to Julie Andrews that endures everything.

Michael Eisner—The Disney chairman is the club's favorite statesman, well bred and enthusiastic, and a man who's made almost no mistakes. Both business and show, and a real fan of talent. The adjective most often used for him is "boyish."

Charles Evans—Snob real estate magnate-brother of Robert Evans who lacks his brother's generosity and spirit. Self-important, he's completely unimportant in the club. Made millions from financing *Tootsie*, but made much of his money from his marriage.

Charles Farrell—Club host, founder of the Racquet Club in Palm Springs, victim for years of strange rumors about his private life. Reportedly anti-Semitic, which was why the club never used him as an actor.

Charles Feldman—Legendary stylish club founder. Agent to the crème of '30s and '40s Hollywood, he went on to produce movies—and live it up in ultimate club style right to the end. Worthy of having a novel written about him.

Sally Field—The only club star with two Best Actress Oscars and a club husband (producer Alan Greisman, who ran Ray Stark's company). Celebrated largely for overcoming terrible early odds: Her mother was a

B contract actress, and she did too many years as *Gidget* and *The Flying Nun*. On her thirtieth birthday the club rewarded her with leading lady status when she won the Oscar for *Norma Rae*. (Uttered the favorite line of the club in the '80s: *You* really *do like me.*) Vulnerable, moody, and not as driven as outsiders think.

Ted Field—Seductive scion of Chicago's Marshall Field fortune, determined to make a mark in the club. So far the producer has produced great parties, and those were in the '80s, when he still owned part of the Harold Lloyd estate Green Acres. Club handicappers don't bet on him to win in the long run. More business than show.

Bert Fields—Unquestionably the most powerful litigator in the club. Lean, unsparing, and intellectual (for a lawyer). Can hold court on the origin of pre-Colombian statuary or the nuances of a back-end deal. Must not be crossed, ever. Represents the crème of the club.

Freddie Fields—The most flamboyant powerful agent of the '70s, he helped launch Barbra Streisand as a movie star and Jeff Berg as a club czar. Also launched a fleet of Young Turks who went on to run the club (Guy McElwaine, Mike Medavoy, Sue Mengers). His friendship-partnership with David Begelman is a true club closeness, outlasting scandals, several wives, more flops than Richard Gere, and every other partnership in the club. Produced the movies *Lipstick* and *Glory*.

Verna Fields—The hall of fame club godmother, largely responsible for the success of *Jaws* (for which she won a Best Editing Oscar, and the loyalty of the Universal executives, who made her the company's first female senior vice president). George Lucas gave her a BMW with her name on the license plate, and the studio gave her carte blanche to headquarter away from the brutal Black Tower. Her premature death in 1983 put a nail in the coffin of women being at the absolute top in the club. Nobody, male or female, has replaced her for nurturing, mentoring, mothering, or editing.

Carrie Fisher—The club's Dorothy Parker.

Harrison Ford—Action star of more blockbusters than almost anyone. He lives as far from Hollywood as he can get. The club liked him best in *Regarding Henry*.

John Foreman—Former club agent who became a producer, and whose career petered out in the '80s. The club yawns when you say his name. Socially charming. Represented Paul Newman and Joanne Woodward at their peaks, and his—in the '60s. In the '70s, he became Newman's producing partner (*Sometimes a Great Notion*).

Bob Fosse—The club considered this director an artist because his movie *All That Jazz* confirmed their suspicions about creative egos.

Jodie Foster—The club admires her because she didn't go under during the John Hinckley mess and become the answer to a trivia question. The club also likes her straightforward style. Best performance: *Bugsy Malone*.

Michael J. Fox—TV star who's built like many club members. Best-liked performance: In Herb Ross' *Secret of My Success*.

Mike Frankovich—Athletic, powerful former club czar who ran Columbia in the '60s, and was forgotten by the '80s. Tall, handsome ladies' man, he made a movie star of Goldie Hawn. One of the few club members to completely lose status, with advancing years.

Arthur Freed—Club producer of MGM musicals in the '40s and '50s. The Freed unit was the best-run production unit in club history, with impeccable output and no star turns. Did not groom a successor.

Dona Freeman—The club's favorite masseuse, she attended everyone from Rosalind Russell and Edie Goetz to Charles Feldman. Petite and philosophical and powerful.

GAC—Formerly General Artists Corporation, this New York-based theatrical agency was bought up in the '70s by the conglomerate that became International Creative Management (ICM). Agents like Sam Cohn and Marty Baum were out of the GAC stable.

Sandy Gallin—The manager-producer who's David Geffen's best friend and one of the club's favorite hosts. Nobody says no to a "Sandy party." Seemingly unconflicted, he's one of the few happy people in the club. Co-producer of Steve Martin's *Father of the Bride*.

Lorraine Gary—nee Gottlieb, now Sheinberg. Has been an agent, packager, producer, actress, and Hollywood wife. More emotionally complex than any other club wife. Played Roy Scheider's wife in *Jaws*, thanks to Steven Spielberg.

David Geffen—The smartest member of the club and the only self-made billionaire. The only club businessman to succeed in the movies, the record business, and on Broadway. The club considers him their Talmudic scholar. His only real touchstone is Barry Diller. His movies: *Beetlejuice, The Last Boy Scout.* Broadway: *Dreamgirls, Cats.* LPs: Joni Mitchell, Don Henley.

Mel Gibson—The worst interview subject in the club—but the camera has orgasms when he appears. Best performance: *Mad Max.*

Bruce Gilbert—The longtime producing partner of Jane Fonda who broke off on his own by producing a screenplay that took ten years to develop, for the Jack Nicholson starrer *Man Trouble.*

Dr. Harry Glassman—The club cosmetic surgeon with the best sense of club history—and beauty; married to Victoria Principal.

William Goetz—Well-liked son-in-law of L. B. Mayer, who amassed the club's first great Post-Impressionist art collection with his social wife, Edie. Best production: *Sayonara.*

Leonard Goldberg—Affable producer who was president of 20th Century-Fox, under Barry Diller. Made his bones in TV, with partner Aaron Spelling. Lives the good life at the top in the club. Socially A. Most profitable movie: *Sleeping with the Enemy,* with Julia Roberts in her prime.

Wendy Goldberg—Had she been born a man, she would have been in the club tribunal. Smarter about Hollywood than some people give her credit for.

Whoopi Goldberg—Club favorite whose talent astounds the club—and whose adopted last name hasn't hurt her.

Leonard Goldenson—A club founder of the TV branch, he's also a founder of ABC. One of the few gentlemen in a vile business.

Milton Goldman—The late New York-based club agent who gave Meryl Streep her break—and gave great Manhattan club parties with his companion, club attorney Arnold Weissberger. Of a style that's no longer current, he had great timing, especially about when to die.

William Goldman—The club novelist-screenwriter with the best understanding of how the club works. By keeping his distance from California, he keeps the club intrigued. His *Butch Cassidy and the Sundance Kid* set a club record for high-priced original screenplays.

Sam Goldwyn—The club mogul of moguls, and the only member to personally bankroll his own movies. Obsessive about detail, beauty, cleanliness, and morality. With his wife, Frances, he gave the best Hollywood parties of the '40s at the top of Laurel Lane in Beverly Hills. His best movie: *The Best Years of Our Lives*.

Sam Goldwyn, Jr.—Independent producer with his own track record. He had the hardest act to follow, and did it quietly and slowly. The label of "Jr." didn't help. His best movie: *Local Hero*.

Larry Gordon—Southern-born producer with deep Japanese pockets, and a taste for action movies. As rich as any modern club deal-maker; a better producer than he was an executive. (It was when he was president of Fox that he suffered his first heart attack.) The club's one true good ole boy. Among his successful movies: *Die Hard* and *Field of Dreams*.

Hildy Gottlieb—The former creative executive for Eddie Murphy, the wife of director Walter Hill, and a former agent. Now runs Meadowbrook, Alec Baldwin's company.

Cary Grant—The club's favorite representative and symbol. Irreplaceable. The club is weaker because no one succeeded him, or ever will. Best performance: *The Philadelphia Story*.

Melanie Griffith—Club's favorite recovery saga. Her vulnerability in *Working Girl* made the club see her differently.

Peter Guber—The warrior, with bodies littered all over town. A club borderline: Brutal to employees, charming to bosses, too brilliant for his own good. Deserves credit for *Midnight Express*, but not for *Rain Man* or *Gorillas in the Mist*; he takes credit anyway. The opposite of a big spender.

Joyce Haber—The most powerful club gossip columnist of her time, and the only successor to Louella and Hedda. Educated at the three Bs—Brearley, Bryn Mawr, and Barnard—she was the *Time* magazine correspondent who handed in the best files. Dropped by the club when she was dropped by the *Los Angeles Times*. Her best-selling novel *The Users* was sequeled as *The Winners*, by Dominick Dunne.

Mel Haber—One of the club's most discreet innkeepers, at his '30s hideaway in Palm Springs. Sinatra drinks at his bar, and George Hamilton goes on tanning binges by his pool.

Gene Hackman—The club's most respected actor, the modern equivalent of Spencer Tracy. Undemanding, productive, presents a good image for Hollywood. Best performances: *The French Connection* and *The Conversation*.

Randa Haines—Club director who worked twice as hard because she's a woman, but may get the last laugh. Considered as capable as any male director, or more so. William Hurt's favored director, after *Children of a Lesser God* and *The Doctor*.

E. Barry Haldeman—The entertainment attorney who was protégé of Norman Garey, and is *consiglière* to Gene Hackman and the brothers who created *Cheers*. A long-distance runner.

Denise Minnelli Hale—The Yugoslavian-born third wife of Vincente Minnelli who gave great parties on a shoestring, in the '60s, and entranced the club with her wit and energy. Social beyond social, and smart as a whip. Her marriage to zillionaire Prentis Cobb Hale made her rich as well as funny.

Jack Haley, Jr.—One of the club's favorite sons. Brilliant at reassembling and understanding Hollywood history, his tenure as studio executive was short-lived. But there will always be room in the club for him, somewhere. Best credit: *That's Entertainment*.

Arsenio Hall—Plays ball with club publicists by throwing softball questions at hard-to-get stars. The new Merv Griffin.

Tom Hanks—In the late '80s, he was one of the three stars who could open a movie. He's the new James Stewart? Best performance: In the underrated *Punchline*.

Aljean Harmetz—Formerly a club scribe, for a dozen years, when she covered Hollywood for the *New York Times*. Takes herself seriously—still. Her book *The Making of the Wizard of Oz* is one of the most thorough Hollywood books ever.

Joan Cohn Harvey—The only woman to marry a mogul (Harry Cohn) and a movie star (Laurence Harvey).

Henry Hathaway—Gruff club director who told off everyone on every one of his movies, including John Wayne. Revered by the club because they couldn't control him. Best-known movie: *How the West Was Won*.

Kitty Hawks—Club daughter (of Howard Hawks) and decorator (of CAA), formerly married to club executive Ned Tanen. Stylish with a capital S.

Goldie Hawn—Club survivor who's savvy about the underpinnings of Hollywood, and brilliant about the overall deals. Knows exactly when to make personal appearances, and is thus a true club movie star. Best performance: *Shampoo*. Worst performance: *The Girl from Petrovka*.

Leland Hayward—The classiest of all club founders, a superior agent to Henry Fonda and Katharine Hepburn, later a Broadway producer and always the best player (at anything) on the club field. To understand him, read his daughter Brooke Hayward's classic memoir *Haywire*.

Katharine Hepburn—The longest-lasting movie star. And the only major star, apart from Garbo, who played Hollywood by *her* rules and not the club rules. Therefore she's the only actress who commands unwavering respect from the club. Best performances: *Alice Adams* and *Little Women* and *The Philadelphia Story*.

Walter Hill—A favorite club director because he's often been on the money, as in *48 Hours*. Best friend of ICM chairman Jeff Berg.

Barry Hirsch—The favorite club lawyer, along with Bert Fields and Kenny Ziffren. Handles major stars and major executives, and ruffles very few major feathers. Not to be made an enemy of.

Alan Hirschfield—A club also-ran who got admitted in the '70s and ousted in the '80s. The Begelman scandal didn't help him, but ultimately it didn't matter—because he wasn't a player. All he is now is a former president of 20th Century-Fox.

Lenny Hirshan—Of the old school of agents—at William Morris for decades. Still handles Walter Matthau.

David Hoberman—The Disney executive who was unwittingly pitted against Disney's Ricardo Mestres. The club is getting bored with this duel.

Dustin Hoffman—Club target because of his perfectionism. His directors talk about how bad his skin is—and how good his acting is. Best performances: *The Graduate* and *Midnight Cowboy* and *Kramer vs. Kramer*.

Bob Hope—The club envies him his real estate.

Brooke Hayward Hopper—Club daughter (of Margaret Sullavan and Leland Hayward) who wrote *Haywire*, one of the best club memoirs, and survived a stormy marriage to club bad boy Dennis Hopper.

Ron Howard—The club's favorite surprise story, the boy who could and did make $100 million grossing movies. Lives away from the club, in Connecticut, but partners with Brian Grazer, whose whole life is spent in the club. The movie that put him on the map was *Splash*. The club most enjoyed his movie *Parenthood*.

Toni Howard—The agent-sister of Wendy Goldberg, one of the main defectors from William Morris to ICM. Considered a player for her careful building (with Sue Mengers) of Anjelica Huston's career.

Ross Hunter—Ultrasuccessful club producer of the '50s and '60s who was victimized by one or two flops in the '70s. Exorcised from the club when Universal insisted the Utrillo in his office be returned when his contract expired—and when Leo Jaffe bumped him off the Columbia lot. Too decent to survive the club in the edgy '80s. Biggest hits: *Pillow Talk* and *Imitation of Life*.

William Hurt—The club's favorite intellectual actor; most members lack the attention span to listen to him go off on tangents, but they respect him. Well-bred in a way the club aspires to. Best liked performance: *Broadcast News*.

Anjelica Huston—The most stylish club daughter—and fairy tale. When she left Jack Nicholson after a decade, and became a movie star, the club felt good about themselves because they knew she deserved the stardom.

Best performances: *The Grifters* and *Prizzi's Honor*. Biggest drama of her life: The great bond between father and daughter.

John Huston—Club legend with superb understanding of complex members like Jack Warner and Ray Stark. Played the town like a gambler, and when he won—he won big. There were also irreversible losses, and a lonely ending. Among his classics: *Moulin Rouge, African Queen*, and *The Misfits*.

Nessa Hyams—Brilliantly instinctive former casting director and studio executive. Had she been a man, she might have run the club. Much respected. Her best credit: *What's Up Doc?*

Peter Hyams—An upward club failure, director of more bad movies than any other major director. Brother of wizard casting director Nessa Hyams, brother-in-law of perennial club executive David Picker. His quirkiest movie, *T. R. Baskin*, gave an early glimpse of Candy Bergen's comedy talents.

Johnny Hyde—Classic, lonely Hollywood agent of the '40s and '50s. One of the few men in the club who gave Marilyn Monroe more than he took. When he foisted MM on John Huston for *Asphalt Jungle*, the career was launched. A regular at the pool at the Racquet Club in Palm Springs.

Martha Hyer—Quintessential club wife of the '70s and '80s, she lived down mysterious rumors by moving to Santa Fe after her husband (Hal Wallis) died. An underrated actress. Best performances: *Sabrina* and *Lucky Me*.

Joan Hyler—Longtime William Morris VP who put Candy Bergen in *Murphy Brown*.

Elliot Hyman—The former agent who made a fortune in the '50s when TV syndication suddenly made reruns profitable. A minor visionary, or maybe just lucky. A co-founder of Seven Arts, one of the most profitable companies of the go-go '60s.

ICM—International Creative Management is the conglomerate name for the David Begelman-Freddie Fields company that was originally Creative Management Associates. In the '70s it was bought by Marvin Josephson

Associates, and then ICM incorporated other, smaller companies like GAC.

Amy Irving—Actress-club wife of the '80s who cashed in beyond imagining, after her divorce from Steven Spielberg. Best performance: *Yentl*, in which Barbra Streisand made her glow.

Michael Jackson—The biggest star of the '80s who wants to become Fred Astaire in the '90s. The club is wishing him luck.

Andrea Jaffe—The marketing woman-sister of Paramount chairman Stanley Jaffe, and daughter of Leo Jaffe, is a '60s radical with deep knowledge of the business, deep financial pockets, and deep-seated drive. Brighter than most of her enemies.

Leo Jaffe—A paterfamilias in the club, chairman emeritus of Columbia, father of Paramount chairman Stanley Jaffe, the long-distance runner who outlived all his peers.

Stanley Jaffe—A club blueblood, son of the Columbia co-chairman emeritus Leo Jaffe. Paramount's Chairman Stanley is considered loyal, lean, and empathic under a gruff exterior. Produced: *Goodbye Columbus*, before he was thirty. He has his enemies, and he knows it.

Mark Johnson—Oscar-winning producer of *Rain Man*, and director Barry Levinson's longtime partner. One of the best-oiled, most affable producers in the club. The member most likely to have been a preppie.

Jennifer Jones—The club recluse until her marriage to Norton Simon. The tycoon rescued her from Synanon and oblivion, not to mention poverty. Best roles: *Tender Is the Night*, *Good Morning Miss Dove*, and *Beat the Devil*. Sexiest role: *Duel in the Sun*.

Pauline Kael—Club critic emeritus, the only print movie critic who made the club tremble. Irreplaceable, and *The New Yorker* knows it.

Stan Kamen—The most popular, powerful agent of the pre-CAA years. Had the client stable of all time, at William Morris: Beatty, Barbra, Goldie, Chevy, Keaton, McQueen, *et al*. Much liked and respected. Ron Meyer is the only one to whom his torch is passed.

Garson Kanin—The writer whose books about show business give perhaps the truest picture of the club. His *Tracy and Hepburn* is the best book ever written about movie stars.

Jay Kanter—The most devoted team player in the club, always at the side of Alan Ladd, Jr. Where Laddie goes, goes Jay. Once the possible successor to Lew Wasserman, Kanter survived the Black Tower, and was smart enough to know when to leave. His heyday as an agent was the '50s when he represented Brando and Grace Kelly.

Gloria Katz and Willard Huyck—The gold-dust club screenwriting couple, survivors of *Lucky Lady* and *Howard the Duck*, who went on self-promoting themselves anyway. The club has paid them extravagant fees, and they respond by taking themselves very seriously.

Jeffrey Katzenberg—The modern L. B. Mayer, with an obsessive touch of David O. Selznick. The Disney studio chairman has the biggest head start of anyone in the club—he's the only member at the absolute top born after 1950. To bet against him is to be a moron (in spite of how bad some of Disney's movies are).

Elaine Kaufman—The den mother of the New York branch of the club. Her salon, Elaine's, is to Manhattan what Chasen's (on a different level) is to Hollywood.

Victor Kaufman—In and out of the club faster than almost anybody. The businessman brought in by Coca-Cola when the company bought Columbia, he proved far more business than show. Responsible for Dawn Steel becoming the first female studio president since Sherry Lansing.

Elia Kazan—Broadway and movie director of the '40s and after who lived in New York and thus didn't become beloved by the club. Best movies: *Streetcar Named Desire, On the Waterfront.* Biggest flop: *The Arrangement*, which was too close to home for most of the club.

Diane Keaton—Club outcast who's no longer a true club star—not because she got older, but because she never played social games. Best role: *Annie Hall.*

Gene Kelly—One of the handful of stars in the club hall of fame, largely because he makes members believe in magic. Best performances: *Singin' in the Rain, Marjorie Morningstar.*

Grace Kelly—Club symbol of the '50s and beyond, who became a club hostess in Monte Carlo in the '60s and '70s. Her death is as verboten a topic in the club as the death of Natalie Wood. Club icon. Best performances: *The Country Girl, To Catch a Thief.*

Kathleen Kennedy—The very rich producer-partner of Steven Spielberg and wife of producer-director Frank Marshall. One of the first female club zillionaires. Biggest hits: *Raiders of the Lost Ark* and *E.T.*

Kirk Kerkorian—The billionaire club recluse who's more business than show. Often blamed for running down MGM in the '70s; lived for a long time ultraquietly in Beverly Hills with the widow of Cary Grant. He's Howard Hughes without style.

Pat Kingsley—The club's favorite publicist (along with Pat Newcomb), she specializes in women: Sally Field, Candy Bergen, Goldie Hawn, Debra Winger, Penny Marshall, the list goes on. A club power broker because of how closely people listen to her advice, including lawyers and agents. She knows she has enemies but her friends are more powerful.

Gene Kirkwood—Brash, hyper producer who got *Rocky* made, and thus has the permanent loyalty of Sylvester Stallone.

Arnold Klein—The club dermatologist and *mensch.*

Marty Klein—The APA club agent who talked Mike Ovitz into letting him keep John Candy as a client. A hero to lower-level members of the club.

Kevin Kline—A club favorite because he's well mannered and straightforward, and so the club trusts him. Best performances: *Big Chill* and his Oscar-winning turn *A Fish Called Wanda.*

Howard Koch, Jr.—A phony with perhaps the unluckiest marital track record of any junior club member. Second-string all the way. Most notable credit: He was the assistant director on *The Way We Were.*

Howard Koch, Sr.—Happy in the role of elder statesman, Koch is really a back-room politico without the finesse of a Hal Wallis or the taste of a Ray Stark. One of the truly luckiest people in the club, especially after the oil-gushing success of *Ghost.* Guilty of upward failure and phony niceness. Among his hits: *Barefoot in the Park* and *Odd Couple.*

Paul Kohner—Legendary club raconteur-agent of Ingmar Bergman and John Huston. Lived at a time in the club when *largesse* counted. An anachronism by the '80s, he was *it* in the '50s.

Sidney Korshak—The most powerful man in the club until the '80s, along with Lew Wasserman and Frank Sinatra. The only club member to be profiled on the front page of the *New York Times* (in a three-part series by Pulitzer-winning reporter Seymour Hersch). The labor mediator *nonpareil* with the best connections, the best meat locker in Bel Air, the blondest wife, and the best understanding of power.

Arthur Krim—The New York club elder, forever at United Artists and a founder of Orion. One of the club's most respected leaders. Mentor, financially, of Woody Allen, and husband of AIDS pioneer Dr. Mathilde Krim.

Harry Kurnitz—Club wit of the '40s and '50s, Oscar Levant without a piano. Best credit: *Witness for the Prosecution*.

Alan Ladd, Jr.—Laddie, the low-key club survivor, is—apart from Richard Zanuck—the only blue-chip second-generation executive club member. His father was a movie star, and his mother was the Sue Mengers of her day, a very powerful club agent. One of the best-liked, least-showy members of the club. Responsible for *Julia* and *Turning Point*, and also responsible for saying yes to *Star Wars*, when five studios said no.

Gavin Lambert—The best Hollywood novelist (*Inside Daisy Clover*) and historian (*On Cukor*) and biographer (*Norma Shearer*).

Burt Lancaster—Hall of fame club star, and stud. Best performance: *Sweet Smell of Success*. Most memorable: *Elmer Gantry*.

Jessica Lange—One of the luckiest club actresses because she seems to play the game by her own rules, and lives as far away from Hollywood as she can get. Her early starlet years would make good reading. Best performances (by far): The back-to-back *Tootsie* and *Frances*, the movies that made her a star.

Sherry Lansing—The beautiful, bright, intuitive, dogged movie producer who's on the set of her movies every single day. Her success in the club—she made history as the first woman studio president—has little to do with luck, and everything to do with love of the movies. Biggest hit: *Fatal Attraction*.

Robby Lantz—Club agent (of Elizabeth Taylor and Anthony Hopkins) who prefers New York to Hollywood, and pays a price in terms of his business.

Abe Lastfogel—"Uncle Abe," the paterfamilias of William Morris, was to agents what L. B. Mayer was to studio chiefs. Monklike in his devotion to the Morris office, he outlived most of his star clients. Responsible for Tracy and Hepburn's off-screen privacy, and Danny Thomas' rise from obscurity.

Peter Lawford—A club provider in the '60s who was dropped in the '70s, and ultimately became a club casualty. Best role: Studio executive Paul Bern in *Harlow*.

Irving Lazar—Club legend at the very top who outlasted, outplayed, outdealt, and outran everyone else. In the '40s he defined the word "independent" for the club, in the '90s he was still giving great parties. The snob agent who gave social climbing a good name, but groomed no successors. Clients have included Joan Collins, Noel Coward, and David Brinkley.

David Lean—The royal elder of club directors, revered as a picture-maker who made classics that made money. All his pictures were his best pictures, from *Summertime* to *The Bridge on the River Kwai* to *Brief Encounter*. Steven Spielberg's idol.

Norman Lear—One of the few strictly-TV people the club takes seriously. Narcissistic visionary. Best feature film: *Divorce American Style*.

Janet Leigh—Actress-club wife of the '50s and beyond who also happened to be a movie star. One of Edie Wasserman's best friends, and one of the club's best tennis players. Operates with a kind of style missing in modern Hollywood. Best movies: *Manchurian Candidate* and *Psycho*.

Felicia Lemmon—Club wife (of Jack) who's too good an actress not to work more often. One of the most patient helpmates in club history. Best role: The misunderstood wife in Billy Wilder's underrated *Kiss Me, Stupid*.

Jack Lemmon—Club hall of fame for his representing the good life in Hollywood without publicly overdoing it. Best roles: *The Apartment* and *Save the Tiger.*

Jean Leon—One of the two savviest modern club restaurateurs. (Wolfgang Puck is the other.) Leon's La Scala is a club legend, and a living one. Still the only place to be seen at Malibu on Saturday night. And the original La Scala, in Beverly Hills, was the best-lit restaurant in club history.

Mervyn LeRoy—A long-distance runner in the club, as producer and director. More major movie credits than almost anyone. Socially astute, he played the club for all it was worth, and they called him "Pops." Best movie: *Mister Roberts.*

Barry Levinson—The Oscar-winning writer-director of mainstream club movies who has the best producing partner in the club, Mark Johnson. Best movies: His personal ones, *Diner* and *Avalon.* Worst movie: *Best Friends,* written with his ex-wife.

Ed Limato—Hardened ICM agent with the loyalty of Richard Gere and Michelle Pfeiffer. His face is a road map of how hard it is to survive in Hollywood.

Bobby Littman—Mouthy, hyper B agent who got famous for five seconds when producer Sidney Beckerman punched him on the patio of Ma Maison circa 1973.

Ernst Lubitsch—Revered as the untoppable club director with the lightest touch. His best comedies, like *Shop Around the Corner,* were soufflés that never fell down. The mentor of Billy Wilder.

George Lucas—Visionary writer-director-producer who cashed in and moved up north, only to become homesick for the system. Was Francis Coppola's assistant, Linda Ronstadt's lover, Steven Spielberg's alter ego. Lacking in social graces—but so what? Will be remembered for the *Star Wars* epics.

Marcia Lucas—The editor-ex-wife of George Lucas, who got one of the all-time great club settlements in her divorce. Edited *Star Wars.*

Gary Lucchesi—The brightest assistant Stan Kamen ever had at William Morris, he went on to executive status at Paramount. Boyish face belies back-room strengths. Is he a survivor?

Ali MacGraw—One of the most savvy club observers, and one of the few people in Los Angeles with true style. Best performance: Sidney Lumet's *Just Tell Me What You Want.*

Shirley MacLaine—One of the handful of stars in the club hall of fame, because she survived four decades at the top in show business. Best performance: *Some Came Running.* Best book: *Don't Fall Off the Mountain.*

Fred MacMurray—Probably the richest man in Hollywood, and thus one of the luckiest. Tighter with a dollar than anyone else in the club. Watching him shop for the cheaper brands of vodka at Liquor Barn was a real Hollywood moment. Best performance: *The Apartment.*

Madonna—She is what Streisand was, even though her main talent may be for self-promotion. Privately, some club members call her a pig. She gave some glamour to the '91 Academy Awards.

Norman Mailer—The club's favorite journalist (*Marilyn*) and least favorite novelist (his books hardly ever become movies). His novel *The Deer Park* is the one modern classic about Hollywood.

David Mamet—Club filmmaker in spite of his scathing Hollywood satire *Speed the Plow.* The club knows just how smart he is. Prolific screenwriter-director whose best work (so far) is *Things Change.*

Frank Mancuso—The ousted longtime Paramount chairman who was in just slightly over his head—his background was always marketing and never creative. If *Godfather III* had been a monster hit, he would have been spared—but it wasn't.

Joe Mankiewicz—Brilliant, brittle club producer in the '30s, writer-director in the '40s and '50s who defected to upstate New York in the '60s. The club never understood why he didn't stay in Hollywood and become an elder statesman, especially after they gave him four Oscars in two years. His *All About Eve* is (along with *The Bad and the Beautiful*) the ultimate Hollywood movie.

Tom Mankiewicz—Club son of Joseph L. Mankiewicz, who grew up to write and direct movies— and be the club's social Boswell. His memoirs would tickle the club. Among his credits: The movie of *Dragnet*, and the TV success *Hart to Hart*.

Rhonda Fleming Mann—The Queen of Technicolor who made a superb transition to club wife when she married mogul Ted Mann in the '70s. One of the most beautiful club wives—and women—of all time. Best performances: *Spellbound* and *Home Before Dark*.

Ted Mann—The most successful movie exhibitor in club history. The one-man owner of the largest chain of theaters in America, who knew just when to sell his portfolio. A master of timing. Married to the most beautiful club wife of her generation, Rhonda Fleming.

Larry Mark—Bright former Paramount executive who became a producer under Jeffrey Katzenberg at Disney. Is one of the best-networked people in the producer branch of the club. Credits include *Black Widow* and *True Colors*. Would have made a legendary gossip columnist.

Garry Marshall—The luckiest movie director in the club, after *Pretty Woman* made him a multimillionaire. Agile, funny, hosts the best club Saturday morning basketball game. Is very aware how lucky he is.

Penny Marshall—The first woman director in the club to make a $100 million grossing picture—*Big*. A sleeper director but a player, she was mentored by Mike Ovitz. The club is proud of her success, and wishes that she would find a husband—as does Penny herself.

Dean Martin—Club star and husband of the '60s, who left the best club wife ever (Jeanne Martin) for a number of second-rate successors. The Dean-Jeanne reconciliation is the only coupling club members of a certain age pray for. Best performance: *Some Came Running*.

Steve Martin—The club movie star who will go the distance. The club likes his taste in clothes and art and movies. Best performance: *Roxanne*, which he also wrote.

Marsha Mason—A club wife in the '70s, an actress before and after, she has the best insights on Hollywood of anyone in the talent branch of the club. Also, firsthand experience, from her marriage to Neil Simon. (He's written so much about her, she now ought to write about him.) Best performance: *Only When I Laugh*, for which she should have won an Oscar.

Carol Matthau—Hall of fame club wife, because of her wisdom about how it all works. Gave a great performance in her friend Elaine May's *Mikey and Nicky*.

Elaine May—The club script doctor, the writer who saved *Tootsie*, the director who blew her shot with *Ishtar*. The club considers her brilliant beyond belief, but creatively self-destructive. The club is afraid to trust her with large sums of money.

Paul Mazursky—Club writer-director who got the town down perfectly in *Alex in Wonderland* and *Down and Out in Beverly Hills*.

David McClintick—The author who wrote *Indecent Exposure*, the best investigative book about the club—ever. (He does not live or work in Hollywood, and never has.)

Roddy McDowall—The one club historian worth having dinner with. Has the best photos ever taken of club members. Probably loves the myth of the community more than anyone. A must as a character in any movie about the club. Best performance: *Camelot*, on Broadway.

Guy McElwaine—An ultimate clubbie. Has played various roles: press agent, studio executive, agent. Has the confidence of people like Spielberg, but his style is too flashy and reminiscent of the '70s. Clients include Kim Basinger and James Caan.

Mike Medavoy—Legitimate boy wonder of the club who helped steer Orion to mass/class status, and went on to become chairman of TriStar before he was fifty. Will go the distance and become a club elder. Responsible for *Bound for Glory*, *Coming Home*, and *Bugsy*, among others.

Dan Melnick—Savvy, artful prototypical club member of the '70s whose best production was *All That Jazz*. A studio executive who wanted independence, he operated best at a time in Hollywood when brunches mattered. Smart, with street instincts and a stylish veneer. A club ladies' man, one of the few. It annoyed the club the way he married up, early on—but his marriage to the daughter of Richard Rodgers didn't last.

Al Mendelson—The Al of Nate 'n Al's, the gold mine deli that elicits real sentiment—and loyalty—from the club. He was richer than many of his very rich customers.

Sue Mengers—Club legend, the first woman to play hardball with the club, and the best club party-giver of the '70s. Among her clients: Mike Nichols, Peter Bogdanovich, Ryan O'Neal.

Ron Meyer—The most popular man in the club, and the spectacular diplomat who handles Stallone, Cher, Madonna, and Alec Baldwin.

Lee Anderson Minnelli—The social publicist widow of Vincente Minnelli, a woman who's hosted more lunches for money (and publicity) than anyone since Elsa Maxwell. Has the best vintage '55 T-bird in the club. As long as Liza lets her live in the big white house on Sunset Boulevard, she'll keep her membership.

Vincente Minnelli—A favorite club director of the '40s and '50s who brought artistry and style to the MGM musical. Alternately gentle and tyrannical. His *The Bad and the Beautiful* is the best movie about Hollywood ever made, and his *Gigi* is the most beautiful musical.

Walter Mirisch—Club stalwart; the man without anecdotes, the vintage president of the Academy of Motion Picture Arts and Sciences who produced classic movies like *West Side Story* and *The Apartment*. (His late brother Marvin was the club's favorite Mirisch.)

Demi Moore—Club joke; the only reason she got the cover of *Vanity Fair* is that she agreed to undress. She's filling the star void—but only temporarily. Best performance: *Ghost*.

Mary Tyler Moore—The club owed her an Oscar for *Ordinary People*, but didn't deliver. And she responded by never again digging as deeply. As talented as she is rich, and far more interesting than she thinks she is.

Maynard Morris—Fussy, anal-retentive agent of the '40s and '50s, known primarily for discovering Brando, and being a screamer.

William Morris—The oldest company in show business, and one of the richest. The management got shook up in the '90s.

Peter Morton—Visionary proprietor of the clubhouse Morton's.

Eddie Murphy—Comedian adopted by the club who became too arrogant for the club. His autobiography could be called *Hubris*. Best performance: *48 Hours*, the original.

Judd Nelson—Club has-been who chose movies badly, and managers badly. A casualty of the Brat Pack. Best performance: He hasn't given one yet.

Pat Newcomb—The club publicist who best understands superstars. On their movies, Streisand and Redford always ask for her. Was Marilyn Monroe's best friend.

Paul Newman—The club loves him more than he loves the club. Best performance: *Sweet Bird of Youth*.

Jack Nicholson—Probably the richest modern club actor, apart from Arnold Schwarzenegger. A long-distance runner who calls his own shots, and has stayed with one agent (Sandy Bresler) since 1967. Best performance: *Chinatown*. Most outrageous: *Batman*.

Rick Nicita—One of the ladies' men at CAA, handling complex actresses such as Debra Winger and Bette Midler; his club marriage to CAA's Paula Wagner makes them contenders for long-term club membership.

Lorena Nidorf—The widow of L. B. Mayer, who went on giving dinners at her Westwood apartment as though nothing happened—when in fact the town had changed radically after her husband's death.

David Niven, Jr.—The dapper film producer-son of the movie star. Most eligible bachelor in the club, once R. J. Wagner remarried. Could probably write the Hollywood memoir of all time.

Nick Nolte—Every three years he's rediscovered by the club, and meanwhile he goes on working all the time. One of the few modern stars who haven't been homogenized—he has temperament. Best performance: Martin Scorsese's segment in *New York Stories*.

Merle Oberon—The club hostess of the '60s, at her seaside villa in Acapulco. Her return to Malibu in the '70s made no waves, even though her Tudor house had the best antique furniture on the beach. Best performance: *These Three*.

Frank Orsatti—Prototypical club agent of the '30s, one of Louis B. Mayer's best friends. Classy and beloved. Mourners at his funeral included Buster Keaton, Buddy Rogers, and Mike Romanoff.

Michael Ovitz—The most powerful man in the club, maybe the most powerful ever. The only dealer nobody double-crosses. A Valley boy who grew up to be a visionary. Clients include Barry Levinson, Penny Marshall, and Kevin Costner.

Alan Pakula—Club producer of the '60s who became a club director in the '70s and '80s. Runs the best club salons in New York, with his stylish writer-wife, Hannah. Best productions: *All the President's Men* and *Sophie's Choice*.

Gene Parsehegian—The New York-based Triad founding partner who represented William Hurt (brilliantly) from the beginning. It was perhaps the best club example of an agent-client relationship that worked until Hurt left in 1991.

Skip Paul—The wizard MCA attorney who made the numbers work for both the Japanese and Lew Wasserman, in the historic 1990 sale of the studio to Matsushita. Sensible instead of slick, he's a true '90s executive, more business than show.

Gregory Peck—The club's favorite movie star, after the death of Cary Grant. A true humanitarian in a town of fake humanitarians. Married to the most beautiful woman in the club, he looks and sounds the way members want to look and sound. Best performance: *Roman Holiday*, because he was relaxed.

Joe Peckerman—The late entertainment attorney who represented Mel Gibson and Dan Melnick, and had a deep understanding of club relationships.

I. M. Pei—The architect the club most reveres, especially after his stunning CAA building.

Sean Penn—The younger version of Dennis Hopper, a club rebel who's talented enough to win in the end. The club figures him to become a director—and to quiet down. Best movie: The underrated *Racing for the Moon.*

Jon Peters—The most emotional person in the club, with true affinity for women, and no time to be bored. *Batman* is the ultimate club movie everyone would like a piece of—and it was Peters' baby from start to stop. More creative than most club executives—hyper and misunderstood. Truly larger than life in a time when almost nobody else is. Just don't cross him.

Michelle Pfeiffer—The Kim Novak of the '80s and '90s, which is not meant as anything but a compliment. Best performance: *Dangerous Liaisons.*

Stevie Phillips—An agent under David Begelman in the '70s, she helped orchestrate Liza Minnelli's movie career and the Broadway production of *The Best Little Whorehouse in Texas.*

David Picker—Always in there plugging. Has run Paramount and Columbia, and produced independently. Titular head of a club family badly in need of a hit movie. His dishiest production: *Won Ton, the Dog Who Saved Hollywood.*

Ed Pine—The late MGM and Disney VP who handled club monsters and control freaks better than any studio publicist since Bob Goodfried.

Polly Platt—The godmother of Jim Brooks' empire, a former set designer and formerly the wife of Peter Bogdanovitch. Should be directing movies, and probably will be. Produced *War of the Roses* and *Broadcast News.*

Roman Polanski—One of the few movie directors the club considers an artist. If he could return to the States, he would work all the time. The club has already (largely) forgotten the Manson murders, not to mention Sharon Tate. Best movies: *Rosemary's Baby* and *Chinatown.*

Bo Polk—Handsome club failure of the '60s who almost got in as an MGM executive, but didn't. Ultimately too handsome for the club to take seriously. (See Chapter 21: Passion and Loyalty—Robert Evans.)

Sydney Pollack—The elder statesman of club directors, with the best track record. Makes movies (*Tootsie, The Way We Were*) the club likes to see and be associated with.

Tom Pollock—An ace club attorney who left law to run Universal Pictures for Sid Sheinberg and Lew Wasserman. Curt, smart, he may be the ultimate company man. Responsible for releasing *Parenthood* and *Born on the Fourth of July*.

Otto Preminger—Club bully of the '40s and '50s who made actresses tremble. Best movie: *Laura*.

Frank Price—Club studio executive who took five years off to play independent producer, and resurfaced as president of Columbia in 1990, before exiting again. As political as Lyndon Johnson, though he never shows his scars. Responsible for the releases of *Tootsie* and *Ghostbusters*.

Wolfgang Puck—The club restaurateur of the '80s and beyond. The only visionary in his field, the only restaurateur who could one day be running a studio. Credits: Spago, Granita, Chinois, and the brilliant kitchen of the original Ma Maison.

St. Clair Pugh—One of the most important media people in the club, he controls access to Liz Smith—and has for two decades. Brash, but only on the surface, and completely misunderstood.

David Puttnam—Club rebel who was made president of Columbia, and promptly began offending club members at the very top. More a symbol (of rebellion) than a player himself. Ultimately too British to grasp American (or Hollywood) neuroses. His moment: The night he won the Oscar for producing *Chariots of Fire*.

Dennis Quaid—The upward failure of the '80s, an actor who got his $3 million price per movie whether or not the movie failed. Best performance: *Postcards from the Edge*, in which he played a version of himself.

Bob Rafelson—Director who goes in and out of the club depending on his output. His friendship with Jack Nicholson is what sustains him, in spite of his flops. His *Five Easy Pieces* was a club classic because the members connected to it emotionally.

Martin Ransohoff—A mainstream club producer, hustling his way through the club maze for almost four decades. Makes good movies and bad movies, but doesn't pretend to be something he's not. Best movie: *Jagged Edge*.

Jack Rapke—A CAA powerhouse expected to accompany Ovitz if Ovitz ever leaves CAA. Strong club future. Most profitable client: John Hughes.

Michelle Rappaport—Bright, well-educated young club producer with moxie and style. Her credits include *White Men Can't Jump*.

Robert Rauschenberg—The modern artist the club most relates to, and most collects. His Joplin collage is a club status symbol, and has been for decades.

Robert Rehme—The failed Universal president who was always being told off by Sid Sheinberg, and who really never recovered. Got in the club on a pass—and was in over his head. Was rescued by the sleeper success of *The Hunt for Red October*, which he co-produced.

Ivan Reitman—Club director and *National Lampoon* alumnus, who will always work because he plays by the club rules. A creation of CAA. He easily survived *Legal Eagles*, one of the most notorious club packages of the '80s.

Kevin Reynolds—The club considers this Spielberg protégé a trouble-maker: His *Fandango* was a dud, and his *Robin Hood* was a horrible experience, maybe ending his long friendship with Kevin Costner. Odds are against him staying in the club.

Molly Ringwald—Club has-been who had the bad taste to snub club legend Claudette Colbert at a *Life* magazine photo shoot. Classic case of a Cinderella who gets dumped—by the club and the public—while still in her twenties. Best performance: James Toback's *The Pickup Artist*.

Stephen Rivers—The media wizard at CAA.

Harold Robbins—Club novelist emeritus who lived the club life (to the hilt) in the '60s, and has paid the price ever since. His *Carpetbaggers* is one of the best-ever Hollywood novels.

Elliott Roberts—David Geffen's first partner; manager of rock stars since the mid-60s. The club likes to hang out on his Malibu deck.

Julia Roberts—The club's first true Cinderella since Barbra Streisand and Audrey Hepburn. But she could wind up living the remake of *Too Much*,

Too Soon. Rumors circulate around her like nobody since Monroe. Most successful movie: *Pretty Woman*.

Cliff Robertson—The club informer, the man who turned in David Begelman in the check-forging scandal. Would play himself (only too willingly) in any movie about Begelman or the club. Won a Best Actor Oscar for *Charley*.

Bill Robinson—Carol Burnett's longtime agent, based at ICM, and always considered one of the gentlemen of the business. When you say his name, almost everyone smiles.

James Robinson—The Baltimore millionaire who put his money in Kevin Costner's *Robin Hood* and became a club contender.

Helen Rose—The club's second-favorite designer of the '40s and '50s (after Edith Head); best friend of Elizabeth Taylor's mother. She did Elizabeth Taylor's cat dress for the original *Cat on a Hot Tin Roof*.

Mark Rosenberg—Sydney Pollack's producing partner, a former Warner's executive, husband of Paula Weinstein, and one of the club's brightest young liberals. His background, not to be forgotten, is the student protest movement of the late '60s. A heavyweight. Co-produced *The Fabulous Baker Boys*.

Howard Rosenman—Co-producer of the remake of *Father of the Bride*.

Herbert Ross—Club director, widower of club favorite Nora Kaye, husband of "Princess" Lee Radziwill. His best movies: The back-to-back *The Turning Point* and *The Goodbye Girl*.

Steve Ross—The club tycoon with the best star relationships. The chairman of Time Warner counts Barbra Streisand and Steven Spielberg among his closest friends.

Ann Roth—The best modern club costume designer. Mike Nichols won't make a movie without her. Her best work: *Silkwood* and *Working Girl*.

Joe Roth—The savior of 20th Century-Fox, and the club member with the best rapport with Julia Roberts. Biggest release: *Home Alone*.

Charles Roven—Well-bred producer, husband of Dawn Steel. Produced *Heart Like a Wheel*.

Kurt Russell—The best father in the club (apart from Ron Meyer)—and the sexiest boyfriend. The club likes him, and hires him. Became a star in Mike Nichols' *Silkwood*. Discovered by Joyce Selznick to play Elvis Presley on TV.

Rosalind Russell—A top-rank club movie star of the '30s and beyond who was married to club producer Freddie Brisson. She gave great club parties at the oval bar in her living room on Beverly Drive. Adored by the club for her style and wit. Best performance: *Auntie Mame*.

Mark Rydell—Savvy club director who knows the ropes but says no to club projects more than he says yes. (See Rule Twenty-six: The club wants what it can't have.) Gets great performances from actors, especially Bette Midler in *The Rose*, and Henry Fonda in *On Golden Pond*.

Winona Ryder—Certain wings of the club believe she will be a movie star, and not just because her name was once Horowitz. Best performance: *Beetlejuice*.

Ilya Salkind—The *Superman* producer who unhinges the club when he gets into hassles. In other words, a troublemaker. (See Rule Six: "He won't do it to me.")

David Sarnoff—The legendary NBC chairman who played with the club when he visited Hollywood.

Bert Schneider—Club snob. Mean-spirited second-generation movie producer who told people he was marrying Candy Bergen before he even proposed. A club casualty of the '60s. Co-produced *Easy Rider* and *Five Easy Pieces*.

Taft Schreiber—The MCA executive whose death from a bad blood transfusion is the stuff of club legend. Rumor had it his politics were incorrect in the eyes of MCA. Very Republican.

Joel Schumacher—Club director, former Bendel's window dresser, he went from being Kitty Hawks' favorite confidant to being Julia Roberts' favorite director. Stylish in the extreme. Best work: The costumes for *Manhattan* and the direction of *Flatliners*.

Arnold Schwarzenegger—The club star who redefined self-promotion, and cashed in at a level that club legends like Clark Gable and Cooper never dreamed possible. Best performance: It hasn't happened yet.

David O. Selznick—Legendary club founder, he was compulsively anal-retentive. Producer of *Gone With the Wind* and other classics, and mentor of Jennifer Jones and Ingrid Bergman. Overall, probably the smartest man in the history of the movie business. Best productions: *Gone With the Wind, Portrait of Jenny, Spellbound.*

Irene Selznick—The daughter of L. B. Mayer, the first wife of David O. Selznick, the best friend of Katharine Hepburn, the producer of *A Streetcar Named Desire*. Would have been a club *macher* if she'd been born a man.

Joyce Selznick—The casting wizard who was denied admittance to the club largely because she was a woman—in the days before the club admitted women. A novelist, executive, pioneer, and a woman before her time. Discovered Tony Curtis on the streets of New York.

Myron Selznick—Prototypical club agent of the '30s who found Vivien Leigh to play Scarlett O'Hara for his producer-brother David.

Terry Semel—Loyal company man, over a decade at Warner's. Has lasted through very high ups and very low downs. Biggest blockbuster: *Batman.*

Norma Shearer—The club wife *nonpareil* of the '30s. As Mrs. Irving Thalberg, she ruled the beach scene at Santa Monica; as a movie star, she was the queen of the MGM lot. Became the longest-running recluse in club history, after Thalberg's death. Best performance: Mary in *The Women.*

Sid Sheinberg—Dour, would-be successor to Lew Wasserman as club king—until Lew sold MCA to the Japanese, and left Sid only wealthy. The truth was always that Lew could barely tolerate Sid at table, which is how most club members feel about him. One must also say that Lew nevertheless invited Sid—to everything.

Sidney Sheldon—The club's favorite best-selling novelist, who's admired for succeeding in TV, movies, and on Broadway. The longest long-distance popular writer. Most popular book-to-movie: *The Other Side of Midnight.*

Cybill Shepherd—Club blonde of the '70s who surprised everybody by becoming the Carole Lombard of the '80s. Brainy and talented. Best performance: *The Heartbreak Kid.*

Dick Shepherd—A club disappointment. Married to club daughter Judy Goetz, he was a front-rank agent in the '60s and '70s who became a middling producer in the '80s. Best movie: *Robin and Marian,* which brought Audrey Hepburn out of retirement.

Judy Shepherd—The granddaughter of L. B. Mayer, the daughter of Edie Goetz, the wife of Dick Shepherd, a walking history of the club.

Mel Simon—A club flop, a supermarket magnate from the Midwest who tried to buy his way in, and couldn't quite. A road company Marvin Davis.

Neil Simon—The only playwright the club feels truly comfortable with, because he understands them. His best work includes: *Lost in Yonkers, Only When I Laugh,* and *Barefoot in the Park.*

Don Simpson—Overexposed producing partner of Jerry Bruckheimer who wanted to *play* the role of producer, as if life was a movie. The showman half of the team, a ladies' man of great extravagance, he's ambitious enough, still, to go the distance. High-concept credits include *Top Gun* and *Beverly Hills Cop.* Spends fifty days a year at Canyon Ranch.

Frank Sinatra—The most powerful man in the club in the '60s and '70s, along with Sidney Korshak. Always able to solve any problem, except his loneliness. An underrated actor—especially in *The Man with a Golden Arm* and *Some Came Running.* And dancer, especially in *Take Me Out to the Ball Game.*

Muriel Slatkin—For twenty-five years, the owner of the Beverly Hills Hotel. At the age of twelve she said to her father, "Daddy, buy me a hotel," and he did.

Lee Solters—One of the club's three favorite publicists. (Pat Newcomb and Pat Kingsley are the other two.) Remembers when a club was a club, and a gossip columnist a gossip columnist.

Sissy Spacek—Her lack of staying power proves club Rule Eleven: You do need to retain sexuality to remain a movie star. Stole the Oscar from Mary Tyler Moore, and lived to regret it. Best performance: *Crimes of the Heart.*

Camilla Sparv—Club beauty and party girl of the '60s and '70s who married Robert Evans, and then married the heir to the Hoover vacuum fortune. (She divorced them both.) The club doesn't want to hear from her now. Her movie roles are not memorable.

Candy Spelling—Conflicted club wife who has the best chance of eventually becoming the club recluse. Living in another decade altogether, she never ever appears happy, except in the role of stage mother.

Sam Spiegel—A club founder, probably the best exemplar of club style. His yacht, docked in the South of France, was the place to be in the '60s. He mentored David Geffen and Warren Beatty, and his New Year's Eve parties were as de rigueur as Irving Lazar's Oscar parties. A true club icon. Also produced *Bridge on the River Kwai, The African Queen,* and *On the Waterfront.*

Rosemarie Stack—The B club wife who will go to the opening of a door.

Sylvester Stallone—Club hero, or close, because of *Rocky.* The living proof that myths exist—he reassures the club that it's okay to do anything to win. So they forgive him even his terrible movies.

Frank Stanton—The former president of CBS scares the club because he represents failure at the top. When William Paley didn't make him his successor, it was over for one of the few broadcasting pioneers. He's what no one in the club wants to turn into.

Fran Stark—Quintessential club daughter (of Fanny Brice), wife (of Ray Stark), sister (of artist Bill Brice), and mother (of the bright Wendy). One of the few club wives with true elegance.

Ray Stark—The most unique—and most powerful—member of the club, from the '60s forward. Blessed with extra energy, Stark is the only producer in the club who counsels executives before flying off to the National Gallery to see the latest Jasper Johns. Probably talks six times a day to Peter Guber and Herbie Allen. Presented Barbra Streisand as a movie star and Neil Simon as a box office screenwriter. Lives grandly in the Bogart-Bacall house in Holmby Hills, and on an extraordinary thoroughbred ranch in lush Santa Ynez. His best productions involved great directors: William Wyler's *Funny Girl* and John Huston's *Fat City* and *Reflections in a Golden Eye*.

Doris Stein—One of the first great club wives, this beauty from the Midwest entertained regally in the early years—and fell asleep often at table in the later years. The most flawless skin of anyone in the club, past or present.

Jules Stein—A club founder, one of the true originals among the moguls. Eye doctor, band-booker, MCA founder, antique collector *nonpareil*. In the '50s, Jules Stein was considered a Renaissance man. Got out of the movie business at the end of his life to make way for his successor, Lew Wasserman.

Frank Stella—Favorite of club art collectors, especially for his spare geometric stripes.

George Stevens, Jr.—A kind of upscale club archivist, who puts together the AFI Life Achievement Awards and the Kennedy Center Honors. His marriage to a woman well placed in Washington politics makes him bicoastal. His best production: The documentary he made about the career of his father.

Robert Stigwood—Outcasted club producer who lives reclusively and richly in the Caribbean. The Bebe Rebozo of the club, who struck oil with *Grease*.

Oliver Stone—Club director because he never stops producing and rarely goes out of the mainstream. His *Platoon* was the club's favorite modern war movie, next to *Casualties of War*.

Meryl Streep—Club leading lady emeritus, an untouchable. Her performances the club likes best were in *Heartburn* and *Postcards from the Edge*.

Barbra Streisand—Club star-star. She has the touch that only David Geffen and Steven Spielberg share—where everything turns to gold. The club careerist whose career shows the most growth. Could have run a studio better than almost anyone who has.

Jackie Susann—The ultimate club novelist because her characters were unfailingly true to life. Of her three books, *Valley of the Dolls* still stands as the best pop novel about show business.

Kiefer Sutherland—Club skeptics who cast him as Eddie Fisher to Julia Roberts' Elizabeth Taylor are misinformed. He's not to be written off, by any means.

Dick Sylbert—The club's favorite production designer because he recreates eras the club is nostalgic for—especially the '30s. Knows who's who and how to handle them, as in Warren Beatty (on *Dick Tracy*) and Roman Polanski (on *Chinatown*).

Elizabeth Taylor—The club's one authentic, lifelong movie star, underrated as an actress. The ultimate newsmaker. Best performances: *A Place in the Sun, Who's Afraid of Virginia Woolf*.

David Tebet—The longest-running TV executive, excepting only William Paley. The man who handled talent like Hope and Benny, and then discovered Johnny Carson. Paddy Chayefsky used him as a role model in *Network*.

Patrick Terrail—The club restaurateur of the '70s who made Ma Maison a legend, before walking away in the '80s. The heir to the Tour d'Argent in Paris.

Irving Thalberg—The true club wunderkind who was revered for taste and sense of what made movies good. Neurasthenic, mother-centered, and the role model for Fitzgerald's *Last Tycoon*. Probably the ultimate club legend. His movies at MGM, where he headed production, included classics like *The Women, Romeo and Juliet*, and *Marie Antoinette*.

Grant Tinker—One of the most respected people in the club, probably the brightest TV executive in modern Hollywood. Especially good at nurturing writers and running tight ships (a contradiction in terms, but Tinker managed it). His palmiest days were as head of MTM, named for his ex, Mary Tyler Moore, where he oversaw the best TV of the '70s.

Steve Tisch—Producer-scion of the Tisch fortune, very determined to be a major player on his own terms. Has backing and brains, and is both show and business. His early hit: *Risky Business*.

Robert Towne—The revered club screenwriter of the '70s—*Shampoo, Chinatown*—who became a club troublemaker in the '80s—*Tequila Sunrise, The Two Jakes*. Highly charged brilliant child of Hollywood who had it all, and got carried away with himself.

John Travolta—Club disappointment, because he let the members down after they gave him superstar status. After *Grease* and *Saturday Night Fever* there was nobody hotter; after *Moment by Moment* there was nobody colder.

TRIAD—After the big three—CAA, ICM, and William Morris—comes this talent agency. Top clients include (from movies) William Hurt, (from TV) Victoria Principal, (from music) Whitney Houston.

François Truffaut—Club hero-director who made the best modern movie about movies—*Day for Night*—and introduced Steven Spielberg to the *Cahiers du Cinéma*.

Kathleen Turner—The luckiest woman in the club. A soap opera actress who got elevated (temporarily) because of a void of stars. Her one good performance: *Body Heat*.

Brenda Vaccaro—Club victim, of usage by former lover Michael Douglas. He dropped her brutally for a young Washington debutante, and she's never really recovered. Superb in *Midnight Cowboy* and *Once Is Not Enough*.

Peter Viertel—Novelist-observer of the club who got it right in his classic *White Hunter, Black Heart*. Longtime husband of former club leading lady Deborah Kerr. Son of legendary club screenwriter (and hostess) Salka Viertel.

Marian Wagner—One of the club's favorite ex-wives, because (a) she has style and (b) she had two club husbands, Stanley Donen and R. J. Wagner. Mother of future club executive Josh Donen. Knows most of the club secrets worth knowing, especially the social ones.

Paula Wagner—The bright agent behind the Tom Cruise career was formerly an actress, and is currently the wife of fellow-CAA agent Rick Nicita. Superb story sense. Stayed behind club movie *Rain Man* when almost nobody else could or would.

Robert (R.J.) Wagner—The club's favorite dinner partner because he's handsome, smart, interested in you, and has beautiful manners. In another era he would have been a matinee idol. Best performance: Brick, in the overlooked TV film of *Cat on a Hot Tin Roof* opposite his wife, Natalie Wood.

Jeff Wald—He's the one you call when you are in big trouble, and he makes a phone call.

Jerry Wald—The ultimate club producer of the '40s and '50s—*Mildred Pierce, Peyton Place.* People said he was the role model for Sammy Glick and he never denied it. A showman of a mold that no longer exists, and a quick thinker. (When he bellowed, "Write me a modern *Kitty Foyle*," Rona Jaffe's best seller, *The Best of Everything*, was born.) High-concept before there was such a term. His widow, Connie, is a club hostess and Audrey Hepburn's best friend.

Hall Wallis—A club founder, probably the most successful production chief in history (at Warner's, in the '30s and '40s). Tasteful, but tight with a dollar, he went on to produce classics like *Come Back Little Sheba* and *Becket*. Brother of Garbo's best friend, club agent Minna Wallis.

Minna Wallis—Probably the first businesswoman in the club (along with Mary Pickford), she had the ear of both Clark Gable and L. B. Mayer. Even Garbo came to her Sunday lunches. Had a conventlike devotion and would be the Mother Superior character in any movie about the club.

Walter Wanger—The producer of Elizabeth Taylor's *Cleopatra* who fifteen years before that shot Jennings Lang between the legs.

Sam Warner—One of the original studio brothers, and club founders.

Lew Wasserman—The godfather. Until the mid-80s, the most powerful man in the club (along with Sidney Korshak and Frank Sinatra). Wholly devoted to MCA, his only real diversions are sunbathing in Palm Springs and spending time with his grandson.

Pilar Wayne—The very social next-to-last wife of John Wayne, a little too Mexican for the club's taste.

Sigourney Weaver—The club child (of former NBC president Pat Weaver) who understands the inner workings and the outer trappings. Best performance: *Gorillas in the Mist*.

Clifton Webb—Dapper, effete movie star of the '40s who hosted the best club gatherings at his house at the foot of Coldwater Canyon. So mother-centered that his mother went on to haunt the house into the '70s. Vintage club polo player, mostly in Palm Springs on the Zanuck estate. Best performances: *Laura* and *Three Coins in the Fountain*.

Paula Weinstein—Liberal former agent of Jane Fonda (in her political period) who went on to produce movies—*Dry White Season*—and to marry fellow producer Mark Rosenberg. They're perhaps the smartest couple in the club under fifty.

Si Weintraub—Sometime producer who's a member of the club because he's a crony of the club. Wealthy from *Tarzan*, a next-door neighbor of Ray Stark, he's a behind-the-scenes player—when needed. Deals in gold coins.

Arnold Weissberger—The most powerful entertainment lawyer in the New York branch of the club. Before his death he gave legendary parties that attracted stars of two continents. His *Famous Faces* is the best photo book about the club ever.

Eric Weissmann—The club lawyer who does 250 phone calls every day and eight sets of tennis every weekend. A survivor of the Holocaust and Hollywood. Clients include Alan Pakula and Paul Mazursky.

Dr. Milton Wexler—Aging, mean-spirited therapist who looks after Carol Matthau and Blake Edwards, and saved the psyche of Jennifer Jones. A star-worshipper, he took co-screenwriting credit on Edwards' satire *The Man Who Loved Women* and even did publicity for the film.

Audrey Wilder—Hall of fame club wife, the most stylish woman in Hollywood. She's the one you want to get up and sing at your parties.

Billy Wilder—The most talented man in the history of the club.

Gene Wilder—The club's favorite tennis player because he amuses members without embarrassing them (especially Mel Brooks). Best performances: *Bonnie and Clyde* and *The Producers*.

Bruce Willis—The former bartender who became the luckiest actor in the club in the '80s. The club now considers him a passing fancy, although he's not completely written off. Best role: *Die Hard*.

Irwin Winkler—One of the wealthiest producers in the club, a member who's made very few mistakes. The *Rocky* pictures were among the club's historically great franchises—and even his directing debut, *Guilty by Suspicion*, was no embarrassment. Has the loyalty of Scorsese and De Niro. One of the few members who knows how to play as well as work; also has one of the best marriages in the club.

Joe Wizan—In the club he's a journeyman producer—not without moxie, but also not a major player anymore. Peaked during his presidency at Fox in the early '80s.

Natalie Wood—The club's second favorite actress of the '60s. *If Elizabeth Taylor wouldn't, Natalie would,* the saying went. Socially adept, she would be a must in any movie about the club. Best performance: *Splendor in the Grass*.

Joanne Woodward—One of the club's favorite success stories, because she got it all: an Oscar, four decades with Paul Newman, and beautiful children. Best performance: *Rachel Rachel*, directed by her husband.

Marvin Worth—Feisty, intense, larger-than-life producer of *Lenny* and *The Rose*.

Talli Wyler—The much-loved widow of William Wyler, courted in the '30s by everyone from Henry Fonda to Jimmy Stewart. A beauty who tested for *Gone With the Wind*, and wound up instead as one of the happiest wives in club history.

William Wyler—The longest-lasting star director, his only peer was Billy Wilder. The nephew of Universal founder Uncle Carl Laemmele, he gave nepotism a good name. More Oscars, and more stellar star performances, than any director. He made Laurence Olivier and Audrey Hepburn and Barbra Streisand movie stars. Married one of the club's favorite starlet-beauties, and lived a charmed life.

Sean Young—In another era, club members would have slept with her, and made her a movie star. In the asexual '80s, they simply found themselves amused by her antics. Best performance: *No Way Out*.

Craig Zadan—The producer of *Footloose*, the biographer of Stephen Sondheim, one of the best handicappers in Hollywood.

Darryl F. Zanuck—Club founder, the tycoon knew "story" as well as any producer or executive who ever lived. An American original, out of Wahoo, Nebraska, he brought dimension and CinemaScope to the movies. Also the only mogul to name a starlet after his wife. (The name Bella Darvi is a combination of Darryl and Virginia Zanuck.) Blurred boundaries in a way no longer possible, he's much underappreciated. Best productions: *Gentleman's Agreement* and *All About Eve*.

Dick Zanuck—First he was the son also rises; now he's the husband also rises.

Lili Fini Zanuck—The determined producer-director-wife of Richard Zanuck who won an Oscar for *Driving Miss Daisy*, against big odds. The first woman who really made Dick Zanuck happy in a town where many women tried.

Bob Zemeckis—A favorite club director who got on the map with *Romancing the Stone*, and makes pots of money for everyone associated with him. Spielberg's most successful protégé.

Evarts Ziegler—Dapper phony who went to Princeton and privately talked like a thug. Used style as a weapon, when the club valued style. Clients included Sydney Pollack and John Gregory Dunne.

Mickey Ziffren—Brilliant writer-wife of the club's most powerful attorney, Paul Ziffren. Had she been born a man, she could have run the club. As it was, she was the club's Madame de Stael in the glory days of the '60s and '70s, when she hosted everyone from Anita Loos to Henry Luce. Was mentored by Helen Gahagan Douglas.

Fred Zinnemann—The last living genius club director, along with Billy Wilder. His last great film was *Julia*.

Adolph Zukor—The founder of Paramount, a founder of the club, and enigma who lived into his hundreds. Everyone knew him, and nobody did.